Authority without Power

STUDIES ON LAW AND SOCIAL CONTROL
Donald Black, Series Editor

AUTHORITY WITHOUT POWER
Law And The Japanese Paradox
John Owen Haley

Authority without Power

Law and the Japanese Paradox

JOHN OWEN HALEY

New York   Oxford

OXFORD UNIVERSITY PRESS

Oxford University Press

Oxford   New York   Toronto
Delhi   Bombay   Calcutta   Madras   Karachi
Kuala Lumpur   Singapore   Hong Kong   Tokyo
Nairobi   Dar es Salaam   Cape Town
Melbourne   Auckland   Madrid

and associated companies in
Berlin   Ibadan

Library of Congress Cataloging-in-Publication Data
Haley, John Owen.
Authority without power : law and the Japanese paradox /
John Owen Haley.
p. cm.—(Studies on law and social control)
Includes bibliographical references and index.
ISBN 0-19-505583-7
ISBN 0-19-509257-0   (pbk)
1. Law—Japan—History and criticism. 2. Social Control.
I. Title. II. Series. Law
349.52—dc20   91-9666

1 3 5 7 9 8 6 4 2
Printed in the United States of America
on acid-free paper

TO SHOEN ONO
Few Japanese lawyers have been as generous
in friendship and support
of foreign students in Japan.

Acknowledgments

This book includes the contributions of far too many persons to name all individually or to express my appreciation adequately. I must begin with Donald Black, who provided the intitial catalyst in suggesting that I write a study for this series on law and social control. I owe my greatest debt, however, to students, colleagues, and friends who over many years have given generously of their time and insights in a continuing dialogue on the themes of this study. They include William P. Alford, Lawrence W. Beer, Thomas L. Blakemore, Taimie L. Bryant, Kōichirō Fujikura, Yashuhirō Fujita, B. James George, Eleanor Hadley, Kōji Hirokawa, Jackson N. Huddleston, Masahirō Iseki, Zentarō Kitagawa, Shumpei Kumon, Eugene H. Lee, Tasuku Matsuo, Toshio Miyatake, Setsuo Miyazawa, Yasusuke Murakami, Shoen Ono, Tomoyuki Ohta, Richard W. Rabinowitz, Lawrence Repeta, Arthur I. Rosett, Stephan Salzburg, Malcolm D.H. Smith, Robert J. Smith, Hideo Tanaka, Tadao Tanase, Frank K. Upham, and Griffith Way.

I must also acknowledge with deep appreciation the help of colleagues in the University of Washington School of Law and Jackson School of International Studies. Donald C. Clarke, Dan H. Foote, and Kozo Yamamura reviewed my manuscript. Hok Lam Chan, Jack Dull, R. Kent Guy, Susan Hanley, and, above all, Dan F. Henderson graciously gave both time and advice. I am equally grateful to Fred G. Notehelfer, Hermann Ooms, and J. Mark Ramseyer of the University of California, Los Angeles, for their efforts in reviewing all or portions of the manuscript. Their suggestions were invariably valuable. All helped to ferret out and correct many of my initial errors. Those that remain are my own.

In addition, I am very much indepted to Sharon Murata and Richard Torrance, two extraordinarily able research assistants who contributed significantly to my research on the legal profession, as well as Art Nishimura and Haruki Sugiyama, who helped to edit the final manuscript.

Special thanks are also due to former comparative law librarian Suzanne T. Lee, her able successor William B. McCloy, and especially Rob Britt of their staff for their many efforts in facilitating my research, as well as to Barbara J. Kennedy and Jeri Miles of the University of Washington Law School staff for their contribution in typing the manuscript, and to editors Valerie Aubry and Ruth Sandweiss of Oxford University Press.

I received research support at various times from the University of Washington Law School Summer Research Program and Asian Law Alumni Fund, the Alexander von Humboldt Foundation, and the University of Washington Japan Endowment Fund, for which I remain very grateful.

Finally, I am indebted to Academic Press, the Faculty of Law of Kobe University, New York University Press, Sage Publications, and the Society for Japanese Studies for permission to reproduce and adapt portions from the following of my articles:

"The Politics of Informal Justice: The Japanese Experience, 1922–1942," in
Abel, R., ed., *The Politics of Informal Justice*, vol. 2 (New York, 1982),
pp. 125–147. ©Academic Press

"The Role of Law in Japan: An Historical Perspective," *Kobe University
Law Review, no. 18 (1984), pp. 1–20.* ©Faculty of Law, Kobe University

"Mission to Manage: The U.S. Forest Service as a 'Japanese' Bureaucracy,"
in Hayashi, K., ed., *The U.S.-Japanese Economic Relationship: Can it Be
Improved?* (New York, 1989), pp. 196–225. ©New York University Press

"Confession, Repentance and Absolution," in Wright, M. and Galaway, B.,
eds., *Mediation and Criminal Justice: Victims, Offenders and Communities*
(London, 1989), pp. 195–211. ©Sage Publications

"Sheathing the Sword of Justice: Law Without Sanctions." *Journal of
Japanese Studies*, vol. 8, no. 2 (Summer 1982), pp. 265–281. ©Society for
Japanese Studies

Seattle, Wash.   J.O.H.
May, 1991

Contents

Authority without Power

Introduction

The Japanese Paradox

From a Western—especially an American—perspective, Japan appears to share many characteristics of other East Asian societies. The legacy of Chinese influence is manifest in Japan's language, its arts, religion, and the most basic perceptions of the individual's relationships to family, community, and nation. These include prevailing social definitions of authority and the role of the state. The Japanese like their East Asian neighbors seem to accept the perogative of those who rule to intervene and regulate nearly all aspects of community life subject, however, to a moral obligation to govern with empathy and benevolence. As reflected in the legal system, these characteristics also include ideological concern for the preservation of personal ties of kinship and loyalty, avoidance of conflict, as well as mediation and conciliation in the settlement of disputes. Also apparent is a tendency to avoid legalistic approaches in the ordering of personal and corporate relationships, coupled with an almost fatalistic sense of the futility of most attempts to control or regulate the future, exemplified in a reticence to rely on law, whether contract or code, as the primary instrument of social ordering.

Although some observers perceive these characteristics to be peculiarly Japanese, they are aspects of Japan's cultural indebtedness to a broader tradition that Japan shares with China, Korea, and other historically sinicized societies of East Asia. One can accurately substitute Korea or China for Japan for many observations, which are usually offered with an explicit or implicit comparison with the West in mind, that purport to depict the distinctive features of the Japanese social, political, or legal environment.

How different Japan appears, however, in comparison with its East Asian neighbors. Relative to Korea or China, Japan is distinguished by its resemblance to the West. Its feudal-like experience with development of martial arts and rule by a distinctively organized military caste, the diffusion of political power, and the scope of community autonomy seem far less Asian and far more Western in kind. From an East Asian perspective, the bonds of family are weaker in Japan than those of territorial or corporate communities and of contract. Japan is also a more litigious, legalistic society, one in which the claims of rule by and of law seem quite relevant in comparison to other East Asian societies.

If few of the most characteristic features of Japan's social order and na-tional polity appear unique—with manifest parallels to either the East or West—the list is still remarkable. It contains an almost endless pairing of opposites. Japan is notable as a society with both extraordinary institutional continuity along with institutional change; of cohesion with conflict, hierarchy with equality, cooperation with competition, and above all else a manifest prevalence of community control with an equally strong impulse toward in-dependence and autonomy. Japan thus presents a multifaceted paradox. It is a nation where political rule appears strong but also weak; governance central-ized but also diffused; the individual subservient but also achieving; the social order closed but also open.

These paradoxical features of Japanese society make it all the more difficult to fit Japan into any prescribed model of social, political, or economic behavior. Japan as well as those who study it seem almost destined to remain separate from the mainstream. One result is that scholars who specialize on Japan are often deeply divided on the most basic issues, such as the contribution of government policy or market competition in Japan's economic growth.[1] Scholarship on Japan is frequently criticized as isolated and uninformed by general theoretical con-structs and comparative research. In response, Japan specialists argue that prevail-ing models do not apply and that too often comparative research fails to integrate effectively the Japanese experience.[2] For those in government or business who deal with Japan directly in negotiating policies or trade, the Japanese paradox can be equally frustrating and divisive. Fundamental assumptions of political and economic behavior do not seem to hold.[3]

Legal scholars and lawyers are not immune from these conflicts. A glance at the contemporary legal literature on Japan reveals equally divergent views. Legal scholars in Japan and abroad disagree over the most basic propositions regarding the role and use of law and the legal process.[4]

Law, however, is a special case. Law is territorial and legal systems are themselves self-defining, cultural belief systems. The nature and role of law are delineated in any society within its particular cultural and institutional matrix. Unlike economic or social theory, law makes few claims to universally valid propositions. Law like language is bound within particular historical so-cial contexts.

It seems especially appropriate for a book about both law and Japan to attempt to explain the Japanese paradox. As a study of a legal order in a specific context, this book is intended to expand understanding of the function and limits of law in society. Japan's legal order thus becomes the focus for a broader exploration of the interrelationships of law, social order, and change. As a study of Japan, however, it is also an endeavor to gain a deeper and more accurate image of Japan and the impact of its history and shared habits on the institutions and processes of law and, in turn, their influence on that history and those habits. The purpose of this book therefore is twofold: to use Japan as a window to law and law as a window to Japan.

At the outset some attempt at clarification of common ground seems in order. The reader is entitled to know something of the underlying theory that informs the analysis that follows and to have the pivotal terms, especially *authority*, *power*, and *legitimacy*, defined. Above all the word "law" can mean many things. There are no universally accepted views of the elements and functions of law or the relationships between law and alternative extralegal or social means of societal ordering and control. The propositions that form the basis of this analysis of Japanese law thus need to be clearly stated at the outset.

The Elements, Attributes, and Functions of Law

By definition, all legal systems, Japan's included, comprise two primary elements—norms and sanctions—and the related institutions and processes for making and enforcing legal rules. The first element requires little explanation: The substantive norms expressed as rules of law and the institutions and processes of their making are familiar in all societies with developed political institutions. We readily recognize, for example, legislatures, administrative agencies, courts, or their institutional analogues and the distinctive procedures of each for recognizing, articulating, or changing, as well as enforcing, identifiable rules and standards as law.

It is by means of the distinctive institutions and processes of lawmaking that legal norms and rules are distinguished from their nonlegal counterparts, which may be similar or even identical in content. Take, for example, law library rules. Those of public universities in the United States are ordinarily subject to rules adopted by a state agency to statutorily prescribed administrative rulemaking procedures and are commonly published in state administrative law codes. They are thus ordinarily treated as justiciable legal rules. Regardless of content or form, those of private universities are not, inasmuch as private universities are by definition not agencies of the state. Their rules are not law.

In any society a wide range of norms thus exist that may be enforced by a variety of sanctions. Yet neither the norm nor the sanction is considered law without special institutional recognition. In both Japan and the United States, for example, to keep one's word or promise and to honor one's parents are widely accepted social norms. The first is recognized in both countries in codes, statutes, and decisional law as the basis for the law of contract. Similarly in neither country is the norm of honoring one's parents a clearly recognized legal norm although in both it is reflected in certain legal rules.

Only a fraction of all the norms and sanctions that order social life in any community are actually defined as law. The choice is made by delineating the specific institutions and processes that make or enforce legal rules. In other words, legal systems must internally define which rules and sanctions are accorded the status of law by designating which institutional processes make and enforce legal as opposed to nonlegal rules. All legal orders must at least implicitly therefore have two separate categories of rules. The first encompasses those norms regarded as the law in that system. The second, however, includes those rules that define which norms are to be included in the first category. The selection of norms and rules defined, to paraphrase H.L.A. Hart,[5] as the "primary" legal rules of the law in a particular legal order is determined by the 'secondary' legal rules of that system. We must keep in mind, however, that secondary rules are particular to individual legal systems. Consequently no universal definition of law is possible. At best only some common attributes of law and legal processes can be described.

First, all societies in which a concept of law has evolved equate it with the rules and sanctions recognized and applied by those who exercise *political authority*. Although perhaps originating in deistic command or the implicit principles of some transcendental order, only in a theocratic state are such commands or principles fully equated with law. Even then, however, religious and political authority are generally combined. Similarly, as explained below, rules and sanctions evolved through custom or established by consensual communities should be distinguished from law, although perhaps functionally equivalent to legal rules and sanctions, unless they are at least incidentally recognized and applied by those with recognized political authority.

Another special attribute of legal norms is their *legitimacy*, in other words, community recognition of the bindingness of the norm and the appropriateness of the sanction for its violation. The legitimacy of legal rules is, however, indirect or contingent in that it derives from the legitimacy of the political authority that promulgates or enforces the law. Dictionary definitions to the contrary notwithstanding, not all law is legitimate. Community judgment of legitimate authority is grounded in culture and custom. Shared religious symbols, social myths, and "folk ways" sanctified by habit and expectation are the ultimate sources of legitimacy. Law as custom, too, acquires a mantle of acceptance. Otherwise rules articulated in a statute, judicial decision, or administrative regulation are legitimate as law ultimately as a result of the legitimacy of those processes themselves. Conversely, if the authority and processes used for prescribing a rule as law are deemed illegitimate, the rules they create also risk being considered illegitimate. If, however, the institutions and processes for lawmaking are themselves viewed as legitimate, they legitimate the rules they create.

This *contingent legitimacy* of law is especially important in order to understand the reception of Western law in modern Japan, which included both the introduction of continental European legal institutions in the late nineteenth and early twentieth centuries as well as the constitutional and other legal reforms under the postwar Allied Occupation (1945–52). The legitimacy of the new legal rules created by those in authority enabled dramatic social change despite conflict with preexisting customary and legal norms. This is not to say that the new Western norms were in all instances overriding. However, as detailed below, in nearly all cases the failure of a new derivative norm to supplant a conflicting customary norm was a consequence of the enforcement process—such as judicial recognition of the customary norm as preeminent or a failure to enforce the new norm altogether.

The attribute of contingent legitimacy also underscores the crucial import-ance of broad societal acceptance of the legitimacy of political authority. Again, the endurance of the legal reforms initiated by the new political leaders of Meiji Japan as well as those nearly a century later of American military commanders during the Allied Occupation can be explained at least in part by the recognition on the part of Japanese society generally that their authority was legitimate. This acceptance of authority was therefore fundamental to Japan's capacity to adapt to institutional and economic transformation without political and social upheaval. Hence the factors that contribute to political legitimacy ultimately also determine legal legitimacy.

"Institutionalized" and "customary" legal orders should also be differenti-ated. At least in so doing we are better able to deal analytically with the role of culture—which for the purposes of this study simply means values, habits, and expectations widely shared throughout a society. An institutionalized sys-tem is one in which either or both the making and enforcing of rules occur through established procedures and institutions—functions exercised by estab-lished political authority. Nearly all contemporary societies have institu-tionalized legal orders in which legislatures, administrative bodies, and courts are the basic institutions for lawmaking and law enforcing. We can easily envision, however, institutionalized systems with much simpler arrange-ments—such as, councils of elders or chieftains—for performing these tasks. Moreover, in complex societies, as noted before, a variety of institutions exist, only a few of which make or enforce law. Nonetheless, whatever the structure, a hierarchy of political authority remains a prerequisite to any institutionalized system.

A noninstitutionalized or customary order, in contrast, is one in which rules are either made or enforced or both by means of consensus and habitual com-munity behavior. Although we would be hard pressed to identify a purely cus-tomary social order—for by definition no hierarchy of authority could exist in such a society and thus equality among all members (however defined) would be required—all societies do contain a variety of constituent customary orders, however peripheral or minor they may seem. In any event, in such an order, both norms, as customary rules and standards, and sanctions exist, but they require community consensus to remain viable. Since custom to be cus-tom depends upon mutual conformity, a norm that ceases to be recognized by the community as a legitimate or binding guide for conduct ceases by defini-tion to be a customary rule. Similarly, only the sanctions a community can and will apply against nonconforming conduct remain viable. No functional distinction exists, of course, between the customary rules in a noninstitution-alized system, although perhaps labeled "law," and the customary rules in an institutionalized order, even if distinguished from the norms defined as "law." What matters is to distinguish between rules and sanctions viewed as "law" in an institutionalized system from what is customary in both.

A primary attribute of legal rules is, as noted above, their indirect or con-tingent legitimacy effected by the legitimacy of the institutions and processes through which they are recognized or created. In contrast, customary norms are by definition legitimate as custom and thus depend directly upon community acceptance or consensus to remain viable. We can identify, for example, customary rules of conduct by conforming conduct. If the conduct changes, the rule is thereby altered. With custom, notes Roberto Unger, "There is a point at which deviations from the rule remake the rule itself. Thus, every act leads a double life: it constitutes conformity or disobedience to custom at the same time that it becomes part of the social process by which custom is defined."[6] As Unger recognizes, to codify custom is to transform it into law. The result, however, is to free what had been a customary rule from dependence upon habit and consent. Instead, as law it becomes dependent like all other legal norms on institutional processes for definition, change, and continued legitimacy. In a sense two rules exist, one is legal and as such dependant on institutional processes and the other customary supported by continued habit. The distinction remains obscure until one or the other changes and conflict between law and custom ensues.

Like custom the viability of legal norms as viable rules or "living law" also depends ultimately upon voluntary compliance and consent. In the end habit and consent sustain law even in regimes of terror, which risk losing the capacity to legitimate norms and sanctions as their political institutions and legal processes themselves lose legitimacy. Institutionalized legal rules are, nevertheless, more resistant as law than custom to changes in community attitudes and impulse in that their legitimacy, unlike custom, is effected by a lawmaking process instead of direct consent. Moreover, because process rather than belief and behavior legitimates legal rules, lawmaking institutions have the capacity to create consensus and thus to introduce new rules. The end result is a third attribute of law: its *consensus-creating capacity*. Imagine, for instance, a community in which there is a shared customary proscription, for instance, against eating meat. As a customary norm such a taboo begins to diminish as soon as anyone in the community begins to eat meat openly. If one person may, then anyone (at least in the same peer group) may, and as such nonconforming conduct spreads, the customary prohibition fades. Conversely, a statute proscribing use or possession of meat may be effective even without universal acceptance of the rule within the community. At least some members of the community can be expected to obey the statute and refrain from eating meat simply because it is against the law.   ·

Omitted in this illustration is the question of sanctions and enforcement. Most definitions of law and discussions of legal systems fail to distinguish lawmaking from law enforcing. To many such joinder may appear necessary as an intrinsic feature of law. Not so. Law without sanctions or lawmaking without law enforcement may be rare but not inconceivable. A rule is no less legitimate and no less binding because the community lacks either the means or will to compel conformity. As noted at the outset, law enforcing is a distinct and separate component of any legal order.

A fourth attribute of legal rules is indeed what might be labeled their *justiciability* or capacity for formal enforcement. As noted, in all communities legal norms can be and are in fact enforced by a variety of extralegal means, some purely social or customary, others more formal and institutional. Only certain institutionalized enforcement proceedings within any legal regime, however, are recognized as appropriate for the enforcement of legal rules. This being so, conversely, any norms that are actually enforced in some formal legal enforcment process are thereby recognized and become legal rules. Take, for example, a purely customary rule that allows the members of a community to forage for wood in private forest land. Such a rule may be enforced for years by community tolerance and refusal to ostracize or otherwise penalize such conduct, yet it is still not recognized as a legal rule. However, once a "right" to forage is raised formally, say, in a lawsuit for trespass by the proprietor, the adjudicator must determine the viability of the customary rule. A decision for the proprietor represents in effect an expansion of private property rights displacing the customary norm, but a decision in favor of the putative trespasser in effect redefines custom as an institutionalized legal rule or, in the private law context, a right. Thus the self-defining nature of law is most evident in the context of enforcement. Since only legal norms are enforceable in formal legal proceedings, law-enforcing processes are in effect also lawmaking processes. Hence any law-enforcing process, especially adjudication, is both a lawmaking and a law-enforcing process.

As explained above, the processes for the creation and change of norms vary. As we have seen, norms are created by custom and various institutional processes. These can be classified as legal or nonlegal, depending upon the secondary rules of each legal system for the recognition of legal rules and standards. In a purely customary process, in contrast, norms depend directly upon consensus and therefore they change as a direct consequence of nonconforming behavior. Law-enforcing processes can be similarly categorized. The processes of formal law enforcement of course include criminal and administrative proceedings. The private lawsuit should also be viewed as a formal means of law enforcement. In addition a variety of extralegal means of enforcing norms exist. Various forms of ostracism, for example, constitute a sanction employed within social groups, either spontaneously without any formalized decision, or as a result of urging by those in authority or with influence. Sanctions are also applied or directed by those in authority within communities or groups from the family to the firm without being recognized by the secondary rules of the particular legal order as law enforcement.

By treating lawmaking and law enforcing as separate components of the legal process, we are able to explain both the fundamental dynamics of legal rules and the pivotal factors that determine the role and limits of law in a given society.

The first proposition is that enforcement frees the viability of a legal norm from consensus. This can perhaps be best stated negatively: unless a legal rule is enforced its viability depends like custom directly on consensus both with respect to the legitimacy of the content of the particular norm itself plus the legitimacy of the norm as law. As illustrated by the taboo against eating meat, the effectiveness of a statute prohibiting use or possession of meat without any penalty depends upon voluntary compliance—that is, consent—or social sanctions for noncompliance. In both instances, the effectiveness of the rule depends on community acceptance. As explained above, the value of having a legal rule rather than simply customary convention or a "private" rule (e.g., a company rule) is its indirect or contingent legitimacy and thus its consensus-creating capacity. The legalization of a rule helps to foster or at least buttress consensus.

By the same token, as noted above with respect to lawmaking by adjudication, a customary rule subject to formal law enforcement becomes viable as a legal rule and indeed inevitably acquires the attributes of the legal rule. A judicial or adjudicatory enforcement process thus operates in fact if not legal theory as a lawmaking process. We also talk of private lawmaking by contract, yet it is not the adoption of the contract rule by private consent but the enforcement of the agreement that transforms the provisions of the contract into legal rules. Were, for whatever reason, a contract to be deemed legally unenforceable, then the rules set out by agreement have neither the force nor legitimacy of law; rather they remain formally unenforceable despite the fact that they might well be readily enforceable through marketplace or other nonlegal sanctions. In this sense, there can be no informal lawmaking.

A second proposition follows from the first. If enforcement determines whether legal rules are viable independently from consent, then, to this extent, those who control the enforcement process control the viability of the legal rule. Prosecutorial discretion, broadly defined to include control over all forms of law enforcement, thus becomes or should become the central focus of any inquiry as to the role of law in society. The answer to the question of who exercises such discretion tells us much about who governs.

Control over the law enforcement process in most legal systems can be divided into two basic categories: public and private. In what I shall call *public law regimes*, control over enforcement is entrusted to those with the political authority to govern, such as officials in the law-enforcing bureaucracies of the state. They may be prosecutors or police, magistrates or judges, or administrative officials of all sorts. Whatever the label, state officials in public law regimes monopolize control over the coercive mechanisms for law enforcement. Although in some instances enforcement may be initiated by private parties by complaint or petition, the prosecution of the case and control over its ultimate resolution, whether by settlement or the application of sanctions, rests with the state.

In contrast, in *private law regimes*, discretion or control over the means of formal law enforcement is exercised by private parties, whose authority to exercise such 'prosecutorial' powers is delineated in a variety of forms, such as standing, capacity, or indeed, the concept of legal rights. A private law regime requires some mechanism to allocate the power to control the application of remedies and sanctions, to determine who could bring what action against whom and for what remedy.[7] A means is found in the concepts of "rights" and "duties" insofar as these notions serve to delineate persons with the legally recognized capacity to enforce prescribed substantive legal rules, whether made by legislative, judicial, or administrative organs or, as in the case of contracts, private citizens with rule-making capacity. Consequently, all private law regimes require some concept of legal "rights" or their equivalent.

Private law as process is central to the Western legal tradition as derived from Roman law. Roman law was after all primarily a system of rights defined as the claims of individuals to protection by specific procedures and remedies. Stripped to its essentials, the notion of legal rights in Western law thus expresses the capacity of the individual to activate and control the process of enforcing legal norms. Although today the term is used more broadly—for instance, to define property—other terms such as interest, estates, or entitlements are more appropriate. The notion of a legal right is meaningful, therefore, only when it entitles the holder to legal protection upon demand. Thus the Roman law maxim *ubi ius ibi remedium* ("where there is a right, there is a remedy") is more than an aphorism. It expresses the crux of private law and the Western legal tradition.

A concept of rights is not necessary, of course, for the enforcement of legal rules. Duties alone suffice. Law in China, Korea, and Japan before the adoption of Western legal institutions did not require a concept of rights for enforcement. The word "law" meant punishment. Codes and statutes were administrative or penal. Legal rules were uniformly proscriptive. There were no rights only duties. Although "civil" or private law rules as defined in substantive terms today can be identified in traditional East Asian law—that is, rules governing family, contracts, property, commercial transactions, and other private matters—they were generally expressed as commands, violation of which was subject to some prescribed penalty[8] or incident to what seems best described as administrative enforcement by an essentially regulatory state.[9] Viewed from this perspective, courts are above all else law-enforcing institutions. From a litigant's perspective, at least, the primary function of litigation is therefore to enforce legal rules, not to resolve disputes. The essential difference between private lawsuits and criminal or administrative proceedings is that private parties instead of state officials control the process of enforcement.

The complexity of social organization should also be kept in mind. No nation or state reflects a single homogeneous, cohesive community governed by a single set of informal or formal institutional arrangements. There are in all societies the lesser communities of neighborhoods, towns, and villages, of families and firms, of voluntary associations, occupational organizations, and other social organizations and subcultures, within each of which formal and informal processes for rule making and rule enforcing operate. Only certain institutions in any society, as noted, however, have the capacity to legislate or to enforce legal norms. These and only these constitute the institutions and processes of the legal system, which in all contemporary industrial societies reflect the power and authority of the state. The horrors of the Stalinist and Nazi systems of justice in which the law and its enforcement were used as integral instruments of state control evidence the error of Max Weber's statement in 1922 that "formal justice is thus repugnant to all authoritarian powers, theoretic as well as patriarchic, because it diminishes the dependency of the individual upon the grace and power of the authorities."[10] By vesting the power to choose what norms to legalize and to enforce in the state and its officials, public law orders provide the instruments for legalized repression and totalitarian rule. The "formal justice" Weber surely had in mind was that of natural law rules and private law regimes in which some rules are beyond state redefinition and control over enforcement rests primarily with private parties. Such a regime had expanded in Germany by the end of the nineteenth century to encompass even criminal justice within its ambit through the *Legalitätsprinzip*, or doctrine of mandatory prosecution, which denies the procuracy discretion over criminal prosecution. Enforcement, however, need not be a formal process. Informal enforcement by private parties may have similar effect as evidenced by the Japanese experience. Private property and contracts do not require state protection under all circumstances.

Having examined the elements and attributes of law, we need to understand also its function. The essential purpose of all rules, and therefore law itself, is to promote conforming conduct or, in the negative, to prevent nonconformity to the underlying norms and values they reflect. Consequently the ultimate aim of law is order; its function is conservative. This is perhaps most evident in the classic definition of a liberal order as one in which rules are kept to the minimum to maintain a necessary degree of order without impairing nonconformity and thus the capacity of the society to change politically and economically. Consequently, in liberal states the most important rules are rules against rules, above all constitutional rules that restrict the powers of government or political organs in order to conserve and protect the liberal order itself.

Viable liberal legal orders, however, require some mechanism for enforcing these rules against rules. Since, as explained, those who exercise the powers of enforcement are ultimately themselves freed from the constraints of most unwanted legal rules they enforce, some institutional mechanism had to be developed. The answer in the West was the independent judiciary without the discretionary prosecutorial authority to initiate the cases for adjudication. To be effective, however, the judiciary must also possess some coercive mechanism for enforcement of its decisions. The common law solution lies in the power of contempt. Other systems rely on the criminal process or administrative penalties. Yet here too extralegal, social means of law enforcement may also function as a substitute for formal processes.

In all liberal democracies in the West the rule of law is far more dependent upon the political process than formal judicial powers. It is the approval or disapproval of the public as expressed indirectly in legislatures but in all events through the electoral process rather than the formal powers of the judiciary that ensures that government officials bow to judicial decrees. But, as stated before, in such cases, the community as ultimate enforcer not the judiciary determines which rules remain viable.

Law operates within the dynamics of this framework. Rules are made and unmade, enforced and left to atrophy. Some are customary; others institutional. Some may be considered law; all impose a kind of order. The nature of the order depends only in part on the institutional arrangements for both law-making and law enforcing—the traditional concern of lawyers and political scientists. Equally relevant are 'cultural' factors: the habits that constitute custom and the values that both shape and sustain consensus and legitimacy. But culture too is dynamic. What I have described here as a 'legal' process is in reality a process of social change. Habit and values are not exempt. They, too, change. What distinguishes one legal order from another, therefore, is less the role or rule of law, but who makes and enforces law by whatever means, and thus whose consensus and whose values control. In short, who enforces, governs.

Authority without Power

With this summary of the elements and functions of law and the relationship between law enforcement and the dynamics of social change in mind, we can return to the main argument of this study. What has been described as the paradox of Japan as a society rests above all on the dichotomy of authority and power. Because in English these terms are so often used interchangeably, the German distinction between *Authorität* and *Macht* may be more useful to delineate these two concepts. By authority or *Authorität*, I mean the legitimacy or socially recognized entitlement to command and to be obeyed; by power or *Macht*, the capacity to coerce others to do something they would not otherwise do. These definitions are not quite as arbitrary as they may perhaps seem. As distinct from power, authority is widely understood to interrelate with notions of legitimacy, moral and legal right, willing obedience, and obligation.[11] Power, on the other hand, can be viewed as both a capacity to influence as well as to coerce.[12] Like the contrast between request and command, influence and coercion are extremes at the ends of a continuum. Toward the middle they merge and cannot be readily differentiated. Law, as explained above, reflects both extremes. As a corpus of legitimate rules, law has the capacity to induce a conforming response, without threat of enforcement. Law in this sense persuades rather than coerces. Yet we usually think of law also as a coercive command at least in enforcement. If only for analytical clarity the distinction is important. Thus a narrow definition of power as coercion is to be preferred. Authority as command and power as coercion are essential to any legal regime. The first, authority as an entitlement to command, is most closely associated with lawmaking as a legitimate process for the creation and articulation of legal norms. The second, power, is most evident in enforcement as the capacity for coercion.

No characteristic of Japanese political life seems more remarkable or intrinsic than the separation of authority from power. As described in the chapters that follow, this separation is represented at the highest political level by the imperial institution. It is also evident in the everyday affairs of contemporary Japan, in the relative weakness of most forms of law enforcement. Japan is thus a society in which in terms of authority to act and intervene, the jurisdictional mandate as it were, government or the state seems pervasive yet its capacity to coerce and compel is remarkably weak. The result is a dependance on extralegal, informal mechanisms of social control as a means for maintaining societal order with a concomitant transfer of effective control over the rules and norms that govern society to those who are able to manipulate these informal instruments of enforcement. There is therefore in Japan both a centralization of public authority and a diffusion—albeit uneven—of coercive power. The effect, I will argue, is to ensure the stability of the basic institutions and patterns of governance and yet also to allow for a high degree of political, economic, and social change.

Law's Domain

Finally, some mention should be made of the problem of gauging the domain of law in legal cultures as different as Japan and the United States. Law, as explained above, is only one of several sources of societal control and ordering. In all communities, markets and morals operate quite effectively to channel and regulate certain economic and social conduct, either together or in competition with legal controls. Societies differ, however, in the scope or breadth of the law's domain as a system of control. In command economies, for example, black markets exist, but legal controls are considerably more pervasive although not necessarily more numerous than in market economies, in which legal controls also exist. Thus while markets may not work without enforceable property interests, property need not be enforced by law.

Were the breadth and density of legal controls of contemporary industrial democracies to be plotted along a spectrum, Japan and the United States would be placed at opposite poles. In no other industrial society is legal regulation as extensive or as coercive as in the United States or as confined and as weak as in Japan. An explanation for this aspect of Japanese reality is one of the primary aims of this book. At the outset, however, it is important for the reader to appreciate the stark contrast with the United States and to guard against a common fallacy of viewing Japan from a totally American perspective. Differences do exist but the United States has no greater claim as model or standard for comparison than Japan. Both societies represent extremes of a kind. Neither reflects the norm, if indeed any norm does exist.

Underlying the contrasts between the two societies are profound differences in concepts of law and morality and the interrelationships between the two, as well as the role of law in protecting the citizen from the state. Until the late nineteenth century, law as understood in Japan did not originate in a religious or moral order. Certain moral norms could be and were, of course, legitimated and enforced by law. Indeed, as noted later, Tokugawa sumptuary edicts were infused with moral proscription. However, Japan inherited from

China a much more "positivist" view of law as a morality-free instrument of governmental control. Legal rules were themselves nothing more or less than commands by those who exercized political authority. However influential the Confucian conception of a "natural" cosmic order in imperial governance, no natural *law* order in the Western sense was or could have been conceived within Japan's sinicized legal tradition. Moral orientations and beliefs did, of course, influence law, but only through a process of purposeful selection and adaptation by those who ruled. Nor did the legal order incorporate a corpus of moral rules that those with political authority were equally obliged to heed.

Indeed, Japan differs from both East Asian and Western societies in its lack of a broadly shared belief in transcendent, universally applicable moral values or standards. Karel van Wolferen expresses this point quite well: "Concepts of independent universal truths or immutable religious beliefs, transcending the worldly reality of social dictates and the decrees of power-holders have of course found their way into Japan, but they have never taken root in any surviving world-view." "The fact," van Wolferen continues, "that Japanese have situational instead of general moral rules and hold particular values rather than universalistic ones" provides crucial "clues to Japanese behavior."[13] He could have also added, to law and its domain. Japanese attitudes toward law, their willingness to circumscribe its applicability and scope, and their acceptance of competing means of social ordering and control, especially consensual patterns of governance, rest in part on their relatively weak sense of transcendent norms as moral imperatives. For whatever reason, the identity of law and morality in the United States, however, has long been extraordinarily durable. As Judith Sklar in a brilliant study of the American ideology of law[14] observes, legalism—that is, "the ethical attitude that holds moral conduct to be a matter of rule following, and moral relationships to consist of duties and rights determined by rules"[15]—has grown luxuriantly in American cultural soil. This coupled with the continuing influence of various versions of natural law theory,[16] has produced a remarkably expansive legal domain.

One consequence of the American ideology of law is both to exaggerate the importance of law and neglect other means for social ordering. The end results are to skew the measurement of other systems and to foster a perilous misunderstanding of law and society. Illustrative is the tendency to equate effective enforcement of contractual undertakings and protection of private property with legal regimes and state power. Japan, I suggest, exemplifies a society in which contracts and property have both been effectively protected without law or state intervention. Thus a closer examination of Japan, it is hoped, will provide a useful antidote. Except in its historical experience, Japan is not unique. While differences in emphasis do exist, we need to understand equally important similarities in kind.

I

Continuity with Change:
The Historical Foundations of
Governance and Legal
Control in Japan

The endurance of past attitudes and values, from familial orientations to a propensity to avoid litigation, is a commonplace theme in much of the literature on Japanese law. Too often, however, whatever aspects of Japanese life that do not seem to conform to occidental expectations of model behavior are labeled "traditional" and left at that without much further analysis or thought. No society, of course, severs the links with its own past. Japan is no exception. Like other facets of Japanese society, Japan's processes of governance as well as its shared attitudes toward law and legal institutions reflect past and present interactions and mutual influence. One cannot understand the present without an appreciation of the past and the role of present perceptions of that past. To appreciate the historical dynamics of Japan's legal tradition is vital both to comprehend more fully the present as well as to predict more accurately the future. In that tradition one expects to discover the source of today's political echoes and the paradigms of contemporary governance. Yet defining Japan's legal tradition is not a simple task.

The historical development of Japan's legal system divides rather neatly into two broadly defined periods. Each features an abrupt infusion of foreign ideas and institutions followed by a gradual process of indigenous adaptation. The first, during which Japan developed what might best be described as an ambivalent tradition, is characterized by the tensions between the ideas and institutions derived from early imperial Chinese law and those forged by native Japanese political and social forces. Japan's legal tradition and its first paradigm of legal control thus began with institutional and conceptual borrowings from T'ang China (A.D. 619–906) in the seventh and eighth centuries. The period ended with short-lived efforts at institutional reform reverting to Chinese models immediately following the Meiji Restoration in 1868.

During the course of this millenium Japan evolved a complex and highly sophisticated mix of legal and social controls. By the mid-nineteenth century Japanese society had well-established institutions and processes for three basic patterns or paradigms of societal ordering and control: the administrative processes of a centralized bureaucratic state, the adjudicatory institutions for a system of judicial governance, and arrangements for indirect governance based predominantly on community-based consensual or contractual patterns of social control exemplified by the rural *mura* or village.

Reception, adaptation, and containment of Western law characterize the second period. Beginning with early translations of French codes and the introduction of French legal institutions of the 1870s, Japan experienced the institutional transformation of its legal order into a modern, predominately German-derivative, civil law system as well as the adaptation and ultimate containment of Western legal institutions during the first half of this century in the midst of rapid industrialization, worldwide depression, war, and defeat. The process continued in postwar Japan, commencing with military occupation and the imposition of American-inspired constitutional and regulatory reforms.

During each of these two periods Japan experienced dramatic changes not only in institutional arrangements but also in shared social values, attitudes, and expectations with respect to the nature and function of law. Yet, since change inexorably also confirms and reinforces something of the past, like all other social orders Japan's too reflects elements of continuity with change. For those who wish to understand both, the puzzle is to identify and fit together pieces of the process and the links between past and present. This then is the aim of the chapters that follow.

1

Emperors and Edicts:
The Paradigm of the Administrative State

Japan's institutional debt to imperial China is difficult to overstate. Borrowed concepts of the state as a political unit with authority to rule vested in an imperial institution as well as borrowed methods of centralized bureaucratic governance transformed seventh and eighth century Japan. From a new central capital, established first in A.D. 710 at Heijo (Nara) and then in 794 at Heian (Kyoto), Japan's centralizing rulers imposed a new administrative structure, legislated a new system of land tenure and taxation, and instituted a new system of rule from the center. Although only parts of a much larger cultural package enveloping the arts, language, religion, and technology, the influence of Chinese legal forms and institutions was pivotal, as acknowledged for the era that followed in the label *ritsuryō*, from the Chinese *lü -ling*, or "penal statutes and regulations." Japan also discovered in Chinese law the procedural forms and devices, as well as evidentiary techniques, of a highly developed system of investigation and rational fact-finding.[1] These were easily adapted and in effect made possible new emphases on judicial adjudication that evolved as Japan began to depart from Chinese patterns. Above all else, however, Japan learned a sinicized version of what law meant and how it was to be used. The primary contribution of the Chinese legal tradition to Japan was thus an appreciation of law and the parameters of its use as a means of social control, of law as an instrument of government control quite separate from any moral or religious order serving the interests of those who exercised paramount political authority.

Public versus Private Law Orders and the
Primacy of State Interests

Japan's earliest formal legal order was grounded in a tradition in which law was no more nor less than an indispensable instrument of state control. By the third century B.C. the principal features of the Chinese legal order had already taken shape. It was conceptually a *public law regime* as defined above. Law was restricted to regulatory statutes and codified administrative instructions defining prescribed duties owed to the court as the embodiment of political authority, with control over the processes for both making and enforcing these rules confined to the court and its bureaucracies. In imperial China, all law was public, commonly defined in contemporary Western jurisprudence to comprise such fields as constitutional law, administrative law, and criminal law. As A.F.P. Hulsewé observes:

> [T]hrough the ages "law" to the Chinese always meant public law; neither ancient China nor traditional China knew an officially established code of private law. Both family law with all its regulations concerning marriage and divorce or inheritance, as well as commercial law were private concerns in China, left respectively to the family and to the guilds. Chinese law was preeminently public law; penal law on the one hand and administrative rules on the other.[2]

This did not mean that Chinese codes and statutes were devoid of rules we would today classify as "private law"—that is, rules on family relations, contracts, property, commercial matters, and other relationships between private persons. Or, as explained previously, that contracts and commercial transactions were not enforced through an adjudicatory process. Creel finds references to rulings for contracts to be carried out in bronze inscriptions from the Chou dynasty (1122–256 B.C.)[3] and Hulsewé notes rules related to family matters in recently discovered fragments of Han dynasty (206 B.C.–A.D. 220) law.[4] The T'ang Code (A.D. 653) included extensive regulations related to marriage, divorce, and other family matters, including disposition of property, as well as miscellaneous provisions on what would now be categorized as contractual and commercial transactions.[5] As early as the Ch'in dynasty (third century B.C.), however, such rules were invariably expressed as proscriptions or commands, violations of which were subject to an elaborate scheme of fixed penalties. Although subsequent codes and regulations contained numerous rules for cases involving family relations, marriage, landed property, and loans, adjudication of such cases was more of an administrative burden with the relatively greater official discretion to hear the case and to devise an appropriate remedy. Such ostensibly "civil" cases were "lumped together" in the words of Shūzō Shiga, not "because their main concern was the realization of a citizen's rights, but rather because they were minor ones involving no possibility of severe punishment."[6] A principal aim of the trial in such cases was to induce performance of public duties or settlement by threat of punishment if necessary.[7] The law-enforcing mechanisms thus remained in the discretionary control of the magistrates. Generally, only conduct considered by imperial officials to impinge on state interests was made subject to legal regulation and control. All other behavior was left principally to other means of social ordering.

In comparison, as law evolved in the West through ancient Greek, Roman, and medieval European systems, private law and an adjudicatory process of enforcement were central. There was of course public law, especially in the late Roman system, with penal and administrative regulation and an enforcing officialdom. Nonetheless, the distinctive feature of the Western legal tradition, as represented by Roman law as perceived and rearticulated in Western Europe from the eleventh through the nineteenth centuries, was the primacy of private law and, more important, a judicial process of enforcement.

As an adjudicatory process for recognizing and enforcing legal rules under the control of private litigants developed, the Roman system produced the prototypical private legal regime of the Western tradition. In private law matters the Roman magistrate functioned with respect to the parties as a neutral arbiter, not a policing or prosecuting official. Citizen claimants or petitioners not only initiated the process, they controlled it. Within the parameters set by the procedural rules that evolved for pleading and forms of action, the litigants themselves defined the issues, the facts to be proven, the evidence to be submitted. They could settle or withdraw the suit—or choose to proceed to judgment. Execution was subject to even greater litigant control. "Judgment given," Crook points out, "the duty of the judge was over."[8] Left to the successful plaintiff were all further steps at coercion. The authorities gave no physical assistance. The law prescribed the consequences but enforcement was left to the parties.

The Chinese magistrate, in contrast, had full authority and control over enforcement. "Once a case had been submitted to the magistrate," Brockman observes, "the plaintiff lost all control over it."[9] Not restricted to issues or facts asserted by the parties nor compelled to do anything more than to commence proceedings, at least with respect to the parties, the Chinese magistrate exercised within the restraints of relevant regulation complete discretion over the application of coercive sanctions or remedies. As might be expected, a magistrate's failure to act became a major cause for the manipulation of pleas[10] and outright bribery.[11] Attempts by higher officials to restrict such discretion were apparently ineffective.[12] Whether by illegal circumvention or legitimate authority, the magistrate in fact controlled the process from start to finish.

The nature of the sinicized legal systems of East Asia as public law regimes also precluded the development of the concept of "legal rights." Again to quote Hulsewé, Chinese law "only knew duties; duties toward the state and duties toward one's elders and betters."[13] In contrast, Roman law was above all a system of rights defined by specific procedures and remedies as the claims of individuals. Legal rights functioned conceptually, as explained previously, to delineate those persons with the legally recognized capacity to enforce certain substantive legal rules, whether made by legislative, administrative, or judicial authorities, or even, as in the case of contracts, private parties given rulemaking authority.

Only within an adjudicatory private law system was a mechanism for allocating control over enforcement necessary: to determine *who* may bring *what* actions against *whom* for *what* remedy or sanction. The notion of legal rights as developed in Western law thus signified the capacity of the litigant to activate and control the process for enforcing the substantive rules or norms of the law as politically legislated or judicially recognized and enforced. In this sense, as noted previously, the concept of legal rights must be distinguished from other, broader uses of the term, for example, in defining property interests or estates. The crux of Western law and all developed private law regimes is therefore the concept of a legal right as legitimate demand for state enforcement of a legal rule. Legal rights have little place, however, in public law regimes. Such regimes recognize no such entitlement or right to the formal procedures for law enforcement beyond the discretionary control of political authorities. That contemporary public law recognizes citizen rights against the state in effect represents one of the most significant contributions of the Roman private law regime in the transference of the private law process to the public law domain.

State control over the process for making and enforcing legal norms assures that state interests prevail. Only those norms and rules deemed important to those who rule are secured and maintained. Not unexpectedly, therefore, one discovers in the codes of successive Chinese dynasties from the Ch'in through the Ch'ing (1644-1911) an emphasis on precepts of respect, loyalty, and obedience to those in authority but not the equally important, reciprocal ethical duties of benevolence owed by rulers to the ruled. Law was an instrument of state control not an instrument to control the state, while the traditional moral order or cosmology regulated both.

The T'ang Code's list of the most heinous crimes—the Ten Abominations of article 6—can all be construed as offenses against the state, such as plotting rebellion, or against those in authority, such as lack of filial devotion. Even the offense of "unrighteousness" (*pu-yi*), which could have included certain violent acts against inferiors, was defined in the commentaries, except for certain sexual offenses, in terms of offenses against superiors, such as killing of department heads, magistrates, and commanding officers, as well as improper behavior by wives in mourning the death of a husband.[14]

Nor is it surprising that so little "private law" is found in the codes and statutes. As in other public law regimes, the legal rules promulgated and enforced by the state reflected the interests and priorities of those who ruled. Equally important, discretion over enforcement enabled the magistrate, their clerks, and others in a position to manipulate the process in their own interests, to control the norms and rules that were enforced. Violation of rules they considered important and the particular cases they could be persuaded to hear could be handled more expeditiously and prosecuted more rigorously. As a result not only were legal rules enacted to deal with private disputes that touched on important state or bureaucratic interests, but also formal rules could be ignored or manipulated to serve the interests of the enforcers.

Most prosecution was initiated by private complaint and pursued by private prosecution. However, at least as early as the T'ang Code two basic prosecutorial procedures were recognized. In cases involving more serious offenses, such as treason or homicide, the authorities were required to act upon an accusation. However, for crimes considered less important in terms of state interests, private prosecution with considerable discretion on the part of the magistrate to avoid judgment and to promote settlement was the rule. The T'ang Code's incorporation of the principles of "retributive punishment" for false accusations and "retributive torture" to ensure equality in treatment between accuser and accused, deterred all but the most determined to make an accusation and prosecute a case.[15] Many scholars, including Noboru Niida, see in these procedural distinctions and the sorts of offenses covered by each, an embryonic dichotomy between criminal and civil litigation.[16] Such categories had no real meaning in the Chinese system. These distinctions reflected no more or less than the gravity of the proscribed conduct as defined by imperial state interests, including the maintenance of peace and order.

For most private disputes, however, out of court settlement was at least preferred if not required. Harmonious settlement of the quarrel rather than an outcome in conformity with norms established by law was generally in the interest of the state and its officials as well as the parties who controlled extralegal processes of settlement. In other words, for most private disputes, the authorities were primarily concerned with peaceful resolution whatever the result, not the enforcement of particular rules or norms of behavior. Emphasis on mediation or conciliation notwithstanding violations of explicit legal rules—whether the settlement of commercial disputes within a guild, village controversies within the community, or family quarrels within the extended household—reflected indifference on the part of the state and its officials to the conformity of the outcome to any prescribed rule or standard. In such instances peaceful settlement, not law enforcement, was the primary official concern. However unlawful, conduct with little impact on sensitive official interests could be ignored.

The emphasis on amicable settlement of private disputes—or more accurately, coerced compromise—tended to preserve if not increase social inequalities, dependency relations, and the influence of those with social and economic power. Kung-chuan Hsiao describes the consequences in China:

> So long as the bulk of the rural population remained largely illiterate and generally poor, they remained also habitually passive and indifferent to public matters, and continued to allow themselves, willingly, unknowingly, or helplessly, to be led and controlled by whoever cared to do so. Indeed they were willing even to allow the task of resolving conflicts at the community level to remain largely in the hands of persons possessing special status or qualifications. It is no surprise, therefore, that compromise both as a result of self-help and of official action did not alter the basic features of Chinese society, even though under the social conditions of imperial China it was for all individuals and groups a safer course of action to take— safer than litigation or settling differences by physical force.[17]

But for some indigenous features unique to China, much the same could have been said for Korea, Japan, or any political order replicating the Chinese use of law solely as a regulatory instrument of state control. To the extent that the outcome of a dispute does not depend upon the social or legal validity of a claim but rather the ability of the party or the others to impose a more favorable compromise, what counts is either the relative power of the parties themselves as in the case of self-help or access to a more powerful intermediary if the parties resort to mediation. Power rules. Thus the lack of private law enforcement becomes in effect a force for stability. It reinforces the existing social order and allocations of power in society.

Secular versus Moral Law and the Pervasive Authority of the State

An even more fundamental contrast in the Western and East Asian legal traditions appears in the relationship of law to religion. In all Indo-European systems law originates in some sort of deistic command. From Hammurabi's code to the Hindu *dharmašâ*, the earliest written statutes explicitly acknowledge a divine source as lawgiver for specific rules and the norms they embodied. Inherent in Judaic concepts of God as lawgiver and judge is a revelation of law as an expression of religious and social norms governing the relationships between God and mankind and among mankind in society. Similarly, drawing on Stoic thought, the lawmakers of ancient Greece and later Rome recognized a "natural law" rooted in religious beliefs, out of which the concept of justice emerges as a set of universally applicable standards of fairness. As expressed by the late Roman jurist Ulpianus: "He who wishes to study law must first know whence the name *ius* derives. Now, it is so called from *iustitia*; for as Celsus nicely defined, *ius* is the art of the good and the fair *(ars boni et aequi)*."[18] And his contemporary, Paulus: "The word *ius* (law) is used in many meanings; in the first place, *ius* is said to be that which is (always) fair and good *(aequum et bonum)*, that is, the *ius naturale*. . . ."[19]

In the West, as exemplified in the word "justice," law as legislation, justiciable custom, or even administrative regulation cannot be fully divorced from moral principles. Law was and continues to be fused with morality. The "good and the fair" still pervades all notions of at least an ideal legal process and ultimately determines the legitimacy of law as made and as enforced. Law as justice also means the existence of an inherent set of legal standards applicable to lawmakers and law enforcers. If law is justice, then legal commands operate as moral commands and moral commands as legal commands that govern the ruler as well as the ruled. Although at best imperfectly realized as the authority to interpret and enforce legal rules remained in the hands of Roman authorities, churchmen, or secular rulers, the notion of justice has been intrinsic to Western law and functions as the wellspring from which the rule of law develops. Not until the emergence of the contemporary nation state in the late eighteenth and nineteenth centuries was this fusion seriously challenged.

Early Christianity might have made possible a radical departure from the existing nexus of law and morality but this separation did not endure. The Gospels and Pauline letters, for example, define moral conduct in terms of avoidance of legal rights and legal enforcement in favor of forgiveness and mercy. Quite properly, the word "justice" never appears in most English translations of the New Testament. Greek legal terminology—such terms as *dike*, *dikaios*, and *endikos*,—is used almost exclusively to express the purely religious concepts of righteousness, justification, and God's ultimate judgment. It appears that at least for a time the essentially charismatic communities of early Christians may have attempted to live out Jesus's admonition to render to God what is God's and to Caesar what is Caesar's by refusing to participate in the political or legal life of the Roman empire. However, with the establishment of the institutional church and Christianity as a state religion, Christianity, too, incorporated the Stoic vision of natural law and justice. Thereafter reinforced by the Gregorian reforms of the eleventh and twelfth centuries and then the Protestant Reformation of the fifteenth and sixteenth centuries, the bonding of law and Christian morality was to constitute, at least until modern times, an essential element of the Western legal tradition.[20] In the United States, the view expressed in the Massachusetts Code of 1648 that "there is no humane law that tendeth to the common good but the same is mediately a law of God and that in way of an Ordinance which all are to submit unto and that for conscience sake" prevailed well into the nineteenth century and is, as argued above, not without influence today.

Used in this sense, "justice" did not exist in traditional Chinese law. "(F)or in China," write Bodde and Morris, "no one at any time has ever hinted that any kind of written law—even the best written law—could have had a divine origin."[21] As Needham explains, "Not only were there no divine edicts in the great tradition of Chinese thought, but no divine creator who could have issued them."[22] Nor, as Needham persuasively argues, could China develop a concept of natural law or a legal order originating in a corpus of universally applicable legal rules.

> The Chinese world-view depended upon a totally different line of thought. The harmonious cooperation of all beings arose, not from the orders of a superior authority external to themselves, but from the fact that they were all parts in a hierarchy of wholes forming a cosmic pattern, what they obeyed were the internal dictates of their own natures.[23]

In the words of Leon Vandermeersch, "Whatever played the part of positive law in imperial China could stem from only one source, the will of the emperor."[24]

Notions akin to justice did exist of course. Legal rules could and did reflect ethical or moral concerns. Indeed, law in traditional China in large part represented an attempt to enforce norms perceived to be necessary to maintain social harmony and hierarchy in conformity with a shared conception of the natural or cosmic order coinciding with state interests. These norms included notions of "the good and the fair" as defined and accepted within the Chinese moral tradition, expressed as "righteousness" [*i*] as well as principles of ritual order embodied in *li*, but such conceptions of fair and correct behavior remained quite separate and independent of law as *fa* or *lü*.

The contrast is exemplified in the difficulty of accurately translating the word "justice" into East Asian languages or, conversely, the Chinese word *i* [in Japanese, *gi*] into most Western languages. The English words "justice"

and even "righteousness" reflect the fusion of law with notions of the good
and fair. Yet in traditional China and Japan, the characters commonly translated as "justice" [*seigi* in Japanese], traditionally bear no relation to law or
legal terminology.

Much has been written on the distinction between law on the one hand
and *li*, the rites or rituals representing the norms of Confucian virtue, on the
other. Studies of traditional Chinese law commonly begin by contrasting the
views of the Legalists, who considered rule by command and punishment essential to proper and effective governance and preservation of order, as opposed to the Confucianists, who insisted that rule by moral example and
practice not legal controls were the prerequisites for effective governance.
Needham, for example, quotes from the *Tso Chuan* (compiled mostly in the
third century B.C.), "Here, at the beginning of the story," he says, "appears
the uncompromising objection to codification which characterized Confucian
thought throughout Chinese history."

> In the third month the people of the State of Cheng made (metal cauldrons
> on which were inscribed the laws relating to) the punishment (of crimes).
> Shu Hsiang wrote to Tzu-Chhan (i.e., Kungsun Chiao, prime minister of
> Cheng), saying:
>
> "Formerly, Sir, I took you as my model. Now I can no longer do so.
> The ancient kings, who weighed matters very carefully before establishing
> ordinances, did not (write down) their system of punishments, fearing to
> awaken a litigious spirit among the people. But since all crimes cannot be
> prevented, they set up the barrier of righteousness (*i*), bound the people by
> administrative ordinances (*cheng*), treated them according to just usage (*li*),
> guarded them with good faith (*hsin*), and surrounded them with
> benevolence (*jen*). . . . But when the people know that there are laws
> regulating punishments, they have no respectful fear of authority. A
> litigious spirit awakes, invoking the letter of the law, and trusting that evil
> actions will not fall under its provisions. Government becomes impossible.
> . . . Sir, I have heard it said that a State has most laws when it is about to
> perish."[25]

Both Legalists and Confucianists assumed, however, the essential separation of law and morality. Legal rules could and did reflect moral concerns,
but the distinction between the two was well understood and accepted. Law
itself, whether considered essential or barely condoned, was accepted as a
necessary if distasteful instrument of state governance. "[L]aw, as Shūzō Shiga
observed, "was that which the ruler laid down, which the bureaucrats abided
by, and which the people merely received the reflective effects of."[26] Law
could reflect moral norms—selectively—but legal rules in the Chinese tradition could not be in and of themselves moral commands. Nor could moral
commands be identified as law. At best law was needed to enforce moral
precepts on those too "vicious" or "depraved" to live according to the standards of virtue through self-cultivation and self-control.[27]

Closely related to the separation of law and morality in the Chinese tradition is what Benjamin Schwartz aptly identifies as the "all encompassing

authority" of the state as "one of the most striking characteristics of Chinese civilization." [28] Schwartz explains:

> The idea of an all-embracing socio-political order centering on a particularly powerful conception of universal kingship seems to have emerged very early within the Chinese cultural world. One can indeed discern its beginnings even in Shang oracle bone inscriptions. The universal king (universal in that he presides over the universal human civilization) surrounded by his ministering elite soon comes to embody within his person both the supreme political authority and the spiritual-ethical authority of the entire society.[29]

The all-pervasive authority of the state as embodied in the office and person of the emperor was, for want of a better term, "totalitarian" in scope. As Schwartz cautions,[30] however, a caveat is necessary that any nuance of conjunction of coercive power or will with such authority is misleading. What distinguishes the conception of the state as embodied in the imperial institution in the Chinese legal tradition is the apparent lack of any bounds or limits to its authority over all aspects of social life. There was no developed concept separating "public" and "private" spheres of activity to contain state authority. Instead, private activity was in effect those areas that the state chose to exclude from its regulatory reach rather than a realm to which its authority could not extend. Traditional Chinese thought did recognize a dichotomy between "public" and "private," but these terms, imperfectly defined, were used more to differentiate more valued, "higher" official concerns, as represented by imperial authority from intrinsically base, selfish, personal interests and behavior. Commerce and family affairs could thus be regulated as "public" matters of concern to the state. Neither was entirely "private." Because the demarcation between public and private spheres of dominion and control remained elusive, individual interest could not be clearly delineated from that of the family or broader community.[31] Nor, without any notion of transcending, deistic legal commands could the traditional East Asian societies evolve a conception of a natural *law* order and, with it, the idea of a rule of law functioning at least as a conceptual restriction over the exercise of state authority. To quote again from Schwartz: "The 'political culture' was indeed unambiguously authoritarian and based on a positive evaluation of hierarchy and status. There was nothing which precluded the *ad hoc*, arbitrary and often brutal intervention of state power in the lives of groups or individuals."[32] "Yet," as Schwartz emphasizes, "the dominant orientation did not ordinarily lead to unremitting intervention by organizational means for either 'good' or 'evil' goals."[33]

One must also keep in mind that the separation of the moral and legal orders did not preclude the vitality of either. Nor does such separation necessarily mean that state power was without bounds and restraints. Much was in fact beyond coercive state control simply because of limitations in resources or political and social limits to official intrusion. The delegation to the household unit of control over most family relations, including property ar-

rangements, as well as to guilds and other organizations of regulation of commercial transactions can be viewed as a reflection of official recognition of
the limits of state power as distinguished from authority. Similarly, the political intrusion of the state produced a variety of protective responses, not the
least of which was a reinforcement of household ties and concomitant impetus
for familial representation within the bureaucratic elite. Still missing, however, was any institutionalized, legal means for restraining state authority and
power. Indeed, the Chinese moral order afforded a separate and, for the Confucianist, vastly superior source of norms controlling the conduct of rulers
and ruled alike. As Alford reminds us:

> The ancient Chinese state was not free to exercise unrestrained power. . . .
> [T]he moral ethos in the *li* and expressed in the mandate of Heaven and
> the ideal of golden age was meant to impose a fiduciary-like set of obliga-
> tions upon those in positions of power and, concomitantly, to generate
> among persons occupying inferior positions clear and enforceable expecta-
> tions as to how that power should be exercised. Thus, although the ruler
> was vested with considerable formal legal authority in order to discharge
> his duty to hear the people, and although the populace typically deferred
> to his presumed greater wisdom and moral insight, if the ruler exercised
> his power in violation of these ethical bounds, he could no longer be called
> a ruler.[34]

What is notable then in traditional Chinese attitudes in comparison with
the West is not only the deference to pervasive state authority but also the
recognition and availability of alternative, nonlegal means of social control,
which included restraints on state power.

Although as in the West, moral values provided standards against which
legal rules and their application were ultimately esteemed and could be
measured; unlike the West, the Chinese tradition and the sinicized systems of
East Asia never had the conceptual tools to resolve any conflict between law
and morals internally within the legal system itself. Thus a theory of law that
would assist in rationalizing legal rules to assure consistency with shared perceptions—theological or otherwise—of the natural order could not develop.
Irreconcilable moral and legal commands may have posed similar dilemmas
for jurists in both East Asia and the West, but neither a Chinese nor a Japanese
magistrate could accept these as inevitable and unavoidable. As official commands, he did not have to "justify" further the rules he enforced. In other
words, law unlike schools of ethical or philosophic thought did not require a
theory or other systematic explanation.

In summary, at a remarkably early point in time, China developed a highly
complex and technically sophisticated public law order in which, as a purely
secular instrument of governance, law functioned independently as a less satis-
factory and perhaps less effective alternative to moral imperatives and custom
as a source of legitimacy and means of social control. Such was the legal
tradition that for over a millennium Japan drew upon to define law and its
role in society.

Redefining the Legacy: Japan's Selective Adaptation of Chinese Legal Institutions

Little is known about Japan's earliest legal order—to the extent one can be said to have existed at all—before the infusion of Chinese concepts and institutions. As organized communities with established political leadership emerged in prehistoric Japan, they tended to be defined and identified by kinship—fictitious or real—and by belief in common deities. Claims to political authority and power in such clans, or *uji*, also tended to be based on kinship relationships as well as the perceived powers of ancestral deities. The clan chieftain, or *uji-no-kami*, combined the functions of king and priest with governance intimately intertwined with religious ritual. As such it is likely that rule by arbitration based on claims of kinship and customary norms supplemented by an occasional political command, if necessary, cast as a deity-inspired utterance, provided the essentials for rudimentary governance without written or institutional law.[35]

By the end of the fifth century, the *uji* controlling the fertile Yamato plain in Southwestern Honshū had emerged as the dominant political force with its chieftain elevated to superior status over other *uji-no-kami* as *sumeramikoto* with both military and religious claims to suzerainty.[36] This process of political consolidation coincided with increasing traffic between Japan and the Asian mainland, especially Korea, and the consequent introduction of a written language, religion, and other elements of the vastly more advanced civilization of imperial China. It was only natural therefore that the emergent political leaders of Japan would also find in imperial Chinese institutions and concepts welcome models for their own statecraft. Thus commencing with the Taika reforms in the mid-seventh century,[37] a process began of selective adaptation of Chinese legal concepts and institutions. This was Japan's first and greatest reception of foreign law.

The legislation of China's newly established T'ang dynasty provided the first models. In A.D. 662, a set of administrative instructions [*ryō*] was promulgated, followed later by the introduction of a series of penal statutes [*ritsu*]. The first known compilation of a complete, integrated "code" of penal statutes and administrative instruction in what became the standard *ritsuryō* legislative pattern came in 702 with the promulgation of the Taihō *ritsuryō*. This legislation was revised by what is now known as the Yōrō *ritsuryō* in 718. These legislative innovations were important not only for the substantive reforms they effected but also in establishing the basic pattern for subsequent Japanese legislation. Moreover, the imperial *ritsuryō*, although increasingly restricted until by the sixteenth century it was only applicable as the law of the court nobility, nevertheless remained in theory Japan's fundamental national law for over a millennium.[38]

What in substance, however, did the Japanese actually take from the Chinese tradition? What did they adapt and enforce in practice? And what did they ignore? Without more complete historical records—today only copies of the Yōrō Code and later revisions remain extant—it is impossible to answer these questions fully or with certainty. It is apparent, however, that the Japanese were selective and gradually adapted much of their conceptual and institutional borrowings. Some fit well and were readily absorbed; others were rejected or forced to atrophy.

As legislated the Yōrō *ritsu* were for the most part a direct copy of the T'ang Code. In the general provisions [*myōreiritsu*, some authorities read the characters as *meireiritsu*[39]], for example, the Yōrō lawmakers adopted verbatim all five forms of T'ang punishment.[40] Of the ten Chinese abominations, the Japanese chose only eight,[41] discarding discord [*pu-mu*] and incest [*nei-luan*]. Only six of the eight T'ang Code 'deliberations' or categories of privileged status [*i* in Chinese, *gi* in Japanese] were included.[42] The Japanese modified the *ryō* even more, including, for example, a very un-Chinese department of shrines in the organization of departments of state.[43]

Preexisting patterns of governance based on kinship ties, for example, precluded the creation of a Chinese-styled, merit-based bureaucracy. Hence in Japan, the offices of Japan's new centralized imperial governance were dominated by powerful families, particularly those with kinship ties to the throne and to the dominant Fujiwara clan. Without an effective, centralizing bureaucracy, the *ritsuryō* institutions served in fact to reinforce and strengthen the domination of the newly defined Japanese polity by a clan-based aristocracy.[44] Indigenous practices and the patterns of political authority, social organization, and control were not fully transformed. Animist beliefs continued, for example, to influence legal proceedings as reflected in the invocation of presumptively powerful ancestral deities and formal oaths.[45] Similarly, even though the Chinese idea of imperial rule transformed a rather primitive form of kingship into a lawgiving sovereign, crucial differences remained between the Japanese and Chinese conceptions of "emperor." The Japanese *sumeramikoto*, retitled *Tennō*, continued to have a distinctive religious role derived from the orientation of the *uji* chieftain as shamanist medium with ritual responsibilities to assure purity and fertility.

Nor could the Japanese incorporate Chinese cosmological claims that centered on the conception of imperial legitimacy as derived from the Mandate of Heaven. Direct biological nexus to powerful, anthropomorphic deities supported the *Tennō*'s claim to authority, thereby establishing the basis for perpetual, unconditional dynastic rule. Indeed, it would have hardly been conceivable for the Japanese to have accepted Chinese conceptions fully. After all, the Mandate of Heaven supported Chinese conceptions of an international order centering on a singular, universal Chinese sovereign. For Japan to have incorporated such ideas as a whole would have thus necessitated an act of political submission. Borrowed Confucianist norms defining crimes and establishing penalties and procedures of the *ritsuryō* could perhaps be adapted to Japanese patterns of kinship relations with relative ease. However, more basic, unstated premises of authority and power on which rule by law rested in the Chinese tradition were not as easily transplanted in the Japanese environment.[46]

Japan also made a significant departure from Chinese models in an early separation of authority from power. In Japan the imperial institution served from the start primarily as the locus and source of political legitimacy. Its power to rule was never absolute. Again preexisting patterns prevailed. A pattern of actual rule by a crown prince in lieu of the emperor was, Ryōsuke Ishii asserts, a compromise between Chinese conceptions of imperial governance and previous Japanese practice obligating the emperor to heed the advice of senior officials.[47] As the system evolved the crown prince would become emperor at an early age and also retire while still young.

Japanese legal historians also point out other significant adaptations. One was apparently a relaxation of the stringent Chinese penalties and rules for prosecution of criminal cases. Influenced in part by Buddhist emphasis on the value of mercy and with less concern for the cosmic phenomenalism mandating exact requital for specific crimes that the Chinese seem to have accepted,[48] the Japanese, it is said, enforced the penal *ritsu* much more leniently.[49] The Japanese *ritsuryō* like its Chinese source was predominately a system of retributive justice.[50] Nevertheless, it appears that the Japanese were not as bound to a system of meting out exact punishments commensurate with specific offenses.

Also, again influenced perhaps by preexisting practice—since no analogous provisions in T'ang legislation have been found—the Japanese seem to have provided for privately initiated adjudication in the earliest *ritsuryō*.[51] Although a source of controversy among contemporary legal historians, according to one view, seventh and eighth century Japanese legal scholars interpreted the *ryō* dealing with forms for official documents and instruments adopted in the Yōrō *ritsuryō* to provide a basis for private litigation.[52] Whatever the explanation, Japanese legal historians generally agree that the *ritsuryō*, like the T'ang Code, did include separate proceedings for dealing with homicide, robbery, larceny, and other serious crimes as opposed to less serious property offenses. For serious offenses under the *ritsuryō* official investigation was to begin once the offense was reported and the accused was to be taken into immediate custody. In the case of lesser offenses, however, upon receipt of the complaint, the officials were required simply to summon the accused. Also, unlike the trial of serious offenses, for which no fixed dates were set, trials for lesser offenses were held during a prescribed period (between the first day of the first month and the thirtieth day of the third month).[53] Apparently there is no evidence in Japanese practice of retributive torture and other efforts to enforce equality between the parties as practiced in Chinese law.

Although not divorced from criminal prosecution, the earliest Japanese legislation thus laid the foundations for the development of judicial adjudicatory institutions that became a distinctive feature of the traditional Japanese legal order, especially under the Kamakura shogunate.

Although only a small part of the package of cultural and institutional borrowings from China, which included Buddhism, a written language, Chinese arts, science, and technology, law was still an important element. The *ritsuryō* provided Japan with the ideas, institutions, and instruments for new, rational patterns of governance and political control. It served as the legal foundation for the political transformation of a relatively primitive tribal society into a highly sophisticated, complex political order. In the end, however, the principal legacy of Chinese law may have been a notion of law itself as an essential instrument of control in an administrative state. What for the Chinese may have been a base, rarely esteemed coercive instrument of rule, associated with the authority of the throne, law in Japan acquired special value as a source of legitimacy and manifestation of authority as well as a tool of power.

2

Castellans and Contracts: The Legacy
of Feudal Law

Japan never fully replicated the political and legal order of imperial China. The political power of the central authorities in Japan was never as complete as in China or Korea. Kinship ties proved stronger than any ideal of merit-based bureaucratic rule. No attempt was even made to establish an examination system to produce a literati-bureaucracy despite the Yōrō code's emphasis on merit for those of privileged status. Any distinction between "public" and "private," in the Western sense, never strong, grew even more tenuous as *ritsuryō* institutions were adapted and legal rules bent to accommodate the status and economic interests of dominant aristocratic households and influential Buddhist orders. Through land grants and tax exemptions, the number of self-governing hereditary domains [*shōen*] increased and the central authorities thereby gradually surrendered control over the state's paramount resource: rice-land. As court-appointed provincial governors chose to remain in the capital as absentee administrators, their power to govern and maintain order correspondingly diminished in favor of those who managed the tax-exempt estates of those with influence in the capital. These stewards, unable themselves to ensure order and control over resources, in turn also yielded to others who could. A new warrior [*bushi*] class emerged. Physical might and lawless coercion began to replace orderly regulation through legal rules made and enforced by court-appointed officials. Although the *ritsuryō* forms of central rule persisted and the authority of the center continued to be acknowledged, the power of the court authorities diminished. Those at the center held to their claims to authority but gradually ceased to exercise the powers of governance. By the twelfth century warriors had assumed a predominant economic and political position throughout Japan. Either by outright seizure or through formal processes of official commendation and investiture or both, they had acquired a substantial portion of all offices [*shiki*] carrying entitlements to the revenues of productive land, their rise to power culminating at the end of the century in the establishment of the Kamakura *bakufu* (literally, "tent government").

As central political and economic power increasingly fragmented into a complex administrative structure of virtually self-governing aristocratic households, *shōen* estates, and emerging warrior rule, clientage became the prevailing pattern of social ordering and control. Expressed, as one might expect, in the customary language of kinship relations, ancient societal patterns seemed to retain more vitality than the transplanted trappings of the Chinese imperial tradition.[1]

Authority, however, continued to emanate from the throne with the legal language of the *ritsuryō* state its primary form of discourse. Might in early medieval Japan did not make right. Full legitimacy came with imperial title and commendation. Like the Chinese ideographic and classical forms in which they were written, the documentary forms of *ritsuryō* prescription had almost talismanic effect in establishing the legitimacy of their purported claims. An equally complex overlay of offices, titles, and official instruments thus enveloped the holders of power and thereby ensured the continuity of political authority in the midst of turbulent competition for power and resources. The administrative rationality of the centralized *ritsuryō* state also served as a model for formal governance, honored in mimicry by household and *shōen* establishments.

In terms of institutionalized rules and processes, a pluralist system of formal legal ordering emerged. With separate offices and regulations for courtier households, the *shōen*, and finally, a warrior caste, Japanese legal historians speak of separate bodies of "law" governing *shōen* estates, temples, and warriors as separate classes. In a purely functional sense without regard to distinctions within the *ritsuryō* legal order itself, the accuracy of such classifications need not be questioned. The scope of imperial-sourced rules and norms contained in the *ritsu*, *ryō*, and supplementary *kaku* and *shiki*—the technical jargon of *ritsuryō* law—had diminished along with the gradual dissipation of imperial power. Thus in functional terms the governing rules and norms for most of Japan were those promulgated or recognized by household administrators, *shōen* estate managers, and warrior overlords. Nevertheless so long as the legitimizing charisma of imperial authority remained, the distinction should be maintained between law with the throne as its source and rules and norms instituted, or as in the case of custom, recognized in the regulation of the affairs of semiautonomous units of society. Unlike Medieval Europe, the lawmaking and law-enforcing functions of the central authorities did not utterly disintegrate and disappear to be fully supplanted by the institutions of feudal governance. In Japan the imperial court remained. Its institutional prerogatives diminished ultimately to the point of near extinction in effect and influence, but still they continued to exist in form. Whether labeled "law" or not, some rules and legal processes as reflected by the terms used to describe them enjoyed attributes of legitimacy, authority, and in the absence of imperial limitation, at least putative application denied to others. Not all rules could be expressed as *ritsu*, *ryō*, *kaku*, or *shiki*.

With the establishment of the Kamakura *bakufu*, we cease to speak of *bushi* bands imposing order by brute force but instead must consider the structure of warrior organization and their exercise of power in terms of institutionalized means of social control both for external rule and internal discipline and cohesion. As territorial governance progressively depended less and less on the administrative regulations of a court-appointed officialdom, access to power too came to rest less on familial relationships and household influence at court and more on the effectiveness of warrior organization as a structured set of relationships for both the mobilization of an effective military force and hierarchical control.

The institutional history of Japan from the late twelfth through the mid-sixteenth centuries reflects the repetition of earlier patterns—the conflicts and tensions between the holders of power at the center and those at the periphery, who in control of greater resources challenged the center and asserted their own independence. In the ensuing conflicts over power and autonomy, new patterns of social organization and control emerged. Those that proved to be the most effective prevailed to become, at least for a time, the dominant patterns.

And what of authority and law? What role did legal rules, processes, and institutions play in the unfolding drama? The period between the twelfth and seventeenth centuries also marked an almost complete separation of authority and power in Japan. Like imperial power, *ritsuryō* law as a coercive mechanism of control also receded, yet as an expression of the authority of imperial rule, *ritsuryō* legislation still remained as the foundation for Japanese law and a source for ultimate legitimacy. By the end of the period, however, the emergence of autonomous daimyo rule in the sixteenth century and the infusion of Chu Hsi neo-Confucianism in the early seventeenth century, had combined to redefine the nature of legitimate rule, its relationship to law, and the Japanese legal tradition. The inherent instability of feudal governance stretched the separation of imperial authority from the holders of political power to the breaking point. It is therefore in the sixteenth century or *sengoku* (literally "warring states") period that Japan parallels most closely the feudal orders of Western Europe in terms of law as a source of legitimacy and instrument of control as well as other aspects of institutional organization.

Early Patterns of Feudal Governance

In assessing the applicability of the label "feudalism" to Japan, John Whitney Hall quotes the "provisional definition" suggested by Strayer and Coulborn:

> Feudalism is primarily a method of government, not an economic or a social system, though it obviously modifies and is modified by the social and economic environment. It is a method of government in which the essential relation is not that between ruler and subject, nor state and citizen, but between lord and vassal.[2]

For our purposes this definition is especially apt. The law of Japan's sinicized system of administrative governance in effect distinguished imperial ruler from subject in terms of the locus of lawmaking authority and those subject to legal control. As an expression of imperial will, law defined rulers by its source and subject by its application. While no articulated conceptual line demarked public and private spheres, the source of legislation and the scope of the law's reach in effect marked a boundary of sorts. Rules promulgated by those without claim to imperial sanction, whether manorial proprietor or warrior overlord, thus lacked the legitimacy of legal rules. And, without similar imperial mandate, institutions and processes for their enforcement, however effective in coercion, could not create legitimized, legal rules or norms by recognition.

Having not replaced the preexisting legal institutions of governance as oc-curred in Europe, the warrior regimes of Japanese feudalism remained at least until the sixteenth century a form of private governance until recognized by imperial authority. By wresting such recognition from the throne, the Kamakura *bakufu* further blurred any distinction between public and private governance. The formal delegation to Minamoto Yoritomo by the court in 1186 of powers of appointment of the constabulary [*shugo*] for all provinces [*kuni*] and tax-collecting stewards [*jitō*] for both public districts and private manors laid the foundation for countrywide warrior rule.[3] Imperial appoint-ment of Yoritomo as shogun seven years later may thus be viewed as confir-mation of power already ceded, but with it came the legitimacy of delegated powers and the capacity to rule by law. Yet, again in contrast to the European experience, such recognition reinforced the value of the authority otherwise so successfully challenged. Not, it appears, until the neo-Confucianist redefini-tion of ruler as lawmaker, as opposed to law as ruler-made, gained a foothold in the seventeenth century, as explained below, was this sustaining need for imperial authority conceptually threatened. Yet no successors to the Kamakura *bakufu*'s powers of nationwide governance in fact long ruled without imperial mandate.

Nor did the Kamakura *bakufu* replace officials of the court or the proprietors of private domains. Instead, it introduced a system of multiple jurisdictions and multiple layers of law and law-enforcing institutions, each paradoxically as interdependent as in competition, preserving both and, in the process, completing the separation of authority from power. Offices and the entitlements to resources they conveyed required authoritative mandate sourced, however remotely, in imperial rule. Conversely, realization of such rewards and grants necessitated a viable threat of coercive force. Consequent-ly, the imperial authorities and the *bakufu* warriors each needed something from the other.

In contrast to Japan, the collapse of the Roman Empire and with it Roman legal institutions in Europe left a vacuum filled by rival claimants to both power and authority. Even conflicts between church and state involved com-petition for both authority and power. The distinction between public and private rule in the Western sense, too, ceased to be meaningful as, in Strayer and Coulborn's terms, the relation between lord and vassal replaced that be-tween Roman ruler and subject. One consequence was the freedom of European feudal overlords to borrow and adapt the conceptual and institutional remnants of the Roman system. To the extent that feudal arrangements repli-cated Roman antecedents, particularly from the eleventh century onward, those who governed acquired a greater measure of legitimacy and acceptance as heirs to the Roman tradition. In Japan, in contrast, so long as the institutions of imperial rule remained, including *ritsuryō* legislation, albeit contained and controlled, the governing warriors of feudal Japan could not duplicate the imperial court or its legislative authority. If only perhaps out of deference to the influence or the benefits of the imperial institution, they chose to remain holders of delegated powers and rivals to its authority.

The relation between lord and vassal was also cast in different molds in Europe and Japan. Indeed, few contrasts illustrate better the impact of differences in the two legal traditions.

The Feudal Contract

In both Europe and Japan the elemental relation between lord and vassal was a consensual undertaking in which protection and reward were given in reciprocal exchange for loyalty and service. In terms of content and revocability there were, it appears, as many variations within Europe as in Japan, at least over time. What distinguishes the two is neither the arrangement nor necessarily its form, but rather its characterization.

For the European the feudal bargain was cast as a contract or covenant, which though ordinarily supported by ceremonial oaths, required little else to establish its bindingness. Whether viewed in Roman legal terms as a species of *contractus*, Judeo-Christian notions of binding covenants, or folk beliefs in the supernatural powers of the oath, the arrangement was binding according to its terms. Hence the obligations undertaken and their mutuality or conditional reciprocity had to be clearly stated.

For the Japanese without any conception of covenant or contract as a legal form, consensual arrangements in and of themselves were not necessarily binding as a matter of law or morality. They were in effect beyond the pale of both. Unless accorded some form of official confirmation, conceptually they had no special legal force. Nor, without some religious recognition, by talismanic or other ritual, did they have moral force.

The problem confronting Japanese warriors was thus to characterize the agreement in some fashion that would ensure its bindingness. From the beginning the answer was found in kinship. By identifying the relationship, not the agreement itself, in familial terms, through marriage arrangements or, later, as adoptive relations in which the vassal became son to the paternal lord, the Japanese found the socially sanctioned glue needed to hold the relationship together. By means of kinship they incorporated into the arrangement shared indigenous and borrowed Confucianist values. By extension, such arrangements also included an intrinsic set of reciprocal duties—those owed between parent and child.[4] The real strength of the feudal bonds in both Europe and Japan varied according to the social and economic circumstances and the rewards and costs of breaches on both sides. However, each characterization had a certain logic of its own with consequences for each society. Whether in Europe or Japan, lord-vassal relations like other consensual arrangements were premised on a measure of voluntary choice between autonomous parties. In neither did the form of public or regulatory law enforcement available to rulers to govern their subjects—or the state, its citizens—fit comfortably a legal order based on agreement. In Europe the covenant between lord and vassal provided the foundation for the social contract and ultimately the rationale for constitutional government. Japan had no comparable legal construct. Continued reliance on real and fictive kinship, combined with neo-Confucianist emphasis on the reciprocal duties of benevolence and loyalty, was similarly, however, to form the basis for the familial characterization of the modern Japanese state.

Neither the social contract nor the familial state, however, sustained feudal governance in either context. How then did Japan's warriors rule?

Order by Adjudication

With the establishment of the Kamakura *bakufu*, a remarkably sophisticated system of adjudication became an integral feature of Japanese governance. As noted, the court in Kyoto remained institutionally intact and maintained a parallel system of law enforcement. The Kamakura rulers, however, were compelled to adapt to new political conditions and demands. Pressed to reestablish order, the warrior-administrators found in adjudication an ideally suited means of legal control. First, adjudicatory emphasis on processes for resolving rival claims and land disputes allowed them to restore and preserve order with minimum cost. A bureaucratic public law regime would have required an extensive force of policing officials and the sort of extensive internal controls of the Chinese administrative state that for Japan had earlier been unattainable. More to the point, an official bureaucracy would have demanded a restructuring of *bakufu* organization—essentially its defeudalization—by either replacing vassals with appointed officials or transforming vassalage into official service, which occurred much later in the sixteenth and seventeenth centuries. Law enforcement by adjudication, on the other hand, amounted to a form of indirect rule with only isolated tests of power. It required less manpower and fewer resources.

Adjudication also complemented *bakufu* authority. Those who dispensed justice did so as neutral arbiters deciding claims based on local practice, custom, and official documents, not legislated codes. Both those who sought relief or defended against a claim could submit to the authority of the Kamakura *bakufu* as equals or near equals obliged to obey out of bonds of allegiance. "Kamakura," as Jeffrey Mass concludes, "thus remained outside and above the suits it sought to resolve, and in the process insulated itself from undue partisanship or criticism."[5]

Without separating the arbiter from the lawmaking official, such neutrality and the sense of fairness it invoked as well as the recognition of the intrinsic autonomy of the parties would have been difficult to achieve. The promulgation and enforcement of newly legislated rules would have necessarily exposed the interests of those in power. Inevitably there would have been rulings against local custom or against application of previously codified rules, in either event undermining any aura of disinterested justice and legitimacy. Although arbiters inevitably also make rules in recognizing and enforcing particular norms of custom or code, the process is more subtle and gradual. With appeals or a process for review, there is time to gauge reaction and test whether the outcome gains consent or approval. It affords authorities an opportunity to correct errors if there is resistance without risking challenge to their authority. It may also be argued that feudal or other systems of decentralized, local governance that seek to maintain order and need to justify their authority to rule tend inexorably to look to custom and precedent as primary sources for legal rules and resort to an adjudicatory or judicial system for their enforcement. As regimes grounded in contracted allegiance, they have neither the authority nor the power to impose an extensive array of legislated rules.

The similarities between the Japanese and European experiences thus suggest that feudal legal orders share certain characteristics as common responses to common problems. In environments otherwise widely separated by space and culture, feudalism in both Europe and Japan was a response to the insecurity and disorder that followed the disintegration of central rule. No community suffers disorder long. Neither complete anarchy nor absolute stability are possible social conditions. The social demand for stability and security and the forces of change are both too strong. Consequently in both Europe and Japan individuals and communities threatened by disorder quickly traded autonomy for protection. In Europe feudal dependency originated in the collapse of the *Pax Romana*; in Japan it resulted from the failed attempt to create a sinicized system of central rule. In consequence, what Marc Bloch said of Europe also applies to Japan: The "usurpation of public rights—mainly those of justice and the *ban*—strengthened the [feudal] lord's grip, and enabled him to extend it to holdings which had hitherto escaped him."[6] While Kamakura justice did not fully displace the law enforcing institutions of the imperial court and dealt primarily with the resolution of claims over land and tenure against or between warrior-stewards and other Kamakura vassals, it nevertheless extended the authority of the *bakufu* throughout Japan and became an indispensable pillar of *bakufu* rule. More important for our purposes, it reinforced and added to the development of the institutions and processes of an embryonic private law regime that had been at least suggested in the *ritsuryō*.

Kamakura jurisdiction extended to three categories of suits. Those involving land tenure and title were classified as *shomusata* and were tried in both Kamakura and *bakufu* offices in Kyoto. What would today be classified as criminal cases—actions involving rebellion, theft, brigandry, homicide, rape, violent assaults, and similar conduct—were tried by special *bakufu* offices in either Kamakura or Kyoto under *shomusata* procedures. The third category of miscellaneous cases, referred to as *zatsumusata*, encompassed various claims to property, other than land, arising from interest-bearing loans, bills of exchange, mortgages, and sales.[7] At least by the fourteenth century these suits were being tried in Kamakura before the *monchūjo* under direct control of the *bakufu*.[8]

Law enforcement by the Kamakura authorities could only be activated by outside complaint or accusation generally, and the process remained subject to the initiative and direction of the litigants. "In this way," Mass correctly observes, "the Bakufu was fundamentally judicial in character and not merely a policing agency."[9] Also evident is the procedural sophistication and inherent rationality of the Kamakura adjudicatory process. Upon receipt of a petition with attached documents, the authorities reviewed it to assure that the controversy was properly within their jurisdiction. If so, the next step was to assign the case to the proper *bakufu* agency, taking into account the parties, the issues, and the location of the property at issue or wrongdoing. Unless the matter could be decided or resolved after the initial pleading, the authorities would subpoena the accused to submit a response and, if necessary, submit to a hearing. The outcome of the process depended primarily upon the persuasiveness of the parties' documentary evidence, especially the availability of official instruments or records issued by the court officials or the *bakufu*. If testimony were needed, the authorities could take statements from witnesses—ordinarily it appears at the request of one of the parties. A witness could be summoned either to appear at Kamakura (or Kyoto) or a convenient site such as the headquarters of the local *bakufu*-appointed military governor [*shugo*]. A form of affidavit or deposition by a witness or the parties (*kishōmon*) could also be arranged by the litigants and submitted in lieu of live testimony. Cases could be reopened for reconsideration, and as the system later evolved, a system of appeals [*osso*] was instituted. As in Chinese practice, no substantive conceptual distinction was made between civil and criminal matters. Coupled with the requirements of party initiative to bring an action, there could be "no penalties for crimes not included in original indictments."[10] Yet, the system represented the mirror image of the Chinese system in its reliance on party initiative and control.

In stark contrast with feudal justice in Europe at the same point in time, there was no trial by contest, reliance on oath taking, or preference for oral testimony over documentary evidence. Nor, interestingly, did the status of the witness determine the probative value of the testimony. Whereas in feudal Europe, for example, the word of a noble or cleric was presumptively accepted as true over the statements by a commoner or serf, in the Kamakura scheme, the legal or social status of the witness had no bearing on the credibility or evidentiary value of his statement.[11] As Mass concludes in evaluation: "Kamakura vassals were assured very high standards of justice. Judicial settlements were basically remedial, with judgments the result of an exhaustive review of evidence submitted by legally equal adversaries."[12]

We can explain the relative rationality of Kamakura procedures as another legacy of the Chinese tradition. The Kamakura authorities did not need to invent entirely new procedures. They could draw upon the borrowed forms and techniques of *ritsuryō* justice, adapting them to their particular aims and needs. Moreover, just as the church absorbed Greek Stoicism and Roman legalism to produce a Christian natural law and the formidable institutions of ecclesiastic justice, so too did preexisting superstitions, pagan practices, and folk law supplant the intrinsic rationality of both the Judaic and Hellenic traditions to produce in the mix a credulous reliance on supernatural intervention to protect the good and the righteous. Similar consequences, while not completely absent, were at least contained in Japan by the separation of law from religion in the Chinese tradition.

In East Asia, the influence of moral values and religious beliefs on law took generally very different form. In Japan, like China, moral strictures tended to operate apart from the law to legitimate authority and as internalized norms at least to some extent to constrain power. Illustrative is Carl Steenstrup's summary of Kamakura magistrate Shigetoki Hōjō's admonition to his eldest son that the obligations of loyalty and benevolence were moral not legal in nature, with a religious rather than legal sanction. "By truthful service to their lord and by displaying benevolence to those they administer, the participants in the feudal system can generate more good karma and transfer it to their own offspring."[13] Equally if not more important, Shigetoki advised his sons on the resolution of the moral dilemma imposed by Buddhist condemnation of killing. Acting in accordance with the law could constitute a moral wrong and moral conduct could be a legal offense.

> Right contains elements of wrong, and vice versa. This is something you should be aware of. Let us consider an example of wrong in right. Suppose you quite justifiably, complain to the authorities about somebody's wrongdoing. Your life is not in jeopardy, but if you pursue your case, the accused will lose his life. If then you proceed according to your right you will have done wrong though you were right.
>
> As an example of the opposite situation, suppose a person has committed all manners of wrongs and deserves to lose his life. But if you do not denounce him he will live. In such case you should keep silent. Your action will be right though the law was wronged.
>
> If you take him to heart, and save lives and subjects, those who see or hear of it will feel affection for you; and just imagine the joy of those whose lives you save! Even if the public and those you have benefited do not rejoice, the Buddhas and gods will love you; they will protect you in this life, and save you in future existences.[14]

How representative such comments were and to what extent they were reflected in practice is unknown and perhaps unknowable. They nevertheless suggest what other scholars refer to as the "quality of mercy" evident in Chinese and Korean legal practice under Buddhist influence.[15] In Japan the potential was perhaps even greater for fusion of Buddhist notions of mercy and the Confucianist ideal of benevolence; the former essential to escape Buddhist hells, the latter a necessary attribute of legitimate rule. Such fusion and its impact on legal control would at least explain the apparent tolerance of feudal authorities toward wrongdoers.

Western cynicism regarding the influence of purely moral constraints should not lead to thoughtless dismissal of any suggestion that such beliefs had much significance. It might be more appropriate to ask why similar Judeo-Christian proscriptions against killing and admonitions for mercy for the repentant had so little effect even in medieval canon law. One explanation, suggested before, is the victory of Roman justice with the conversion of Constantine and the substitution of ecclesiastic for secular rule. Buddhist mercy could influence only where a tension existed between competing systems of order and definitions of good; East Asian societies were not required to merge moral and legal norms to do "justice." Neither secular nor religious leaders had to resolve the tensions and dilemmas between conflicting definitions of what was just or "good"—the mercy of the moral rule or the penalty of the legal rule. The result in the West was the need for a mutually conforming redefinition of both law and morals.

As indicated previously, however, the separation of law from morality does not preclude the enforcement of religious or moral values as legal norms. The legislated rules of imperial Chinese and *ritsuryō* law reflected generally accepted moral values, at least those that served state interests.[16] Adjudicatory regimes also incorporate moral norms and standards of behavior as rules of decision. The question remains therefore what rules or standards, if any, were applied by the Kamakura magistrates in deciding the disputes before them and whether their decisions could be predicted in advance on the basis of consistently enforced norms. In other words, did the Kamakura regime develop a recognizable body of legal rules or norms in the process of adjudicating cases?

It is difficult to answer any of these questions with more than a highly qualified yes. As described above, a system of regular, predictable procedures did develop out of a combination of edict and practice. There was also reliance on administrative precedent,[17] as well as the legislated proscriptions of either the imperial or *bakufu* authorities. However, there seems to be little law in the Western sense of a corpus of doctrine and principles from which more specific, generally applicable rules could be deduced and predictably applied. The outcome of the vast majority of cases depended upon the fact of official appointment or investiture as evidenced in official records or commercial and other contractual instruments relating to debts, land, and distributions of property. By consistently acknowledging the validity of claims based on such documentary evidence, one might argue, the Kamakura magistrates did develop in effect a type of precedential "notarial" law. A prominent example was the development of rights of proprietorship beginning with the enforcement of offices [*shiki*] entitling their holders to income from particular parcels of land.[18] Moreover, the repeated judicial enforcement of consensual undertakings, such as compromises, by denying further judicial relief did, as Steenstrup points out, create a sort of law of contract out of the "interstices of procedure."[19] Nonetheless, the adjudicatory emphasis of Kamakura rule could not overcome the conceptual constraints imposed by Japan's Chinese legacy. Without a conception of principled judicial reasoning or a belief in any universally applicable set of norms it could not evolve beyond the institutional framework for a private legal order.

This is not to say that legislated legal rules and documentary evidence were the only bases for decisions by Kamakura judges. There was also resort to *dōri*, or "reason." As Steenstrup notes:

> The parties appealed to [dôri] in their pleadings to the courts. The judges based decisions on it, when the parties or their own experience had not supplied them with stronger arguments, such as rules or clear precedents. And Bakufu legislators used it, when they felt that a deviation from imperial law was necessary for the new ruling class of warriors.[20]

Dōri, however, did not embody a set of norms capable of consistent articulation or application. In the end it came to mean the prevailing consensus of the warrior community,[21] which, "inextricably bound to all the facts and imponderabilia of the individual case,"[22] could only add unpredictability rather than certainty to the outcome.

The emphasis on adjudication should not divert us from noting that, as the *bakufu* government matured (and, it should be added, weakened politically), it, too, began to issue an impressive corpus of orders and edicts, including the fifty-one-article *Jōei* Formulary [*Goseibai shikimoku*] issued in 1232 in the form of written instructions to adjudicating officials, and the series of supplementary regulations promulgated during the decades that followed.[23] To a notable extent these regulations concentrated on adjudicatory procedures, representing a significant departure from imperial Chinese legislation. Their promulgation also reflected a desire by the warrior-rulers for greater legitimacy. Lawmaking had become a legitimizing exercise. The *Kenmu* Formulary [*Kenmu shikimoku*], issued as one of the earliest actions of the first Ashikaga shogun in 1336, is thus characterized as "an attempt to legitimize his coup d'état."[24]

Neither formulary should properly be labeled a code in either traditional Chinese or modern Western usage. Both were designed primarily as a compendium of hortatory admonition, injunctive prescription, and above all, restatement of customary or precedential rules for use in adjudication by *bakufu* officials. Their purpose was to ensure greater uniformity and fairness by *bakufu* magistrates. Supplemented by later edicts, especially in the case of the *Kenmu* formulary, they also became the official compilation of *bakufu* law. Their promulgation may also indicate a deterioration of adjudicatory standards as *bakufu* control began to weaken, at least if one assumes they were issued in response to a perceived need.[25] As the title *shikimoku* suggests—the term *shiki* denoted supplementary regulations to the *ritsuryō*—the formularies reflect the formally delegated lawmaking authority of the *bakufu* with respect to the governance of warrior houses. Both were subsequently treated as fundamental sources of warrior law.

Finally, above all else Kamakura adjudication was a method of control over the conduct of its vassal constables and stewards who had been dispatched to the provinces to parallel court-appointed officials for purposes of policing and administrative oversight. However effective the Kamakura scheme of adjudicatory law enforcement may have been in maintaining order and legitimacy, in the end it proved to be inadequate as a means of internal administrative discipline.

Kamakura law enforcement was, it appears, remarkably lenient or weak. Officials guilty of serious offenses might lose their titles, but, as described by Mass, rarely suffered any other penalty. In most cases, "defaulted taxes were simply ordered paid, stolen goods were ordered returned, abused residents ordered secured, and illegally seized office or land rights ordered terminated." "Where," asks Mass, "was the coercive element in Bakufu justice?"[26] The frequency of suits suggests they had some benefit to both the petitioners and adjudicatory authorities. The lack of sanctions imposed for disobedience of *bakufu* orders and edicts as well as the nonfinality of most suits[27] nevertheless prompts one to wonder what other means of control existed. One possibility is that in this era of "notarial law" in most cases the loss of title and with it any legitimate claim for redress against more powerful rivals may have been sufficient sanction. The real threat may not have been the Kamakura authorities but some more powerful rival claimant. The Kamakura and Muromachi regimes, it seems, only managed to impose a superficial order on a much more turbulent reality.

Impulse toward Power and Autonomy

Without adequate means to control their vassals the Kamakura rulers and their Muromachi successors could not contain the impulse toward power and autonomy. Just as the scions of Heian court families sent from the capital as official representatives of the throne in the provinces gained independent power as they asserted dominion over local resources, so too the *shugo* and *jitō* vassals of the Kamakura and Muromachi shogun emerged as local overlords and independent proprietors. The destruction of the Kamakura *bakufu* along with its headquarters in 1333 by forces loyal to Emperor Go-Daigo only briefly restored a semblance of imperial rule. Three years later Takauji Ashikaga, who had led the campaign for the emperor, established his *bakufu* in the Muromachi district of the capital. Central rule progressively weakened, however, until effective central governance ceased entirely. Authority and power could not be joined. Power had become too diffuse to control. In the ensuing rivalry for domination, the real contestants were the warrior-lords. Only those who were able to devise new methods to sustain effective oversight and the cohesion of their forces would run the course.

By the mid-sixteenth century the feudalization of Japan was complete. As summarized by Hall:

> [T]he distinction between boundaries of legal jurisdiction and outright control had been largely obliterated. Within this area, the complex division of rights which characterized the *shōen* system had given way to the holding

of land in fief. By now the absentee interests of courtiers or distant temples had been almost entirely squeezed out. In other words, the vertical lines of authority and control had been pulled short and taut. Very little administrative and almost no fiscal contact existed between the provinces and Kyoto. The individual daimyo domains were essentially independent. Within them the power and authority relationships consisted of a hierarchically structured system of allegiances in which military service was exchanged for grants of fief. Furthermore, the exercise of the functions of government coincided with those relationships. It is this situation which can be compared most closely with the model of decentralized feudalism in Europe.[28]

Control through Dependency

The demands of an age of constant warfare beginning with the Ōnin War in 1467 and ending only at the dawn of the Tokugawa hegemony in 1600—known as the *sengoku* [warring states] period—produced radically new solutions to the problem of governance. The extended feudal structure of the Kamakura and Muromachi regimes disintegrated. Smaller, more cohesive warrior units developed, whose survival depended upon improved methods of hierarchical command and oversight. The older, consensual forms of vassalage thus gave way to new patterns based more on submission than bargain. The logic of fictitious kinship was taken to its logical conclusion with retainers characterized as "quasi-children" [*yoriko*] submitting to a local warrior chieftain in the role of a protective parent [*yorioya*]. Organized more on functional lines with hereditary ranks replacing ties of kinship or personal vassalage, military units subject to a more efficient hierarchy of command supplanted warrior alliances. Most important, the prototype of the new order had become the small warrior band whose members lived in close proximity with their leaders, sharing a common fortification and dependent on their leaders for stipendiary remuneration instead of proprietary rewards of rent from or tenure to specific parcels of land.

The *sengoku* daimyo were acutely sensitive to the need for more effective means of control over their immediate retainers and their domains in general, having themselves risen to their positions of power by rebellion against their overlords. With the barest mandate from an atrophied *bakufu* ruler, much less formal imperial authority, they sought to devise more effective means of political and social control and, on that account, were impelled to find new rationales to legitimize the exercise of power such methods entailed. Their innovations included establishing the first castle towns to which they required their samurai retainers to relocate from the villages, holding "hostage" the kin of close retainers, and initiating land surveys for more accurate assessment of taxes, which served also as a basis for allocating ownership. These and other measures first introduced by individual *sengoku* daimyo were subsequently adopted and applied nationwide in the process of reunification that began in the mid-sixteenth century under Nobunaga Oda (1534–82), the first of the "Three Unifiers" of medieval Japan.

Under Nobunaga and, after his assassination in 1582, Hideyoshi Toyotomi (1526–98), the foundations for the hegemony of the third and most successful of the three, Ieyasu Tokugawa, were laid.[29] Hideyoshi's cadastral surveys [*taikō kenchi*] effected the transformation of the country with the village [*mura*] as the basic administrative and economic unit and a registered list of landholders [*naukenin*] in lieu of the complex variety of preexisting communities and forms of land tenure. In addition Hideyoshi brought all land under governmental control. Local daimyo became recognized proprietors [*ryōshu*] with official entitlements to tax and administer land under their territorial control. Other notable reforms initiated under Hideyoshi were a new system of taxation based on calculated yields of rice-land payable in kind rather than cash and regulations requiring the separation of samurai from the village [*hei-nō-bunri*]. All of these changes took place in the context of one of the pivotal events in Japanese history, the establishment of the castle town [*jōkamachi*].

Within a remarkably brief period of time—only about three decades—at the end of the sixteenth century, one local daimyo after another established a capital with a castle headquarters in which warrior-retainers were ordered to establish residence. Almost overnight villages and undeveloped land were transformed into urban centers. Thus were Edo, Osaka, Nagoya, Sendai, Hiroshima, Okayama, Himeji, Fukuoka, Kumamoto, Takamatsu, Matsuyama, Tokushima, Kōchi, Fukui, Kanazawa, Tottori, Shizuoka, Kōfu, Hikone, Fushimi, and Takasaki founded. Concomitant with the creation of these new urban centers and their impact on the economic and commercial development of Japan, was the relocation of the samurai from the village to the castle towns as a consequence of Hideyoshi's *hei-nō-bunri* edict. This coercive "push" out of the village and "pull" to the castle and the resulting resettlement of the samurai led not only to the expanded development of officialdom and judicial legal controls in urban centers but also to intensified forms of extralegal social controls in the village.

In return for relocation in the castle town, the samurai retainers received for themselves and their heirs a guarantee of status as an officially privileged caste and a measure of security in the form of fixed stipends calculated in terms of rice yields from land that, had they been free to remain in the village, they could have exploited directly. Daimyo overlords thereby not only subjected their followers to direct, local supervision but also denied them independent access to resources that in the past had repeatedly provided the basis for autonomy and rival centers of power. They created a control system through dependency. No longer subject to direct supervision and oversight by resident officials of an imperial court or the retainers of a more distant feudal lord, the village, in turn, gained a rarely experienced measure of autonomy and internal peace. Mutual dependency within the village community similarly ensured the effectiveness of community control. Both developments were to be intensified under the Tokugawa in the two and a half centuries that followed.

Power without Authority: Law and the Redefinition of Legitimate Rule

The idea of law that had held sway in Japan from the eighth century rested on the legitimacy and exclusive political authority of the imperial institution. Law took the form of penal proscription, and administrative regulation issued from the throne or by delegated mandate shared the attributes of *ritsuryō* legislation. Similarly what distinguished public from private spheres of activity was the exercise of imperial will. Thus, for example, *shōen* estate administration, including adjudication, was private insofar as it was not carried out on behalf or under the authority of the throne.

Before the influence of Chinese political and legal models, limits on the exercise of power by the emperor already existed. These became an even more intrinsic aspect of Japanese governance in the Heian court. The expansion of warrior governance, however, further widened the rift between possession of authority and the exercise of power to such an extent that the implicit exclusivity of imperial political authority and with it notions of legitimacy and law were jeopardized. Nevertheless, so long as imperial mandate remained a prerequisite for legitimate rule—as measured by the value those exercising political power placed on imperial entitlements and imperial delegation of the authority to make official appointments—the separation of authority and power could endure. The dissipation of *bakufu* power at the end of the fifteenth century, however, nearly broke the tension of mutual necessity that sustained this separation, and Japan drew closer to the European experience in which the power of governance, including the coercive use of law, ultimately determined the authority to govern.

As the daimyo of the *sengoku* period consolidated control within their domains, they too, like the *bakufu* rulers, became lawmakers. In one domain after another in the mid-sixteenth century the ruling overlords issued rules for governance in the form of "house codes" [*kahō*], resembling in most respects the formularies issued under the Kamakura and Muromachi *bakufu* for the regulation of the warrior class and the administration of justice under warrior rule. Neither the *Jōei* nor the *Kenmu* formularies purported, however, to supplant imperial *ritsuryō* in nature or in scope. Quite the contrary, they represented specific instructions, admonitions, and prohibitions for limited purposes and audience. In purport they merely supplemented the *ritsuryō* as a set of special legal rules for the warrior class, consonant with the shogunate's authority to maintain social order and administer a system of adjudicatory justice for those under the *bakufu*'s direct jurisdiction. Neither formulary, it should be emphasized again, constituted a comprehensive code for general governance as evidenced by their specificity and lack of coherence. Rather they were intended for the most part to deal with acute problems requiring immediate attention.

The daimyo house codes of the sixteenth century were notably different. In contrast to the *bakufu* formularies, their scope extended beyond the regulation of samurai retainers [*kashindan*]. They were territorial in scope, directed to the general populace of the domain. While they reflected a continuation of the primacy of adjudication in the scheme of warrior governance, evidenced by the substantial portions devoted to proscriptive rules to be applied by domain courts, they tended also to include a heavy dose of hortatory admonition and moral instruction similar to the household precepts [*kakun*] a daimyo would leave for his heirs. As argued by Shizuo Katsumata, these features reflected a broader aim to regulate the domain as an autonomous political entity. Such intent was evident in the frequent use of the word *kokka*, a composite of the characters for *kuni* and *ie*, or in the nearest equivalent English, "province" and "house" (in the sense of "household").[30]

They also modified existing rules to enforce their control. This is exemplified by house code rules punishing both sides to a quarrel, a condemnation of self-redress similar to European anti-dueling statutes. Prior rules had recognized a limited right to revenge.[31] Other measures included the regulation of coinage, weights and measures, shrines and temples, guilds and markets, not to mention debt moratoria [*tokusei*], all of which extended beyond the daimyo's warrior retinue to encompass all domain inhabitants regardless of class or status. The *sengoku* daimyo in effect relegated to themselves both the authority and power to legislate well beyond any official mandate they may have been able to claim.

They proceeded in effect to resolve the issue of their authority by redefining conventional views regarding the nature and source of legitimacy as well as the role of law. A threshold issue was the supremacy of daimyo edicts as preeminent commands valid against preexisting entitlements, privileges, and customary practices. This was achieved first by redefining *bakufu* law. The *Jōei* Formulary, long viewed as fundamental law for warrior houses, attracted special attention in the *sengoku* period. Copied and recopied, and the subject of extensive commentaries, it was treated with a reverence ordinarily reserved for sacred text.[32] The *sengoku* house codes, which in form and content were quite similar, thus acquired by reflection some of the formulary's glory.

The daimyo lawmakers asserted the supremacy of their edicts more directly in promulgated rules. Katsumata, for example, cites article 39 of Date Takemune's *Jinkaishū* forbidding anyone wounded by a sword in a quarrel to retaliate despite warrior principles [*riun*] to the contrary. This is, he says, "one of many examples of, to use the contemporary phrase, the kind of 'law that overrides principle' (*ri o yaburu hō*)."[33] By retainer demand, the seeds of an even more radical idea—the supremacy of law over the daimyo themselves— was introduced. Again to quote Katsumata: "The classic documentary expression of this was the *Rokkaku-shi shikimoku* [of Ōmi], which was explicitly intended to curb arbitrary rule by daimyo." The example given is article 37: "ITEM. It is forbidden for the *daimyo* to hand down and enforce a judgment in a trial without a full inquiry or without allowing the defendants an opportunity to explain the circumstances."[34] In other words, daimyo edicts had supremacy over principle and precedent, but even the daimyo was bound by what would today be categorized as procedural fairness.

The primacy of law alone did not fully resolve the dilemma of daimyo rule. The legitimacy of their assertions of political authority, too, needed to be confirmed. The substitution of terms used to describe the Chinese state, such as *kokka*, or, especially in the case of Nobunaga, *tenka* (literally "under heaven"), for the territory under their control, enabled them, in Katsumata's words, "to claim legitimacy for their rules as a 'public' or 'official' authority (*kōgi* or *kubō*) under the shield of a concept of *kokka* or 'state' they themselves had created."[35]

Underlying the notion of *kokka* as an independent polity was the equally pregnant notion of the legitimizing nature of wise and benevolent rule found early in Chinese political thought but given new vitality at least in Japan through the medium of neo-Confucianist teaching. Concomitant with the institutional changes that gave rise to the need for a new ideological basis for warrior rule, neo-Confucianist ideas began to permeate the warrior class. The idea that the authority and powers of governance should ultimately devolve to the ruler who is virtuous and also able to maintain security and social order was a core element of traditional Chinese political thought. For the *sengoku* daimyo, it provided a needed independent source of legitimacy. The idea of virtuous rule interwoven with the concept of their domains as *kokka* thus became the pervasive rationale for daimyo governance.

In summary, by the end of the sixteenth century two equally profound changes had occurred in Japanese conceptions of authority, power, and law. The idea of the supremacy of law as command had begun to take hold, and Japan had also rediscovered the Mandate of Heaven and, with it, the ideological underpinnings for rule by benevolent might. Law had become more than an instrumental adjunct of governance. Adherence to codified prescriptions and procedures of the past and basic elements of procedural fairness had become integral to legitimate rule. For a brief time, therefore, Japan hovered on the verge of a radically new political order, one that, as in Europe, could build the foundations of legitimate governance on the quality of rule by law and perhaps by gradual extension the rule of law.

3

Magistrates and *Mura*: The Ambivalent Tradition of Tokugawa Japan

The unification—or perhaps more accurately, pacification—of Japan under Ieyasu Tokugawa and his successors in the seventeenth and eighteenth centuries culminated the consolidation of daimyo power begun in the late sixteenth century by Nobunaga and Hideyoshi. Successfully synthesizing methods of feudal governance that had evolved from the Kamakura *bakufu* through the *sengoku* era, the early Tokugawa rulers established a delicately balanced political regime, arresting on hindsight, however, the potential for further evolution toward the joinder of authority with power and fuller synthesis of law and legitimacy. The Tokugawa regime endured until the forcible opening of Japan by the West in the mid-nineteenth century. Ultimately the Tokugawa rulers could not retard a gradual but perceptible shift once again of power away from the center. Western demands for Japan to end its self-imposed policy of seclusion and open to commerce and trade exposed the regime's inherent weakness and provided the catalyst for its collapse.

For most Japanese today the institutions and processes of Tokugawa governance appear to define their legal tradition. This is not unreasonable. Among the achievements of Tokugawa governance was the fusion of elements of a sinicized bureaucratic tradition with the institutions of judicial governance in a context that included a critical new element, the semiautonomous village. In this combination we find paradigms of governance that help explain the peculiar contours and multifaceted paradox of law and social control in contemporary Japan. Ieyasu Tokugawa and his heirs introduced few radical institutional innovations into the Japanese polity. They grounded their regime and secured their dominion instead on foundations already laid by adapting, expanding, and perfecting mechanisms of political control that others, particularly Hideyoshi Toyotomi, had previously instituted.

The perfection of Hideyoshi's reforms, especially his means of consolidating political power and maintaining control, was among their major achievements. Yet they also consciously drew upon earlier sources. The ostensible model to which Ieyasu Tokugawa and his immediate successors gave express homage was that of Kamakura. In a sense they thereby arrested Japan's apparent institutional evolution. Yet they found within the past the means to transcend earlier patterns and create a very different order from any that had existed before. Theirs was thus an ambivalent tradition, one that remained on

51

the edge between a radical break with and a reaffirmation of older forms of authority and rule.

The basic patterns of Tokugawa governance were firmly established within its first half century. The institutions and methods of social control are misleadingly static. Their apparent continuity and endurance over a span of two and a half centuries tends to veil the dynamics of economic and social change that political and legal controls could not contain. Nevertheless, the Tokugawa rulers did achieve their primary aim to establish and perfect a regime that would withstand any challenge from daimyo rivals. To this end, Ieyasu Tokugawa and his first two successors redrew the political map of Japan, confiscating the domains of scores of daimyo houses and either bringing them under direct Tokugawa rule or redistributing their lands to Tokugawa kinsmen or loyal daimyo. Immediately after Ieyasu's victories at Sekigahara and Osaka in 1600 secured his military dominion over Japan, he eliminated eighty-seven defeated daimyo and established sixty-eight of his senior retainers as independent *fudai* daimyo, along with two new cadet [*shinpan*] daimyo houses. The strategic relocation of daimyo domains—now referred to as *han*—and assertion of rule over the crucial commercial center of Osaka and foreign trade at Nagasaki, as well as the imperial capital in Kyoto, ensured direct Tokugawa presence in all regions of the country and possessory control over nearly a sixth of all productive land.[1]

Quest for Legitimacy

Like all military rulers whose initial claims to rule are based on battlefield success and force of arms, having established an hegemony of power, Ieyasu Tokugawa and his successors sought corresponding legitimacy. Ieyasu first followed the precedent of the Kamakura and Muromachi *bakufu* to secure legitimacy by means of imperial appointment as *Seii-tai shōgun* in 1603 and somewhat dubious assertion of Minamoto lineage. Imperial mandate as shogun and Minister of the Right endowed Ieyasu and his successors with the traditional trappings of political legitimacy. But more was wanted.

A skeptic might well ask at this point what need did Ieyasu or his successors have for the court. Once the Tokugawa shoguns had effectively consolidated political power, Edo replaced Kyoto as Japan's political center. And whatever leverage the court retained by virtue of its control over imperial appointments had surely dissipated in the absence of any credible military rival to Tokugawa dominion. Why then did Ieyasu or one of his successors not simply do away with the emperor? Herman Ooms's response to this question is persuasive. The Tokugawa shoguns, he argues, must have perceived that at least some vestige of imperial authority remained; so simple and final a solution would have "deprived their power of legitimacy."[2]

Instead of eliminating the throne, Ieyasu successfully sought to control and use it while appropriating its prerogatives of appointment, the principal manifestation of imperial authority as well as source of political leverage. By retiring as shogun in 1605 in favor of his son Hidetada, Ieyasu managed to free himself from obligations of service to the court without sacrificing the gains of initial imperial office. More important, however, was his successful assertion of control over imperial conferral of rank and office to warriors, which denied the throne the means of independent political manipulation, along with the trappings of authority. Such maneuvers evidence, however, the residual authority of the throne.

Again following the lead of Nobunaga and Hideyoshi, Ieyasu sought additional grounds for nationwide rule independent of imperial authority. These he found in a mix of native and imported sources. Wrapping his person with Shinto ritual and in death with deistic claims, exemplified by the massive mausoleum at Nikkō, Ieyasu and his successors established the Tokugawa claim to hereditary rule without reference to Kyoto. Ieyasu's "Testament" (written anonymously after his death) even went to the extent of appropriating the ancient symbols of imperial authority of mirror, sword, and jewel.[3] Neo-Confucianism, however, served as the primary ideological foundation, justifying Tokugawa rule apart from imperial appointment. Reinterpreting Japan's past and the nature of rule, successive Confucian scholars sponsored by the shogunate created an enduring rationale for Tokugawa authority.[4]

Neo-Confucian thought provided a justification for rule that, like law in Europe, made it possible to reconcile might with right and join power with authority. The rediscovered Mandate of Heaven could legitimate virtuous rule however initially acquired. Thus in the early decades of Tokugawa hegemony, neo-Confucianism was rapidly established as the primary component of an officially encouraged ideology. Explicit in neo-Confucian tenets was the conditionality of authority and legitimate power on wise and benevolent rule. Neo-Confucianism taught a cosmology of constraint, requiring those claiming its justification for political authority to ensure order through virtue. The impact on law was considerable. As expressed by Sokō Yamaga (1622–1685), one of the early proponents of the School of Ancient Learning [*kogaku*], "virtuous rule" could not be achieved until "rites and music, law enforcement, and political administration have been put in order."[5] Once internalized by those in power, the values intrinsic to neo-Confucian legitimacy would inexorably produce rulers whose self-justification of power would require them to rationalize their conduct in terms of a paternalistic benevolence expressed in law. Neo-Confucianism thus included an ideal of principled governance that, although separate from legislated rules, nevertheless, held both the ruler and his laws accountable.

For those subject to Tokugawa rule, neo-Confucianism similarly established a discourse for social protest and political redress. As recent studies show, eighteenth and early nineteenth century peasant uprisings almost invariably couched grievances in terms of appeals to virtue[6] without express challenge to the authority of those who ruled. Nonetheless, implicit in the mere fact of collective opposition and this demand for benevolence was a threat to legitimacy. Whether for this reason or as a result of the force of collective action or, most likely, both, these rural tax revolts were also exceptionally successful in outcome.[7]

The inherent contradiction between traditional notions of imperial authority and a shogunal Confucian mandate could not be reconciled. Whether construed in terms of the tension between a Shintoist emphasis on sovereignty and authority and Confucian orientations as suggested by David Earl[8] or simply in terms of the dilemma posed by traditional conceptions of the imperial authority in relationship to shogunal power, neo-Confucianist views of suzerainty were more than inadequate in rationalizing the respective roles of emperor and shogun. As shogunal power waned, neo-Confucian orthodoxy could not foreclose a resurgent stress in political discourse on imperial authority.

Hidetada, the second Tokugawa shogun, tied these claims to daimyo oaths of submission and fealty required of the western daimyo in 1611 and the eastern daimyo in 1612. Each pledged "to obey with respect the laws and practices [*hōshiki*] of the shogun [*kubō*] as established from age to age since the time of the General of the Right [*Yoritomo*]" and "any regulations [*mokuroku*] issued from Edo."[9] In so doing the Tokugawa regime implicitly added its identification with the laws and legal institutions of the Kamakura *bakufu* and lineage to imperial mandate as a basis for legitimacy. Buttressed by custom and precedent, law too had become an acknowledged source of authority and validation of power.

The daimyo fealty oaths also signaled the new regime's intention to be the primary if not exclusive source of law for the nation as a whole. As the *sengoku* daimyo had appropriated exclusive lawmaking prerogatives within their domains, so the Tokugawa assumed the role as lawmakers for Japan, all but extirpating the throne as the primary source of law and vestiges of dual jurisdiction that remained from the Kamakura era. In 1613 the shogunate issued the first of two early regulatory fiats addressed to the nobility [*kuge*] that included—albeit indirectly—a command to the throne to order the nobility "to limit themselves to study and refinement" (article 1). It also included an order for the punishment of any noble who violated the law, including shogunal edicts [*hatto*]. This was followed two years later first by *Buke shohatto*, a similar edict issued to all daimyo houses, and then by the *Kinchū narabini kuge shohatto*, a more detailed edict regulating the nobility and, for the first time in Japanese history, the throne itself.

Echoing similar provisions in *sengoku* house codes, each of these enactments also firmly expressed the Tokugawa shogunate's view of the supremacy of law, especially its law. In the 1615 edict directed to the court, for example, article 12 stated that any crime or offense committed by a member of the nobility or court official was to be punished in accordance with the *myōreiritsu* [general provisions] of the *ritsuryō*, which included the basic criminal offenses.[10] The *Buke shohatto* went even further. Article 3 not only prohibited any daimyo from providing sanctuary to anyone violating shogunal edicts, but also went on to extol the supremacy of law even over reason: "Law [*hō*] is the foundation of ceremonial decorum [*reisetsu*]. Law [*hō*] prevails over reason

[*ri*] and reason yields to law. To disregard the law (as laid down by us) [*hatto*] is an offense not to be treated with leniency." Despite deletion of this provision in later edicts governing the warrior class and the subsequent shift of emphasis—more a return to past convention and practice—as a result of which reason [*dōri*] became, in Henderson's words, "the primary rule to be applied by Tokugawa judges,"[11] shogunal edict constituted the paramount source of legislated rules. In other words, law sourced in the will of the shogun not the throne had become a primary instrument of *bakufu* rule. The Tokugawa synthesis thereby transformed on a national scale law and lawmaking from simply an expression of legislated regulation, custom, and precedent into a manifestation if not source of legitimacy as well.

Return to the Administrative State

The administrative structure of the Tokugawa regime itself developed gradually. Military units of *sengoku* warrior organization were adapted to serve administrative needs and members of the hereditary samurai class were transformed into a functional administrative elite. Peace and security restored, hereditary samurai retainers in both the Tokugawa and other domains, settled in or near castle towns with fixed stipends, quite naturally acquired administrative functions. Thus, well before the end of the seventeenth century, Japan had restored a partially centralized public law order with a warrior officialdom as the literati-officials of this new version of the Chinese-styled administrative state. By the end of the seventeenth century, the regime had completed the formation of a complex structure of functional offices designed for the administrative control of the Tokugawa domains and the urban centers under its direct rule. The patterns of Tokugawa governance also influenced other domains as they were borrowed and adapted by individual *han*.

The most important functional administrative units within the Tokugawa domain were the three *bugyō* offices: the Temple and Shrine Commission [*jisha bugyō*], the Edo Town Commission [*Edo machi bugyō*], and the Finance Commission [*kanjō bugyō*]. Each had both administrative and judicial functions. The Temple and Shrine Commission enjoyed the highest status of the three, with initially three and later four *fudai* daimyo appointed to the post. The officers of both the Edo Town Commission and the Finance Commission were filled with samurai of bannermen [*hatamoto*] rank, two to three for the Town Commission and four to five for the Finance Commission. In addition to fiscal supervision and tax receipts, the Finance Commission was also responsible for most ordinary judicial functions in Edo. It was also charged with administrative oversight of *daikan* (deputies), the primary Tokugawa official outside of Edo and the other urban centers or special districts under direct shogunate control, such as Kyoto, Osaka, Nagasaki, Shizuoka, Hakodate, Niigata, as well as Nara, Nikkō, and Sado Island. The *daikan* was thus the only official link between the central offices of the shogunate in Edo and the vast majority of Japanese who resided in rural villages within directly ruled Tokugawa domains.[12] There were, however, only ten *daikan* offices with only forty to fifty *daikan* officials for all Tokugawa domains.[13] Each of the *han* developed similar functional administrative offices. Like the shogunate itself, they were concentrated in the castle town or at the residence each *han* was required by the shogunate to maintain in Edo.

Coupled with the obligation imposed on all daimyo to spend every other year in residence in Edo [*sankin kōtai*], the hostage-taking requirement that their families reside permanently in Edo was the shogunate's most trenchant means of daimyo control. Others included an elaborate network of spies, forced contributions to maintain Edo castle and other public works, and restrictions on the construction of castles. Having successfully asserted a prerogative to govern the daimyo, the nobility, and the throne alike, the shogunate felt no restraint in following the *sengoku* example by extending their lawmaking authority to all aspects of economic and social life within the Tokugawa house domains. Thus the Tokugawa rulers and other daimyo followed *sengoku* daimyo precedent to prescribe by edict and decree the status and conduct of all inhabitants within their respective domains. Regulatory measures designed to control the inhabitants of Tokugawa domains and cities under direct shogunate control in general included the imposition of censorship, the expansion of five-household units [*goningumi*]—introduced by Hideyoshi in 1597—for mutual supervision, prohibition against conspiratorial factions [*totō*], and above all, new personal and household registration requirements. For census purposes the shogunate reinstituted personal registries—a practice that had atrophied in the mid-Heian period. All births, adoptions, marriages, and divorces were subject to registration in the *ninbetsuchō* registries maintained for each village and urban district [*machi*]. Census registration also enabled the shogunate to regulate more effectively the restrictions initially introduced by Hideyoshi's 1591 *Hitobarai* edict prohibiting vocational mobility among warrior-officials [*hōkō*], peasants [*nōmin*], and townspeople [*chōnin*]. The Tokugawa regime intensified and further elaborated these restrictions by establishing a hierarchy of hereditary vocational castes: the nobility [*kuge*], warriors [*bushi*], Buddhist and Shintō priests (*sōni* and *shinkan*), peasants [*hyakushō*], artisans [*shokunin*], merchants [*chōnin*], and outcast communities [*eta* and *hinin*]. The four primary occupational categories of warriors, peasants, artisans, and merchants corresponded to the Confucianist four-tiered status scheme although reversing the Chinese original, which exalted scholars and ignored warriors.

Additional controls were devised to enforce the shogunate's ban on Christianity (also precedented by an expulsion edict issued by Hideyoshi in 1587). One was the expansion of the five-household unit system to all villages and urban districts. Another was the requirement that households register with a local Buddhist temple. Thus, at least within Japan's urban centers the regulatory controls of the public authorities were increasingly intensified and perfected. The complexity of samurai ranks and status increased along with the complexity of their administrative and ceremonial duties. The economic and social lives of merchants, artisans, and common laborers became increasingly regimented and restricted. Such ancient Chinese methods of supervision and control as registration, the five-household units, and vicarious liability were adapted and refined as effective means of indirect regulation and control. In short, urban Japan experienced, in John Whitney Hall's words, "a density of administrative supervision that few peoples have ever matched."[14]

Judicial Governance

The influence of Chinese practice was also evident in the Tokugawa regime's approach to litigation. The regime's emphasis on neo-Confucianist ideas necessitated a devaluation of the adjudicatory institutions. Consequently, the judicial functions of government were ostensibly reduced to criminal trials and ordered dispute resolution as in China and Korea. Harmony and the preservation or restoration of peaceful, if not amicable, relations between disputants became the official aim of private dispute adjudication. In theory at least, the procedural barriers to private petitions for relief by Tokugawa magistrates were substantial. Those seeking enforcement of legal claims or remedies against suffered wrongs were required to exhaust all means for mediation and settlement. Those who persisted were themselves subject to potential sanctions and instruction by the authorities as to their misconduct. Conciliation—or in Henderson's apt phrase, "didactic conciliation"—became a central feature of Tokugawa justice. Nonetheless, lawsuits continued to be brought in increasing numbers, as commerce increased and the country prospered. The institutions and processes of feudal adjudication were thereby expanded and perfected.

The ambivalence of the Tokugawa judicial tradition is manifest in the restricted devolution of Kamakura procedures for private suits with a concomitant expansion of litigation. Tokugawa law did recognize what were in effect private legal claims, but they were apparently conceptually less developed than the miscellaneous cases categorized as the *zatsumusata* of Kamakura and Muromachi practice. By the eighteenth century, Tokugawa had codified procedural rules distinguishing between adjudication initiated by petition [*deirimono*] as opposed to persecutions brought by the authorities [*ginmimono*]. With some justification contemporary scholars usually classify these as "civil" versus "criminal" actions,[15] focusing on the issues in dispute. This procedural dichotomy, as noted previously, could, like procedures for lesser offenses in Chinese law, also be accurately described as a distinction between claims of lesser or greater concern to the lawmakers. Those of lesser importance tended to be what would today be categorized as "civil" matters. In contrast, as Henderson observes, claims important to the shogunate were given full procedural protection as officially instituted actions.[16] Article 15 of the *Osadamegaki* (1742) is illustrative; it provided that no matter of concern to the shogunate could be tried as an adversarial action initiated by private petition.[17] Monetary claims came in numbers that forced recognition by the authorities. New categories for "money suits" [*kanekuji*] had to be devised to channel if not contain what was in effect a burgeoning private law order. In such cases conciliation requirements became less mandatory and more a *pro forma* hurdle. Indeed, Ryōsuke Ishii observes, by the end of the Tokugawa era the principal function of the *daikan* had become his role as an adjudicating magistrate in lieu of any administrative or policing duties as a shogunate deputy.[18] Moreover, despite the ban on representation of litigants in shogunate judicial proceedings, allowance for stand-ins in the event of infirmity and similar circumstances, as well as the requirement that litigants lodge at special inns, led to development of an incipient legal profession.[19] Judicial precedents grew in number. Later Western observers would marvel at the role of the Tokugawa magistrate and the development of judicial law.[20]

Autonomy with Dependence: The Enforced Cohesion of the *Mura*

The pivotal element of the Tokugawa legal order was not, however, this amalgam of regulatory and adjudicatory legal controls. Instead it was the paradox of a highly judicialized administrative state characterized by the autonomous village. The bureaucratic apparatus of the Tokugawa system was not pervasive. Urban centers may have been "overgoverned" as Hall puts it,[21] but the Japanese *mura* remained largely autonomous. Unlike Europe, no warrior-ruler remained to become the manorial lord and ultimately the local gentry and landed aristocracy of a postfeudal generation. Nor was Tokugawa Japan like Yi Korea where a *yangban* aristocracy remained close at hand. Legal controls did not penetrate to the village level through a resident official *yamen* "runner" as in imperial China or the *sōri* clerk as in Yi dynasty Korea. The Japanese *mura* was linked to the Tokugawa or *han* authorities solely through the formal accountability of the headman. However, any sense of responsibility or loyalty felt by headmen toward the ruling authorities was diluted by their identity of personal interests and priorities as well-placed villagers with those of the village community in general. As a result the vast majority of Japanese were freed from effective oversight and control by either a European-styled aristocracy or a Chinese-styled officialdom.

The Japanese *mura* as a self-contained, semiautonomous economic and political unit was also a product of the late sixteenth century. The dissolution of the *shōen* estates and the consolidation by Hideyoshi of various local units—the *shō*, *gō*, *hō*, and *ri*—into a single unit called the *mura* had enabled it to become the smallest territorial unit of a three-tiered political structure—provinces [*kuni*], districts [*kōri*], and villages [*mura*]—of the Tokugawa domains. Hideyoshi had also successfully defined peasant status through a series of edicts: the prohibition against peasant possession of swords and other implements of warfare, restrictions defining exclusive occupational roles for warriors and peasants, and removal of the warrior from the village. All served to reinforce village identity as separate community and caste.[22]

Once the *mura* was recognized as a basic administrative unit, village offices were also established. The most important was that of headman. Completing a triad of village officers were the offices of *kumigashira*, comprising the three or four heads of leading households who assisted the headman, and *hyakushōdai*, representatives from a board of overseers that included all landholding families. Thus within the village a hierarchy of rank and status, presumably determined at least initially by wealth, prevailed. With the vicissitudes of economic change, however, family pedigree was as often divorced from wealth in the village as the town.

The office of headman was, at least in Tokugawa domains, ostensibly appointive or at least subject to formal *daikan* approval. In practice, however, in some villages the position became an hereditary office, while in others the headmen were selected by agreement among those eligible and not uncommonly rotated at regular intervals. In some instances, the headman held the office for life.[23] Several of the village documents collected by Henderson hint at the intrigue involved in the process of selection. In one, six village elders meet and agree to rotate the office among themselves and their descendants for five-year terms. Anticipating, however, the possibility of a retirement or the appointment of an outsider, they agree that one of the six would keep custody of a copy of village survey records and maintain a common front.[24] In another, unable to find a successor, a village contracts with a neighboring headman to assume its office as well. In return all agree to cooperate, put an end to past disagreement, and pay their respective share of village taxes as instructed by village officials.[25] In a third, the village apparently preferred the appointment of a more wealthy farmer who lacked the requisite family status. The solution was an arrangement separating authority from power at the village level by supporting the appointment of a person who was eligible but, by agreement, recognizing the other as the one with actual responsibility.[26]

Viewed from above, the *mura*, like its urban counterpart the *machi*, appeared to be an intensively regulated community. At least there was no dearth of regulatory proscriptions, and no facet of personal or community life was beyond the potential purview of administrative fiat. In addition to registration, tax, and corvée labor obligations, villagers were increasingly subject to a wide variety of regulatory controls designed primarily to maximize revenue yields from rice production and closely related efforts to restrict social and geographic mobility. Villagers could not possess weapons, alienate land, or legally leave the village. Even dress was prescribed to inhibit social mobility. In Akita *han*, Kōta Kodama reports, an 1807 edict prohibited peasants from wearing any rain gear other than straw hats and straw coats.[27] Liability for any individual infraction was vicarious, with households, the five-household groups, and the village as a whole collectively liable for any individual misconduct and the headman individually accountable as well.

Focus on the volume and scope of regulatory edicts alone is misleading, however. Viewed over time, Tokugawa legislation manifests a consistent pattern. The greater the decline of shogunal and *han* resources and power in favor of an increasingly prosperous and autonomous rural elite, whose growing manufacturing and commerce activities were outpacing their agricultural income, the more stringent became the legal controls imposed in the Tokugawa village. Susan Hanley and Kozo Yamamura conclude in their seminal study of economic and demographic change during the Tokugawa period:

> The rising income of peasants [especially from commerce and manufacturing], rural entrepreneurs' advantages in obtaining labor relative to their urban counterparts, monopolistic and monopsonistic restrictions practiced by city guilds, and the changing Bakufu policies towards commerce and manufacturing—all contributed to the growth of the rural economy.[28]

From the mid-eighteenth century most Tokugawa and *han* legislation directed toward the village reflected an attempt to increase the resources under their control and at least to contain the threatening processes of economic and social change taking place in rural Japan. The shogunate's supreme legislative effort in the 1742 *Osadamegaki* and the *Kyōhō* reforms that preceded it under Yoshimune Tokugawa, the eighth shogun (1716–1745) were themselves an attempt to deal with the destabilizing effects of rapid economic changes, evidenced by shortages in the rice-based tax system, rising commodity prices, and above all, a mounting caseload of money suits. In response to these social ills—all symptomatic of the diversification and growth in nonagricultural sectors of the economy—the authorities renewed old proscriptions and imposed new controls on the alienation and reclamation of land, commodity markets, rural mobility, and the administration of lawsuits.[29] These and other attempts to stem the tide of social change by edict failed. The regulatory apparatus of the Tokugawa administrative state was incapable of preventing the erosion of the foundations of Tokugawa rule.

By the end of the eighteenth century Japan had a total population of about 26.5 million persons. Eighty percent of the population comprised peasant farmers residing in one of 60,000 plus villages.[30] Roughly four to five million lived in Tokugawa domains. With only forty *daikan* in ten districts to oversee their activities, the impracticability of adequate enforcement of Tokugawa controls is evident. Without the cooperation of village officials Tokugawa edicts could not be effectively enforced. Moreover, since most if not all Tokugawa regulation took the form of instructions issued to *daikan* and other shogunate officials and were usually not made public, even the remote possibility of voluntary village compliance was also quite limited. Where restrictions were widely publicized, villagers—especially the leading landowning families and most active commercial entrepreneurs who dominated official village posts—can hardly be expected to have submissively complied with legal restrictions designed to transfer wealth to outside authorities or deny them new sources of income. To the contrary, official reliance on village self-government and indirect rule through the mediation of village headmen enabled the village to disregard unwanted restrictions. One of the most telling of Henderson's village documents is indicative of the most likely village response. In 1832 officials from six neighboring villages colluded to resist *daikan* approval of a petition to open a new field in a nearby river bed. In addition to details on the apportionment of expenses, the memorial of their agreement even anticipated and attempted to preclude the prisoner's dilemma: "If a single village or individual [among us] should be interrogated alone, in accordance with [this agreement] petitions for opening of new fields will not be accepted no matter where [the proposed reclamation might be located]."[31] Japanese villagers were, it appears, quite adept at collective action to protect their own interests.

Autonomy had a price. For the community and the individual, conflict avoidance and deference to authority were the prerequisites of self-governance and independence. So long as peace prevailed and taxes were paid, there was little to draw official attention and scrutiny. However, any open conflict or breach of peace threatened that autonomy and invited investigation and more stringent controls. By suppressing intracommunity quarrels and satisfying formal fiscal obligations, a village community could restrain or avoid unwanted official regulation. The consequence was an institutional structure that in allowing evasion of official legal controls also promoted external deference and internal cohesion. In effect the village had the security of the administrative state along with the freedom of the outlaw.

To achieve or maintain such autonomy with ostensible conformity the community itself had to develop mechanisms of control. The most prominent included the psychological sanction of collective community displeasure as well as more severe forms of community coercion, such as ostracism and expulsion. Because rice cultivation necessitated a high degree of cooperation, community action had substantial coercive impact. Moreover, as the protection afforded by the community rather than outside or higher official authority was more important to the individual and the household, the threat of community sanctions became an even more effective means of control. Outside one's village the individual no longer shared the material or psychological benefits of membership. The alternative was flight to urban centers without introduction and guarantees, often in defiance of legal restrictions on travel and change of residence, possibly offering the unattractive alternative of more direct supervision and stringent legal regulation within *machi*, which were also semiautonomous and subject to similar community controls. Consequently, community sanctions of both formal and informal stripe, not the samurai's sword, were the real deterrents to wrongdoing in Tokugawa Japan. Moreover, inasmuch as such sanctions were as readily imposed on the family for the misconduct of its members, as other village documents in the Henderson collection suggest,[32] the family tended to parallel the village in both its need for a means to control its members and the forms of coercion it used.

In this environment individual interests were generally subsumed by community and family concerns. Yet at each level of social organization from the larger village to the nuclear family and the individual, a greater measure of effective autonomy was achieved by outward display of dependence and deference to authority. All stood to gain, therefore, by overt submission to those with power at each level in the hierarchy of authority and to control by whatever means the conduct of others for whom one might be vicariously liable. In other words, the Tokugawa scheme of indirect governance set into motion a process that fostered social cohesion as a means of maximizing autonomy, coinciding neatly with the neo-Confucian norms of loyalty and respect for authority. In other words Japan evolved a self-enforcing process of autonomy with dependence.

Community—and to a lesser extent family—control over sanctions also meant that the community had a significant degree of control over the viability of legal norms. As evidenced in the process of regular adjudication, those who enforce legal rules invariably make legal rules. Only the rules and standards the community was willing to enforce by the threat or application of sanctions could be effectively implemented within its confines. It is therefore reasonable to assume that offenses against Tokugawa or *han* policy that did not affect community concerns or at least were contrary to community interests would not have been penalized unless they might come to the attention of the officials. At each level of social organization from family through the village, overt and superficial conformity to legally prescribed rules of conduct would thus be emphasized at the expense of actual compliance. Truly secret behavior would not matter. To be caught rather than to commit became the crime. Unintended support for such disregard for internalized norms can even be found in neo-Confucian thought. As the neo-Confucianist Shundai Dazai (1680–1747) wrote:

> Now, in the Way of the Sages, the good and evil at the bottom of someone's heart are never discussed. The teachings of the Sages are devised to enter from without. Anyone who, in his personal conduct, upholds the rites of the Early Kings; in dealing with everything follows the righteousness of the early Kings; and has the outward decorum of a Gentleman, is to be considered a Gentleman. What is inside his heart is not in question. Regardless of what is inside his heart, if someone adheres outwardly to the rules of proper conduct and does not violate them, he is a Gentleman.[33]

What mattered was outward behavior, not private thought. It was an easy step to include unnoticed conduct and secret acts. Thus there was ideological underpinning for an institutional structure that promoted external submission and dependency but also permitted evasion of official legal proscriptions.

Two and a half centuries of domestic peace and stable government under the Tokugawa regime produced what we today tend to take for granted as the basic features of Japan's distinctive legal culture and tradition. Commonly ignored are the changes forged in the Tokugawa synthesis of older concepts, institutions, and process. On the one hand, successive Tokugawa rulers were able to perfect as never before the centralized institutions of the regulatory state embodied in the *ritsuryō* system. With a well-organized, dependent corps of samurai administrators, Tokugawa and *han* rulers could as never before attempt to replicate the Chinese administrative state. It is not surprising, therefore, that interest in learning more from Chinese models grew steadily with the shift from military to administrative rule, and the endurance of the Pax Tokugawa. By the mid-eighteenth century, Henderson reminds us,[34] Chinese law and legal literature, especially Ming statutes and code commentaries imported into Japan in the early eighteenth century, had awakened interest in imperial Chinese law among the shogun's neo-Confucian advisors and in several *han*, especially those, such as Kumamoto in the vicinity of Nagasaki, the then port of entry. Not since the mid-Heian period had Japanese paid special attention to Chinese legal sources.[35] By the mid-eighteenth century translations of both the Ming and Ching codes with commentaries had been made. Their influence on the shogunate's legal reforms, as well as eighteenth century *han* codes, was considerable.

This resurgence of interest in Chinese legal models also ensured that the Japanese legal tradition would remain captive to the conceptual constraints of imperial Chinese law. However close *sengoku* and Tokugawa legislation may have seemed to approach contemporary Western notions of law as a fundamental source of political authority, Tokugawa legislation was hardly more than what Thomas Stephens aptly describes as a set of "disciplinary" rules.[36] At no time before Japan's mid-nineteenth century engagement with the West did Japanese undertake to define law as a corpus of abstract principles or endeavor to use juridical discourse as a vehicle to explicate social or political values. It is misleading folly to attempt to cast the Japanese legal culture in contemporary Western legal molds. To presume, nevertheless, that attitudes and understandings regarding the nature and role of legal forms and principles as expressed in eighteenth century shogunate and *han* legislation as well as the *ritsuryō*, feudal formularies, and sixteenth century daimyo edicts were unrelated to the justification of political power and the definition of political authority would be equally erroneous. The importance of Chinese models and the sudden spurt of legislative activity from the mid-eighteenth century attest to the importance of law as an emblem if not a source of political authority as well as a more mundane tool for the effective exercise of political power.

The propagation of neo-Confucian and Chinese juristic thought, albeit instrumental in buttressing the claims and conduct of Tokugawa governance, also tended, however, to retard the development of less compatible processes and institutions, especially adjudicatory or judicial institutions and the processes of a more private law order. Although commercial growth compelled the extension of judicial institutions and procedures to accommodate increasing numbers of "money suits," their place within the total scheme of Japanese governance remained ambivalent. Adjudicatory processes in which contracts, commercial instruments, and other private claims could be enforced with predictable certainty were difficult to reconcile within a legal order that defined legal status and social obligations within a hierarchy of neo-Confucian absolutes. Thus official pronouncements and procedures were designed to discourage litigation and sought to substitute compromise and conciliation for assertive claims to enforce nascent rights. Nonetheless, the hold of custom and precedent as well as commercial activity and the perennial need to maintain order prevented any atrophy of Japan's indigenous judicial institutions.

The Tokugawa legal legacy was, therefore, above all institutional. By the mid-nineteenth century Japan had perfected the official forms, processes, and procedures of an intricate web of bureaucratic controls within which, however, the adjudicatory institutions of an incipient private law order were also prominent. Adapted and transformed by indigenous political and economic needs, legal institutions of imperial Chinese origin had evolved quite differently in contrast to Japan's East Asian neighbors to include the basic elements and mechanisms of a developed judicial system.

More influential than either the administrative or judicial instruments of governmental control and ordering, however, was their containment. Indirect governance of the *mura* and the *machi* prompted resort to a complex variety of consensual or contractual means of social control. Reinforced by registration, *daikan* approvals, and other administrative restraints, they were never completely isolated from the larger regulatory environment. Yet beneath the surface of an intensively regulated, overgoverned society was the reality of a dense fabric of informal, social controls that affected the everyday life of a far greater proportion of the Japanese population than edict or officialdom. Law was not inclusive. Moral and ethical strictures were conceived quite apart from law as totally separate sources of value and constraint. Nor—except by those who ruled—was law accepted as a desirable or protective instrument of control. Most Japanese thus lived in an environment in which their lives were ordered by economic needs and community norms and sanctions. For them, formal legal controls usually constituted unneeded and unwanted restrictions imposed by others over whom they had no authority and little if any influence. Formal legal rules were best acknowledged with an obsequious bow but kept at arm's length and, if possible, ignored or evaded. In a functional sense a parallel, informal "legal" order existed in which conventional property interests and consensual undertakings were enforced by means of accepted community and market sanctions. Within this order, the community—and those within it with customary status and economic influence—controlled. Their values and interests prevailed.

Not even the Tokugawa rulers, however, could permanently escape the paradox of authority. Unwilling or incapable of breaking completely with Japan's imperial tradition, they could not fully resolve the dilemma of legitimacy. At least from hindsight, although perhaps overstated, it appears that rule from Edo was not absolutely secure insofar as Kyoto remained a locus of residual political authority. As the administrative state reached new levels of institutional maturity, its eroding power became increasingly evident, and the idea of a revival of imperial rule began to stir those dissatisfied with Tokugawa hegemony. The existence of the imperial institution did not determine the shift in power and political change. But for the court, however, the changes that were perhaps inevitable would surely have taken different forms and been channelled in different directions. Major institutional changes thus threatened Japan well before Perry's "Black Ships" arrived in Edo Bay to force the opening of Japan to the West. The regime's incapacity to enforce its seclusion policy against the newly industrializing Western powers merely provided the catalyst for impending political change.

However inexorable the events leading to the collapse of the Tokugawa regime and restoration of imperial rule may seem in hindsight, their timing was not. The Western world to which Japan opened was itself at the end of a process of major political and legal change, one in which liberal political systems with codified private law regimes were deemed in the smugly self-confident, newly industrialized West to be close to the final stages of a progressive evolution toward a utopian society. That Japan would emulate the West in law as well as technology seems almost inevitable as it began to remake its own political and legal order under the newly enthroned Meiji emperor. That the model was nineteenth-century Western law was profoundly important.

4

Constitutions and Codes: The Making of the Contemporary Legal Order

No linear nexus links traditional practices to the formal institutions and procedures of Japan's contemporary legal order. They did not evolve from the past. Nor do they reflect a cultural consensus of shared values and preferences of the Japanese people as if the product of some sort of nationwide referendum. Rather in nearly all respects, Japan's contemporary legal order was an imposed system. Like the formal institutions of Heian, Kamakura, *sengoku*, and Tokugawa justice, those of contemporary Japan were the creation of ruling elites, with later embellishments imposed by an alien occupying army.

Constitutions, codes, and other formal institutions do not, however, complete the definition of a legal order. Institutions and institutional processes function within the more inclusive environment of shared values, habits, and expectations—in other words, culture—derived from yesterday's experience. Culture is always a legacy of the past, a subject of change and redefinition in the present that shapes the practices and patterns of the future.

Meiji Japan (1867–1912) may have witnessed a radical institutional transformation but this did not—could not—include a similar rupture with Japan's cultural tradition. The sudden infusion of Western law institutions that had not themselves evolved within Japan's historical experience, like Chinese law twelve centuries earlier, faced or threatened new habits and expectations and a change in values as well as the new institutions themselves. In the ensuing confrontation and conflict both institutions and culture yielded to produce something more than a mere blend or composite, but rather a different institutional and cultural compound, a hybrid of both. The making of Japan's contemporary legal order is therefore the story of the sometimes destructive but always creative interaction between new, imposed legal institutions from the West and the habits and values of Japan's past.

The Meiji Transformation

The making of the legal system of modern Japan began with the opening of Japan to the West in the mid-nineteenth century. The first phase ended at the turn of the century with a nearly complete institutional break with the past and the creation of a new legal order based on Western, predominantly German, models. Mindful of the immediate need to consolidate power internally, the leaders of the Meiji government were particularly sensitive to Japan's weakness relative to the external forces they faced. They were fully cognizant of Western encroachment in other parts of Asia and Japan's inability to resist a similar fate. The goal for the new government was clear—to build a strong and independent nation. The means were equally apparent. Like modernizing rulers in nineteenth century Czarist Russia, the Ottoman empire, and Ch'ing China, Japan's new leaders felt compelled to emulate the West. Law and legal institutions were high on the list of immediate reforms.

That external pressures contributed to this decision should be neither overlooked nor overemphasized. Included in the 1858 Treaty of Amity and Commerce with the United States was provision (in article VI) for consular jurisdiction over American nationals in Japan in both criminal and civil cases. This pattern was repeated in the treaties subsequently concluded between Japan and the European powers. Although regarded as natural in earlier eras when law was personal and legal rights and duties integral to nationality or religious identity, extraterritoriality during the nineteenth century reflected self-congratulatory judgments in the West that theirs were the "civilized" systems of law. It followed logically that they should therefore claim protection for their nationals from inferior systems even beyond the territorial reach of national sovereignty. The Japanese perceived very quickly that such attitudes, if not the reality, constituted an affront to national sovereignty and pride. Thus the conditioning of elimination of consular jurisdiction (in addition to Western control over Japanese tariffs and foreign trade policies) to the establishment of a modern—hence Western—legal system added impetus to the Japanese efforts.[1]

The outcome was not, however, the predictable product of a predetermined scheme. Neither the process nor the substance of the Meiji legal reforms followed a previously charted course. Instead codification came only after a series of incidental and often *ad hoc* changes. In some instances, as illustrated by Shinpei Etō's influence in the establishment of the Department of Justice, Western patterns could be adapted to advance the power or prestige of particular individuals.[2] In other cases, as with the Meiji Constitution, Western models could be used to serve the more generalized interests of those in power. Practices proposed by a French or German advisor were also often adopted without necessarily much thought or concern as to their impact or implications simply because they were "modern" and "western" and thus had a particular legitimacy and attraction to the self-conscious makers of modern Japan. Above all else, however, their break with the past was complete. As Thomas C. Smith pointedly observes:

> As revolutionary leaders are likely to be, the Meiji leaders were desperately harassed men. They had come to power by destroying old institutions and impairing old loyalties, and, until these were replaced, their grip on power was necessarily nervous and insecure. But if their destructive work deprived them of the support of part of the past, it also saved them from the illusion that trapped Chinese leaders: that the past could be preserved

intact. Having burned bridges, they had to go forward—to find new solutions rather than refurbish old ones.[3]

The commitment of the Meiji leaders, whatever their motives, to full-scale legal reform is not in doubt. Nor should their achievements be slighted. The legal reformers of Meiji Japan undertook their task with deliberate care and without undue haste notwithstanding pressures for revision of treaty provisions on custom control and extraterritoriality. Despite the formidable obstacles of learning alien languages and adapting alien concepts and institutions, by the end of the century the Japanese had established a modern legal system with independent courts, trained legal professions, and an inclusive corpus of codified law. New institutions were created and new procedures introduced as courts and ministries were established and judicial and administrative practices developed. A new officialdom of professional judges, procurators, and police were selected and trained. Other careers in law became possible with recognition of the need for lawyers and legal scholars. Even the language of the law was almost completely rewritten. Japanese translators either invented new compounds of Chinese characters [*jukugo*] or adopted older ones for the terminology of Western law. In definition hardly a single term of Japanese legal language survived the transformation. An entirely new vocabulary was created, with new categories, new concepts.

There had already been significant progress by the mid-1870s. The process of translating foreign law codes and drafting new ones with the aid of foreign legal advisors (among whom Gustave Émile Boissonade de Fontarabie and Hermann Roesler were to be among the most important) had commenced. As time went on, interim regulations and laws enacted and revised as transitional measures began to depart increasingly from traditional patterns and to incorporate principles and practices of Western origin.

Institutionally, the process began in 1871 with the organization of a Department of Justice [*Shihōshō*], which replaced the Finance Department's jurisdiction for civil adjudication as well as a short-lived *ritsuryō*-styled office of criminal law [*Keihōkan*], which had been established in 1868.[4] By 1872 local courts had begun to be organized as officials from the Department of Justice, initially sent to local administrative offices, began organizing independent offices labeled *saibansho*, or courts. In the same year the first formal program for legal education, known as the *Meihō-ryō* Law School, was organized as a bureau of the Justice Department. By the end of 1872 under the direction of Shinpei Etō, the new Minister of Justice, the department expanded its jurisdiction to engulf the entire legal system from courts to prisons, procurators to police, judges to lawyers.

Three years later, in April 1875, the Great Court of Cassation [*Daishin'in*] was established along with a system of higher courts and local prefectural courts, patterned as the common English translation suggests for the most part on French models. The role of private advocates [*daigennin*] in civil actions was also recognized. During the succeeding months, the system grew as the prefectural courts were renamed "district courts" [*chihō saibansho*] and their branches became local ward courts [*ku-saibansho*]. Although some modifications were made in 1882, the earlier system was largely reinstituted under the Court Organization Law of 1890.[5] Thus by the end of 1876 the basic structure of Japan's judiciary as it exists today had been completed.

As the court system formed, so new procedures for civil and criminal adjudication developed. Until 1881 Japanese procedural law was a slightly modified amalgam of Tokugawa law and practice. Yet one by one traditional forms yielded to Western patterns. Finally, in 1890 the Japanese government adopted a new Code of Civil Procedure based on separate drafts prepared by German (Techow) and French (Boissonade) advisors, which fully replaced any remaining vestiges of traditional procedural law.

A similar process of transformation occurred in substantive law. Best known is the making of the Meiji Constitution[6] and the Civil Code.[7] The development of commercial and criminal law codes followed similar paths.[8] In each instance Western legal forms and rules first supplanted traditional institutions and practices through a gradual and often piecemeal fashion while a general code or statute was being drafted. In many aspects the codes represented less a departure from the immediate past than confirmation of rules that had already been put into practice.

By the late 1880s the process neared completion. In 1880 a criminal code and a set of regulations for criminal procedure were adopted, which were later (1890) enacted as the first Code of Criminal Procedure[9] with minor modifications. These were followed in 1889 by the Meiji Constitution,[10] and in 1890 by the first Civil Code,[11] the first Commercial Code,[12] the Court Organization Law, the Administrative Court Law,[13] and the Code of Civil Procedure.[14]

Critical changes took place during these years, however, in Japanese outlook and attitudes toward the West, Western culture, and Western law. First, esteem for French law had waned in Japan as in Europe as deference to German legal science (and German economic and military power) grew. Moreover, reaction had set in against what was undoubtedly an excessively naive preference for all things Western during the early Meiji years.[15] Thus the first phase of the legal reforms did not culminate until the enactment of the second Criminal Code in 1907,[16] by which time all but the already predominantly German procedural codes had been redrafted along German lines.

Several aspects of the Meiji transformation of Japanese law illustrate the adaptability of Western law as well as the residual problems Japan encountered. The first is a point too often neglected: For the most part, Western legal institutions, processes, and even derivative legal rules proved to be easily integrated into the Japanese cultural and institutional matrix. This transferability can be explained on the one hand by the existence of analogous institutions, processes, and even norms in Tokugawa law. As one observer— presumably John Henry Wigmore—wrote in a long series of essays for the *Japan Weekly Mail*, nearly all of the presumably new, Western-derived institutions of the 1890 Codes with respect to property rights and commercial practices were analogous to preexisting institutions and practices.[17] Although stressed by Wigmore for purposes of influencing enactment of the 1890 Code, fundamental similarities in practice did exist. The series concluded:

> We have seen that the leading ideas of Code and custom (where comparison is possible) have the same content; that where latitude could be given, the new Code has allowed to local varieties of usage the freest play; and that where novelties or inflexible rules have been determined on, the conditions were such as to admit the exercise of legislative discretion. Looking once more over the detailed comparisons of the foregoing chapters, we cannot see how there can be more than one answer to the question we started with—the answer that in any fair sense the Codes are not in conflict with existing custom.[18]

Japan had also long been familiar with registry systems, complex procedures for adjudication, and sophisticated commercial instruments. Official land registers were maintained in village offices throughout Japan. They recorded the names of proprietors, the location and size of the parcel, as well as the assessed yield for tax purposes. The Tokugawa shogunate had also—as noted previously—expanded personal registration with Buddhist temples as a means of enforcing its ban against Christianity as well as with village officials for census and other control purposes. Births, marriages, adoptions, and deaths were all recorded and reported to *daikan* officers and ultimately to Edo.

As discussed in previous chapters, the Japanese had developed sophisticated trial procedures by the thirteenth century. These were expanded in the seventeenth and eighteenth centuries with the growth of commercial activity. The 1742 *Osadamegaki* was itself essentially a manual of instructions on policies and procedures addressed to adjudicating officials in Tokugawa domains.

With respect to commercial instruments, by the end of the eighteenth century Japanese merchants and traders were using a wide variety of commercial instruments analogous to contemporary, Western forms. These included shares [*kabu*] in commercial enterprises, guaranty certification [*hikiawase*], various types of bills of exchange [*kawase*], and promissory notes [*tegata*]. Special summary trial procedures [*naka-nuki-saiban*] for actions on commercial paper had also been introduced.[19]

The drafters of Japan's new codes also took particular care not to incorporate derivative rules or norms that directly contradicted desired preexisting ones. As Boissonade would later point out in defense of the 1890 Civil Code and Code of Civil Procedure, the code drafting commission had before it extensive sources on traditional law and procedure.[20] These included a set of 7556 volumes of manuscripts and other materials containing countrywide records evidencing extant customary practices encompassing the last two centuries of the *bakufu*, a Ministry of Justice compilation of local judicial practices in ten volumes, and a summary of the Ministry of Justice compilation prepared for the draftsmen of the civil and commercial codes.[21] The drafting process was methodical. Every effort was made to ensure continuity.

Individual Japanese were quick to take advantage of new institutions introduced from the West. As shogunate and *han* restrictions on internal trade and entry into new occupations were abolished, enterprising Japanese from all classes took advantage of their new opportunities. For example, Japan's first modern banking regulations[22] were promulgated in 1872. These were quite restrictive, requiring newly formed national banks to transfer over half of their cash holdings to the government in return for government securities. Only four banks were established under the regulations, with an aggregate capital of about two and a half million yen. The restrictions were eased by amendments decreed in 1876,[23] and by 1880 Japan had 151 banks with an aggregate capital of over 43 million yen.[24] Not then nor thereafter did anyone seriously question the applicability of new commercial institutions and norms.

It would be a mistake, however, to view the growth of new commercial ventures, whether joint-stock companies, banks, or other Western-inspired forms of commercial enterprise, as the product of law reform, new statutes, and codes. As Ryōsuke Ishii notes, a number of new banks were initially organized as joint-stock companies and were actively engaged in the banking business before 1876, only they could not be called banks.[25] For the most part the new codes and statutes were responses as a means of regulation and control rather than catalysts to entrepreneurial activity. New legislation was prompted less by the desire to initiate or stimulate economic growth than a felt need to channel and control economic activity. The lawmakers of Meiji Japan thus construed Western law in traditional East Asian terms: law as an instrument of the pervasive administrative state. Only gradually, if at all, did they adjust to the underlying premises of private law in a liberal political order. This divergence in the enthymemes—the unstated premises—of law itself is perhaps best revealed in the initial Japanese reactions to Western law, the controversy over the enactment of the first Civil Code and Western misconceptions of the Meiji Constitution.

Reform and Reaction

The European nations to which Japan opened in the mid-nineteenth century were themselves in the grip of pervasive economic, social, and institutional change. A self-conscious faith in enlightened progress and cultural superiority was evident. To Europeans, mankind had broken through barriers of ignorance and superstition to a world of evolving perfection and triumphant reason. Contemporary conceptions had just emerged of the state and its relationship to society, of citizenship and individual autonomy, as well as of law and its primacy as an instrument of social ordering. Confronting Japan was a Europe that defined claims to supremacy in terms of its own break with a feudal past, the glorification of the nation-state, and a rational legal order.

Nowhere were these currents stronger than in post-revolutionary France. Hence France led in the movement toward codification of law, impelled by the ideal of a rational system of unified national law in codes, accessible to the ordinary person, in which the rights and duties of all citizens would be articulated coherently and clearly. No wonder that Japanese encountering the French codes just before the Restoration were impressed. The French example seemed to meet all of the needs of a new modern Japanese state.

Nineteenth-century European and Japanese notions of the state were not identical, however. Strong as statist impulses in Europe may have been, the authority of the modern European state could not be defined in totalitarian terms. Dichotomies of public and private, of secular and sacred, denied the state the authority to intrude in certain spheres, while corresponding economic, religious, and social institutions politically limited state powers accordingly. Moreover, the idea of the liberal state fostered by eighteenth-century British political economists now waxed with the expansion of British economic and military prowess. Simply put, the preeminent function of the state was deemed to be the maintenance of an order within which autonomous individuals could by industry and skill realize their fullest potential. Although the role of the state in promoting the welfare of its citizens through education, health, and other services expanded, along with growing skepticism and outright disbelief in the neutrality of the state as to the allocation of resources within the order it maintained, this premise of the ultimate purpose of government stood largely unchallenged for over a century.

Liberal views of the role of the state led inexorably to the primacy of private law. If the principal aim of the state (government) was to maintain order as a means, at least in part, to foster the realization of gains to the common welfare resulting from autonomous individual effort, it followed that the preferred legal order was one that both ensured the most effective maintenance of social order and also enabled individuals to determine without state direction the norms governing their relationships with others. Consequently, nineteenth-century European law focused on private civil law, particularly contract.

The pivotal element was the distinction between *jus cogens* and *jus depositum*—that is, between mandatory rules that could not be modified at the will of the parties involved and optional rules that could. Nearly all rules in the continental civil codes, especially the law of obligations (of which the law of contract is the most significant part), were optional. The predominance of optional rules within an ordered system of law could not, however, also include autonomous choice to avoid regulation by law. Freedom of contract also meant the loss of individual autonomy to change one's mind in the future and unilaterally to break past promises. Any modification of the optional rules of the codes by consent of the parties was as binding and as enforceable as any legislated rule of law, optional or mandatory. And without new consent by all parties, all were also bound by their prior agreement.

The private law systems of nineteenth-century Europe also denied to the state the power to enforce legal rules without the consent of the parties affected. Unlike public law rules, enforced through an administrative or criminal process, the state does not initiate or control the action to enforce private law rules. As a result, those with the capacity to cause enforcement—in other words, those who hold the "rights" to be enforced—have the freedom to renounce, settle, or compromise their claims as they will irrespective of public policy or the common good. Consequently, the only legal rules that are enforced are those someone with the capacity to sue wishes to enforce. The civil codes of nineteenth century Europe were thus grounded on conceptions of the state and legal ordering that were almost completely alien to the East Asian tradition. Although property interests and commercial transactions were recognized and enforced both in formal adjudication and informal practice, early nineteenth-century Japan still had no abstract conception of legal rules subject to private control over content, application, and enforcement or law as a means of private, autonomous ordering. Legal rules as opposed to custom were, as described before, no more or less than the regulatory commands of those who ruled and the customary and precedential rules they recognized and enforced.

The reaction of the first Japanese who came into contact with Western law is not surprising. Simply construing what they saw within their own frames of reference they viewed Western private law as a remarkably inclusive set of regulatory, state-directed rules. Masamichi Tsuda, for example, sent to Leiden to study Western philosophy by the shogunate in its last days, discovering the Dutch civil code, began a translation in which he coined the term "*minpō*" or "citizen's law" used today to denote both civil code and private law. As explained by Robert Epp, Tsuda saw in the codes "an excellent instrument for regulating the people."[26] The impressions of French civil law by Joun Kurimoto while serving as the Meiji government's first ambassador to France were similar. Upon his return Kurimoto described the French codes in a published pamphlet. The French Civil Code, he exclaimed was "truly unparalleled and without precedent . . . I think that nothing short of the genius of Confucius could even have imagined it. Almost every order issued by Napoleon [III], the present emperor, is rooted in this code."[27] Lost on Kurimoto was any distinction between public and private law or between coercive, regulatory rules enforced by the state and optional legal norms whose enforcement was subject to the initiative and control of affected parties as defined by an allocation of rights and duties. Instead he, like most Japanese in his day and perhaps even some today, thought of law in sinicized terms as rules and regulations issued by those who rule and subject to their discretionary enforcement. Yet although Kurimoto may have misconceived the nature of Western private law rules and the processes of their enforcement, he did perceive correctly their expansiveness as a means of social ordering. Kurimoto wondered at the domain of law and the pervasiveness of legal controls over all aspects of social life.

For the lawmakers of Meiji Japan, the codification process thus represented more than the codification of modern legal rules or preexisting customs and precedents into a new code of national law. It represented the dominion of the Meiji state and an expansion of the instrumentality of state regulation to coincide more fully with conceptions of its political authority. As Masao Maruyama has observed:

> Whereas in the West national power after the Reformation was based on
> formal, external sovereignty, the Japanese State never came to the point of

drawing the distinction between external and internal spheres and of recognizing that its authority was valid only for the former. . . . [T]he Japanese State, being a moral entity, monopolized the right to determine values.[28]

Maruyama might have added that just as in the West law and the state's formal processes for law enforcement reflected the limits of state authority and power, so in Meiji Japan the adoption of Western law represented an expanded use of law as an instrument of state influence on social values. The codes thus had very different aims and predicted effects to Japanese from those assumed by Western advisors and observers.

The Civil Code Controversy

The final drafts of a civil code, compiled under the guidance of the French scholar, Gustave Émile Boissonade de Fontarabie, were completed in 1888 along with a commercial code and a code of civil procedure, which Hermann Roesler, the German jurist best known for his contribution to the Meiji Constitution, had helped to draft. After consideration and approval by the cabinet and other government organs, it was submitted to the House of Peers in the First Diet. Almost immediately a vehement and highly emotional debate began, focusing primarily on the provisions of the Civil Code dealing with family law and succession.[29] Although all three codes were initially enacted in 1890 with all but the Civil Code scheduled to go into effect as early as 1891, only the Code of Civil Procedure survived. Because of the controversy over the Civil Code, in 1890 the Diet postponed the Commercial Code's enforcement until 1893. In 1892 the Third Diet postponed the effective date for the Civil Code. Completely redrafted, a new code was enacted and enforced in 1896 (the books on general principles, real rights, and obligations) and 1898 (the books on family law and succession). Out of necessity the provisions of the 1890 Commercial Code on trading companies, partnerships, bills, and bankruptcy became effective in 1893 but only pending the enactment of a revised code, which did not occur until 1899.[30]

Few problems, it should be emphasized, were encountered with specific provisions of the codes, particularly those dealing with property, mortgages, and other security devices. As the *Japan Weekly Mail* articles indicated, most of the code provisions had been carefully drafted to take into account customary practices. The review process by the government authorities was also thorough, with participation by officials at all levels.[31] The provisions on family relations and succession were more sensitive. Although most of the specific rules were apparently based on customary practices,[32] few could refute the assertion that underlying these provisions were premises far less compatible with the Japanese tradition.

The telling aspects of the Civil Code postponement controversy relate to perceptions of critics that the codes were in some way incompatible with Japanese tradition. The few American lawyers and legal scholars who have examined the debate in detail seem uniformly to question the intellectual content of the controversy. The criticisms of the code, by their opponents are described as "almost grotesquely exaggerated,"[33] and both sides are charged with having avoided "confrontation of intellectual principles."[34] Japanese scholars tend to agree. Some emphasize the controversy as a factional contest between the "English" and "French" schools of Western jurisprudence with the ultimate selection of German civil law as the dominant model, a compromise between the two.[35] Others interpret the dispute in more political terms as a reactive response by traditionalists alarmed by changes the code symbolized that they feared were sweeping away traditional values and patterns of behavior.[36] Some go even further to cast the proponents of the codes as progressive internationalists engaged in a struggle with ultranationalist political reactionaries.[37] In no scenarios were Boissonade's 1890 Civil Code or any of the other codes the central issue at all. Having won postponement, the codes' opponents could therefore afford to be magnanimous and to accommodate without a murmur of protest revised codes equally Western in derivation.

However characterized or evaluated, the dispute over the codes revealed deeper tensions dividing Japanese political and intellectual elites. Just as surely as some entered the fray out of concern for personal factional or political interest, others reacted from a commitment to change and desire to institutionalize what they perceived as advances toward a better social order or with a genuine sense of despair over the magnitude of the transformation of social attitudes and values, as exemplified especially in what was considered the "decadent" lives of those in positions of political authority.[38] The debate should not be divorced from its historical, political context. The popular rights movement and debate over the constitution had culminated in the Meiji Constitution of 1889. Concessions offered in secret negotiations for treaty revision, begun in 1886, had become public, causing popular uproar, the resignation of Foreign Minister Kaoru Inoue, and an end to the negotiations in 1887. New groups and periodicals had formed and were expressing vehement anti-Christian and anti-foreign sentiments.[39]

Questions remain, however, whether the criticisms of the codes had merit and whether the opponents did in fact make valid points in opposition at least from the perspective of Japan's cultural tradition. In my view, they did. The arguments made by the codes' critics were valid not so much with respect to specific provisions or features of the codes themselves (such attacks were rather early rebutted by their proponents), but rather insofar as they correctly identified the unstated premises on which the codes rested. The underlying issue was, as Miyagawa correctly observes, the ideology of law.[40]

Nearly all the published attacks appeared in the two magazines of the *Hōgakushi-kai*, a club formed in 1885 by founders and supporters of the English Law School (later to become Chūō University). The first, *Hōri Seika*, began publication in 1886 but was suspended by government order in 1891. It was succeeded in April 1891 by *Hōgaku Shinpō*. Published in the fifth issue (August 1891) of *Hōgaku Shinpō* was the best known and most influential attack: the essay by Yatsuka Hozumi entitled "*Minpō idete, chūkō horobu*" (Civil Code enacted, filial piety destroyed). Hozumi's essay was representative of the ideological criticism of the Civil Code. For Hozumi and other critics, the Civil Code was in effect a Trojan horse that threatened Japan's traditional order. Hozumi argued that intrinsic to Western private law was a radical individualism that could only erode Japan's historical orientations and understandings involving the family, authority, and the state. He accurately perceived that the private law systems of the nineteenth-century European codes were premised upon individual action and will. By treating the individual as prime actor, the Civil Code necessarily defined the family in terms of partners to the marriage and their offspring. In so doing, the Code redefined Japan's historical orientations based on a broader conception of familial relationships to include reverential ancestral ties. In similar fashion the notions of individual autonomy underlying the code also threatened historical understandings of authority and the state. Hozumi was right, of course. The assumptions underlying Western private law with respect to individual autonomy and the relationship between citizen and state were inconsistent with Japanese tradition. In the Japanese tradition law had become an expression of legitimacy and moral values. Therefore for the state to approve these premises by enacting the Western private law did pose a threat to Japan's traditional system of values. Unfortunately for Hozumi and the other critics who won postponement, no real compromise was possible. The next lot of drafters could look to Germany instead of France for models, but, so long as Western legal forms were to be used—as they inevitably were—this threat to tradition was equally unavoidable. As the Meiji Constitution revealed, one could hardly articulate the fundamental premises of the Japanese polity of authority and its awkward relationship to power in Western legal terms.

The Meiji Constitution Reconsidered

The restoration of imperial rule in 1867 reestablished the *ritsuryō* ideal of centralized imperial governance. As Japan opened to the West and the Meiji transformation began, Western legal conceptions of sovereignty, the state, and legitimate authority began to supplant those of ancient origin. Only from the nineteenth century can we speak accurately of Japan's sense of nationhood or Japan as a state, of sovereignty, or even of law with the assurance that as used in Japanese these terms have comparable frames of reference. They were all new ideas whose inclusion in Japanese political discourse evidenced the extent of Western influence and the impact of the West on Japanese cultural norms. Although it was possible to draw comparisons and analogies between Japan's historic institutions and processes of governance with those of the West in functional terms, not until the nineteenth century did the vocabulary become the same.

The challenge facing the political architects of Meiji Japan was to design the institutional scaffolding of a modern Western state that would incorporate those features of Japan's tradition they desired to preserve. After all, they came into power as leaders of a "restoration" not a social revolution. Thus they sought in Western forms and formulas institutions and ideas that would secure what they wished to preserve from the past and yet also effect the reforms they wished to realize. The Constitution of the Empire of Japan—or, as it is better known, simply the Meiji Constitution—was their solution.

Writing in 1957 George M. Beckmann summarized the prevailing view of the 1889 Meiji Constitution: "By the Meiji Constitution, the oligarchs established a body of authoritarian political principles in Western forms as the ultimate defense of their positions in the Government."[41] The source of this authoritarian character is found in the limited accountability of most organs of government to the electorate. In outline, the constitution provided for ministers of state as the basis for a cabinet government who were to "advise" the emperor on matters of state and take responsibility for advice given.[42] A Privy Council to deliberate on matters of state "when consulted by the Emperor"[43] completed the executive organs of government. A judiciary with powers to adjudicate "in the name of the Emperor" civil and criminal cases but not hear direct appeals from administrative measures was also recognized.[44] In addition, the constitution provided for a two-house legislature, the Imperial Diet. The upper chamber was a House of Peers comprising "members of the Imperial Family, of the orders of nobility, and of those who have been nominated thereto by the Emperor."[45] The only governmental organ with any direct accountability to the electorate was the House of Representatives [Shūgi-in].[46] On the one hand, all statutes required the consent of both houses of the Diet and countersignatures of each minister of state. On the other, however, administrative ordinances [meirei] required no legislative action, only ministerial advice. Thus, except for the elected House of Representatives and the autonomous judiciary, all other branches of government were either constituted by or accountable only to the throne. In the words of the constitution:

> Article IV. The Emperor is the head of the Empire, combining in himself the rights of sovereignty, and exercises them, according to the provisions of the present Constitution.
>
> Article V. The Emperor exercises the legislative power with consent of the Imperial Diet.
>
> Article VI. The Emperor gives sanction to laws and orders then to be promulgated and executed.
>
> * * *
>
> Article IX. The Emperor issues or causes to be issued, the Ordinances necessary for carrying out of the laws, or for the maintenance of public peace and order, and for the promotion of the welfare of the subjects.

The Meiji Constitution did not even in theory, however, grant the imperial institution absolute powers. Chapter II set out an extensive list of constitutionally protected fundamental rights of all subjects. These included the "freedom of abode" or freedom of all Japanese subjects to determine their permanent and temporary residence;[47] freedom from arrest, detention, trial, and punishment except in accordance with law;[48] the right to judicial trial;[49]

freedom from unlawful entry and searches;[50] freedom from censorship of correspondence;[51] guarantee of property rights with a right to compensation for lawful takings in the public interest;[52] the freedom of "speech, writing, publication, public meetings and association";[53] and the right to petition.[54] These were not empty guarantees. The phrase "as provided by law" or equivalent did hedge each provision, but the English translation is misleading. The Japanese "*hōritsu ni yoru*" referred to statutory law.

The Meiji Constitution was therefore less absolutist and authoritarian than it first appears. The constitution by its own terms bound all institutions including the emperor, and these rights could not be modified except by statute requiring the consent of an elected lower house. The absolutism of the Meiji Constitution thus depended on how broadly the electorate was defined, as provided by separate statute, not the constitution itself. Nevertheless, no change from the initial institutions established under the control of those in power in 1889 and 1890 would be possible with the affirmative action of the upper chamber and the ministers of state. The Meiji Constitution had created a system that would be remarkably resistant to change.

More detrimental than the controls against unwanted progressive change, however, was the role of the emperor. For Hermann Roesler and other Western jurists, the imperial institution was pivotal for a workable constitutional order. The accountability of the political and administrative organs of government to the emperor meant that the throne in exercising its prerogatives and powers could ensure desired change and adjustment of conflict. As Roesler explained in his commentary to article 1:

> The Empire shall be reigned over and governed by the Emperor. This confirms not only the abolition, as effected by the late restoration of imperial government, of any divisional power of government, as it has been exercised in Japan by the territorial princes (Daimyos) or by a military commander (Shōgun). It confirms also the entire unity and concentration of the monarchical power in the person of the Emperor. It has been said by a modern French political (Mr. Thiers) that the king reigns, but does not govern. According to this opinion, the monarch would enjoy the honors of royalty and might also exercise a certain sanctioning power over parliament, but the governmental or executive power would be a separate ministerial power, independent of the monarch and not responsible to him. Such a division of monarchical power cannot be admitted in Japan.[55]

Roesler was wrong. He misunderstood the function of the imperial institution and the nature of authority and power in Japan. The Meiji Constitution was consistent with Japanese tradition. The emperor was to be the locus of national sovereignty and the authority of the state, but the occupant of the imperial throne was not to exercise power or be responsible for the consequences of decisions made pursuant to the imperial will. In turn, responsibility and access to the throne meant autonomy and accountability.

The lawmakers of Meiji Japan confronted a dilemma they did not fully appreciate or articulate. Only by describing the authority of the imperial institution in absolutist terms as exercisable power could they maintain the sanctity of the institution as the locus of sovereignty and source of all authority and power. To have attempted to separate the emperor's authority from exercisable powers and to have described accurately his institutional role in a written constitution would have been impossible. To do so would have impaired the full sovereignty of the institution. This is perhaps tacitly understood in the United Kingdom and explains why the role of the crown is not defined in a written instrument of law.

The consequences were profound. Japan's new constitutional order had a fatal flaw that, by misconstruing the role the emperor could play, Western advisors like Roesler failed to appreciate and thus to correct. Without an active emperor, no institutional mechanism existed to regulate or to mediate the inevitable tensions and conflicts between Diet and cabinet, or between the military and civil bureaucracies. Each branch or institution of governance accountable only to the emperor with seemingly limited powers to "advise" or consult. No organ or branch of government was supreme. None had the power to direct or check the others. Only the judiciary could claim full autonomy from all direct outside interference—hence judicial independence—as it alone had both the authority and power to act "in the name of the Emperor." The military would at a later time similarly base its claims to independence from control from the civilian political branches of government on the emperor's prerogative as commander-in-chief and the "right of supreme command."[56] In other words, by centralizing all legal powers in the person of the emperor who by convention could not or would not exercise them, the Meiji Constitution ensured that there could be no effective centralized control. The consequence was, to paraphrase Masao Maruyama, a failure of political integration and a fatal fragmentation of governance.[57] Western legal forms were unable to express or articulate the basic premises of the Japanese political tradition, the separation of power from authority.

II

Cohesion with Conflict:
The Containment of Legal Controls

By the end of World War I, Japan had concluded nearly three decades of experience with its Western-derived legal system. The institutional framework was completed with the promulgation of the Meiji Constitution in 1889 and enactment of the Court Organization Law and Administrative Court Law in 1890. By 1907 the long process of drafting and legislating a comprehensive set of substantive and procedural codes had come to an end with the enactment of the Criminal Code. By then Japan also had a well-trained career judiciary and procuracy as well as a rapidly growing practicing bar, including a small community of foreign lawyers who regularly represented foreign clients in Japanese courts. In addition to a growing legal profession, law faculties, especially that of Tokyo Imperial University, had become Japan's most prestigious educational establishments. In addition to those of the newly established imperial universities in Tokyo (1886) and Kyoto (1897), an increasing number of private universities were also creating law departments. Prominent among them were Chūō University (the former English Law School), Waseda, Keiō, Hōsei, Nihon, and Dōshisha. By 1920 over 700 students a year were graduating in law from the two imperial universities alone.[1]

Scholars from these new law faculties increasingly made their almost mandatory pilgrimages abroad—especially to Germany—to understand more fully the codes and other laws they studied and taught. They brought back the legal theory encasing the black letter rules of the codes. This reception of predominantly German legal theory was especially influential as provisions in the codes borrowed from French and even English law tended to be modified or completely ignored as German theoretical gloss permeated the interpretation of the codes.[2] Returning scholars also opened Japan even further to new ideas and the legal changes taking place in the West.

Japan's leaders could justifiably boast of success in their adoption of a Western-based legal system. Their pride was evident. Those responsible for the constitution and codes wrote extensively on their achievements.[3] Japanese themselves viewed their experience as a model for other non-Western societies to emulate.[4] Their success, however, owed much to the foundations on which the legal system rested. As detailed above, from commercial practices to registries, ample indigenous analogies existed to the codes, statutes, and institutions Japan borrowed from the West. Moreover, most departures from traditional forms and patterns were also accommodated quite easily. Western law provided new but easily adapted forms for both entrepreneurial economic activity and governmental control. Yet not all elements of Western law fit comfortably within the Japanese tradition. Underlying premises and assumptions about law and its role were not as mutable as codified rules or institutional forms. Some aspects of Western law were thus less compatible with Japan's traditional legal culture than others. By the turn of the century an inexorable process of adaptation and revision of both had also begun in earnest.

Judicial institutions matured and defined their special niche in the scheme of Japanese governance. A legal profession came into being, expanded, and ultimately, prospered, as it too discovered a distinctive identity. Borrowed codes and statutes were interpreted and applied as often as not to conform to existing social arrangements. Practice also followed legal rules as Japanese changed the ways they did things to take advantage of the benefits and opportunities offered by new laws and institutions. An existing legal order was not simply recreated in the image of a foreign one. Nor, however, did Japan's new legal order become a mere façade behind which customary patterns continued to flourish. Instead, elements of diverse legal traditions, both native and foreign, merged to create a contemporary legal order characterized by contained law enforcement and the dominance of consensual mechanisms of social ordering.

5

Lawsuits and Lawyers:
The Making of a Myth

Historically the Japanese have been quite litigious. Adjudication, as we have seen, is among the oldest and most developed processes for social control in Japan. By the end of the eighteenth century, the substantive rules of Japanese law were as much the product of a well-established judicial process of articulation and enforcement as administrative fiat. Japanese procedural law rivaled the rationality and sophistication of any European system. Judicial duties had become a major function of the *daikan*, the frontline Tokugawa samurai official. Even a prevenient legal profession had emerged. In a narrowly defined class of claims recognized as "money suits," an adjudicatory enforcement process had evolved and expanded with the rise of commerce in the eighteenth century. That said, however, Japan still did not have a fully functioning private law order in the sense of an adjudicatory process controlled by the parties for the redress of grievances and enforcement of recognized legal obligations.

The values and practices of both the sinicized administrative state and the *mura* excluded the notion of remedial rights. Neo-Confucian imperatives of loyalty and filial piety precluded any conception of a litigant's assertion of a claim as a legal right to be enforced by a neutral arbiter. Judicial governance in Japan represented an assertion of political power to maintain a stable order and to enforce only those legal rules of value or important to those who ruled, or an accommodation out of commercial necessity. Certain claims might be so regularly and consistently enforced that one could say a nascent system of private law had emerged, but Tokugawa officials retained control over the process and the discretion to deny relief. Japanese institutions for the administration of justice were designed in conformity with their Chinese antecedents for a system of penal and administrative rule enforcement. Any use of adjudication for private claims had evolved out of political and economic need. The primary aim was not an instrumental one to enforce claims to achieve ends reflected in legal rules, but to ensure order and stability. Although private claims may have been more justiciable in Japan than China or Korea, those who governed were less concerned with their enforcement or remedial relief than to resolve unwanted disputes and restore peace irrespective of the outcome.

For a potential litigant a lawsuit often meant the invocation of not only protective official powers but also official scrutiny and oversight of otherwise concealed affairs. It entailed a submission to those who ruled and a concomitant loss of autonomy over the matters being litigated.

The primacy of private law in nineteenth-century Western legal systems and the consequent emphasis on justiciable rights meant that intrinsic to the new Japanese legal order were a set of premises quite antithetical to fundamental precepts shared by Japan's political and social elites. As lifeless abstractions, legal rights would have perhaps caused little concern, but their exercise in court could only be perceived as a threat to Japan's social and political order. They also, however, introduced a radically different scheme for social ordering by empowering those without access to the informal levers of persuasion and power within the community or governmental institutions. Effective enforcement of the legal rights articulated in the new codes and statutes would in effect require nonconforming practices to yield, including longstanding practices and understandings protecting community or influential individual interests. The power of the state could thus be used to enforce a process of uncharted, unplanned social change as a neutral arbiter of private rights.

Much depended, of course, on the substantive content of the rights to be enforced and the nature of the social order envisioned under the new codified private law regimes. As noted with respect to the Civil Code controversy, Japan's neotraditionalists won the debate. The result, however, was less a recodification taking into account actual practices than a restructuring of the code based on German models. In terms of family law—the primary focus of the debate—the result was the incorporation in fixed legal form of an idealized version of samurai familial relations. This was especially evident in the sweeping authority granted to the head of the greater family unit or house [*ie*], whose consent under the Meiji Civil Code was required for marriage, divorce, adoption, residence, and even certain transfers of property by members of the house. The neotraditionalist concern was to fix in the Civil Code as in the Constitution the principle of authority in a familial state. Less problematic than the legal principles these provisions expressed, however, was their formulation in Western terms as presumptively enforceable legal rights.

Western law within its own domain could not articulate restraints on an exercise of these rights imposed by societally recognized, reciprocal obligations of compassion and just conduct. Nor, as in the case of the authority of the emperor in the Meiji Constitution, could the code confer authority without power. Western law necessarily cast the concept of family, and hence the state, into a far more absolutist mold than had the traditional order. However, unlike the emperor—a single individual who could be taught to understand customary cultural constraints that divorced power from authority—with family law the entire population was involved. The consequences were predictable. Having been granted legal rights, people began to exercise them, thereby eroding the residual restraints of traditional ethics. The code had begun to live, threatening unwanted social change. Disputes occurred, lawsuits were filed, and Japanese courts quickly faced the issue of enforcing the new rights.

Adaptation, Revision, and the Rediscovery of Tradition

In an increasing variety of contexts, Japanese judges displayed their ingenuity in harmonizing the new legal rules with traditional norms and values. In disputes over changes of residence they relied on the French doctrine of "abuse of rights" to restrain arbitrary exercises of the rights of house-heads.[5] When house-head consent for registration precluded legal marriage, they found in contract theory a basis for offering some legal protection to the all-but-legal bride and in the process created a new category for spousal relationships, the *naien* marriage.[6] Outside of family law the pattern was repeated in urban and rural tenancy cases[7] as well as early pollution cases.[8] In lawsuit after lawsuit where the consequence of casting traditional relationships in terms of enforceable rights produced harsh results for those who could otherwise have claimed the protection of traditional moral admonitions of just conduct, the courts modified and adapted the rules of the code to conform to accepted, customary norms. In these early cases the courts also introduced a standard that would continue to recur as a leitmotif of judicial lawmaking: So long as conduct being challenged or asserted conformed to the "general consensus of the community" [*ippan shakai no kannen*], it was acceptable irrespective of its apparent inconsistency or variance with the norms set out in the codes. Like Kamakura magistrates, Japan's twentieth-century judges in effect applied *dōri* as they understood it. Only now *dōri* was no longer the norm of a warrior society but that of contemporary Japan. Not immutable, *dōri* could and would change along with other changes in Japanese attitudes and expectations.

By the end of World War I, it had become apparent—at least to some—that it was the process not the principles of Western private law that threatened traditional values. The courts could prevent unconstrained exercise of legal rights and harmonize new legal doctrines with traditional practices, but only in the context of litigation, a process that was itself subversive to the traditional moral order.

In June 1919 Japan's first party cabinet appointed a special commission to study and recommend reforms in the Civil Code. The timing was not coincidental. Preservation of familial values had long been the concern of those who, like Yatsuka Hozumi, linked the legal concept of family to the political order. The reinforcement of familial values and relationships of mutual dependence and the corollary rejection of liberal and individualist premises were increasingly viewed as ways of avoiding or curbing the unwanted social conflicts caused by industrialization. It was hoped that preserving what was essentially a Japanized neo-Confucian orientation would reduce, if not eliminate, the social frictions and disintegrative effects of economic growth. Deepening social conflicts in Europe following World War I were to many Japanese fearful omens of the social discord that would engulf Japan unless measures were taken to alleviate the dislocations caused by rapid industrial growth. The collapse of the European political order, the spreading symptoms of impending social upheaval in Japan, such as the Rice Riots of 1918, and the menace perceived in the Russian Revolution simply made the Japanese task appear all the more urgent.

The commission—formally titled the *Rinji Hōsei Shingikai* (the Ad Hoc Commission for the Study of Legal Institutions)—contained the elite of Japan's legal establishment. Chaired by Japan's leading academic jurist, Nobushige Hozumi, it also comprised as vice-chairman, Kiichirō Hiranuma, then procurator-general and future justice minister, chief justice, Privy Council president, and prime minister; and as members, Masaaki Tomii, also one of the principal drafters of the Civil Code; Keijirō Okano, another future justice minister who had assisted in the drafting of the Commercial Code; Kisaburō Suzuki, who would become minister of justice in the Kiyoura and Inukai cabinets; and Tatsukichi Minobe, who was already recognized as one of the nation's leading administrative and constitutional law scholars. Nearly a third of the members were practicing lawyers heavily involved in party politics, including Yoshimichi Hara and Heikichi Ogawa, two of the few practicing attorneys ever to hold the post of minister of justice, and Takuzō Hanai, the lawyer appointed to defend Shūsui Kōtoku, the ill-fated anarchist in the Great Treason trial of 1910. Three other members would also become ministers of justice; two, the chief justice of the Great Court of Cassation; and two, the president of the Privy Council. The staff included Shigetō Hozumi, Nobushige's eldest son and a professor of law at Tokyo Imperial University, Eiichi Makino, one of Japan's leading prewar legal scholars, as well as two future procurator-generals and another future chief justice.

Prime Minister Kei Hara outlined the objectives of the commission at its first meeting. The commission, he announced, was to recommend changes in the Civil Code that would conform the law to Japan's "virtuous ways and beautiful customs" [*junpū bizoku*].[9] A second aim—for some the primary—was to draft legislation creating a jury system that would allow public participation in the judicial branch of government. The twin goals were quite in keeping with the thrust of earlier reform proposals—to meet the crisis of stability by reinforcing traditional values while widening participation in the political process.[10]

Political divisions within the commission apparently prevented agreement over changing any of the substantive provisions of the Civil Code. There was consensus, however, about the desirability of conciliating family disputes. In 1922 the commission recommended the creation of the separate family court that would conciliate civil cases involving family matters. In the language of the commission's report: "The existing system in which family disputes are resolved by means of formal trials fails to maintain the beautiful customs of old."[11] In other words, the commission could scarcely agree on any item except the threat to Japan's familialist tradition posed by litigation. (They also recommended establishment of a jury system.)

In fact the actual number of family cases in court was quite low. As indicated in Table 5-1, never more than ninety-three actions per million persons per annum were even filed between 1898 and 1941. Although the absolute number of cases had increased steadily since the turn of the century, the litigation rate relative to population actually peaked in 1919. Moreover, there already existed significant procedural constraints on family cases. For example, only district courts [*chihō saibansho*] had trial jurisdiction in cases involving the family law provisions of the Civil Code. Since during most of this period there were only 51 district courts located in major cities, as compared with 281 more widely dispersed ward courts [*ku saibansho*], it was much less convenient to bring a suit involving an issue of family law than an ordinary civil action.

The effort to deal with family disputes established a pattern that was to be repeated throughout the 1920s and early 1930s. An outbreak of disputes viewed by Japanese governing elites as a threat to social order first produced attempts to ameliorate the causes through substantive legal reform. When this failed, as it generally did, formal conciliation was introduced. Although the Diet failed to implement the 1922 recommendation for a family court, it did approve the Land Lease and House Lease Conciliation Law[12] that year and the Farm Tenancy Conciliation Law[13] in 1924. In both instances conciliation was viewed as a means of reducing social conflict exacerbated by a regime of private law.

As in the case of family law, by redefining leaseholds in terms of enforceable rights and duties, the Civil Code had again eliminated the paternalistic familialism inherent in the traditional landlord–tenant relation, especially evident in rural areas. As described by Ann Waswo in her perceptive study of rural tenancy disputes in the 1920s:

> Many tenant families in the Meiji era had farmed the land of the same landlord family for generations. In some cases, whether true in fact or not, the two families claimed a common ancestry, and their economic relationship was reinforced by kinship and religious ties. Even where kinship ties did not exist, the tenant was conscious of continuing a relationship with his landlord which his father and grandfather before him had initiated and which had provided his family's livelihood for a half-century or more. Born into and brought up in a status of dependency, he grew accustomed to hardship and to obeying the landlord's orders. Although he might occasionally feel that the treatment he received was unduly harsh, it did not occur to him to question the landlord's right to exercise whatever power he possessed.[14]

As Waswo explains later, landlord "rights" to exercise power were tempered by the obligations to their tenants and the community for fair and compassionate treatment. Although when times were good landlords could perhaps claim higher returns, when yields were low from bad weather or other causes, they were expected to ease the burdens on their tenants. This reciprocity provided the mutual self-interest that reinforced the traditional relationship. "Tenants accepted the wealth and power of landlords not only as part of the natural order of society, but also because both were useful in as-

TABLE 5-1. New Civil Actions involving Family Matters, 1898–1941

Year	Number of Actions	Number of cases per one million persons
1898	1733	40.4
1899	3441	79.3
1900	3347	77.2
1909	3464	71.3
1910	3600	73.2
1911	3738	74.9
1912	3905	77.2
1913	3762	73.3
1914	3957	76.1
1915	3573	67.8
1916	4061	75.9
1917	4320	79.9
1918	4750	86.8
1919	5115	93.0
1920	5129	92.4
1921	5035	88.8
1922	5032	87.7
1923	4690	80.7
1924	4916	83.5
1925	5366	89.9
1926	5384	88.7
1927	5287	85.7
1928	5168	82.6
1929	5679	89.4
1930	4895	75.9
1931	4763	72.7
1932	5015	75.5
1933	5151	76.4
1934	5415	79.3
1935	6148	88.2
1936	6189	88.3
1937	6323	89.6
1938	5866	82.6
1939	5947	88.3
1940	6413	89.2
1941	6704	92.9

Source: Nihon Teikuku Shihôsho (Ministry of Justice of the Empire of Japan), Minji Tōkei Nenpō (Report on civil case statistics), Tokyo, 1900, 1911-14.

suring their own survival and well-being."[15] The adoption of conciliation for landlord–tenant disputes fit the paradigm perfectly.

In contrast, the Civil Code converted the basic duties of tenants into enforceable rights of the landlord but did not give similar recognition to the latter's traditional social and moral obligations. Indeed, as redrafted after the code postponement controversy, the German-based 1896-98 code placed landlords in an even more favorable position in the reclassification of a lease from a property right or real right [*bukken*], as provided in the French-based 1890 code, to an *in personam* obligation [*saiken*] with an enforceable right only against the original landlord, not subsequent landowners. Although the code did recognize real rights in ground-rent arrangements as property rights in the form of superficies [*chijōken*][16] or rights of emphyteusis [*eikosakuken*],[17] these were insufficient to give full protection to tenants, who otherwise would have had what was, in effect, a perpetual lease. For one thing, each was subject to restrictions on duration that generally favored landlords. Ordinary leases were limited to a maximum of twenty years.[18] An emphyteusis could run no longer than fifty years,[19] and unless the term was provided by express agreement or custom, the landlord could appeal to the court to terminate a superficies after twenty, but before the expiration of fifty years.[20]

These provisions gave landlords the legal right to terminate many existing leases. Moreover, even where an existing lease was valid, if the landlord breached the lease and sold the property, the third-party purchaser had the apparent right to evict the tenant, the latter's only redress being a claim for damages against the original landlord.

Japan's rapid industrialization soon produced the economic incentives for urban landlords to exercise these rights. The dramatic expansion of economic opportunities, especially during the period between the outbreak of the Russo-Japanese War and the end of World War I, resulted in a comparable growth in urban population. As the demand for housing in Japan's major cities outpaced supply and shortages became increasingly acute, prices and speculation rose precipitously.[21]

Industrialization also had disruptive effects on rural landlord–tenant relations. Since many rural landlords were among those attracted to the cities by the advantages of urban life, the number of absentee landlords increased, particularly in areas adjacent to the most prosperous urban centers, such as the Kinki region of southwestern Japan. Although their tenants, as a result, may actually have been better off economically, absentee landlords could not carry out the variety of paternalistic obligations they owed to their tenants and the village community and thereby sacrificed some of their traditional status and claim to respect and loyalty.[22]

As landlords began to exercise their new found legal rights and abandon their traditional roles, the number of rural and urban tenancy disputes increased rapidly, both in court and out.[23] In rural areas, for instance, the number of reported cases increased from 256 in 1918 to over 2700 in 1926.[24] The majority were in the Kinki region. The initial response to this outbreak of cases was to reform the code. The early attempts were directed at the urban situation, but they failed because of landlord opposition in the upper house of the Diet. The only reform approved prior to the 1920s was one article of the proposed Law for the Protection of Buildings, enacted in 1909, which provided for registration of both ground-rent agreements and superficies in order to protect those who rented the land but owned the buildings against third-party claims. More significant reforms were delayed until 1921, when the Land Lease Law and the House Lease Law were enacted. These statutes gave tenants

in the major urban centers substantial protection through what amounted to
rent control and a lifetime lease. Yet the Diet was actually codifying existing
case law, for Japanese judges had reached similar results in a long string of
earlier decisions.[25]

The first statute to authorize formal conciliation in civil cases was passed
the following year—the Land Lease and House Lease Conciliation Law of
1922. Like the Land Lease and House Lease laws themselves, it applied only
to major urban areas. The message was clear, however. Conciliation was considered a critical adjunct to substantive law reform. In presenting the bill to
the Diet, the government noted: "Last year at the time the Imperial Diet approved the Land Lease and House Lease bills, hope was expressed in both the
House of Representatives and House of Peers that a separate means for conciliation outside of formal judicial proceedings would be established for land
lease and house leases."[26]

Tenant unrest in rural Japan caused greater alarm. As Waswo observes,
"By the early 1920s a sense of crisis prevailed in official circles. Not only
were tenancy disputes more numerous than industrial labor disputes; they
revealed the existence of discontent in that very part of Japanese society, the
rural villages, long regarded as the nation's ultimate guarantee of social
stability."[27] This "sense of crisis" prompted various attempts at substantive
reform, all of which failed. The significant political actors agreed that resort
to the formal legal process was not a suitable means for resolving rural tenancy
disputes. Consequently, in 1924, the Diet approved the Farm Tenancy Conciliation Law. As explained by Hatasu Nagashima (one of the drafters), conciliation was essential in order to restore harmony and the spirit of compassion
and benevolence [*nasake*] to rural Japan.[28]

Harmony and compassion were also concerns in Japanese labor relations.
Japan's new industrialists had long resisted the enactment of Western-style
labor legislation, echoing the arguments of those who opposed family law
changes that legal reform would subvert the traditional master–servant
relationship:

> The situation is entirely different here from what it is in those countries
> where rights and obligations are set by law. To create laws hastily without
> realizing this fact would, in short, destroy our beautiful national customs
> and create a people who are cold-hearted and without feelings. If workers
> confront the factory managers with coldness, the factory managers will be
> unable to feel warmth. Ultimately the two will be in constant conflict over
> matters of wages and hours.[29]

Business attempts to prevent labor reform were moderately successful, but
rising levels of labor agitation and unrest following World War I demanded
some response. An active labor movement had emerged from the war. The
mood was combative as a host of new labor unions were formed. Faced with
organizing efforts, strike-backed demands for improved working conditions,
and increasing labor mobility, managers responded with lockouts, blacklists,
and agreements not to hire workers who had left other employment.[30] In 1926

the Diet passed the Labor Disputes Conciliation Law,[31] which provided for conciliation of industrial labor disputes by an administrative committee. Once again the pattern of prior statutes repeated: Labor agitation and unrest produced a new process for resolving disputes rather than substantive changes in legal rules relating to the conditions of workers.

Each of the conciliation statutes enacted in the 1920s reflected a response to increasing litigation in peculiarly sensitive areas of Japanese social life subject to traditionalist moral regulation. Interest in conciliation as a more general alternative to litigation had begun to increase, however. It was difficult to argue, for example, that conciliation satisfied special social needs in commercial disputes. Nonetheless, the government statement in support of a bill to establish extensive conciliation procedures for commercial disputes (drafted while Chū Egi, one of the original members of the *Rinji Hōsei Shingikai*, was justice minister), asserted that the law would ensure "continuing harmony in future dealings between the parties."[32] Underlying this argument was the assumption of governmental responsibility for preserving cooperation in ongoing commercial transactions—a presage of things to come.

By the 1930s worldwide economic crisis made conciliation even more attractive in Japan. The economic crisis of the late 1920s and early 1930s fiercely tested the resilience of the political system in all industrial states. Initially at least, they turned to collectivist solutions for security. In the United States under the early New Deal these took the form of state-enforced industry codes under the National Industrial Recovery Act of 1933.[33] In Germany and later Japan, similar policies were pursued through mandatory cartel legislation. The rise of what Ronald Dore has aptly labeled a "collectivist ethic"[34] was thus not unique to Japan. The forms of collectivism did vary by political system and social culture, and for Japan expansion of conciliation was therefore predictable.

As those who championed collectivist values and rejected a liberal legal order increased in influence, conciliation was viewed with greater frequency as the preferred means for resolving every dispute. Consequently, by the end of the 1930s nearly all civil disputes had become subject to conciliation. The impetus toward conciliation thus culminated in 1942 with the Special Wartime Civil Affairs Law,[35] mandating conciliation of virtually any civil dispute and authorizing judges to enter enforceable judgments without trial based on the conciliators' recommended settlement if the parties refused to accept it voluntarily.[36]

Under the early statutes, conciliation had been an optional alternative to litigation, one that a party could choose. The Land Lease and House Lease Conciliation Law as originally enacted, for example, provided that trial proceedings would be stayed upon receipt of a petition for conciliation by one of the parties.[37] The petition could state the particulars of the dispute, and if it was inappropriate or the court deemed the petition frivolous, this was to be dismissed.[38] By 1924 the Diet had amended the law to enable the judge to initiate conciliation on his own motion.[39] The Farm Tenancy Conciliation Law differed only slightly from the amended version of the preceding statutes in that it provided for conciliation of disputes that had not been filed as regular civil actions. Thus a petition for conciliation could be filed not only with the appropriate district court but also with the mayor of the town or village.

Only one step was needed to completely contain the private law process. That was to remove the freedom of the parties to reject a recommendation by authorizing the conciliator to make a recommended settlement binding. Thus the 1932 Monetary Claims Temporary Conciliation Law provided in article 7 for "judgments in lieu of conciliation":

> If the court deems it proper, when conciliation is not reached in the conciliation committee (*chōtei inkai*), [the court] ex officio may render a judgment in lieu of conciliation, ordering modifications of interest rates, term, and other contractual relations after listening to the opinion of the conciliation committee, considering fairly the interest of both parties, and allowing for their resources, the nature of their business, amount of interest, fees, and payments made by the debtor, as well as the other circumstances.

The Agricultural Land Adjustment Law[40] included a similar provision that made it possible to compel the parties to accept the settlement recommended by local farm tenancy conciliators [*kosakukan*] and judges.[41] Comparable provisions for coercive conciliation were included in all subsequent conciliation statutes to the point where, as noted previously, the Special Wartime Civil Affairs Law gave all conciliation settlements the effect of enforceable final judgments.

The expansion of conciliation to cover all civil disputes and the progression toward coercive conciliation are critical factors in evaluating the motivation for these statutes. By the late 1930s the rejection of litigation as incompatible with collectivist values had become the primary explicit justification, but in the 1920s other explanations were voiced. Delay in court had become chronic, and some argued for conciliation as a means of ensuring prompt justice. Shigetō Hozumi, for example, praised the efficiency of conciliation as a means to provide prompt resolution of land and house lease suits.[42] Disputes that had festered for two or three years were now resolved in a matter of weeks because lawyers had been eliminated. Yet in advocating a family court and conciliation of family disputes, Hozumi had been more forthright in arguing that the settlements would more accurately reflect Japanese morality. Conciliation was viewed primarily as a corrective for social conflict, not as a speedier means for enforcing legal rights.

Indeed, from the first conciliation statute to the last, the central purpose of proponents was to ensure that the outcome of any resolution of social disputes reflect Japanese morals rather than law. As stated in the government report in support of the Land Lease and House Lease Law, "Conciliation means resolution [of disputes] not by adjudication of the rights between the parties but rather in terms of their own morality and their particular circumstances."[43] Similarly, a spokesman for the drafters of the Commercial Affairs Conciliation Law explained that in Japan, unlike other countries, even commercial disputes should be settled in terms of harmonious cooperation; a resolution based on human feelings [*ninjō*] and morality rather than law was the ultimate purpose of conciliation.[44] In other words, adjudication by law initiated by an assertion of rights, whether by landlord or tenant, parent or child, businessman or worker, should be opposed as incompatible with a "moral" resolution. "The emphasis on harmony precluded the view of society as a balancing of conflicting self-interests. The demand for recognition of one's rights was itself unworthy. All should have the interests of the collectivity at heart."[45] The utility of conciliation in advancing a "moral" resolution for social conflicts was not, however, just a matter of the outcome. As Henderson emphasizes in his comparison of Tokugawa and modern conciliation in Japan,[46] the critical feature of the traditional process was its "didactic" quality: Conciliation provided an effective opportunity for officials to instruct the parties with respect to their moral and social obligations, not merely their legal duties. During the course of the proceedings, the judge or other conciliator could castigate one side of the controversy or both for failing to live up to traditional moral standards and still show his benevolence by recommending an equitable compromise.

The proponents of conciliation thus spoke in the language of Japan's neo-Confucian tradition, with all the claims to legitimacy it afforded. Not all agreed, however. Objections were raised. Not surprisingly, the most vocal critics were lawyers. From the last years of the 1920s through the mid-1930s, with some frequency, such widely read professional periodicals as *Hōsō Kōron* and *Hōritsu Shinbun* carried articles and comments increasingly critical of the trend toward more inclusive and more coercive conciliation, reaching a crescendo soon after the enactment of the Monetary Claims Temporary Conciliation Law in 1932.[47] Because the statute covered almost all actions to recover money owed, conciliation could no longer be viewed as an exceptional response to special categories of disputes. As more than one observer noted, the temporary conciliation laws had become permanent.[48] By the end of the 1930s the political climate precluded open criticism. The trend had become irreversible and opposition futile.

No doubt the lawyer-critics were motivated in part by self-interest. Conciliation, as Shigetō Hozumi had remarked, reduced the need for legal representation. In fact, attorneys were actively discouraged from participating.[49] Whatever their motives, however, their arguments were sound. They raised perceptive questions about the operation and effect of conciliation. Of course, not all lawyers were critical. Many supported formal conciliation, even arguing for its expansion,[50] but the majority of critics, or at least the most vocal, were lawyers.

The critics understood that conciliation did not just embody the neo-Confucian ideals of the bureaucracy and other members of Japan's conservative elite. It also offered significant economic advantages to some. Conciliation compelled creditors to compromise their claims regardless of how legitimate or just they might be from a legal or moral perspective. The conciliation statutes, especially those authorizing conciliation in ordinary commercial and debtor–creditor cases, were thus criticized as debtor-relief measures.[51] Conciliation in rural tenancy disputes in the 1920s and 1930s resulted in significant reductions of rent to the benefit of tenants.[52] Ann Waswo's statistics indicate, however, that tenants won over five times as often as they lost in the 1920s and nearly four times as often as they lost in the 1930s in cases not subject to compromise through conciliation. Moreover, tenants won an average of over eight times as many cases as they lost in the years before the conciliation statute became effective.[53] Without an objective examination of the facts of each case, it is impossible to determine whether tenants or landlords would have been better off without conciliation. Nevertheless, it appears that neither judges nor conciliation committees were unsympathetic to the plight of Japanese tenant farmers, and it is thus not unreasonable to assume that the conciliation compromises favored tenants, although efforts were made, one assumes, to restore an essentially paternalistic relationship. Writing in 1937, Wolf Ladejinsky, who later assisted in the Occupation land reform efforts,[54] estimated that conciliation procedures during this period tended to benefit tenants, with an estimated 30 percent reduction of rents.[55] Similarly, conciliation of monetary claims was said to operate as a de facto reorganization of small and medium enterprises to rescue them from the burden of overindebtedness.[56]

This does not mean that those who opposed conciliation were unsympathetic to the plight of persons struggling to maintain a decent livelihood in the midst of depression or to tenants and others with relatively weak bargaining positions pitted against overreaching landlords.[57] Rather, they attacked what they saw as indiscriminate, across-the-board measures that relieved all debtors of responsibility for even their just debts[58] and argued that reform of substantive law was the proper way to protect the disadvantaged.

One answer to such criticism was that conciliators and judges were well placed to ferret out debtors who used conciliation improperly and would recommend a settlement that did not unduly disadvantage the creditor. Moreover, as noted before, conciliation was a "didactic" process in which the conciliators could be extremely severe in instructing the parties on how to conduct themselves in the future.

What troubled the lawyer-critics most deeply was the opportunity for abuse that conciliation measures provided. Their most common complaint was that defendants invoked the process as a procedural device for delay and obstruction, that the statutes were being used to avoid debts, not to promote "harmony."[59] Apparently judges would entertain petitions of reconciliation throughout the course of a regular action. One lawyer complained that in landowner suits to vacate land and houses it was common for the defendant to petition for conciliation after the action was filed in order to stay the proceedings, and that even after the conciliators had sent the case back to trial, the defendant would file another petition, causing further delay.[60] This, in turn, was said to lead to more frequent use of legal devices, such as notarial deeds [*kōsei shōsho*], which allowed creditors to obtain civil execution for collection of debts without a prior judgment conforming the indebtedness.[61]

The critics recognized that conciliation contradicted the underlying tenet of private law—the enforceability of legal rights. As one of the more vehement opponents described the process:

> The ideal of conciliation laws is to achieve in the particular circumstances of a dispute an harmonious resolution by reaching a mutual understanding and carrying this through by voluntary assent. The parties may not be family enemies or sibling opponents acting as though they are irreconcilable—fighting it out in court, a spark having set them off. In fact in most instances there is just a confrontation of economic interests and feelings. Even in these cases this ideal of resolving conflicts of interest is based on both sides yielding to a sense of morality, reconciling their feelings toward each other. And there is of course no objection to this . . . but it is a pipe dream. Reality is not so simple. Whatever is said, conciliators are laymen. They do not understand that the facts and circumstances of a dispute must be determined by a showing of evidence. Refusing to follow this reasoned approach in deciding how to settle disputes, they ignore the facts and reach a resolution with only one side, the debtor. . . . As a result the creditor's rights receive no protection.[62]

Inherent in conciliation was the notion that the legal rights of the parties must give way to the conciliators' sense of morality. Conciliation was criticized as a procedure in which the legal rights of all parties were compromised, and such denigration of rights was viewed as undermining the private law system and a liberal legal order.[63] Nevertheless, so long as conciliated settlements remained subject to the parties' mutual agreement, there was little likelihood that either side would agree to a compromise too far removed from the perceived outcome of a judicial judgment. However, once the "judgment in lieu of conciliation" provisions were added, the parties lost control. The judicial conciliators could effectively ignore their legal rights and impose their view of a "just" settlement.

Critics of the conciliation measures thus also attacked their constitutionality. Article 24 of the Meiji Constitution guaranteed the right of Japanese subjects to be tried by judges. Some argued that this applied to civil as well as criminal cases and noted that the conciliators were not necessarily judges (although judges participated in many cases).[64] Others maintained that withdrawing protection from legal rights similarly raised constitutional questions,[65] but the absence of any constitutional provision specifically guaranteeing a right to trial in civil cases led most to reject the first argument.[66] Indeed, Japan's leading constitutional law scholar, Tatsukichi Minobe, replied to the cited bar association survey on conciliation: "I do not believe it is unconstitutional."[67] The guarantee of the right of access to the courts in the postwar constitution thus had particular overtones for the Japanese. The epilogue was the invalidation of the "judgment in lieu of conciliation" provisions of the Special Wartime Civil Affairs Law by the Supreme Court in 1960.[68]

Both the proponents and critics of prewar conciliation correctly perceived the role of litigation in Japan's modern legal system, if at times only dimly. As the lawyer-critics were quick to point out, legal rights are meaningless unless enforced. This was indeed the underlying premise of Western law. Yet it was equally true that the process of enforcement was indeed subversive of

Japan's tradition. Thus the real issue was not the value of conciliation as an alternative to formal trials but rather whether Japan should continue to progress in the direction of a liberal legal order. In the mid-1930s the answer was clear. The military and civil bureaucratic elites chose cohesion over conflict, a collectivist ethic over liberal values.

By the end of the 1930s almost all civil disputes had become subject to conciliation procedures, with judges and special commissioners empowered to require the parties to conciliate. The Special Wartime Civil Affairs Law of 1942 capped the progression by providing for conciliation in all civil disputes and empowering judges to impose judgments without trial where the parties failed to reach a voluntary settlement. For those Japanese who reached maturity in the late 1930s and the years of war, defeat, and occupation that followed, the politics of conciliation would have profound and enduring impact. As the prewar experience receded into the past, the next generation of Japanese were thus enveloped by the ideological currents described by Justice Tsuyoshi Mano in his dissent in the postwar case of *Suzuki* v. *Ishigaki*[69] as "a tendency to regard lawsuits as a kind of vice."[70]

Postwar observers, in making a myth of the Japanese propensity to avoid litigation, tended to view modern conciliation statutes as reflections of a more pervasive societal desire for a less formal alternative to lawsuits. Empirical evidence refutes such views, however. Despite enactment of conciliation statutes, the number of lawsuits increased dramatically in the 1920s through the early 1930s. In 1934 the number of civil cases filed began to decrease precipitously, but as illustrated in Figure 5-1 and tables 5-2 and 5-3, this decline in litigation was parallelled by a similar decline in the number of conciliation proceedings as well. Conciliation did not displace litigation. Its availability as an alternative to formal trials—even when subject to discretionary judicial resolution notwithstanding lack of agreement between the parties—did not lead to a decrease in lawsuits. Instead, the creation of an additional process for formal enforcement of legal claims led to an even greater increase in the number of disputes channeled into a formal process. Conciliation did not reduce conflict. Instead it provided—at least until the late 1930s and the 1940s—an alternative remedial system for the parties. The statutes of this period were themselves in fact to have little lasting influence. However, the attitudes they fostered—that of conciliation as a culturally preferable means of conflict resolution and thus conflict resolution instead of law enforcement as the primary function of the courts in private law cases—were to have enduring impact.

Advance and Retreat: Lawyers in Prewar Japan

The 1930s also marked a watershed for the legal profession. For half a century the profession had grown continuously in size and influence. By regulation

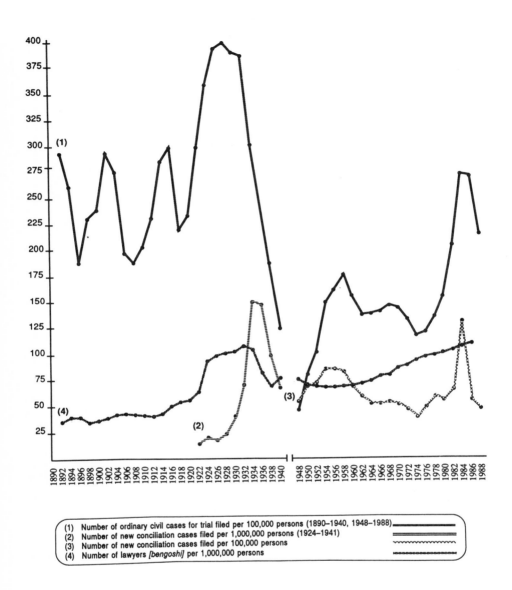

Figure 5-1. Comparative Trends: civil suits, conciliation, and Lawyers, 1890–1988

Cohesion with Conflict

Table 5-2. New Civil Cases Filed for First Instance Trial Proceedings (*soshô*),
1891-1941, 1948-88

1891	136,589	1922	169,239 (295)	1959	156,366
1892	118,474 (293)	1923	188,164	1960	146,855 (157)
1893	111,246	1924	208,774 (355)	1961	134,848
1894	107,442 (261)	1925	225,429	1965	131,411 (138)
1895	90,241	1926	237,244 (391)	1963	127,863
1896	78,546 (187)	1927	248,999	1964	134,900 (139)
1897	83,927	1928	248,406 (397)	1965	131,923
1898	98,564 (230)	1929	242,757	1966	138,304 (140)
1899	105,736	1930	249,980 (388)	1967	139,146
1900	104,739 (239)	1931	261,761	1968	148,131 (146)
1901	121,346	1932	255,187 (384)	1969	143,245
1902	132,758 (295)	1933	228,224	1970	147,842 (143)
1903	144,084	1934	204,731 (300)	1971	151,928
1904	127,004 (275)	1935	196,782	1972	173,137 (133)
1905	100,681	1936	180,510 (257)	1973	130,277
1906	90,956 (193)	1937	158,881	1974	127,759 (116)
1907	85,489	1938	132,069 (186)	1975	127,558
1908	90,570 (189)	1939	106,294	1976	135,199 (120)
1909	94,386	1940	88,160 (123)	1977	147,312
1910	99,900 (203)	1941	74,835	1978	155,475 (135)
1911	106,499	1948	36,833 (46)	1979	161,642
1912	117,049 (231)	1949	42,959	1980	181,081 (155)
1913	130,598	1950	66,746 (80)	1981	201,501
1914	148,177 (285)	1951	76,592	1982	242,976 (205)
1915	162,545	1952	86,308 (101)	1983	273,258
1916	159,351 (298)	1953	99,719	1984	326,789 (272)
1917	132,531	1954	132,483 (150)	1985	343,685
1918	120,641 (220)	1955	143,065	1986	328,879 (270)
1919	118,825	1956	145,106 (161)	1987	307,592
1920	129,152 (233)	1957	150,384	1988	264,307 (215)
1921	145,850	1958	161,865 (176)		

Sources: The statistics for 1891-1941 are from *Nihon teikoku shihō* (Ministry of Justice of the Empire of Japan), *Minji tōkei nenpō* (Annual report on civil case statistics), (Tokyo 1943), at Summary, pp. 103-104. Those for 1949-88 are from Saikō Saibansho (Supreme Court), Shihō tōkei nenpō, Minji (Annual report of judicial statistics, civil cases), (Tokyo), 1960-65, at p. 6; 1969, at p. xviii; 1976, at pp. 12, 14; 1988, at p. 6.

Note: These statistics represent the number of actions filed for ordinary first instance trial proceedings in civil cases in district courts and ward courts (1891-1941) or summary courts (1949-88). They do not include actions involving summary or special proceedings (such as suits or provisional remedies and summary proceedings or bills and notes). The statistics for 1949 through 1988 include administrative cases. The figures in parenthesis indicate the number of new civil suits filed per 100,000 persons.

and statute the professional role of attorneys as representatives for litigants was gradually recognized officially. Bar associations were formed and their membership swelled.

Initially the numbers were small. In 1900 Japan had only 1244 career judges [*saibankan*], 473 procurators [*kensatsukan*], and 1590 practicing lawyers [*bengoshi*], the latter reflecting a ratio of 36.3 attorneys per one mil-

Table 5-3. New Cases Filed under Special Conciliation Statutes, 1922–41

	House lease land lease	Farm tenancy	Commercial affairs	Monetary claims	Personal affairs	Total
1922	224	—	—	—	—	224 (14)
1923	6,035	—	—	—	—	6,035
1924	10,013	31	—	—	—	11,837 (20)
1925	6,780	1824	—	—	—	8,604
1926	7,901	2564	400	—	—	10,865 (18)
1927	10,380	3663	2278	—	—	16,321
1928	9,800	2919	2505	—	—	15,224 (24)
1929	12,121	3657	2994	—	—	18,772
1930	19,523	2838	2485	—	—	255,346 (40)
1931	18,285	3358	2796	—	—	24,439
1932	19,233	3206	2581	22,376	—	47,396 (70)
1933	20,133	4883	2616	73,798	—	101,430
1934	19,254	5015	2175	75,533	—	101,977 (150)
1935	20,158	6778	1666	84,668	—	113,270
1936	18,587	7469	1561	75,627	—	103,244 (147
1937	15,503	5717	1457	63,031	—	85,708
1938	12,751	5277	1281	51,064	—	70,373 (99)
1939	9,785	3576	1535	37,991	5236	58,123
1940	7,432	3765	1067	29,400	6899	48,563 (67)
1941	7,472	3139	1042	22,889	5493	40,035

Sources: Nihon Teikoku Shihōsho (Ministry of Justice of the Empire of Japan), *Minji tokei nenpō (Annual report on civil case statistics), (Tokyo), for 1922-40 (1942), at Summary, pp, 99-101; for 1941 (1943), at Summary, pp, 88-93,*

Note: Figures in parenthesis indicate number of new conciliation cases filed per 1,000,000 persons,

lion persons. In comparison, for example, with the United Kingdom and Germany, these numbers are not especially impressive, even given the novelty of the legal profession in Japan. Richard L. Abel estimates that there were about 4000 barristers in England and Wales at the turn of the century with a total law society membership of 7260 persons, a ratio of about 123 barristers per 1 million population.[71] This represents an average growth of only 231 barristers per year between 1880 and 1900. In Germany, with admission to practice as *Anwälte* partially deregulated in 1879 by granting admission to all persons who passed the two state examinations for full status as a jurist (*Volljuristen*),[72] the number of practicing attorneys increased rapidly from 4091 in 1880 to 7835 in 1905, for a ratio of 129.2 *Anwälte* per 1 million population.[73]

In the 1920s and early 1930s, however, the number of lawyers in Japan reached new peaks, increasing from 3082 in 1920 to over 7000 by 1932. Their political influence in the Diet also rose. Suddenly, without easily identifiable cause, in the mid-1930s the number of practicing lawyers fell precipitously from 7082 in 1934 to less than 5000 in 1938. Between 1934 and 1938 nearly a third of Japan's lawyers had left the profession; their decrease in numbers paralleled declines in litigation and formal conciliation cases. Not until two decades into the postwar period did the ratio of lawyers per capita recover to its prewar peak, and the postwar percentage of lawyers in the Diet was never to duplicate the prewar experience.

As reflected in the regulatory regime gradually established for the legal profession, Japanese governmental authorities displayed an attitude of benign tolerance of the Japanese bar. Recognition of the lawyer's professional role came quite early, reversing Tokugawa edicts prohibiting representation of litigants except in cases where because of sickness or similar cause the litigant could not appear in person.[74]

The first official acceptance of professional representation of parties in civil litigation was contained in regulations governing judicial [shihō] occupations issued in 1872.[75] These regulations coined the term *daigennin*, from the French *avocat*. Four years later in 1876 the Ministry of Justice issued the first regulations for *daigennin*, which did little more than authorize use of that title by persons licensed after examination in separate judicial districts.[76] *Daigennin* did not, however, enjoy an exclusive right of representation nor was their role extended to criminal cases. Nonetheless, by the end of 1876, 174 persons had become duly licensed *daigennin*.[77] New regulations issued in 1880[78] empowered the Ministry of Justice to conduct the licensing examinations, granted *daigennin* the right to represent litigants in civil cases before all courts, and provided for the organization of bar associations.[79] The right of representation in criminal cases was not recognized until 1882 under the first criminal code.[80]

In 1893, the Second Diet enacted the first statutory regulations[81] governing lawyers, discarding the *daigennin* label in favor of the new title *bengoshi*, a translation of the English barrister. Under the 1893 *Bengoshi hō* the scope of practice was limited to "matters dependent on laws in ordinary courts," specifically excluding representation of parties before special courts, such as the Administrative Court and military tribunals.[82] As a result the role of the licensed *bengoshi* was formally confined to trial advocacy in civil and criminal cases. The statute made no provision for the unauthorized practice of law, hence the *bengoshi* like the *daigennin* did not have an exclusive right of representation even as advocates. Foreign lawyers, for example, not only fully engaged in preventative legal counseling, they also commonly represented foreign litigants involved in lawsuits in Japan.[83] A subclass of de facto lawyers—generally referred to pejoratively as *sanbyaku daigen*—also developed, especially in rural areas.[84]

Throughout the period between 1893 and 1933, when the second *Bengoshi hō* was enacted, government policy at least tolerated the growth of the profession. Until 1933, the government consistently resisted efforts by the bar to regulate unauthorized practice and to define the *bengoshi*'s role more broadly to include representation before all official adjudicatory tribunals or even to restrict representation before the regular courts to licensed *bengoshi*. Governmental policy also encouraged new entry. Under the 1893 statute all graduates of imperial university law faculties, including graduates of the former Tokyo University law faculty and old Ministry of Justice law school, holders of a doctorate in jurisprudence [*hōgaku hakushi*], career judges, procurators, and others who had passed the examination for judicial officers [*shihōkan*] were entitled to admission without examination.[85] The government also refused bar requests for self-governing autonomy. The 1893 statute continued to vest regulatory authority over the profession in the Ministry of Justice.[86]

The profession grew rapidly under the 1893 regime. As indicated in Table 5-4, between 1894 and 1930, the number of licensed *bengoshi* in Japan increased from 1562 to 6599, while the number of judges and procurators remained almost constant. The rapid growth of the bar, particularly after 1915, caused concern, principally, it appears, within the profession itself. As described by Rabinowitz, the legal profession in the 1920s was considered by "those who were at all familiar with the situation . . . to be in a state of acute crisis."

> The number of lawyers had increased greatly, and a survey undertaken by the Japanese Bar Association showed that the profession was in a truly alarming economic state. More than 2,400 lawyers out of a total of 4,100 reported that they failed to make their living expenses, and 240 had not even managed enough to pay office expenses.[87]

In 1923 the statutory provision allowing special treatment for graduates of imperial university law faculties was repealed to become effective in 1926.[88] New entry into the profession slowed somewhat but the number of licensed lawyers continued to rise.

By the early 1930s the political influence of the profession had increased substantially. In 1890 only 8 percent of the members elected to the lower house of the Diet were lawyers.[89] This percentage increased in almost every election until 1936. By 1928, lawyers were a near plurality in an occupational breakdown of the Diet, second, with 15.6 percent, only to businessmen. It is not surprising therefore that after years of effort by the profession, in 1933 the government finally introduced new legislation for regulation of practicing attorneys. The 1933 law[90] recognized a broader scope of practice by lawyers to include "legal affairs related to the laws" and in separate legislation for the first time provided for controls against unauthorized representation of parties involved in legal disputes.[91] It also provided for licensing by registration of foreign lawyers.[92] Ironically the bar opposed the statute because it left enforcement to the Ministry of Justice, which they feared would not actively discourage intervention by *sanbyaku daigen* in contentious cases.[93]

The 1933 statute did not become effective until 1936; nevertheless, the number of registered lawyers began a drastic decline beginning in 1934. By 1936 nearly 20 percent of the bar had withdrawn from practice, and by 1938, the number of practicing *bengoshi* had declined by another 15 percent. The number of licensed *bengoshi* rose slightly after 1938, however. Thus there were more licensed lawyers in Japan during the immediate prewar period and during the Pacific War than in 1938.

Table 5-4. The Japanese Legal Profession

	Law faculty graduates	Judges	Procurators	Private attorneys
1891		1531	481	1,345 (34)
1892		1532	482	1,423 (35)
1894		1221	383	1,562 (38)
1896		1221	383	1,478 (38)
1898		1244	473	1,464 (34)
1900		1244	473	1,590 (36)
1902		1208	363	1,727 (38)
1904		1197	374	1,908 (41)
1906		1179	379	2,027 (43)
1908		1239	401	2,006 (42)
1910	1,366	1125	390	2,008 (41)
1912		1129	390	2,036 (41)
1914		898	386	2,256 (43)
1916		903	389	2,665 (50)
1918		1004	478	2,947 (54)
1920	1,431	1134	570	3,082 (56)
1922		1150	578	3,914 (68)
1924		1155	574	5,485 (93)
1926		1121	564	5,936 (98)
1928		1245	656	6,304 (101)
1930	12,481	1249	657	6,599 (102)
1932		1345	628	7,055 (106)
1934		1370	648	7,082 (104)
1936		1391	648	5,776 (86)
1938		1470	686	4,866 (69)
1940	12,429	1541	734	5,498 (76)
1942		1581	625	5,231 (72)
1944		1188	610	5,174 (70)
1946		1232	668	5,737 (76)
1948		1197	857	5,992 (75)
1950	24,070	1533 (2261)	930 (1673)	5,862 (70)
1952		1595	930	5,872 (68)
1954		1597	980	5,942 (67)
1956		1597	1000	6,040 (67)
1958		1617	1000	6,236 (68)
1960	63,897	1687 (2367)	1044 (1761)	6,439 (69)
1962		1730	1059	6,740 (71)
1964		1760	1067	7,108 (73)
1966		1787	1082	7,687 (78)
1968		1803	1097	8,016 (79)
1970	140,000	1838 (2605)	1132 (1983)	8,868 (85)
1972		1900	1173	9,483 (88)
1974		1905	1173	10,197 (93)

continued on next page

Table 5-4. *(continued)*

	Law faculty graduates	Judges	Procurators	Private attorneys
1976		1912	1173	10,792 (96)
1978		1935	1173	11,308 (99)
1980	166,875	1956 (2718)	1173 (2088)	11,759 (101)
1981		1970	1173	12,002 (103)
1982		1976	1173	12,251 (104)
1983		1983	1173	12,486 (105)
1984		1992	1173	12,701 (106)
1985		2001 (2740)	1173 (2092)	12,937 (108)
1986		2009	1173	13,159 (108)

Sources: For statistics on the legal profession, *Juristo (Bessatsu)* (1987), at p. 85. For the number of law graduates, *Japan Statistical Abstract* for year indicated.

Note: The figures after 1948 do not include summary court judges or assistant procurators. For comparative purposes, these are included in the figures in parentheses. Some law faculties combine law with political science. The figures in parentheses indicate the number of lawyers [*bengoshi*] per 1,000,000 persons.

This decline is not easily explained; it cannot be attributed to a single cause. General economic conditions and the availability of more attractive alternative employment opportunities, however, seem to have been significant factors in both the growth and decline of bar membership. For Japan the Great Depression came early and struck hard. With the collapse of overseas markets in 1920, the economic boom generated by World War I ended with increasing bankruptcies and worker layoffs. Industrial growth continued, but at a much slower pace. For the majority of Japanese employed in the agricultural sector during the 1920s, economic conditions also deteriorated drastically. Stagnant rice prices and declining land values and farm income caused serious dislocation. The Great Depression's worldwide impact combined with the deflationary policies of the Hamaguchi government (1929–30) exacerbated an existing crisis. By 1930 over a million Japanese workers were unemployed.[94] Graduates from elite universities were not immune. Japan's major enterprises were firing workers and not hiring replacements. Andrew Gordon cites the observation by a 1932 law graduate of the Kyoto Imperial University that less than 10 percent of his classmates got the jobs they wanted.[95] For law graduates, especially those from imperial universities, bar membership at least offered some employment status and the potential for income. However grave the economic plight of the lawyers during the 1920s, the alternatives seem to have been even worse.

The year 1934 marks the end of the Great Depression in Japan. As a result of the fiscal and monetary policies initiated in 1931 by Finance Minister Korekiyo Takahashi, Japan's average growth rate per year more than doubled between 1931 and 1937.[96] Thus between 1930 and 1940 industrial employment increased by nearly two and a half million in industry and almost one million in the professions, many returning from rural areas.[97] "By 1937," Andrew Gordon notes, "an acute scarcity of skilled labor afflicted the economy."[98] Agricultural prices had also returned to normal levels by 1935 and with the reduction in rural population and new income from family wage-earners in nearby urban centers, average farm income also increased significantly.

Economic recovery also meant new employment opportunities for lawyers and, it appears, a large number left the profession for positions with *zaibatsu* firms and other major commercial and manufacturing enterprises.[99] Lawyers active during this period recall that acquaintances who left practice did so in order to join major industrial companies.[100] Because so many qualified law graduates after 1934 were accepting employment in private companies, the Ministry of Justice began to nominate new judges and procurators several months earlier than previously.[101]

Economic opportunity was not the only factor at work during this period. In addition to the economic incentives to leave the profession, less tangible disincentives discouraged remaining. The status of the profession had reached its nadir. Being a lawyer was to many—especially the military and others in civilian bureaucracies—simply not a legitimate occupation. The Japanese press, in particular, portrayed the lawyer with notable contempt. Daily accounts of *bengoshi* accused of bribery, embezzlement, extortion, and other disreputable conduct were common fare.[102] One scans the major Japanese newspapers during this period in vain for any favorable depiction of the profession.

Finally, the rise of militaristic nationalism also had an impact. In relating his own personal experience during this period, former Supreme Court Justice Shunzō Kobayashi recalled that the military were particularly prone to disparage the profession. He remembered an officer's questioning why, as he listed occupation as *bengoshi* when registering for conscription, he "didn't go out and get an honest job" [*shōjiki na shokugyō*].[103] There is, however, no reliable evidence that the military or civilian government officials contributed in any overt or concrete way to the decline in the number of lawyers.

The legal profession's retreat in the 1930s was, like the decline in litigation, symptomatic of deeper cultural changes engulfing Japanese society. Japan responded to the economic and political crises of the 1930s by redefining themselves and their culture. Drawing on certain elements of their tradition but ignoring others, they reinterpreted both their past and present. An acute societal need for cohesion and cooperation in the face of mounting domestic and international conflict and the fragmentation of political power produced a highly ideological emphasis on harmony and collective identity. Solidified in the crucible of war and defeat, the attitudes and perceptions of the 1930s were to become enduring elements of Japan's postwar legal culture.

Occupation Reforms and Postwar Patterns

The reforms carried out under the Allied Occupation to demilitarize and democratize Japan included a new constitution and a series of conforming statutory revisions. The legal reforms related to code revisions and changes in court organization and the legal profession were carried out under the supervision of the Courts and Law Division of Government Section. Headed by Alfred C. Oppler, a German émigré to the United States in the 1930s and former administrative court judge under the Weimar Republic, the Courts and Law Division was charged with the task of ensuring that codes and other laws basic to the legal system conformed to the new constitutional order. Consequently, much of the work of the Division consisted in review of the codes and other statutes to eliminate provisions that appeared to conflict with the new constitutional mandates for equality of the sexes, abolition of the *ie* system, and procedural protections in criminal proceedings. Oppler's deputy, Thomas L. Blakemore, was one of the few American lawyers in the General Headquarters of the Supreme Commander of the Allied Powers (SCAP) who had prewar legal experience in Japan and Japanese language ability. Unlike many of their superiors Oppler and Blakemore viewed their role in limited terms. They shared an aversion to any attempt to remake the Japanese system along American lines and an appreciation of the merits of Japan's adaptation of continental European institutions. Their attitude is perhaps best summarized in an undated draft of a memorandum Blakemore addressed to the chief of Government Section:

> Time and time again, SWNCC [State-War-Navy Coordinating Committee] directives and the declarations of policy-making officials have recognized that the reform of Japanese institutions is primarily a Japanese problem. SCAP's relationship toward reform is simply that of a stimulant, or at times when necessary a spur, to the development of genuinely Japanese solutions. Only when all efforts to incite self-reform have failed, and only when the subject matter is of vital importance to the objectives of the occupation, should SCAP draft and initiate legislation. . . .
>
> I am also quite concerned over the heavy American flavor of the changes proposed in this Revision [of the Code of Criminal Procedure]. The impression gained from reading through the draft is that existing Japanese law is altered, in many cases, not so much because of basic weaknesses or errors, as because it happens not to coincide with criminal procedural patterns of the United States.
>
> The debate over the respective merits of Civil and Common Law has gone on for centuries, and the discussions concerning Criminal Procedure always have been sharp. Anglo-American lawyers, proud of the many common-law safeguards of personal liberty, point to abuses which at times appear in countries following the continental pattern. On the other hand, continental scholars refer to the high crime rates in many English-speaking countries, and to the striking successes of codes in democracies such as the Scandinavian countries, Switzerland, Holland, and France.

Perhaps it might have been better for the Japanese to have modeled their criminal law upon Anglo-American patterns, when they were drafting codes sixty or seventy years ago. The decision, however, was to the contrary, and Japanese legal concepts have now crystalized in continental patterns. A general shift to Anglo-American practices, now, would require a major transformation of legal thought, in contrast with the ease with which Civil Law concepts filled a vacuum during the Meiji era.

No one can question for a moment the necessity of substantial reforms in Japanese criminal procedure and practice. It does not follow, though, that future Japanese law must break sharply from Civil law patterns. After all, there is democracy in Switzerland, as well as in Iowa.[104]

Blakemore went on to write that a far sounder disposition of proposed revisions was to present them "*informally* to the appropriate legal revision committee of the Japanese government, making it crystal clear that the proposals contained in no way constitute a SCAP directive, nor even a consensus of SCAP opinion as to what should be contained in a Japanese revision. . . ."[105]

The Courts and Law Division thus viewed its task as corrective, holding more assertive SCAP officials at bay to prevent unwanted reforms while attempting to respond to Japanese suggestions for revision. One consequence was for the division to play a sponsorship role for reforms those Japanese who had their ear wished to see enacted. An example was the 1949 *Bengoshi hō*, which achieved many of the long-sought reforms of the Japanese bar.

The principal changes wrought by the 1949 statute were provisions giving the bar self-governing autonomy subject to rules made by the judiciary. The Ministry of Justice was no longer to exercise any regulatory authority over the profession except with respect to criminal prosecution for unauthorized practice, the second reform won by the bar.[106] For the first time in Japanese history, the practice of law—still defined in terms of representation of clients involved in litigation or formal judicial and administrative proceedings—was made the exclusive province of the licensed *bengoshi* with unauthorized practice subject to criminal prosecution.[107]

Most important, no distinction was to be made between the qualifying procedures for *bengoshi* and those for career judges and procurators. There was now a unified profession with entry based on admission to a two-year apprenticeship program operated by the administrative arm of the Supreme Court. Admission to this reconstituted two-year Legal Research and Training Institute [*shihō kenshū sho*] was by national examination with all graduates thereby qualified as *bengoshi* as well as judicial officers, subject to appointment by the Supreme Court as assistant judges or the Ministry of Justice as procurators.

The effect of the new system for qualification was to tie entry into the profession to the number of admissions to the Legal Research and Training Institute. Since "legal apprentices" [*shihō shūshūsei*] in the institute received government stipends, additional budgetary constraints also determined the number to be admitted each year. As indicated in Table 5–5, despite an increase in the number of persons admitted each year to the institute from 265 in 1949 to about 500 in the mid-1960s, the number of applicants during the

Table 5-5. The Japanese National Legal Examination

Year	Applicants	Persons passing examination (and entering the Legal Training and Research Institute)	Percentage of successful applicants
1949	2512	265	10.5%
1950	2755	269	9.8
1951	3648	272	7.5
1952	4765	253	5.3
1953	5141	224	4.4
1954	5172	250	4.8
1955	6306	264	4.2
1956	6714	297	4.4
1957	6920	286	4.1
1958	7074	346	4.9
1959	7819	319	4.1
1960	8302	345	4.2
1961	10921	380	3.5
1962	10802	459	4.2
1963	11725	456	3.9
1964	12728	508	4.0
1965	13681	528	3.9
1966	14867	554	3.7
1967	16460	537	3.3
1968	17727	525	3.0
1969	18453	501	2.7
1970	20160	507	2.5
1971	22336	533	2.6
1972	23425	537	2.3
1973	25259	537	2.1
1974	26708	491	1.8
1975	27701	472	1.6
1976	29088	465	1.5
1977	29214	465	1.6
1978	29390	485	1.7
1979	28622	503	1.8
1980	28656	486	1.7
1981	27816	446	1.6
1982	26317	457	1.7
1983	25138	448	1.8
1984	23956	453	1.9
1985	23855	486	2.0
1986	23869	486	2.0

Source: Ministry of Justice, Legal Training and Research Institute.

same period increased more than fivefold from 2,512 to 12,728 with a corresponding decline in the passage rate from 10.5 percent to 3.9 percent. Since the late 1960s the passage rate has hovered between 1.5 percent to 3 percent. The result has been a major barrier to entry to the profession and, even more important, severe restraints on the number of judges and procurators.

In per capita terms the number of judges in Japan has declined drastically since the turn of the century. In 1890 Japan had one judge for every 26,063 persons. By 1970 the number of judges had decreased to one per 38,586 persons. Although the number of procurators per capita doubled during the same period, Japan today still has less than 2,500 procurators for the entire country, a ratio of about 1 procurator for 50,000 persons.[108]

Litigation rates since the end of World War II have also declined. As indicated in Table 5-2, over twice as many new civil cases per capita were filed for formal trial proceedings in 1928, the prewar peak, as compared to 1958 and 1968, the postwar peaks prior to the 1980s. More new civil cases were filed per capita in 1896 and 1908, the two prewar years with the lowest number of new filings, than in any postwar year until 1980. Yet court congestion and delays remain chronic. In 1969 district courts in Tokyo and Osaka had caseloads in excess of 1500 cases per judge.[109] The total caseload per judge reached 1708 in 1974.[110] In 1970 an average of 12.8 months elapsed between docketing and the completion of a first instance trial in Japanese district courts; first [kōso] appeals in high courts (which can involve a full trial of the facts) required an average of 40 months, and second [jōkoku] appeals to the Supreme Court an additional 66 months (see also Table 5-6).[111] In 1970 over 75 percent of the civil cases decided by the Supreme Court took longer than 3 years to complete from initial docketing for trial to final disposition by the Court. Fourteen percent were decided between 7 and 10 years after docketing and 11 percent took over 10 years to complete.[112]

The contrast with West German trials is stark. In 1965 in civil cases 48 percent of first instance *Landgericht* trials (the German equivalent to Japan's district courts) were completed within six months from the date of filing. By 1984 the percentage had increased to 64.4 percent with 80.1 percent of first appeals in West German *Oberlandesgerichte* (high courts) completed within 12 months and 41.2 percent completed within six months.[113]

In the late 1920s and early 1930s Japanese jurists expressed concern with the capacity of the courts to handle the volume of cases being filed. High litigation rates and a lack of judges were common complaints.[114] Even greater congestion and delay in the postwar period, however, has not produced similar complaints. Instead of decrying the extent of litigation and lack of institutional capacity, the common response has been to ignore these issues altogether behind the assertion that the Japanese are an unusually nonlitigious people.[115]

The myth of Japanese aversion to litigation has been remarkably resistant to change. Most commentators—Japanese and non-Japanese alike—attribute to the Japanese legal culture a pervasive and deeply rooted aversion to all formal mechanisms of adjudication and a corollary preference for mediation. Most versions of the myth today additionally posit an aversion to litigation that precludes an effective judiciary and limits the effect of legal rules and the efficacy of legal ordering. Japanese reluctance to litigate thus goes beyond a desire to preserve autonomy and control by not surrendering the power to decide a dispute to a third party or to avoid the costs and delays of a lawsuit in favor of more expeditious means to similar ends.

Table 5-6. Delay: Ordinary Civil Actions and Appeals, 1984 (April) through 1985 (March)

	Pending cases, April 1984	New actions filed	Total number of cases completed	Within							
				3 mos.	3 to 6 mos.	6 mo. to 1 yr.	1 to 2 yrs.	2 to 3 yrs.	3 to 4 yrs.	4 to 5 yrs.	Over 5 yrs.
District courts	107,443	107,677	104,745	33,111	21,276	17,415	16,530	7,564	3,784	2,395	2,739
			By judgment, 48,759	(2,700)*	(1,553)	(1,126)	(820)	(349)	(154)	(64)	(73)
				[1,107]†	[940]	[847]	[659]	[132]	[132]	[51]	[66]
			By compromise, 32,697								
High courts (Koso appeals only)	11,081	10,224	10,584	945	2,221	3,461	2,734	763	279	126	173
			By judgment, 5,062	(55)	(107)	(150)	(115)	(27)	(10)	(4)	(2)
				[44]	[94]	[193]	[141]	[30]	[11]	[3]	[3]
			By compromise, 4,003								

Civil cases only

	Pending cases, April 1984	New actions filed	Total number of cases completed	3 mos.	3 to 6 mos.	6 mo. to 1 yr.	1 to 2 yrs.	2 to 3 yrs.	3 to 5 yrs.	5 to 6 yrs.	7 to 10 yrs.
Supreme Court (Jokoku appeals only)	1,616 (Civil and administrative cases)	1,930 (Civil and administrative cases)	1,783 Appeal dismissed without oral proceedings, 1,637	243	741	313	164	61	36	9	1

*Actions for purchase price under sales contracts ().

†Actions for payment of objection under promissory note, bill of exchange of check []. The number of actions based on an objection is greater than the number of payment actions.

Source (for Tables 5-6 and 5-7): Saikō saibanshō Jimu Sōkyoku (Supreme Court General Secretariat). *Shihō tokei nenpo, shōwa 59 nen, minijiken* (Annual report of judicial statistics, 1984, Civil cases), pp. 6-7, 120-121, 128-129, 170-171, 172-173, 194-197.

Like most myths, this one too has elements of truth. As discussed below, autonomy is a scarce resource in Japan and the decisional power of a judge or arbitrator is not readily accepted by many potential litigants. In few societies is litigation thought to be more than a necessary evil or pursued except as a last resort for either redress or resolution of disputes, and, as indicated below, the majority of parties to a dispute in most societies including the United States[116] may in fact prefer negotiated settlement or mediation. The claim of a special cultural aversion to litigation in Japan depends on something more—a willingness to forego perceived benefits of litigation out of such aversion to formal adjudication. Those who may assert this proposition, however, ignore not only comparative data on litigation rates and preferences in other societies, but also Japan's own historical experience. "And whatever the attitudes of academics," J. Mark Ramseyer aptly quips, "Japanese barbers, taxi drivers, and bureaucrats still lose no time in telling American law professors that the Japanese, being Japanese, think suing is un-Japanese (and hate lawyers to boot)."[117]

Why? How does one explain the persistence of a belief despite so much evidence to the contrary? The experience of the 1930s provides only a partial answer. To understand more fully Japan's self-conscious identity in the postwar period, one needs to be reminded that much of what the Japanese understand about themselves is based on comparative frames of reference. If European notions of progress informed prewar Japanese views of law and their society, comparisons with the United States have permeated Japan's postwar identity. That Norway or Sweden may have lower litigation rates than Japan is beside the point;[118] the only external point of reference that counts is the United States. Japan's immediate prewar and wartime experience and rapidly rising postwar litigation rates in the United States thus combined to produce a perception of Japan's distinctive and praiseworthy, nonlitigious legal culture.

Beliefs are often self-fulfilling. The more widespread the view of Japan as a peculiarly nonlitigious society, the less the public is apt to press for any increase in the number of judges or other changes in government policy that would make the courts more accessible. Similarly, the inability of the courts to process existing caseloads in timely fashion fosters resort to alternatives to litigation as a means to remedy grievances. The impact runs full circle as the lack of political demand for expansion of institutional capacity plus substantial reliance on alternatives to the courts for legal relief are in turn viewed as proof of the validity of the myth.[119]

Judicial incapacity is unquestionably a direct product of governmentally imposed restrictions on the number of persons admitted to the Legal Research and Training Institute. Whatever the motives behind such policy, limited entry into the legal profession is not a consequence of either self-selection or market demand for legal services as many casual observers often suggest.[120] Explaining the causal factors behind the government restrictions is a more controversial and difficult task. Some suggest that the limits on admission to the Institute reflect a more or less premeditated concern by the Japanese bureaucracy to reduce or at least contain litigation and judicial activity.[121] No one, however, has yet presented any persuasive evidence of such motives. The attitudes of Japanese bureaucrats are equally well explained by their acceptance of the myth. There is no reason to believe that Japanese officials are immune from accepted wisdom about Japanese society, much less firmly entrenched beliefs regarding fundamental features of Japan's legal culture. In response to suggestions that the judiciary be expanded, a Ministry of Finance official preparing the national budget is as likely as anyone else to reply, "Why should we provide for more judges? We are after all a peculiarly nonlitigious people."

A more persuasive explanation for the failure of the government to expand the number of judicial apprentices and thereby increase the number of judges is a combination of opposition by the bar and a sense on the part of the government officials that enlarging the institute is likely to increase the number of lawyers without alleviating the need for more judges. For at least the past two decades, both the Supreme Court and the Ministry of Justice have had increasing difficulty in persuading institute graduates to choose judicial or procuratorial careers instead of becoming practicing attorneys. As the differentials in income between lawyers in private practice and those in government service have widened along with the legal profession's gains in social status, the highest ranked graduates of the institute have tended increasingly to go into private practice. As a result, both the Supreme Court and the Ministry of Justice face mounting recruitment problems. Simply increasing the number of judicial apprentices in the institute, many fear, would not solve the problem. The consequence would be instead simply to expand the number of lawyers at government expense.

The bar's opposition is also a major factor. As detailed below, the policy-making process in postwar Japan has been one of bargained-for-consent by those whose economic and political interests are most closely affected. As a result, bar opposition to an expansion of institute enrollment is a major impediment to change. The bar's reticence should not be viewed, however, as simply a defensive gesture to protect a privileged economic interest. The bar's experience of the 1920s and 1930s looms large and the issue of a significant increase in the number of *bengoshi* touches very sensitive concerns related to the value placed on individual autonomy in Japan.

Autonomy with Security: Freedom from Control as a Scarce Social Resource

Ask most Japanese *bengoshi* why they chose the legal profession as a career and invariably the answer will be that the practice of law enables one to have both security and autonomy. As in the United States, today lawyers in Japan have a relatively high degree of economic and social security. The income of most Japanese attorneys is considerably higher than their counterparts in either government or business. Most work fewer hours and individually enjoy the less tangible rewards of elite social status as well. As important for the *bengoshi*, however, is a second attribute of legal practice in Japan: autonomy—the freedom from control by others that the profession offers.

The importance of autonomy—that is, freedom from control, not freedom to act—to the Japanese lawyer is difficult to exaggerate. As mentioned, Japanese attorneys almost invariably list autonomy as one of the two primary reasons they decided to enter the profession. The lawyer's freedom from control by others is thus one of the central concerns of Japanese professional ethics. For instance the Preamble to the proposal for a revised code of Professional Ethics adopted October 18, 1988, by the Ethics Committee of the Japanese Federation of Bar Associations begins: "Bengoshi make the defense of fundamental human rights and social justice their mission. For the realization of this mission, occupational freedom and independence must be assured and the highest degree of autonomy must be guaranteed."[122] Conflicts of interests and the issue of client confidentiality are secondary to this concern over the attorney's freedom, independence, and autonomy.

This emphasis on freedom from control is not new. The 1933 *Bengoshi hō* included a provision precluding the employment of *bengoshi* without special bar association permission,[123] a rule that remains in force today.[124] As any Japanese attorney will confirm, this rule is not merely a *pro forma* matter; such permission is not readily given.

The prevalence of concern for autonomy within the legal profession in Japan helps to explain why Japanese lawyers are rarely able to establish stable law firms with more than a few partners. In terms of the number of *bengoshi*, the largest law office in Japan today has only thirty-nine *bengoshi*. Even this office reflects at least three successive splits since the original was founded in the late 1960s, and less than half of the *bengoshi* associated with it have been in practice for more than five years. Even a firm this size is the rare exception. In a 1981 survey by the Japan Federation of Bar Associations, only 3 out of the 4489 respondents (nearly 40 percent of all lawyers in practice) indicated that they were working in law firms with more than twenty-four lawyers. Over 50 percent were sole practitioners and 82.7 percent practiced in offices with three or less lawyers.[125] A similar survey taken a decade earlier in 1972 revealed that 59 percent of Japanese attorneys were sole practitioners. Only one out of the 350 respondents (4 percent of the Japanese bar) indicated that he or she worked in an office with ten or more attorneys.[126] Most firms with more than one lawyer are office-sharing arrangements with a senior attorney assisted by one or two young lawyers, who, once they develop their own client base, move on to establish their own separate firms.

The value placed on autonomy by Japanese attorneys also directly contradicts popular conceptions of Japan as a "group-oriented" culture in which some sort of ingrained behavioral pattern dictates a preference for group activity and organization. Nothing could be farther from the truth. The concern of the Japanese lawyer for autonomy is a value shared by most Japanese. What makes the lawyer—and one might add the physician—exceptional is not their concern for freedom from control but rather their relatively unique opportunity to enjoy such freedom within an occupation that also assures status and financial security.

The prototypical "group-oriented" Japanese salaried employee of a major enterprise or official in an elite government ministry is more likely than not a law graduate of Tokyo University or some other major public or private university, sharing with the typical Japanese lawyer a common educational and socioeconomic background. What distinguishes the lawyer is the fact that he or she passed the national examination for admission to the Legal Research and Training Institute. The vast majority of those Japanese who have the choice between careers with large organizations, which offer security but little autonomy, and legal practice, which offers both, choose to become attorneys. Typically less than 1 percent of all legal apprentices choose careers other than judgeships, the procuracy, or private legal practice.

This point is not new. Chie Nakane uses the lawyer to illustrate the vertical structure of Japanese social organization. She writes:

> The best illustration of such a process [of vertical organization and its "fissures"] is the traditional manner of establishing new agricultural households or new mercantile shops by a second son, an adopted son, a servant or tenant of the original household or shop. Among modern occupations a similar process operates, for example, among lawyers and doctors. It is customary for a young lawyer or doctor who has just finished training to enter one of the well established offices, under the guidance of the head of the office, and after some years' work to set up his own independent office. . . . *Indeed, the ambition of any such young capable Japanese would be to have an independent office of his own.* There is not a system of partnership in the sense that obtains in Britain or America, for it is very difficult for Japanese to form a partnership on Western lines. [Emphasis added.][127]

The worth or value of autonomy in Japan is indicative of the complex role of relationships in Japanese society that effectively deny most Japanese freedom from organizational control without a life of substantial social and economic risk. The vast majority of Japanese face at best a Hobson's choice between autonomy with insecurity or security without autonomy. They either accept submission and dependency in return for a greater measure of protection against social and economic risks or they must sacrifice such security in order to retain greater freedom from control. Japanese salaried employees and dependent subcontractors do not need to be reminded that Japan's bankruptcy rate among small and medium enterprises is among the highest of any major market economy.[128]

Economic and social insecurity in Japan thus operates as a powerful lever to force dependency and control by others. To anticipate somewhat the topics of later chapters, the principal instruments of social ordering and control in Japan thus turn out to be those of community, family, and firm, not of public authorities and the state. Neither judicial governance nor the regulatory state provide the dominant paradigm. Instead, as detailed in Chapter 8, the *mura* offers the best model for understanding how Japanese society is ordered and governed. The weakness of all paradigms of legal ordering, in turn, however, reinforces the pervasive influence of extralegal, community controls. By the same token, the effectiveness of those controls also function to weaken and restrain the effectiveness of the instruments of legal ordering. Take, for example, the well-known (at least in Japan) case of the lawsuit brought by the parents of a child drowned in a backyard pond against the neighbor who had volunteered to look after the child while the mother went shopping.

The mother had asked her neighbor if her three-year-old son could stay at the neighbors' home and play with their son, a preschool classmate. While the boys were playing near a public pond behind the house, one of the boys fell in and drowned. The parents sued both the neighbors for negligent care of the child and the municipality for failure to maintain a safe pond. The Tsu District Court found negligence on both sides and, apportioning damages accordingly, awarded the plaintiffs 5,266,000 yen or about 35,000 U.S. dollars (at 150 yen to one U.S. dollar). The municipality was held not liable.[129]

The most significant aspect of this case was its aftermath. The parents were ostracized throughout the community and, once the lawsuit caught the attention of the media, the nation. Even shopkeepers in the neighborhood refused to serve the mother. The case also gave rise to much discussion about Japanese attitudes toward litigation. Prominent Japanese legal scholars analyzed the case, its implications, and the public response it elicited.[130] Some viewed the reaction as more alarming than the case itself. As one young attorney wrote, the criticism resembled the "dangerous ideas" of wartime Japan that disputes should be settled to preserve "harmony," avoiding the exercise of rights established by law.[131]

The Tsu case was exceptional. Similar cases have not resulted in at least reported community recrimination against the plaintiffs. What distinguishes this case, however unusual, from what might have happened in the United States and perhaps other societies is less the criticism by the community of the suit itself than the ostracizing actions taken against the plaintiffs. In other societies such a lawsuit might have provoked similar condemnation and perhaps a degree of outrage at the unfairness or injustice of successfully suing a (presumably uninsured) good Samaritan neighbor. One suspects most American juries would have denied recovery. However, one wonders whether an American community would have been willing to ostracize or refuse to trade with the hapless plaintiffs. Would resort to social sanctions have been considered acceptable or effective? However hostile public opinion in the United States might have been, the view that the community should not "take the law into its own hands" by imposing social penalties is as strong a feature of American legal culture as the willingness to use such sanctions is in Japan.

The Fallacy of America as Model

The persistence of the myth of an unusual Japanese reluctance to litigate is explained in part, as stated, by the tendency of at least postwar Japanese to define their own identity in comparison with the United States. The relative dearth of litigation in Japan in comparison with the United States thus fuels the view on both sides of the Pacific that resistance to litigation is a peculiar phenomenon of Japanese culture. For the Japanese, such emphasis buttresses a sense of national identity as a homogeneous and unusually conflict-free society, fostering the notion of nonlitigiousness as a recurrent theme in the profusion of *Nihonjinron* literature, a rather narcissistic form of impressionistic anthropology. In the United States this view of the Japanese has similar appeal for those who seek to find at least in one modern industrial society social harmony and goodwill. Differences in the number of lawsuits in Japan and the United States can be explained, however, by several factors that have little if anything to do with aversion to formal adjudication—some institutional, some cultural.

Certainty of Result: The lack of a jury system in Japan and the career judiciary with frequent transfers fosters a greater uniformity of result. Moreover, in Japan as in other civil law systems there are general societal as well as institutional expectations that justice requires certainty with consistent and equal treatment of similarly placed litigants. Considerable efforts are therefore made to prevent disparities in compensation awards and other judgments. Japanese judges, adjudicating similar sorts of claims, meet regularly to compare notes and to ensure that they are applying the same standards and reaching consistently similar outcomes. Potential litigants are thereby able to calculate better the value of a claim and thus have more incentive to settle rather than incur the costs of litigation. In contrast, American courts offer casino justice. The jury system and the autonomy of individual judges produce substantial variations in outcome. In a study of civil jury awards in Cook County, Illinois, by Mark A. Peterson for the Institute for Civil Justice of the Rand Corporation, awards for similar injuries were found to vary by a factor of 10 depending upon whether the injury was incurred at the workplace or as a result of an automobile accident.[132] Such disparities and the uncertainties thus produced make the American system a gambler's delight.

Registration: Another institutional difference is the Japanese registry system (also common in other civil law systems). The registry systems for real property and family relationships preclude the need to use the courts in a wide variety of cases, including adoption, divorce, real property transfers, and succession. In the United States, all divorce is based on a judicial decree, hence litigation; there is no divorce by consent alone. Similarly, even the most routine change in land title may require judicial action, hence litigation; there is no simple registration adjustment.

Mediation: At work also in Japan is a significant cultural factor: the effectiveness of third party intervention. The availability of suitable third parties who are willing and able to perform the role of mediator reduces the need to invoke formal judicial intervention. At the outset, mediation requires the presence of persons who, because of position or personal relationships, command respect and are able to exercise some measure of authority. In other words, to be effective, the mediator must be someone who can command the parties' trust and their obedience. Effective mediation thus requires persons who are not only in a position of power or authority in relation to the parties to a dispute but, equally important, who are also willing to become involved and exert their influence on both sides.

As one might anticipate, suitable third parties are more readily available in a stable, closely-integrated, and hierarchial society like Japan than in a more geographically mobile, less cohesive society like the United States, in which privacy and social equality are given ideological emphasis. Societal expectations and habits are equally relevant. Where there is repeated reliance on third parties to settle disputes, the role of mediator becomes increasingly legitimate for both the mediators themselves as well as for the parties to disputes. The acceptance of responsibility for the conduct of others is an integral thread in the Japanese social fabric. The contrast in police attitudes toward their role as mediators in Japan and the United States pointed out by David H. Bayley[133] is especially telling in this respect. Japanese commonly rely on the police for assistance in settling disputes.[134] Popular demand in the United States is quite similar. "What is different," says Bayley, "is that American police organizations have not adapted willingly to perform this function."[135] Another contrast in Japan's favor are the mediating services some companies provide for employees involved in traffic accidents.[136] In short, the Japanese may be more successful in avoiding litigation because of social arrangements and values more conducive to mediation as a means of dispute resolution rather than simply an aversion to litigation.

Interdependency: Closely related to mediation is the prevalence in Japan of ongoing interdependency relationships. As Stewart Macauley's studies on the use and nonuse of contracts in the United States show,[137] there is far less need for "law" and certainly far less likelihood of litigation between persons who have ongoing relations, such as family or business partners. The extent of close interdependency relationships in Japan, from family ties to business dealings, therefore precludes resort to court in far more instances than in the United States.

What emerges from comparisons between Japan and the United States is the picture of the latter as a society in which conflict is less easily resolved without litigation and direct intervention by the state. High litigation rates and a more frequently utilized judiciary do not necessarily mean, however, that courts play a more significant role or that law and legal rules are more determinative.

To Sue or Not to Sue

The efficacy of the courts as an agency for law enforcement is not determined by their volume of business. So long as potential litigants can and will resort to the court, when they perceive that they have something thereby to gain—in other words, that the prospective outcome of a litigated case is more beneficial than other avenues of redress or settlement—low litigation rates may evidence the efficacy rather than the failure of the process. In cases where the litigated outcome is certain and informal mechanisms for negotiated or mediated settlement are readily accessible, with, what the economists would label, low transaction costs, there should be fewer lawsuits. Yet there should also be at least equal if not greater conformity to legal rules in comparison with cases where either the litigated outcome is uncertain or alternative forms of dispute resolution are less accessible. In other words, where both the certainty of the applicable legal rules and effective means for out-of-court resolution pertain, settlements approximating the perceived outcome of litigation less its costs—the discount for delay and the litigant's out-of-pocket expenses—should prevail. The recently published study of the pattern of insurance settlements in cases involving automobile accidents in Japan by Mark Ramseyer and Minoru Nakazato provides a textbook example of the efficacy of Japan's judicial process in achieving a high level of compliance with legal rules with infrequent resort to court under such conditions.[138]

Such analyses proceed from an initial proposition that the party invoking the process by bringing a lawsuit is motivated by a desire to have the legal rule enforced but will settle without suing so long as the result is equally beneficial. The evaluation of the efficacy of the courts as an agency for the enforcement of legal rules in a private law system thus hinges on the potential plaintiff's decision to sue or not to sue.

As Ramseyer and Nakazato explain, cases involving automobile accidents share special characteristics that make them especially conducive to out-of-court settlement in conformity with legal rules. First, they involve disputes between strangers. The potential plaintiff's decision as to whether or not to sue is therefore not complicated by concern over the implications a lawsuit or this single incident of conflict with other relationships between the parties. Second, as noted, litigation is sufficiently frequent in similar disputes for the parties to be able to calculate with reasonable certainty what the litigated outcome would be. Third, the remedial powers of the court are effective in these instances in providing the relief sought by the plaintiff. The plaintiffs in automobile accident litigation simply seek money damages against insurers whose assets are readily reached through civil execution of a court award.

Even so, institutional incapacity resulting from inadequately staffed courts and available lawyers does have a negative impact. The lack of judges and lawyers increases delay and attorneys' fees and, as a result, the costs of litigation and the discount in calculating the relative value of an offer for settlement. In cases where any one of these three conditions of unrelated parties, certainty of litigated outcome, and the effectiveness of judicial enforcement are not satisfied, the model breaks down, and the role and efficacy of the courts must be reexamined.

Inasmuch as private law orders depend upon the initiative of the parties not the state to enforce legal rules, the extent to which the potential litigant has a sufficient sense of grievance to invoke state protection—or, as the case may be, desire for revenge to seek state-imposed sanctions[139]—becomes a determinative factor. The use of apology and other customary practices that serve to reduce feelings of having been wronged may themselves preclude the enforcement of otherwise applicable legal rules. Acceptance by Japanese women of unequal treatment, for example, helps to explain why constitutional and statutory proscriptions of gender discrimination were not heretofore challenged until recently with any frequency.[140]

Above all else, however, the potential litigant must also perceive that he or she has something to gain by litigation. The judicial remedy or sanction must be sufficient to outweigh the costs of a lawsuit. Difficulties of proof and low monetary awards for antitrust violations, for example, discourage the resort to private damage actions in Japan as a means of antitrust enforcement.[141] The disincentives to sue are even greater, however, in cases where a plaintiff seeks any form of relief other than a monetary award. As in other civil law systems, Japanese courts do not enjoy the broad equitable powers of common law courts to fashion remedies, nor do they exercise contempt powers. As described by John Henry Merryman, in the civil law tradition in the interests of greater certainty the judiciary functions with much narrower remedial powers: "But in the civil law tradition to give discretionary powers to the judge threatens the certainty of the law. As a matter of legal theory, the position has been taken that judges have no *inherent* equitable power."[142] Merryman goes on to note that "[t]he very idea of giving a court the general power to compel individuals in civil actions to do or to refrain from doing certain acts under penalties of imprisonment or fine or both is repugnant to the civil law tradition."[143] In most other civil law systems, some form of civil or criminal sanctions exist for the enforcement of court orders.[144] In German law, for example, violations of court orders are made subject to fines up to a half a million deutsch marks (approximately 250,000 U.S. dollars) or up to two years' imprisonment.[145] Administrative officials also have the power to enforce their orders with fines or attachment without resort to either the civil or criminal process—that is, without direct judicial oversight.[146] Not so in Japan. Few means of coercion to enforce compliance with judicial orders exist.

Yet, in Japan, the demand for injunctive and other forms of nonmonetary relief are substantial. For example, Japanese procedures allow the courts to issue preliminary injunctions and to make preliminary attachments of property in addition to the courts' powers of execution. As indicated in Table 5–7, more actions were filed for such provisional relief and civil execution each year than the total number of ordinary civil actions.

The greater the uncertainty of outcome and the less effective the available forum of relief becomes, the greater the adverse impact of institutional incapacity becomes as a disincentive to sue. Under such circumstances potential plaintiffs are more apt to compromise their legal rights or to rely upon extralegal forms of relief. In either instance the legal rule may still regulate the ultimate outcome, but it will be subject to an even larger discount and, in the event of resort to self-help or third-party enforcers, may significantly enhance the social position and powers of extrajudicial agencies for enforcement. The legal rule may still apply, but the judiciary's role may be jeopardized.

Table 5-7. New Civil Actions Filed in District Courts,
1975 (April) through 1985 (March)

Year	Ordinary civil actions (*tsujo minji sosho*)	Civil conciliation (*minji shotei*)	Expedited bills & notes actions (*tegatta, kogotte sodho*)	Provisional remedies (*kari-shobun, kari-sashiosae*)	Civil execution (*kyosei shikko*) Against immovables	Against contract and other obligation rights
1975	74,907	2828	17,507	37,920	7,435	43,560
1976	81,075	2877	21,306	42,759	8,007	45,255
1977	89,544	2651	24,578	49,355	8,613	51,421
1978	91,545	2334	22,196	46,534	8,899	51,454
1979	93,732	2330	21,364	46,697	9,017	53,236
1980	105,559	2118	21,513	50,315	10,306	54,370
1981	113,253	2104	19,476	50,709	11,982	40,643
1982	110,873 (6,407)*	2245	17,361	50,629	13,741	46,198
1983	92,515 (6,522)	1777	13,297	48,973	15,471	53,444
1984	101,257 (6,420)	1693	13,942	53,997	17,828	66,979

*Personal status actions, primarily divorce, in parentheses.

Where, for example, governmental bureaucracies or private groups become the law's primary enforcers, as Frank Upham's narratives reveal so well, they not the courts define the rules being enforced and control their efficacy. To be sure, the judiciary may continue to play a role and determine the outer boundaries of the law, but it is a much diminished and less efficacious one. The containment of the judiciary's role thus both restricts the law's domain and empowers other agencies—public and private—of enforcement.

6

Policemen and Prosecutors:
Crime without Punishment

Constraints in Japan's criminal justice system parallel the relative weakness of Japan's judiciary in terms of institutional presence and the range of effective coercive sanctions other than those for collection of monetary awards against unconcealable assets. With fewer than 2200 procurators [*kensatsukan*] to handle not only all criminal prosecutions but also administrative and civil litigation involving Japanese governmental entities, institutional incapacity is at least as serious a problem for Japan's criminal justice system as it is for civil law enforcement.[1]

Falling Crime Rates but Chronic Delay

The institutional constraints on Japan's criminal justice system are generally overlooked in view of Japan's extraordinary achievement in crime prevention. Alone among all industrial states in the postwar period, Japan has enjoyed substantial declines in crime rates in almost all categories, except for criminal traffic and other motor vehicle violations. Table 6-1 indicates the number of known major criminal code offenses between 1948 and 1980.

As Charles Fenwick observes:

> Despite unparalleled industrial growth, modernization, and increased population density, the total number of non-traffic penal code offenses in Japan significantly decreased during the 1948-1979 period. Between 1969-1979, the population of Japan increased by approximately 23%. During that same period, the incidences of major crimes declined by approximately 17%. During the 1975-79 period, the number of murders declined 16%, rapes—32%, robberies—16%, and assaults—27%.[2]

Even so, however, the demands on the procuracy have increased. From statistics reported by the Ministry of Justice,[3] the number of offenses under special statutes more than doubled between 1932 and 1987, with a sixfold increase between 1932 and 1967, followed by a significant decline after 1968 and 1969. This decline is attributable to the establishment of a traffic infraction notice procedure [*kōtsū hansoku tsūkoku seido*] for minor traffic offenses, such as first-time parking tickets and minor speed limit violations.[4] Under the

Table 6-1. Offenses on Police Records, 1948-80

Offenses	1948	1953	1955	1964	1968	1970	1973	1975	1977	1980
Penal Code offenses										
Murder	1,034	1,022	1,228	2,366	2,195	1,986	2,048	2,098	2,031	1,684
Bodily injury & manslaughter	21,208	52,525	65,978	61,282	57,822	50,836	43,385	34,136	32,479	26,264
Battery	5,796	25,105	30,808	46,965	36,268	32,028	27,079	21,944	19,931	15,301
Rape	1,936	3,517	4,046	6,857	6,136	5,161	4,179	3,704	2,945	2,610
Robbery	10,854	5,296	5,878	3,926	2,988	2,689	2,000	2,300	2,095	2,208
Extortion	25,691	18,777	28,419	40,892	19,030	18,775	14,652	14,255	10,964	8,830
Theft	1,246,445	931,791	1,056,974	1,057,531	975,347	1,039,11	973,876	1,037,942	1,073,393	1,165,609
Fraud	133,666	141,000	124,633	75,891	60,706	58,340	55,473	53,647	56,120	58,958
Embezzlement	31,241	27,789	22,197	16,734	9,657	9,362	10,172	10,575	13,891	21,391
Negligent homicide & bodily injury	3,297	27,341	42,550	224,383	510,593	654,942	540,790	441,374	438,337	456,781
Others	122,097	110,319	95,491	72,914	61,737	59,164	55,072	51,752	52,809	53,119
Total	1,603,265	1,344,482	1,478,202	1,609,741	1,742,479	1,932,401	1,728,726	1,673,727	1,704,995	1,812,755
Special law violations	1,269,961*	389,213	355,696	167,187	206,070	142,460	142,627	167,811	153,952	189,650
Grand Total	2,873,226*	1,733,695	1,833,898	1,776,928	1,948,549	2,074,861	1,871,353	1,841,538	1,858,947	2,002,405
Nontraffic Penal Code Offenses										
Number	1,599,968	1,317,141	1,435,652	1,385,358	1,231,886	1,277,459	1,187,936	1,232,353	1,266,658	1,355,974
Rate per 100,000 population	1,999	1,514	1,608	1,426	1,216	1,232	1,080	1,101	1,110	1,160

Source: Hōmushō (Ministry of Justice), *Hanzai hakusho* (White paper), cited by Yoshio Suzuki, "Crimes," *Kodansha Encyclopedia of Japan*, Vol. 1 (Tokyo; Kodansha International, 1982), at p. 44.

*Including all types of traffic violations; figures for other years exclude all traffic offenses under special statutes.

new procedure, offenders are simply ticketed and can pay a fine without the stigma of a criminal prosecution. According to the 1969 Summary of the White Paper on Crime, six months after inception, over two-thirds of all traffic violations were being processed under the new procedure.[5] The automobile accidents and more serious criminal traffic violations still account for the vast majority of these cases (see Tables 6-1 and 6-3); and while they do not detract from Japan's achievement in preventing crime, they continue to pose significant burdens on law enforcement authorities.

Consequently, although the number of procurators tripled between 1932 and 1987, the total number of reported offenses quadrupled. Since the ratio of indictments to reported offenses did not vary to any appreciable extent, as a result, the total caseload per procurator increased from an average of 272.2 indictments per procurator filed between 1932 and 1937 to 1,121.8 indictments per prosecutor filed between 1982 and 1987. Moreover, under prewar criminal procedure, major cases were referred to the judiciary for preliminary investigatory proceedings. Judges questioned suspects and handled other aspects of the investigation. Although supervised by procurators, whose office was attached to the courts not the Ministry of Justice as today, their burden was somewhat less onerous and time-consuming than under the postwar system. Postwar comparisons are equally stark, however. Between 1947 and 1967 the number of procurators increased by a factor of 1.45 but the number of reported offenses more than quadrupled. In short, Japan's criminal justice system suffers the same sort of relative institutional incapacity evidenced in civil cases.

However insubstantial the number of criminal prosecutions or civil lawsuits may be in Japan in comparison with the United States and other industrial democracies, there is no dearth of criminal or civil cases relative to Japan's judicial and prosecutorial capacity to handle those cases efficiently and effectively. The inexorable results are delay coupled with internal pressures to use extralegal mechanisms to avoid prosecutions to reduce the burdens on the system. As with the pressures on judges to induce the parties in civil cases to compromise their claims, so in criminal cases, police, procurators, and judges seek alternatives to manage their caseloads.

Writing in the early 1960s, then-Counselor of the Criminal Affairs Bureau of Japan's Ministry of Justice and subsequent Supreme Court Justice (1984–88) Atsushi Nagashima noted that delay in criminal trials had increased in the postwar period despite falling crime rates.[6] He cited statistics showing that in the late 1920s through the mid-1930s over 75 percent of all criminal trials from the filing of information to trial disposition in the first instance were completed within one month.[7] Even then, German observers criticized the extent of delay in Japanese criminal trials.[8] However, by the late 1950s less than 17 percent of criminal trials in Japanese district courts were being completed within a month, with over 20 percent requiring over a year throughout the decade (as compared to less than 10 percent taking over six months in the prewar period). By the 1980s procedural changes for minor traffic offenses as well as dramatic reductions in crime rates in Japan helped to ease the problem of delay. Thus, as indicated in Table 6-2, between 1980 and 1987 about 80

Table 6-2. Duration of Criminal Trials in Japanese District Courts
(from the first trial date through disposition)

Year	Cases	Within 15 days	1 mo.	2 mos.	3 mos.	6 mos.	1 yr.	2 yrs.	3 yrs.	Over 3 yrs.
1962	55,799	17,414	8,228	10,104	5271	6307	3759	2299	940	948
(%)	100.0	31.2	14.7	18.1	9.4	11.3	6.7	4.1	1.7	1.7
1969	49,190	11,761	6,581	10,471	5861	7261	3479	1791	562	896
(%)	100.0	23.9	13.4	21.3	11.9	14.8	7.1	3.6	1.1	1.8
1980	65,309	23,748	9,731	13,286	6389	6406	2685	1174	480	786
(%)	100.0	36.4	14.9	20.3	9.8	9.8	4.1	1.8	0.7	1.2
1981	64,289	23,677	9,848	13,703	6353	5912	2249	864	315	811
(%)	100.0	36.8	15.3	21.3	9.9	9.2	3.5	1.3	0.5	1.3
1982	64,335	28,780	9,716	14,276	6374	5826	2079	771	360	509
(%)	100.0	44.7	15.1	22.2	9.9	9.1	3.2	1.2	0.6	0.8
1983	64,769	24,692	10,024	14,324	6195	5567	1975	741	206	472
(%)	100.0	38.1	15.5	22.1	9.6	8.6	3.0	1.1	0.3	0.7
1984	66,311	25,505	10,420	14,465	6404	5624	2015	671	205	436
(%)	100.0	38.5	15.7	21.8	9.7	8.5	3.0	1.0	0.3	0.7
1985	65,553	26,628	9,795	13,617	6274	5568	1894	714	196	293
(%)	100.0	40.6	14.9	20.8	9.6	8.5	2.9	1.1	0.3	0.4
1986	63,204	26,058	9,327	13,163	5870	5354	1931	642	144	289
(%)	100.0	41.2	14.8	20.8	9.3	8.5	3.1	1.0	0.2	0.5
1987	61,995	25,280	9,302	13,000	5879	5139	1850	647	192	257
(%)	100.0	40.8	15.0	21.0	9.5	8.3	3.0	1.0	0.3	0.4

Source: Saikō Saibansho Jimu Sōkyoku (General Secretariat Supreme Court of Japan); Shihō tōkei nenpo (Annual report of judicial statistics) (Tokyo, 1980–1987) at p. 11 (for each volume).

124

percent of all district court trials were completed from the first trial date within three months and less than 5 percent of all cases took a year or more. Since multiple hearings are apparently necessary, the delay in trial is a matter of months (mostly the period between hearings). In West Germany, in contrast, nearly fifty percent of all criminal trials are complete in one hearing session of less than two hours and complex cases take only about two days.[9] Japan has yet to reduce delay to prewar levels.

The available options for dealing with criminal caseloads and delay are limited by both institutional and cultural considerations. Both police and prosecutors have to select among options permitted by procedural and institutional requirements and also compatible with values and preferences shared within Japanese society generally and the community of law enforcement officials in particular. How to reduce delay continues to be a principal topic of discussion at meetings of judges, procurators, and lawyers held annually in each judicial district. A variety of solutions have been proposed and attempted. One is for prosecutors and defense counsel to reach agreement on what documentary evidence may be submitted by the prosecution without challenge prior to trial. Since, as noted below, there is no guilty plea, without such prior agreement even an uncontested case could require two or three separate hearings on admissible evidence. Such cooperation can reduce the time required in uncontested cases to less than an hour, corresponding to current German standards.

Attempts have also been made to handle criminal actions in a concentrated trial or at least to shorten the interval between hearings. In cases involving separate indictments against an individual defendant for multiple crimes, prosecutors are urged to file all additional indictments [*tsui kiso*] as quickly as possible to permit a single trial. Higher penalties for multiple crimes tried separately also encourage defendants and their lawyers to cooperate in the consolidation of cases for trial. However, the relative scarcity of lawyers and the prevailing practice of overburdened trial attorneys to prepare their cases on a piecemeal basis in the intervals between hearings are among the factors that tend to work against any efforts to speed the process.[10]

Institutional Options

The criminal process in Japan in effect moves along two parallel tracks. The first involves a formal institutional process similar to most contemporary legal systems derived from continental European models. Detailed substantive and procedural rules set out in the constitution, codes, and statutes govern each stage of the formal process from the investigations and apprehension of offenders by the police to formal sentencing and trial appeals by judges. Few if any of Japan's institutions reflect adaptations of traditional practices and procedures. Even the most exceptional often turn out to be innovations derived indirectly from Western models. Japan's system of discretionary prosecution, for example, is a notable departure from German practice. However, Japan's apparently unique system for citizen review of exercises of prosecutorial discretion through an "inquest of prosecution" or prosecution review commission [*kensatsu shinsakai*][11] was in fact designed by Thomas L. Blakemore as a compromise to fend off superiors in SCAP's Government Section who wished to include an American-styled grand jury system as a component of the criminal procedure reforms.[12]

Japan's formal system of criminal justice is therefore somewhat of a hybrid. It combines basic features of continental European, especially German, law and practice with elements of American law, particularly the procedural protections included in provisions of the postwar Constitution and the revised Code of Criminal Procedure. The most striking departure from German and other European practice, which dates to Japan's earliest regulations on criminal procedure in the mid-nineteenth century, is the extent of discretion enjoyed by police, prosecutor, and judge alike.

The process begins with investigation of a reported crime and the identification of a suspect as the offender by the police, who exercise considerable discretion in reporting to the procuracy cases involving "minor crimes." For example, in 1978, Japanese police identified suspects in 599,302 cases out of 1,136,448 reported offenses.[13] In these cases they identified 231,403 suspects, many apparently responsible for several offenses, who could be subjected to prosecution. However, only 168,646 suspects were actually reported to the procuracy; 62,727 (21.12 percent) were instead released without further process pursuant to article 246 of the Code of Criminal Procedure authorizing the police to close "simple" cases [*bizai shobun*]. In this manner, between 1975 and 1980 the police disposed of nearly 18 percent of all Criminal Code offenses (not involving violations of motor vehicle traffic laws and other special statutes).[14] An even higher figure is given for the Tokyo Metropolitan District. It is estimated that the police fail to report about 40 percent of all referrable cases.[15]

For cases reported to the local procurator's office, several avenues are open. After a second investigation, the procurators may transfer the case to another procurator's office on jurisdictional grounds, close the case for lack of sufficient evidence or other reasons, prosecute in either summary or ordinary trial proceedings, or suspend prosecution.[16] For example, as indicated in Table 6-3, in 1987 Japanese procurators had a total caseload of 3,441,024 cases, of which 1,169,185 represented criminal code offenses (including certain traffic-accident related offenses like bodily injury or death resulting from professional negligence), 2,084,152 criminal motor vehicle and traffic violations under special statutes, and 187,687 other offenses under special statutes, such as possession of illicit drugs, violation of Japan's gun control law, and electoral law violations. Of the total caseload, only about 50 percent were prosecuted. Twenty-seven percent were transferred to other procurator offices or to family courts (cases involving juvenile offenders, constituting 14.5 percent of the total caseload). Less than 2 percent were closed for lack of suffi-

Table 6-3. Disposition of Criminal Cases by Japanese Public Prosecutors, 1987

								Transferred to	
	Caseload	Prosecuted Cases	Formal Trial	Summary Proceedings	Suspended Prosecution	Closed for Insufficient Evidence	Closed for Other Reasons[+]	Other Prosecutor's Office	Family Court[*]
Total offenses	3,441,024	1,742,508	125,421	1,617,087	356,283	37,631	13,991	782,834	496,140
Criminal code	1,169,185	377,407	79,732	297,675	266,537	33,521	8,618	233,409	247,198
Homicide (art.199)	2,989	1,060	1,060	—	57	129	1,538	37	84
Bodily injury	39,722	15,607	4,604	11,003	3,625	494	179	9,459	10,244
Larceny (art. 235)	220,434	37,513	37,513	—	30,067	1,678	1,175	15,216	134,674
Indecency through compulsion (art. 176) & rape (art. 177)	2,382	771	771	—	106	70	630	61	742
Rape or death in course of robbery (art. 241)	930	423	423	—	12	45	77	14	343
Robbery (art. 236)	874	449	449	—	41	51	67	17	245
Fraud (art. 246)	19,462	10,095	10,095	—	4,237	2,219	210	1,615	812
Motor vehicle violations	2,084,152	1,282,320	10,725	1,271,595	64,351	824	4,763	497,821	226,384
Other offenses under special statutes	187,687	82,781	34,964	47,817	25,395	3,286	610	51,604	23,258

Source: *Hōmushō (Ministry of Justice), Hōmu nenkan shōwa 62 nen* (Yearbook on Administration of Justice 1987), at pp. 320-321 (1987).

[*]All cases transferred to Family Court involve juvenile offenders (ages 14 through 19).

[+]Includes cases reported by the police that are deemed to be nonconvictable as well as conduct referred by police or private parties that do not constitute criminal violations, cases not prosecuted because of withdrawal of the victim's complaint, e.g., rape, are also listed under this category.

cient evidence or other reasons. Prosecution was suspended in the remaining 10 percent.

As mentioned there is no guilty plea in Japanese criminal procedure. In all prosecuted cases—including those subject to simplified procedures—the procurators must provide the court with sufficient evidence of guilt to convict. However, the vast majority of all prosecuted cases (93 percent) are adjudicated with only documentary evidence in uncontested summary proceedings [*ryakushiki tetsuzuki*] in which the maximum penalty is 200,000 yen (less than $1500 at prevailing exchange rates).[17] Formal trial proceedings—with or without a defense—were used in 1987 in only 7 percent of all prosecuted cases and less than 4 percent of the total caseload.[18] Summary proceedings are an available alternative for any offense for which the penalty of a fine is an available statutory option. Serious offenses punishable by mandatory jail terms must be tried in ordinary proceedings. These include such offenses as homicide, rape, larceny, robbery, fraud, and extortion. Thus a far greater proportion of ordinary proceedings—63 percent—involve these and other criminal code offenses.

The police report very few suspects who are not convictable. As indicated in Table 6-3, in 1987, out of 3,441,024 reported offenses, only 37,631 or 1 percent were dismissed by the procurator's office for lack of sufficient evidence. This percentage has been constant for over a decade.[19] Those who are prosecuted are almost always convicted. Prevailing conviction rates hover at about 99.5 percent.[20] Since guilt is not contested in the vast majority of cases,[21] the conviction rate in cases where guilt is at issue is probably closer to 90 percent.

Few offenders, however, are punished with more than a minor penalty. As noted, in summary proceedings the maximum penalty is a fine of 200,000 yen, less than $1500 U.S. dollars. Most offenders pay considerably less. For example, in 1987 over 70 percent of all defendants convicted in summary proceedings were fined less than 50,000 yen (about U.S. $360 at prevailing exchange rates). Nearly 43 percent were fined less than 30,000 yen (about U.S. $215). Only 0.5 percent received the maximum 200,000 yen fine.[22]

Defendants subject to more stringent penalties than those allowed in summary proceedings are treated upon conviction with similar leniency. With hardly any variation for over a quarter-century, Japanese first instance trial courts annually sentenced between 60,000 to 65,000 defendants to prison terms or detention a year. In slightly more than 50 percent of all cases, the court suspends the sentence. About 5 percent of all convicted defendants are sentenced without suspension to prison terms of less than six months; 12 percent to terms of six months to a year, 12 percent to terms of one to two years; 5 percent to terms of two to three years, and only 2 percent to terms of 3 years. Less than 2 percent of those convicted are sentenced to prison terms of more than five years.[23]

Even in cases involving violent crime the courts suspend sentences in a relatively large number of cases. In 1977 and 1987, for example, sentences were suspended in 25 percent (1977) or 20 percent (1987) of all homicide cases, 46 percent (1977) or 35 percent (1987) for all arson convictions, 47 percent (1977) or 37 percent (1987) of all rape cases, 32 percent (1977) or 26 percent of all robbery cases, and in 55 percent (1977) or 52 percent (1987) of all convictions for bodily injury. Moreover, lenient parole requirements have meant that more than half of the relatively few offenders Japan imprisons are paroled before the expiration of their terms.[24]

Even pretrial detention is rarely used except in cases involving violent crimes. More than "four-fifths of all suspects," observes David Bayley, "are handled without arrest on an 'at home' basis."[25] He continues, "[I]n 1972 88 percent of all suspects were examined by prosecutors without detention; only 12 percent were actually arrested."[26] (Bayley's estimate may be somewhat low, at least for the present. Ministry of Justice figures for 1989 show that about 22 percent of suspects were arrested.[27]) Of those suspects actually indicted, Bayley notes, fewer than 10 percent were detained in 1972 (most of whom were subject to summary proceedings).[28]

In other words, by almost any standard criminal justice in Japan is extraordinarily lenient. Large numbers of offenders identified by the police are never reported as suspects to the procuracy. Of those reported, most are convictable. Yet the vast majority are allowed to take advantage of summary proceedings that result in minor fines equivalent to a few hundred dollars. For many others prosecution is routinely suspended. Even though prosecution of those that remain seems tantamount to conviction in ordinary trials, sentences are generally suspended in more than half of all cases. Except for detention during police interrogation, few offenders, it appears, ever see the inside of a jail. This is the outcome of the informal "second track" of Japanese criminal justice.

Confession, Repentance, and Absolution

The police, procurators, and judges take a variety of factors into account in their decisions on how to treat a particular suspect or defendant. They include considerations common to most criminal justice systems: the gravity of the offense relative to the stigma for the offender of a criminal conviction, the circumstances and nature of the crime, the age and prior record by the offender. Added to this matrix in Japan, however, are additional factors that appear to be missing elsewhere—at least in the West.[29] First, the attitude of the offender in acknowledging guilt, expressing remorse, and compensating any victims, but also the victims' response in expressing willingness to pardon, are determinative elements in the decision whether to report, to prosecute, or to sentence the offender.

Minoru Shikita, former director of the United Nations Asia and Far East Asia Institute for the Prevention of Crime and Treatment of Offenders (UNAFEI), describes the role of the police:[30]

> [T]he police, with the general accord of the chief public prosecutor of a district, need not refer all cases formally to the prosecution, but may report

cases in consolidated form monthly, provided the offenses are minor
property offenses, the suspects have shown repentance, restitution has been
made, and victims forgive the suspects.[31]

Even in the cases referred to public prosecutors, Shikita notes, "the police
invariably recommend a lenient disposition if a suspect has shown sincere
repentance about his or her alleged crime and the transgression against a social
norm is not particularly serious."[32]

Similar considerations motivate prosecutors in deciding whether to
suspend prosecution. The critical factors include "the existence of a confession, sincere repentance by the suspect and the forgiveness of the victim."[33]
In an excellent account of Japanese prosecutorial practice, Marsha E. Goodman relates several instances to illustrate the typical factors prosecutors take
into consideration in deciding the charge and whether or not to suspend prosecution.[34] In one case an older and wiser procurator overruled the initial
decision by a young prosecutor in charge of the case to proceed with the in-
dictment for "causing death by negligence" of a mother whose baby had suf-
focated under a pile of newspapers that had fallen on top of the infant while
the worker was out of the house on an errand. The senior prosecutor concluded
that the mother had suffered enough and that "to prosecute would be not only
useless, but cruel."[35] In other cases the prosecutors displayed their concern
that the victim be compensated—in one case facilitating the negotiations between a former lover and the woman he had attacked on the street, breaking
three fingers—as well as demonstration by suspects and their families of their
remorse. Other cases were "too serious to ignore" and were prosecuted despite
victim compensation and offender contrition.[36]

Japanese judges also uniformly confirm that a defendant's acknowledgment of guilt and sincerity in displaying remorse, evidenced in part by compensation of the victim and the victim's forgiving response, are pivotal in their
decision on whether to suspend sentence. One senior Japanese judge is said
to have refused even after conviction and sentencing to allow defendants to
leave the courtroom until they confessed and expressed remorse.

Typically, the suspect not only confesses, but through family and friends
also seeks letters from any victims addressed to the prosecutor or judge that
acknowledge restitution and express the victim's sentiment that no further
penalty need be imposed. So customary are such letters that most Japanese
attorneys have some sense of the amounts usually required.

The victim thus participates in the process. Restitution is ordinarily made
and the victim has a voice in the authorities' decisions whether to report, to
prosecute, or to sentence the offender. The experience of an American resident
of Tokyo is illustrative. His summer house was burned down by a burglar in
a clumsy attempt to destroy any incriminating evidence. Once the suspect was
apprehended and charged, intermediaries arranged for the suspect's father to
meet with the American owner. In response to an offer to pay for the entire
amount of the damage, the American first insisted that this was not necessary
because the house was insured. Only after the father prostrated himself, beg-

ging to pay some amount in compensation, with the intermediary explaining that some restitution was necessary as a matter of social custom, did the American relent and agree to accept money for the uninsured furniture and other personal belongings destroyed in the fire. In return, he wrote the necessary letter to the authorities explaining that compensation was paid.

In this way the victims participate in the process but do not control it. Ultimately they must defer to the authorities' decision. The burglar-arsonist in the preceding account was in fact prosecuted, convicted, and served some time in prison. The process, however, does give the offender an incentive to make amends and the victim an opportunity to forgive. The victim does not assume the role of adversary or prosecutor nor is the victim enabled to use the formal process as a means of retribution and revenge.

Most studies of the criminal process in Japan note the evidentiary importance of confession but seldom proceed further either to analyze its implications or to note the victims' role in the process. A few depict the dark side and more, its cultural underpinnings. Futaba Igarashi is among the best known critics of the use of confessions in the Japanese criminal process. As an attorney she has written extensively on the use of torture and threats by police interrogators to coerce confessions from suspects, especially in cases involving violent activities by political dissidents.[37] The English language studies of the Japanese police have been more positive.[38] They also focus on the evidentiary value of the confession, but they generally conclude that the Japanese not only share a propensity to confess but also expect lenient treatment explained in large part by child-rearing practices and other cultural phenomena. Conceding "the temptation" of the police and procuracy to coerce confessions from seemingly unrepentant suspects, Bayley argues: "Despite these factors in favor of pressing for a confession, most informed observers— lawyers, criminal reporters, law professors, and prosecutors—contend that instances of abuse of persons in custody are rare. Celebrated cases have occurred but the incidence is small. . . ."[39] Instead, he notes the strength of "the psychological compulsion to confess"[40] and the "enormous moral authority"[41] of the Japanese police. "So," he concludes, "guilt is admitted in Japan for a variety of reasons: because it is a moral imperative, but also because it is a *quid pro quo* for leniency."[42]

One of the most extensive and detailed works on the criminal investigatory process in Japan is the study by Kobe University legal sociologist Setsuo Miyazawa.[43] Miyazawa's research depicts police motives and behavior more critically than Ames, Bayley, Clifford, or Parker, but he is less excoriating in his findings than Igarashi. Japanese police detectives, according to Miyazawa, are motivated by a variety of concerns. Among the strongest is their drive to apprehend the offender as quickly and as efficiently as possible and to ensure before arrest the adequacy of their evidentiary findings to sustain conviction.[44] For both reasons confessions are considered indispensable, not, however, because a confession alone is sufficient to convict, but rather because confessions generally lead to further disclosures of additional evidence of guilt. As a result, obtaining a confession becomes a primary aim in all investigations, and as a result, police detectives emphasize the necessity for direct interrogation of suspects and, for such purpose, their detention before arrest.[45]

Finally, Chalmers Johnson, too, treats the role of confession at some length in his study of the Matsukawa cases. "It is," he states, "the decisive element of proof sought by every procurator before he takes a case into court and the single most important item in determining the reception his efforts are likely to receive from most Japanese judges when he gets there."[46] Johnson criticizes exclusive emphasis on the evidentiary value of confession and the consequent resort by the authorities to psychological inducements and, in some instances, physical abuse to obtain them, as well as cultural explanations that stress Japanese behavioral norms that "predispose prisoners to confess to anything that authorities want them to." Instead, he argues, both coercion and culture operate to produce the extraordinarily high Japanese rate of confessions and convictions.[47] One might add that such views also suffer from a restrictive ethnocentricity.

The focus on the evidentiary importance of confessions to the exclusion of its rehabilitative effect, whether or not elaborated by charges of abusive coercion, is generally premised on Western-derived notions of the primacy of the formal process and the exclusivity of its function to ascertain guilt. Prior to sentencing, the criminal justice system is conceived to have a single overall objective—to identify accurately the offender. This premise inexorably leads to a predominate emphasis on the credibility of evidence of guilt as well as procedural controls to prevent error in the investigatory and trial process. American observers tend to be particularly sensitive to such concerns because confessions and plea bargaining play so significant a role in reducing the burdens on the criminal process in the United States.[48] While Japanese judges also display great concern with the probative value of coerced or induced confessions, they do not neglect their correctional value.[49]

No person in Japan is convicted solely by confession. As noted previously, unlike the United States, the United Kingdom, and other common law jurisdictions, there is no guilty plea in Japan, eliminating the need for a trial on guilt. In all cases, even summary proceedings, an evidentiary hearing to determine that a crime has been committed and the guilt of the accused is necessary.[50] Even where there is a confession, the prosecutor has the burden to prove it was made voluntarily and proffer at least collaborative evidence of the crime.[51] Miyazawa's study demonstrates police concerns for conviction, but it should be emphasized, premised on belief that the suspect is telling the truth when confessing. Moreover, the judge in the trial has the duty to clarify evidence and, as the finder of fact, be convinced of guilt and thus the reliability of any confession.[52] Although prosecutorial and judicial scrutiny of collaborative evidence is not likely to be as vigorous if the accused has confessed and offers no defense, nevertheless, such procedural protections may not be as relevant to accuracy as the concern of judges as well as police and prosecutors over the "sincerity" and truthfulness of the confession and demonstrated remorse. The second track includes telling tests of credibility.

A fundamental aim of the criminal process in Japan is correction, not just determination of guilt or punishment of the offender. Law enforcement officials at all levels tend to share this objective, in what Shikita refers to as an "integrated approach" to criminal justice.[53] Thus, their roles are not confined to the formal tasks of apprehending, prosecuting, and adjudicating. Rather once personally convinced that a suspect is an offender, their concern for evidentiary proof of guilt shifts to a concern over the suspect's attitude and prospects for rehabilitation and reintegration into society, including acceptance of authority. Leniency is considered an appropriate response if the correctional process has begun. The sincerity of confession and remorse therefore becomes a significant factor in deciding whether correction is likely. Since confession and repentance provoke leniency—and most do confess—law enforcement authorities also generally expect offenders to confess and to behave with remorseful submission. For a suspect the authorities believe to be guilty not to confess thus poses a dilemma. Either they have erred and the suspect is not guilty or he is unrepentant and less correctable. Under these circumstances, it is not surprising—nor, one hastens to add, excusable—that police, prosecutors, and judges are tempted to induce or coerce acknowledgment of guilt. The more convinced the authorities become that the suspect is guilty, the more likely they are to resort to harsh and abusive measures. Yet there is also an incentive for them to reexamine more carefully the evidence of guilt before attempting to coerce the suspect.

Many instances of physical coercion by the police detailed by Igarashi involve suspects who do not contest the facts of the case against them but as political dissidents steadfastly refuse to acknowledge wrongdoing. Their refusal to defer to authority and conform to community norms better explains the vehemence of police reaction than police concern for proof.

Cultural explanations tend to be equally, albeit more subtly, ethnocentric by quarantining the Japanese experience and denying its relevance outside of Japan's peculiar cultural setting. There is no question that history and societal values underpin the pattern of confession, repentance, and absolution in Japan. East Asian legal orders all place extraordinary emphasis on confession. At least as early as the T'ang dynasty, codified Chinese law provided for more lenient treatment to those who confessed voluntarily. If the commission of the crime itself was unknown to the authorities, confession resulted in pardon,[54] and for all categories of crime voluntary confession gained a reduction in penalty.[55] Similar patterns are observed in contemporary China.[56] Yet it appears that the Chinese aim has also been predominantly evidentiary. Confession was a means of protecting the officials from error and maintaining the legitimacy of their authority. Thus the authorities pressed for confession and in turn, regulations were imposed on torture and other means of coercion to protect the credibility of confessions as evidence.[57] During the era of Mongol domination under the Yüan dynasty (A.D. 1280-1368), greater emphasis was placed on the victims' restitution and penalties were reduced.[58] Apparently in the succeeding Ming (1368-1644) and Ch'ing (1644-1912) dynasties the severity of penal sanctions was restored although compensation of the victim continued to be demanded as an additional penalty.[59]

The historical origins of contemporary Japanese practice are unclear. Ryōsuke Ishii's description of Japanese penal proscriptions during the *ritsuryō* period parallels Chinese practice[60] which, as noted, permitted reduction of punishments for those who confessed prior to official discovery of the crime. He also remarks on the relative leniency of mid-to-late Tokugawa criminal justice.[61] The extent to which confession, remorse, and victim compensation played any role is difficult to determine.

Although Japanese insistence on prosecutorial discretion represented a major departure from its otherwise faithful adaptation of German models in the Meiji era,[62] there appears to be little evidence that such discretion was used in any systematic, pervasive fashion to suspend prosecution for offenders who acknowledged guilt and expressed remorse as a means of rehabilitation and reform. An unsuccessful effort in the early 1920s to amend the Code of Criminal Procedure to include express authorization for procuratorial discretion to suspend prosecution in cases involving "repentant" offenders[63] suggests to the contrary that prosecutors felt unable to use their apparent discretion in such instances.

The first well documented use of lenient treatment as a quid pro quo for repentance and behavioral change were the interwar thought-control prosecutions under the 1925 Peace Preservation Law and related thought-control measures.[64] In return for public renunciation of radical ideological beliefs— *tenkō*—the leaders of Japan's Communist movement received significant reductions in sentences. The life imprisonment sentences for Manabu Sano, Sadachika Nabeyama, and other Communist Party leaders convicted under the Peace Preservation law in 1932, for example, were reduced to fifteen years' imprisonment after they issued a joint statement on June 9, 1933, repudiating the Comintern and Japan's Communist Party and affirmed their support for the *kokutai* (or 'national polity') and their allegiance to imperial rule, including full support for Japan's actions in Manchuria.[65] The defection of Sano and Nabeyama had an immediate impact. By 1935, 469 of the 741 Communists awaiting trial issued similar *tenkō* renunciations. The September 5, 1933, issue of the *Tokyo Asahi shinbun* noted that of 1370 persons imprisoned under the law, 415, or 25 to 30 percent, had recanted, with another 393 in the process, and 548 remaining ideologically intransigent.[66] In the words of Hideo Sakamoto, a noted expert on thought-control of that period:

> Penal punishment and strict laws . . . were by themselves inadequate; it was a mistake to depend only upon the overly harsh Peace Preservation Law, and, since wrong ideology could only be countered by correct ideology, the nation's strongest weapon in the thought war was love. [The idea was to] make the proletarians love the country and the country must also love them[.] Thus, the urge to reform instead of punish, to suspend sentence instead of imprison, was strongly felt in justice circles; and from this basic feeling evolved a positive policy of parole and reintegration for the majority of thought offenders.[67]

Success in using leniency as a trade-off for *tenkō* in the prosecution of Japanese radicals may have stimulated broader use of leniency as an effective means of rehabilitation and reform in cases of ordinary crime. Justice Minister Raizaburō Hayashi seemed to echo Sakamoto's thoughts in his 1936 appeal to the procuracy that they be guided by a spirit of benevolence and compassion [*jin'aishugi*] in the treatment of all offenders.[68] Thus, like the myth of the reluctant litigant, the origins of Japan's postwar emphasis on confession, repentance, and absolution in criminal justice may lie in the redefinition of traditionalist values of the 1930s.

In other words, it can be argued that, faced with mounting postwar caseloads and unable to expand institutional capacity to relieve the resulting congestion, Japan's criminal law enforcement authorities expanded and in effect institutionalized an approach to criminal justice that had worked with such spectacular success in the 1930s. This renewed emphasis on correction and social reintegration of offenders was not necessarily premeditated or planned. It seems likely that it reflected a seemingly natural response to the demands of Japan's postwar environment, a response that drew on past success buttressed by broadly shared values and attitudes regarding what actions are appropriate by a fair and benevolent state.

Prevailing societal values in Japan, whatever the historical origin, do encourage the use of confession and, more important, permit a lenient response. As many have pointed out, repentance and forgiveness is a pervasive theme in Japan evident throughout the society from adaptations of Western fairy tales[69] to conventional behavior.[70] In this respect perhaps the West, not Japan, should be considered peculiar. The moral imperative of forgiveness as a response to repentance is surely as much a part of the Judeo-Christian heritage as the East Asian tradition.[71] For whatever reason, Western societies failed to develop institutional props for implementing such moral commands. Instead the legal institutions and processes of Western law reflect and reinforce societal demands for retribution and revenge. Indeed as one recent comparative study shows,[72] American and Japanese attitudes toward punishment differ considerably. In the United States punishment is favored as the primary response to crime. In Japan, compensation is considered far more important. Such studies, like most cultural explanations, however, depict reality in static terms; they offer rationalizations for what exists and miss the critical contrasts between the reinforcement and disintegration of similar values in different societies. The Japanese may well prefer compensation because their system works. Americans, on the other hand, may seek punishment because theirs does not.

Unfortunately, little attention has been paid either within Japan or beyond its borders to the implications of confession and compensation in the criminal process. Apparently Japanese authorities keep few statistics on confessions or compensation, nor have Japanese criminologists displayed much interest in assessing the positive impact of confession and compensation on either the offender or the victim.[73] Studies by the National Research Institute of Police Science, one of the premier criminological research programs in Japan, typi-

cally concentrate on the clarification of factors that contribute to criminal behavior. One searches their voluminous publications in vain for a description
of the informal process much less its effects. Academic criminologists and
criminal law specialists have also been preoccupied with Western approaches
to the neglect of indigenous patterns.[74] The Japanese no less than their
counterparts in the West tend to view Japan's experience in static cultural
terms, seemingly buttressed by the somewhat smug belief that Japan's success
is largely the product of a unique cultural identity.

There is, however, evidence to justify the hypothesis that the Japanese pattern—acknowledgment of guilt, expression of remorse including direct
negotiation with the victim for restitution and pardon as precondition for
lenient treatment, and sparing resort to long-term imprisonment—does contribute to a reduction in crime. What is lacking is comparative data to validate
the hypothesis. The most recent empirical study of recidivism among those
released after suspension of prosecution is a 1980 study by the Ministry of
Justice Research and Training Institute. It found that recidivism, as defined
by criminal conviction within three years, increased with the severity of the
initial disposition, but remained less than 50 percent in all categories except
upon release after incarceration for the term of the sentence. The aggregate
rates by disposition were as follows: suspension of prosecution—11.5 percent;
fines—16.3 percent; suspension of execution or sentence—21.5 percent;
suspension of execution of sentence with probation—35.4 percent; release by
parole—44.5 percent; and release after termination of sentence—57.2 percent.[75] These findings confirm an earlier 1968 study. Out of a sample of 9,296
of approximately 246,000 persons whose prosecutions for nontraffic offenses
were suspended in 1964, only 1,243 (13.4 percent) were identified from
fingerprint records kept in the National Police Academy to have committed a
new offense through February 1967.[76] Although the accuracy of the 1968 findings were challenged,[77] most law enforcement authorities in Japan considered
them to be a reasonably reliable measure of the success of the system of
suspension of prosecution as a means of rehabilitation and correction.[78] The
1980 figures support this view. Recidivism rates for offenders who serve
prison terms are apparently considerably higher in Japan than the United
States.[79] This is to be expected, however, since a larger number of those imprisoned in Japan compared to the United States are repeated offenders.[80]
From the studies it seems reasonable to conclude that the authorities have
been relatively good predictors of the likelihood of offender recidivism, or
the correctional emphasis of Japanese criminal justice has been notably successful, or, possibly, a bit of both.

The Japanese experience also confirms a growing literature on the importance of acknowledgment of guilt and restitution of victims to the psychological rehabilitation of offenders and attitudes of victims toward the offender and
the criminal justice system.[81] Studies have found that offenders attempt to
relieve distress experienced after committing a crime involving harm to others
by justification, derogating the victim and denying responsibility, or restitu-

tion.[82] Consequently, there is considerable empirical support for the notion that encouraging remorse and restitution reduces recidivism.

An arguable added benefit of the Japanese approach is that the emphasis on victim compensation and pardon reduces societal demands for revenge and retribution and thus facilitates efforts by law enforcement authorities to provide effective means for offender rehabilitation. In other words, as societal demands for punishment as retribution are reduced the authorities are then able to respond with greater leniency. Albeit sparse, empirical evidence on victim participation in the legal process in the United States and Canada indicates that victims who have some voice in the process are not only more satisfied with the process itself,[83] but also, if negotiated restitution is attempted, may be less inclined to view whatever penalty is imposed as inadequate.[84] This would also explain why Japanese are more tolerant of leniency and are more willing to accept than the Americans surveyed by Hamilton and Sanders reductions in the penalties the law prescribes.[85]

Thus it is at least arguable that the Japanese second track contributes to a process of positive reinforcement in which rehabilitation is both more likely to succeed and, in turn, to be ethically or socially a more acceptable objective. The second track of confession, repentance, and absolution of the Japanese criminal process may provide insights for other industrial societies seeking to establish a more humane and effective system of criminal justice, one free from the human and economic costs of overcrowded prisons, increasing crime, and victim alienation.

Typical of American views is a study of Tokyo undertaken in the early 1970s by the Citizens Crime Commission of Philadelphia.[86] The Commission identified two dozen differences between Japan and the United States that would account for significantly lower crime rates in Japan. Some were purely cultural: Japan's ethnic homogeneity, its insularity, the cohesion of the family unit, a sense of self-discipline, the influence of meditative religions, high literacy rates. Other explanations were more structural or institutional: the accommodation of unskilled workers in the work force, a unified, national crime control system, an emphasis on counseling and mediation of disputes, police recruitment and training, the family court system. Nowhere did the report mention how offenders or the victims of crime are actually treated within the system. Nor do any of the factors listed explain how crime in Japan has been reduced as opposed to being maintained at low rates of increase.

Charles Fenwick provides a more thorough and thoughtful look. In addition to the more shopworn explanations, from Japan's homogeneity and history as an isolated "island nation" to the economic well-being of its citizens—most if not all of which are shared by at least one other industrial society, Sweden, which has not been able to contain crime[87]—Fenwick adds a number of other critical factors. Some are what he calls "justice factors," such as the use of the formal state-provided mechanisms of law enforcement only as a "last resort" and, citing Bayley, not retributively.[88] He also praises the "overall coordination, control, centralized planning, and standardization of operating procedures,"[89] as well as clearance rates (i.e., apprehension of offenders) for all major crimes of between 68 and 71 percent as compared to a U.S. average of 26 percent.[90] And, of course, he gives credit to Japan's success in controlling drug use.[91] Japanese criminologists would generally add effective gun control to the list.[92]

Fenwick goes further, however, emphasizing two additional factors: strong, societal deviance control mechanisms and public participation in the justice system. Citing Bayley and quoting extensively from Clifford, Fenwick concludes:

> Indeed, where crime exists in this Asian nation, it is often of a subcultural nature and involves such activities as organized crime, juvenile delinquency, and political extremism. What we basically find is that conformity is more a function of the threat of exclusion from social groupings rather than formalized punishment that might be meted out by the criminal justice system. . . .
>
> What the above suggests is that social structure[,] conditions and processes are major determinants not only of normative human social conduct but also of crime causation/control. The effects of mutual dependence are consistent with findings [by various cited U.S. sources] concerning the relevance of social control on crime.[93]

Yoshio Suzuki expresses similar views. "More important" than Japan's ethnic homogeneity, he remarks, "small and intimate groups control the behavior of their members. Informal social control through traditional institutions like family, school, and local community still functions with reasonable effectiveness."[94] [B]elonging to a group," he continues, "nourishes and reinforces conformity to social norms."[95] Or, at least, he might have added, those norms the group chooses to enforce.

Whether or not a factor in either the prevention or reduction of crime, what both Fenwick and Suzuki describe is a fundamental aspect of the relationship between the postwar Japanese state and society. Behind the trappings of ubiquitous authority is a state far less powerful and far more dependent than most Western observers have fathomed. Although norms articulated as law in constitution or code may thereby gain greater legitimacy and societal acceptance, the reliance by the state and its instrumentalities for their enforcement on informal, social mechanisms of control represents a transfer of power. Inasmuch as the efficacy of legal norms ultimately rests with those who control their enforcement, by depending upon informal social mechanisms for crime control, the Japanese state has in effect abandoned the most coercive of all legitimate instruments of state control. In contemporary Japan these powers thus reside with the society at large and its constituent, lesser communities of family, firm, and friends.

In effect, state institutional incapacity and the successful emphasis on reintegration of repentant offenders into society and corollary reliance on informal social means of crime control have reinforced the capacity of social groups to exercise coercive controls usually reserved in the West as an exclusive prerogative of the state. The consequence is a weaker state and stronger, more autonomous and cohesive society.

7

Bureaucrats and Business: Administrative Power Constrained

The paradigm of the administrative state has long been the dominant vision of governance in the modern Japanese state. Governmental intrusion into all areas of life has been widely viewed as characteristic of Japan since the Meiji era. The power, prestige, and ubiquitous presence of Japanese officialdom has been a constant theme. Views may vary from Robert Ward's restrained understatement that "since the Meiji restoration . . . the bureaucracy has been very important in the Japanese political system"[1] to Dan Henderson's hyperbole that in Japan, "[r]ather than a rule of law, a rule of bureaucrats prevails."[2] Some even see in Japan new and menacing models of bureaucratic dominion to achieve mercantilist economic goals as "Japan Incorporated,"[3] "Japan's New Capitalism,"[4] or the "Developmental State."[5] Whatever the name, and however varied the harmony, the melody remains the same. Whether a "triumvirate"[6] or "a system,"[7] political, economic, and bureaucratic leaders in Japan form a powerful elite that directs the political economy to achieve self-centered, nationalist aims. Japanese society is thus directed by a state controlled by a small clique of power holders.

Each of these views presupposes the capacity of the state or "system" to exercise power with authority in conscious, willed aims and directions. Japan's economic success is thus the product of intentional, planned policies executed effectively by the state. To the extent that market forces have played any role, this would primarily also be a consequence of intentional choice by prescient officials and their political and business partners in governance. Such analyses leave little room for accident, luck, or circumstance. The operating premise is that what Japanese bureaucrats wanted, they got.

By all appearances such observations are quite accurate. The administrative state has been a preeminent pattern of governance in Japan since the sixth century. It is also the dominant model in all industrial democracies. Many features of Japanese bureaucratic presence are merely reflections of the expanded role of the administrative organs of the state in all societies, industrial and developing. They sometimes appear to Americans as well as to Japanese who tend to use the United States as the measure for self-defining comparisons to be peculiar to Japan because the organization and diffusion of political and administrative authority (with power) of the American presidential system are mistakenly taken as the norm against which Japan is compared.

Many of the features considered from an American viewpoint to be distinctively Japanese are in fact, however, reflections of distinctively American institutional arrangements. Take, for example, the policy-making or legislative role of the bureaucracy. Bureaucratic involvement in setting the legislative agenda and determining the content of legislation is prevalent in all industrial societies, the United States included.[8] However, many Japan specialists in the United States use data on the dearth of private or member bills introduced in the Diet and the overwhelming percentage of government-sponsored and bureaucracy-drafted legislation as an indication of an unusually influential bureaucratic establishment. Chalmers Johnson, for example, sees in such data evidence that "the influence of former bureaucrats within the Diet has tended to perpetuate and actually strengthen the prewar pattern of bureaucratic dominance."[9] However accurate this conclusion may be on other grounds, the bureaucracy's influence on legislation does not provide its proof.

Bureaucratic Influence in Japan: A Comparative Perspective

With respect to legislation, Japan's experience does not differ significantly from that of the United Kingdom, Germany, France, or other parliamentary systems. In the United Kingdom, for example, legislation is prepared and drafted as a matter of course within the administrative department with jurisdiction over its subject matter after consultation with affected interests.[10] Private member bills in the United Kingdom constitute a "very small proportion of the work of Parliament, and then only those which embody policies acceptable to the government are passed."[11] In the Federal Republic of Germany, three-quarters of all legislation is estimated to originate in the ministries.[12] The same is true for France.[13] "The political system of the Fifth Republic," writes Ezra Sulieman, "has conspired to place the deputy in an impotent position, at the mercy of the government and the administration."[14]

Another often-stated source of bureaucratic influence in the legislative process in Japan is the participation by former bureaucrats within the ruling Liberal Democratic Party. The presence of a significant proportion of former bureaucrats in leadership positions in the Party is commonly cited as an explanation for the Japanese bureaucracy's pronounced influence.[15] After all, it is noted, during the thirty-four-year period between 1946 and 1980, for all but five years (1947–48, 1954–57, 1972–76) Japan has been governed by cabinets led by prime ministers who began their careers in one of five national ministries.[16] It is argued that former bureaucrats within the political parties and the Diet tend to retain ties and allegiances to their former ministries analogous to the relationships maintained by former union officials to labor union bureaucracies under Labor Party governments in the United Kingdom, Australia, and New Zealand.

Direct participation by former bureaucrats in the Liberal Democratic Party is explained in large part by the near monopoly of power that elite civilian bureaucrats enjoyed under and immediately after the Allied Occupation. As Chalmers Johnson points out:

> Ironically, it was during the Occupation that one fondest dreams of the wartime "control bureaucrats" (*tōsei kanryō*) were finally realized. With the militarists gone, the *zaibatsu* facing dissolution and SCAP's [Supreme Commander for the Allied Powers] decision to try to set the economy on its feet, the bureaucracy found itself working for the *tennō* [MacArthur] who really possessed the attributes of "absolutism" (*zettai-shugi*).[17]

The decision by SCAP to rule occupied Japan indirectly, unlike occupied Germany, through the existing civilian bureaucracy precluded any massive purges of civilian officials who had supported or participated in Japan's war effort and secured the political influence of Japan's bureaucratic elite for at least a generation. The members of this elite created the ruling political parties of postwar Japan. The contrast between the postwar and wartime careers of Shigeru Yoshida and Konrad Adenauer or between Nobusuke Kishi and Ludwig Erhard is instructive. The political leadership of postwar Japan was drawn from the prewar or wartime bureaucracy. In postwar Germany, they were either prewar political figures opposed to Hitler's National Socialist regime or political newcomers. Bureaucratic influence in the postwar political process in Japan was thus more a consequence of Occupation policies than some less mutable institutional or cultural feature of Japanese politics.

Gradually, almost imperceptibly, however, the postwar constitutional order has functioned to reduce rather than increase this influence. Except for the 1949 Diet election, in which 37 former government officials, including 25 of Prime Minister Yoshida's recruits, entered the Diet, and 1952, in which 48 former officials, including several depurgees such as Nobusuke Kishi, were elected; ex-bureaucrats have not made significant political gains in any postwar election.[18] Rarely has the number of newly elected former bureaucrats exceeded a dozen.[19] As the careers of former Prime Minister Kakuei Tanaka and Yasuhiro Nakasone illustrate, the political influence of career politicians and members of their staffs with strong bases of local support has slowly increased from election to election during the postwar period at the expense of bureaucratic elites at the center.

Even granting that former officials exercise significant influence in the ruling party and the Diet, here too Japan's experience merely approximates other parliamentary systems. Aberbach, Putnam, and Rockman, for example, show that in 1973 about 38 percent of the members of the West German Bundesrat were government officials on leave.[20] Of those elected a decade later, over 10 percent were high civil service officials in federal, state, or local government at the time of their election. With about 20 percent of the LDP members of the Japanese House of Representatives identified as former government officials,[21] Japan is thus comparable to the Netherlands.[22]

From an American perspective, the coercive powers of the Japanese bureaucracy seem impressive also for their reach. The scope of coercive bureaucratic intrusion into the economic and social life of Japan is often described as if it were several degrees greater than in the United States or other industrial democracies. Japanese officialdom appears to be "so confident, prestigious, and effective, as well as officious."[23]

Such observations are equally flawed. Government in the United States is far more intrusive in its coercive impact than in Japan. Except perhaps for family registration and the neighborhood police, there is little if any evidence that the average Japanese citizen has any more contact with government than his or her American counterpart. The volume and coercive intrusiveness of governmental controls in the United States—from taxation through consumer and environmental regulation—is in fact greater than in Japan. The volume of new regulatory enactments in the United States each week exceeds the annual quota of all new legislation and administrative regulations combined promulgated by Japanese authorities. There is in fact no evidence to support the widespread belief that bureaucratic influence is any greater in Japan than in other developed parliamentary democracies. Once again, we confront a persistent and unyielding myth.

Even in comparison with the United States the extent of administrative intervention in Japan is hardly remarkable. Despite differences in priorities and emphasis, governmental measures designed to foster economic growth were at least as extensive in nineteenth century America as Meiji Japan. The Meiji government's efforts to encourage industrial development through model factories, new government-managed enterprises, and subsidies pale in comparison with the massive transfer of public land and timber and mineral resources for promotion of the railroad, timber, and mining industries. By the 1880s, however, as the Meiji government completed its liquidation of government enterprises and the remaining mining and other resources owned by its Tokugawa predecessors, the United States had already begun the regulatory era. Whereas the Japanese continued to pursue their goal of economic growth through the promotion of private industry, by the late nineteenth century the United States was regulating major sectors of the economy purportedly in the public or consumer interest. The result in the United States was the burgeoning state and federal administrative apparatus of regulatory commissions, departments, and agencies. As Kenneth Culp Davis reminds us, "almost one-third of all federal peace-time administrative agencies were created before 1900 and another third before 1930."[24] The array of regulatory controls quite familiar in the United States by the eve of World War I were unknown in Japan until after World War II. Those who describe the power and presence of the postwar Japanese bureaucracies generally ignore the fact that nearly all of Japan's basic regulatory legislation in effect today was drafted and imposed by its American occupiers between 1945 and 1952. No Japanese Diet has extended the powers granted to the Japanese bureaucracies by the Occupation authorities.

Nor at any time in modern Japanese history has Japan maintained as large a bureaucratic establishment as the United States. In 1910, for example, Japan had an estimated 185,045 national government civilian employees including imperial appointees, minor officials, and other salaried government employees—that is, one government employee per 265.8 persons. In the United States in 1910 there were an estimated 388,708 federal government employees, including postal workers, or 1 federal employee per 237.7 persons. By 1970 both the absolute numbers and ratios had increased significantly in both countries, with as might be expected, the United States leading Japan by a wide margin. By 1970 the number of Japanese civilian government employees had increased to 832,174, almost doubling the number of government employees per capita to 1 per 146.9 persons. During the same period the number of United States federal government employees rose to 2,981,574 or 1 government employee to every 68.4 persons.[25]

What makes the role of the bureaucracy distinctive in Japan is neither its influence nor its size. It is instead the conjunction of broad, seemingly limitless authority without, however, even a relatively normal degree of coercive legal powers. That most assessments of the Japanese bureaucracy fail to convey its role accurately can best be explained by fundamental differences in language and conceptual premises.

Seldom articulated with much precision, governmental regulation and bureaucratic influence in most industrial democracies is assumed by economists, political scientists, and lawyers alike to relate to policies articulated in legislation or legally binding administrative pronouncements and then implemented by governmental authorities exercising a variety of coercive legal powers. The prevailing paradigm of the administrative state in the West depicts legislatures, administrative agencies, and, occasionally, the courts as the fora with legislators, administrative officials, and judges, the primary actors. Despite formal procedural controls, particularly in the United States, most administrative activity tends to be informal. Moreover, by necessity or design, those whose economic, ideological, and political interests are affected usually participate both in the process of formulating policy and in its implementation. Notwithstanding procedural requirements structuring how decisions are to be made, informal negotiation and compromise are dominant aspects of the process. There is thus always some element of consent by those most affected. Government officials remain, however, the primary actors. They are the ones who make the decisions, they decide whether to accept or reject a compromise and issue the final rule or order.

Administrative regulation in the Western democracies also has limits. Governmental controls are restricted to specific areas of activity. As exemplified by economic regulation, governmental directives and controls do not cover a broad expanse of economic matters but instead reflect in conception particularized intervention as a substitute for otherwise private or marketplace decisions. Whether a regulated or command economy, however, the nature of state coercion through statutory or administrative fiat is essentially the same. The difference between the two lies more in the pervasive scope of state direction, not in the nature or efficacy of the state's coercion or control in areas subject to state intervention. In both law is the primary instrument of the coercive powers of the state.

The Japanese pattern must be distinguished. In terms of *authority* governmental activity in Japan tends to be as unlimited in scope as in a command economy. In terms of *coercive power*, however, government officials have only the legal powers granted to them by statute plus whatever extralegal levers of influence or persuasion may be available. The result is a pervasive, ostensibly unrestrained capacity to intervene without, however, the means of coercive legal control that may be necessary to achieve official aims unilaterally, lacking the consent of those affected.

The Japanese administrative process is more aptly described therefore as a form of *consensual administrative management*. Yet even this phrase may mislead insofar as it implies an exercise of power by state officials in determining or implementing policy. In the context of contemporary Japan, consensual management encompasses a process of governance in which the state may have the authority to intervene but not necessarily the power to insist on unilateral decisions. Ministries and other administrative bodies become in consequence the situs for decisions, but officials are not the primary actors. Their influence and control depend upon their ability to achieve consent among those most directly affected by the policies being implemented and whose cooperation is necessary for their effective implementation. Behind the appearance of official direction and control is a process of governance by negotiation in which the state must by necessity bargain in both the making of policy and its enforcement. In such circumstances, distinctions between "public" and "private" blur and "regulation" takes on new meaning, as those apparently subject to governmental direction gain a significant and often determinative voice in the process of formulating and implementing policy. Unlike expressions of consent expressed through formal electoral and similar institutionalized channels in other industrial democracies, the consent of those governed in Japan is less the product of intentional political choice than necessity born of Japan's unique institutional history.

Regulation by Cartel: Origins

As we have seen in previous chapters, the separation of authority and power has been a consistent motif in Japanese patterns of governance. Seldom if ever did central authorities in Japan exercise powers of government as extensive as their authority to govern. The capacity of the Japanese state to coerce has rarely matched its authority to do so.

Also as noted, until the 1930s few attempts were made to regulate the Japanese economy. For the most part government intervention in the Meiji, Taishō, and early Shōwa periods was limited to permissive legislation enabling or promoting economic activity in desired private sectors of the economy.

Until the mid-1920s agricultural policy had greater priority than industrial policy.[26] Even then, government policy was generally more reactive, responding to economic crises, than planned. Large-scale projects, such as operation of Yawata Steel and subsidization of shipbuilding were more an element of military policy than economic planning. The main targets of Japanese support were medium and small enterprises; the principal means chosen for their promotion were the encouragement of cartels and cooperative associations in lieu of direct subsidies or managerial support.

Even Japan's wartime controls, except briefly, amounted to little more than the systematic extension of mandatory cartels in which privately owned and managed enterprises, especially the *zaibatsu* conglomerates that had begun to emerge by the turn of the century, preserved extensive autonomy.

The Japanese government's reliance on mandatory cartels and industry associations as a vehicle for wartime allocations of resources and procurement is indicative of the chronic weakness of direct administrative controls. A compromise between the military's demands for improved coordination and the interests of the civilian economic bureaucracies and their "client" industries, particularly *zaibatsu* firms who benefited most, the wartime industry "control" associations seriously handicapped Japan's war effort. The effect on the direction of Japan's wartime economy was, by one account, "chaotic,"[27] preventing full mobilization of Japan's already scarce resources. The counterproductive impact of such indirect means of control was evident even before the outbreak of war with the United States. "Production of consumption goods, such as textiles, food products, and paper (including pulp)," states Takafusa Nakamura, "had already fallen to 60 percent of its prewar level [1937] by the time Japan entered the Pacific War."[28]

The most ambitious attempt to secure a more unified, coordinated system of control during the war was the creation in 1944 of the Munitions Ministry out of the Ministry of Commerce and Industry by the Tojo Cabinet. It also failed. As described by Jerome B. Cohen:

> The theory was good. In practice, it can be categorically stated that the desired unification was never achieved. The services continued to operate independently, some control associations continued to administer allocations and priorities, an adjustment between orders and supplies was never achieved, production was consistently overestimated, the special priorities were never observed. It is only fair to add, however, that in view of the economic realities which confronted Japan in 1944 and early 1945, no matter how expert the planning, how cooperative the agencies, and how thorough the unification in one body, it could never have succeeded. Wholly aside from administrative controls, good or bad, the ship losses and the consequent shrinkage of raw material supply which occurred made inevitable a drastic decline in output of finished munitions. The incompetent planning, of which the Japanese were guilty, only intensified their plight.[29]

The cartelization of the Japanese economy immediately before and during the war should be understood for what it really was, a compromise between government and industry to preserve a greater degree of autonomous action by industry vis-à-vis the government and the civilian bureaucracies vis-à-vis the military. Japan's wartime cartels reflected the inability of even the military in wartime Japan to impose needed reforms on resistant business firms and civilian bureaucracies. Japanese government officials had faced similar obstacles in the imposition of mandatory cartels in the early 1930s.

Japan is commonly believed to have been widely cartelized like Germany by the early 1930s. Not so. From the late nineteenth century through the early 1930s, the differences between Japan and Germany were striking. Cartels had become so dominant a feature of German economic life by the mid-1920s that it is often described as the "fatherland" of the cartel movement. From the moment of German unification in 1871, the number of cartels in Germany increased at a rapid pace. By the eve of mandatory cartel legislation under the Nazi regime in the mid-1930s, all significant portions of Germany industry had become subject to some form of private anticompetitive agreement.[30] Germany was not exceptional. In the interwar period, voluntary cartels and government marketing restrictions had proliferated in nearly all industrial countries.[31] Few agricultural products, minerals, or chemicals escaped restriction. In the United States by 1939, even after the demise of the initial New Deal experiment with cartelization as national economic policy, an estimated 47.4 percent by value of all agricultural products and 86.9 percent of all minerals produced are estimated to have been subject to cartel restrictions.[32]

Japan was in fact more victim than player in the international cartel game. In contrast with its industrial trading partners its economy was characterized by fierce competition. The *zaibatsu* did not gain their dominant position in the Japanese economy until after the military buildup of the mid-1930s. Available evidence suggests that among themselves the *zaibatsu* were more likely to compete than collude.[33]

Dependent upon imports for nearly all foodstuffs, chemical fertilizer, minerals, oil, and other raw materials, Japanese consumers were forced to buy from the most successful international cartels while Japanese producers, mainly textile manufacturers, sold in the most competitive international markets. Attempts were made in Japan to restrain competition, but there is little evidence that they were successful. The first trade associations had been organized in the 1880s, beginning with the textile industry, but it was not until the turn of the century that they made any serious effort to restrict competition.[34] During the first Sino-Japanese war in 1894–95 and at other times before World War I, a few voluntary cartels were tried, mostly among small-scale exporters. Most were ineffectual and short-lived.[35] Without greater external control Japanese firms remained too rivalrous. The 1897 Major Export Goods Trade Association Law[36] and the 1900 Major Products Trade Association Law,[37] as well as other legislative measures enacted by the Meiji government, did facilitate the organization of trade associations and thus the mechanism for price and output restrictions among competitors, but indicative of the contrast with Germany, a government decree in 1916 prohibited price fixing.[38] Other legislative measures, such as the 1927 Banking Law, effectively barred new entry into a variety of fields, but positive state intervention to encourage cartels did not come until 1931 with the enactment of the Major Industries Control Law,[39] designed to aid small and medium enterprises. At that time Japan is estimated to have had only twenty-four legally recognized cartels, most of which were inactive. Four years later despite "mandatory" controls, there were still only twenty-five compulsory and fourteen voluntary cartels and eighty trade associations, again mostly among exporters.[40]

The imposition of control associations as a mechanism for wartime economic regulation was thus not simply an extension of a prior pattern of industrial organization by the military. It reflected the incapacity of the Japanese government, even the military in wartime, to resort to needed coercive direct state controls on resistant business firms and other bureaucracies.

The wartime use of industry associations as a conduit for implementing economic policy established a pattern that still persists. Despite the elimination of the control associations under the Allied Occupation, which Japanese business and government leaders resisted to the last, and SCAP's attempt to subject trade associations to rigorous antitrust regulation, by the mid-1950s trade associations had become the principal fora for business-government negotiation of economic policy and a crucial device for enforcement. Once again, the origins of the prevailing postwar arrangement are found in the mid- to late 1930s.

Occupation Regulatory Reforms

The contributions—many unintentional—of the Allied Occupation to the patterns of governance in postwar Japan are difficult to exaggerate. The basic features of the Occupation reforms are well known. A new constitution and implementing statutes created a bicameral parliament to which the executive cabinet and administrative organs were accountable. The constitution included an extensive list of fundamental human rights with an American-styled judicial branch explicitly granted the power of judicial review to assure their enforcement. The imperial institution was retained as the "symbol" of the people with ceremonial functions normally assigned to a head of state. The military establishment was abolished and any national right of belligerency renounced. Executive accountability to the Diet through the electoral process and political parties along with the elimination of imperial prerogatives of governance removed the most critical defects of the Meiji constitutional order. Legislative supremacy among the political branches of government and ultimate accountability to the electorate have worked—albeit gradually and in ways often unappreciated by outside observers—to assure a government that is responsive to the desires and interests of the electorate.

The Occupation also introduced extensive regulatory reforms. Some, like land reforms, *zaibatsu* dissolution and new, stringent antitrust controls, new labor legislation, and capital market regulation, were intended as permanent reforms to achieve long-term goals for a stable Japanese democracy. Others,

especially foreign exchange and trade controls, and foreign investment regulation, were designed as temporary, emergency legislation to cope with immediate economic and social needs. Less extraordinary than the nature and scope
of the reforms themselves, however, has been their endurance. Nearly all of
the fundamental regulatory statutes in effect in Japan today are a legacy of
the Allied Occupation; some, like the constitution itself, without amendment.

Two factors help to explain why the Occupation reforms have lasted
throughout the postwar period. First, most of the reforms had politically influential beneficiaries, who have resisted any attempt to alter the new status
quo. The gains for former tenants of land reform are perhaps the most obvious.
Any change that threatened to eliminate or reduce their benefits from land
reform would have met with strong political opposition. Similarly, it has
proven to be almost impossible, for example, for the Ministry of Finance to
overcome objections by Japan's securities firms to eliminate the American-
inspired restriction on commercial banks from engaging in the securities business.[41] And, as noted below, public opposition in 1958 prevented the Kishi
Cabinet from winning Diet approval for an amendment that would have significantly weakened Japanese antitrust controls.[42] Even the 1953 amendments
to Japan's antitrust statute were less severe than most critics imply.[43] Time
and again throughout the 1950s attempts to undo unwanted Occupation
reforms, including amendment of the postwar constitution itself, failed. The
political reforms to assure responsive, democratic government were effective
in assuring that other reforms could not be undone without the political support of those most affected by them.

A second, closely related explanation is the utility of many of these statutes
to Japanese officials themselves. No effort has thus been made on the part of
the Japanese officials to repeal any Occupation-imposed reform that has empowered government officials. Many an Occupation reform has thus survived
because of official enthusiasm. Much of the regulatory legislation enacted at
SCAP's suggestion or request granted Japan's economic bureaucracies legal
powers they had never before exercised and probably would never have been
able to wrest from the Diet. For perhaps the first time in at least modern
Japanese history, Japan's administrative officials enjoyed legal powers corresponding to their authority. In this respect no Occupation legislation rivaled
in importance the Foreign Exchange and Foreign Trade Control Law.[44]

The first direct governmental controls restricting trade and investment by
foreign nationals in modern Japanese history were established by SCAP.
Within weeks of Japan's surrender, SCAP had imposed a wide range of restrictive controls over nearly all foreign trade and investment activities with Japan.
These early controls gradually evolved into a comprehensive regulatory structure covering Japan's economic relationships with the rest of the world. The
need for specific foreign trade and foreign exchange controls originated within
SCAP, which invited Jan V. Mladek of the newly established International
Monetary Fund to Japan to advise a joint Japanese and American drafting
committee. Mladek prepared a draft for a statute on the basis of which a
Japanese government committee drafted a second version. Both were used by

the final drafting committee.[45] Describing the process is a memo to Government Section by Robert H. Neptune, a lawyer with the Legislation and Justice Division of Legal Section (before 1948, the Courts and Law Division of Government Section), headed by Alfred C. Oppler. Neptune wrote:

> The Japanese draft of the bill departed from Mladek's recommendations in that it endeavored to detail much of the matter of substance which Mladek would have left to Cabinet Order under a broad delegation. Even so, the standards or Cabinet Orders or Ministerial Ordinance had to be broad, such as that stated in Par. 2, Article 48 of the approved bill. Difficulties in drafting the substance of the bill arose from jurisdictional disputes among the Japanese. The Foreign Exchange Control Board was hoping to get considerable power at the expense of the Ministries. The Ministries were likewise endeavoring to prevent the FECB from gaining any veto or control over their actions. Arguments lasted into the early morning hours on several occasions, and but little progress was being made toward the objective. The Chairman, Lt. Col. Ryder, finally decided that in any case of jurisdictional dispute, the issue would be settled by including in the substantive provision that "the competent minister, may ***(Here, the substance was stated)*** *in accordance with Cabinet Order*." This method left it to the Cabinet Order to determine what Minister or Agency has the function prescribed.[46]

In other words, the broad delegation of discretionary power to Japan's economic ministries, particularly the Ministry of International Trade and Industry (MITI) and the Ministry of Finance, were pressed upon them, over their initial objections, by the American Occupation authorities. "[Chief of the Legislation Division, Government Section, Justin] Williams," Neptune notes, "did not consider such objections important in view of the urgency of, and peculiar nature of, the legislation desired."[47]

The process leading to enactment of Japan's first statutory foreign investment restrictions followed a similar path. SCAP's initial controls following the surrender in September 1945 also included restrictions requiring explicit SCAP approval for all "financial, commercial, or business contacts" by Japanese nationals "with any concern which was foreign owned or controlled."[48] Except for foreign nationals who had resided in Japan continuously during the war, acquisitions of any equity interest in Japanese enterprises were prohibited.

As United States policy toward Japan shifted toward an emphasis on Japanese economic recovery in the wake of communist gains on the Chinese mainland and heightened tensions between the United States and the Soviet Union in Europe from mid-1947 through 1949, SCAP began to ease the restrictions against investment in Japan. In August 1947, pursuant to SWNCC direction, SCAP permitted resumption of private international trade, allotting for the first time since the surrender a restricted number of entry permits to certain foreign businessmen from Allied countries. In 1948 the quotas were removed for certain categories, and for the first time, foreign businessmen without prewar investment and trade interests were allowed to enter to explore new investment and trade opportunities. Not until January 1949, however, were

SCAP's regulations eased to permit new investment in Japan subject to specific procedures for validation.[49] On March 15, 1949, the Yoshida Cabinet issued a cabinet order creating a Japanese institutional framework for SCAP's regulatory schemes.[50] The order established a Foreign Investment Commission attached to the Prime Minister's Office as an independent agency.[51] Paralleling the SCAP circular, the order empowered the new commission to review and validate applications for any proposed acquisition of corporate stock, real property interests, and industrial property rights as well as any purchase agreements for a term in excess of one year for a portion of the output or sales of any Japanese manufacturing enterprise.[52] Under the order applicants were required to show that their acquisition was necessary: (1) to carry out preexisting commercial activities if the applicant had been continuously resident in Japan since the date of surrender; (2) to resume a prewar commercial activity, in cases involving applicants with "a legitimate restitution claim"; or (3) to pursue new commercial activity "which will improve Japan's foreign exchange position or positively aid in Japan's economic rehabilitation."[53] The acquisition also had to be "indispensable for attaining the object of the business activity."

The need to open Japan to foreign trade and investment was widely acknowledged within SCAP, Japanese government and business circles, and in Washington. Although Japanese government and business leaders privately agreed that some restrictions were necessary to preserve the "autonomy" of Japanese enterprises, even the Communist Party limited its opposition to inducement of foreign capital that would contribute to "monopoly capitalism."[54]

The principal proponents of restrictive controls were within SCAP itself. Officials in the Economic and Scientific Section "feared" a "large influx" of foreign capital.[55] Special Assistant to the Chief of the Section Theodore Cohen, for example, wrote in July 1948 in support of strict regulation of the business activities of foreign investors then resident in Japan and any new equity investment.[56] General William F. Marquat, Chief of the Economic and Scientific Section, expressed similar support for comprehensive regulatory controls "required in a planned economy such as of necessity exists in Japan today."[57]

A year later in January 1950, the process of drafting began for Japan's first statute governing foreign investment. Although the Japanese negotiators initially did not perceive any need for the law, claiming that it would be "superfluous" because of the newly enacted foreign exchange controls, both sides evidently agreed that "strong, comprehensive screening measures be included in any foreign investment law."[58] The draft that emerged, enacted on Saturday, March 31, 1950, as the Law Concerning Foreign Investment, was promulgated on May 10, 1950, and remained in force until January 1, 1980. Until the mid-1950s, neither the Foreign Exchange and Foreign Trade Control Law nor the Foreign Investment Law appear to have had major restrictive impact on foreign investment. Fears of overall political instability in Asia in combination with what appeared at the time as the more attractive investment opportunities in a more quickly recovering Europe and in North America contributed to a general disinclination by all but a few U.S. firms to enter Japan in the early 1950s. After 1955, however, the door closed. These two statutes promptly became the principal instruments of Japan's First Five-Year Plan and successive efforts to expand Japan's industrial capacity and economic performance by a policy of export expansion and import substitution. These statutes, initially designed as temporary expedients, also endured in the radically altered economic environment of the 1960s and 1970s as the source of the principal legal powers for the implementation of Japan's domestic and international economic policies.

Regulation by Cartel: Postwar Patterns

Elimination of Japan's wartime control associations was also high on the list of Occupation priorities for economic reform. MacArthur had expressed this aim within the first months of the Occupation.[59] The utility of the associations as an instrument for economic coordination between government and industry served to stiffen Japanese resistance. *Zaibatsu* dissolution in fact proved to be an easier and more successful effort. The Occupation authorities, too, may have discovered that it was easier to use industry associations as a device for communicating and implementing policy than dealing with individual firms directly. Whatever the cause, however, the enactment of permanent antitrust legislation prohibiting domestic and international cartels was delayed until 1947,[60] with a supplemental Trade Association Law[61] postponed to a year later in July 1948. By then SCAP had discontinued the efforts to eliminate major concentrations of economic power as a result of political controversy in the United States.[62]

The importance of trade associations to the economic ministries is evident in that the first measures the Japanese government took once the Occupation ended on May 1, 1952, were to repeal the prohibition against the use of the *zaibatsu* names and to amend the Trade Association Law.

Also enacted within weeks after Japan regained complete sovereignty was the Law Concerning Special Measures for the Stabilization of Small and Medium Enterprises[63] and the Export Transactions Law.[64] A portent of things to come, the Export Transactions Law exempted from antitrust proscription—albeit subject to Japanese Fair Trade Commission (FTC) approval—certain cooperative export arrangements among competitors. A year later in September 1953 the Japanese government achieved a sweeping amendment of the basic antitrust statute. In addition to a new exemption for resale price maintenance for commodities designated by the Japanese FTC and easing somewhat the quite stringent prohibitions against restraints of competition, the 1953 amendments also introduced new exemptions for "depression" [*fukyō*] and "rationalization" [*gōrika*] cartels, subject to Japanese FTC approval. Although perhaps deservedly criticized as an indication of the disregard Japanese economic officials had for antitrust policy and the dawn of over a decade of lax enforcement, the amendments themselves were not extreme measures. The new exemptions paralleled quite closely the exclusions and exemptions being proposed for the new West German anticartel statute, which was generally hailed as strong antitrust legislation.[65] More significant than the 1953 antitrust amendments was the series of legislative enactments that followed. The Law Concerning Special Measures for the Stabilization of Small and Medium Enterprises[66] and the Export Transactions Law were also renamed and amended. The new Export Import Transactions Law,[67] for example, introduced exemptions for import cartels and, equally important, gave MITI rather than the Japanese FTC authority over approvals. Between 1953 and 1961 the Diet enacted over twenty statutes permitting formation of cartels in nearly every industry in the Japanese economy. Some, like the Medium and Small Industry Stabilization Law, and enabling legislation for cooperatives applied to broad segments of the economy. Others were industry-specific. As described by Kozo Yamamura:

> More legal cartels, in addition to "recession" and "rationalization" cartels, were also authorized by more than a score of industry-specific laws enacted during the fifties and sixties to "promote," stabilize," or "adjust the demand and supply" in the industries selected to achieve rapid increases in productive capacity and international competitive power. The Marine Products Export Industry Act and the Ammonium Sulphate Industry Rationalization and Ammonium Export Adjustment Temporary Measures Act of 1954 were the first of these [industry-specific] laws to be enacted. Those that followed during the next two decades enabled shipbuilding, cement, iron, steel, chemical, machinery, electronics, textile, and other industries to form cartels and benefit from subsidies, low-interest loans, and other inducements to achieve the policy goals.[68]

This proliferation of cartel-authorizing statutes is difficult to explain as the product of a coherent economic plan. The first statutes were enacted several years before Japan's first five-year economic plan in 1955 and there is little if any evidence to suggest that anyone in industry or government in 1952 had a determined vision of economic policy for the late 1950s and certainly not for the 1960s other than recovery and growth of Japan's prewar industries.

The emphasis on cartels as the keystone of Japan's postwar economic policy seems more likely a reflexive continuation of past practice, a product of political expediency rather than premeditated planning. Like the wartime control associations, reliance on cartels and trade associations ensured industry, particularly the dominant firms, a decisive voice in any allocations of resources within an industry. To the extent that decisions regarding new investment, prices, and output were not to be left entirely to individual firms and the unfettered forces of the marketplace, at least reliance on the consensual cartel mechanism and collective agreement within industry associations precluded unilateral direction by government officials. For those in MITI, the Ministry of Finance, and other economic bureaucracies, reliance on cartels and trade associations as conduits for economic policy also had special attractions. First, and perhaps foremost, they represented an accustomed pattern of government intervention in the economy. Japan's postwar ministries were, after all, dominated by men who had entered government service in the late 1920s and the 1930s. They were familiar with the wartime system of regulatory controls. It was only natural therefore for them to revert to past practice.

Political constraints also limited the options. The Occupation ended with several strong regulatory regimes in force, particularly, as noted, those for foreign trade and investment. No regulatory framework existed for an assertive industrial policy. To the contrary the only significant contribution of the Occupation to the legal framework for the regulation and direction of the domestic economy were antitrust controls solely administered by an American-styled, independent regulatory commission. For the Japanese government to sweep those controls away entirely and to substitute an extensive bureaucratic establishment for economic planning and direction would have been unthinkable. Bureaucratic rivalry and industry opposition alone would have been sufficient to scuttle any such attempt. The United States would almost surely have also protested with expressions of deep concern and the domestic political reaction would have been no less hostile.

In fact, however, there is no evidence that anything of the kind was even considered. What is described today as a successful "industrial policy" carried out by an elite corps of Japanese technocrats[69] can be more accurately characterized as a series of ad hoc adjustments to immediate economic needs and circumstances by government and business cooperating when their interests coincided, but often in conflict as they pursued their own individual aims.

The officials in Japan's postwar economic ministries were not technocrats in any meaningful sense. Predominantly graduates of a single law faculty, they had no special expertise in economics, business, or any area of science and technology. They were law-trained generalists who understood economic policy from what they had experienced within their respective ministries. They laid no claim to unique ability or vision. The justification for their authority and leadership has rested on a carefully inculcated sense of mission and broad public acceptance of their role.

A Mission to Manage

A sense of mission is widely recognized as one of the chief attributes of the Japanese bureaucracy. John Maki, writing in 1947 as a critic of bureaucratic influence, viewed the select economic ministries as a small elite sharing "a common training, a common tradition, a common ideology, and a common desire to monopolize what the group regarded as the skills of government."[70] Writing three decades later Ezra Vogel elaborated:

The esprit that unites a Ministry's five hundred or so elite bureaucrats rests on a sense of group mission. Although not immune from political pressures, bureaucrats do not hesitate to unite against politicians who obstruct their perceived mission. Responsibility for success in any important matter rests with a work unit, and all in the unit are judged by their unit's contribution to the Ministry. Superiors do not promote someone who cannot win the liking and cooperation of his peers, for an individual's value to his unit is determined by his capacity to work effectively with his peers, his superiors, and his subordinates. Each bureaucrat is personally identified with the mission of his work unit and the Ministry as a whole.[71]

Generally absent, however, from such descriptions of the esprit and sense of mission of MITI and other economic bureaucracies is any clear definition of what that mission is. Chalmers Johnson comes close. In his study of the Ministry of International Trade and Industry, he demonstrates how MITI officials by choice and chance emerged as one of the dominant actors in setting Japan's economic agenda. Theirs was no narrow, technocratic mission to manage or control carefully defined sectors of Japan's economy. Their objective was instead a broad, undefined mission to manage the economy overall.[72] In effect, Japan's bureaucratic establishment divided the totality of Japanese economic life and allocated to each ministry responsibility for the management in their respective spheres with MITI at the center. As a result, governmental intervention in the economy appears to be totalitarian in scope with unbounded administrative discretion. Ministry establishment laws [*setchi hō*] became blueprints for territorial divisions, allocating managerial jurisdiction over specific segments of the total terrain. This claim to authority above all other factors sets Japanese governmental agencies apart from the regulatory, policing agencies of the United States as well as the more "managerial" approach of bureaucracies in other industrial democracies.[73] The managerial mission of Japan's economic officialdom establishes an underlying premise that has had as much to do with their organization and behavior as history or even shared values and expectations of the Japanese society at large.

The mission of Japan's bureaucracies is not, however, unrelated to either history or culture. Both are essential aspects of bureaucratic authority that cannot be separated from the more general societal acceptance of the bureaucracy's role. While denying the utility of cultural explanations for Japanese economic success, Johnson nevertheless subscribes—perhaps inadvertently—to what is essentially a cultural analysis of the bureaucracy's role. As he explains:

> The "aura" formerly attached to samurai can still be found in some of the terminology now associated with bureaucrats. For example, the common term for governmental authorities is "those above" (*okami*). It is also said that Japanese do not normally question the authority of the government because they respect its "samurai sword" (*denka no hōtō*), which refers directly to a samurai family's heirloom sword. Such a jeweled sword symbolized the status of a samurai household rather than being a weapon designed for killing people. Yamanouchi[74] says that use of the term reflects

the popular consciousness of the law as being a symbol of authority, not something the possessor of authority need actually use. The change from the old constitution to the new, Yamanouchi argues, did little to change this attitude.[75]

In other words, Japanese bureaucrats enjoy widespread public acceptance of their authority to govern, an authority that, like the heirloom samurai sword, is symbolic and does not necessarily denote the powers of actual rule. The postwar constitution did not radically alter the prewar system. Continuity exists. Popular sovereignty may have replaced imperial rule but the bureaucracy has managed to perpetuate its claim to authority absent imperial delegation nonetheless. The ultimate justification for the postwar bureaucracy's mission to manage has thus been a shared societal expectation, a general public consensus, based on a perceived tradition and historical perspective. Bureaucratic authority in Japan does not necessarily include the prerogatives of power.

The Political Limits of Bureaucratic Power

Even at the height of bureaucratic influence in the mid-1950s, the elite economic ministries did not exercise political or economic control. As many scholars have begun to recognize, the formulation and implementation of economic policy in Japan involved complex interrelationships within individual firms and industries as well as among the various bureaucracies and political institutions at each level of government. Bureaucratic rivalries, industry objections, and public opposition prevented MITI, the Ministry of Finance, and other bureaucracies from receiving the formal legal powers most governmental agencies in the United States and other industrial democracies take for granted. One culls post-Occupation statutes in vain for legal enforcement powers commensurate with the bureaucracy's managerial role. The Export Import Transactions Law, for example, is almost entirely permissive. It authorizes the establishment of a variety of anticompetitive export and import arrangements subject to MITI disapproval if these arrangements are unduly restrictive. Under the express terms of the statute, MITI is empowered to intervene to impose restrictions only in cases where an export or import cartel has been voluntarily created but would be ineffective because of nonparticipating outsiders. In such cases alone is MITI authorized to order outsiders to abide by the agreed price, quota, or other restrictions. Under the statute MITI has no powers to direct or otherwise induce firms to enter an export or import cartel agreement. Export and import cartels are to be voluntary.

Notwithstanding this lack of legal authority granting MITI or any other administrative department even colorable powers to direct Japanese manufacturers or exporters to form export or import cartel agreements, the Japanese government has consistently maintained that the Export Import Transactions Law, along with the Foreign Exchange and Foreign Trade Control Law provide the legal basis for governmentally compelled export restraints. In a letter sent to U.S. Attorney General William French Smith, in connection with the "voluntary" export restraints imposed on Japan's automobile industry in May 7, 1981, for example, Japanese Ambassador Yoshio Ōkawara asserted that MITI had legal authority to maintain orderly exports and to establish at its discretion quotas on the exports of automobiles to the United States without subjecting automobile exports to formal restrictions under the Foreign Exchange and Foreign Trade Control Law. Only if a company threatened to exceed the limits set by MITI would the Japanese government "then enforce the export maximums it established for each company by refusing to license exports in excess of these maximums."[76]

In retrospect, the enactment of the 1953 amendments and the decade of limited enforcement that followed represented the high water mark of effective MITI opposition to antitrust policies in postwar Japan. Despite the new exemptions and the underlying rejection of the Occupation's pro-competition policies, the basic framework for antitrust enforcement remained intact. Although antitrust enforcement was severely reduced, unlike nearly all other independent regulatory agencies established under the Occupation, the FTC was not abolished or absorbed into MITI or some other ministry. It remained an independent agency and thus a vehicle to promote more vigorous antitrust enforcement and to serve as a political counterbalance to the economic ministries, especially MITI.

The most significant test of the political influence of MITI came in the late 1950s, coincident with the first major slowdown in the Japanese economy after the Korean War and demands by the United States for Japan to liberalize restrictions on foreign trade and investment. The response of officials in the economic ministries and the government led by Kishi was predictable. In October 1957 the Kishi cabinet appointed a special commission to study further amendments in the Antimonopoly and Fair Trade Law. Four months later the commission proposed a series of major changes that all but eliminated significant antitrust proscriptions and significantly increased the legal powers and authority of MITI.[77]

A bill was promptly introduced into the Diet in April 1958. Little more than the ultimate extension of the pattern begun in 1955, its main features were (1) substantial easing of the standards and procedures for approving recession cartels, (2) broadening the scope of permitted rationalization cartels, (3) recognition of mergers for purposes of "rationalization," and (4) a variety of critical changes in FTC procedures. Under the bill the FTC would have also effectively lost any claims as an independent agency through the requirement that it "listen" to the opinions of the competent ministries before taking any corrective action or granting or denying approval. In a remarkable showing of support for antitrust policy as well as political influence, consumer groups, labor unions, agricultural organizations, and medium and small business groups rallied and killed the measure in committee.[78] Thus ended the last frontal assault on the Antimonopoly and Fair Trade Law in the postwar period.

Led by MITI, the government next attempted to achieve a similar result through the most ambitious special exemption measure ever proposed—the

Designated Industries Promotion Special Measures bill (abbreviated in Japanese as the *Tokushinhōan*]. The *Tokushinhōan* was designed to permit certain industries, particularly automobile, petroleum, and specialty steel manufacturers, to achieve greater concentration and restrictive specialization. The envisioned level of government intervention and supervision, especially by MITI, was too great for the industries concerned as well as the rival Ministry of Finance. The combined opposition of MOF and various industrial, consumer, and other groups prevented enactment. The bill finally died in 1963 after having been introduced three times in the Diet.[79] One option left for those who sought to avoid the constraints of the Antimonopoly and Fair Trade Law was evasion through extralegal support for private restrictive practices.

Denied express legal powers to make and implement desired economic policies, MITI resorted to indirect and extralegal means of persuasion. Although many have construed this pattern of administrative direction as a reflection or even a source of bureaucratic power, unless one concedes that MITI's influence within the LDP and the Diet was limited—that ministry officials could not get what they wanted—it is difficult to explain MITI's failure to obtain express statutory authority that would have legitimated its intervention. Surely Japanese officials would have preferred express powers to back up their guidance instead of having to resort to implied powers or extralegal means of coercion. Surely legally exempt restraints on competition were preferable to illegal secret cartel arrangements. The expanded use of administrative guidance was, as Chalmers Johnson notes, "a direct result of the loss of significant portions of its license and approval authority"[80]—a product of political and legal weakness, not strength.

Barely able to preserve, much less expand, any express legitimizing statutory authority, MITI was forced to rely primarily on legal powers inherited from the Occupation. Foremost among these were foreign exchange and foreign trade controls. The legal requirements for export and import licenses and prior approval for access to foreign exchange gave both MITI and the Ministry of Finance substantial leverage in implementing domestic economic policy. The availability of these indirect levers of coercion, however, diminished as Japan liberalized. Equally important, as Japan prospered and Japanese firms grew less and less dependent on direct access to foreign exchange and import and export licenses, their effective use and MITI and Ministry of Finance leverage decreased. The economic ministries—especially MITI—thus operated on borrowed time. Governmental management of the economy and bureaucratic determination of economic policy and its implementation could continue only as long as indirect controls remained viable and a national consensus continued giving economic growth priority over other domestic concerns.

Many observers familiar with Japan in the 1950s and early 1960s would reject outright this description of bureaucratic weakness. It flies in the face of both personal experience and much of the literature on the role of the bureaucracy. What outside observers see, however, is the end result; policies being implemented as if established by bureaucratic fiat. However, closer examination of individual policies and their implementation reveals a consistent pattern of compromise and negotiation both in making and implementing government policies that can only be characterized as a reflection of failure on the part of the economic bureaucracies to achieve their original goals. Veiling such failure from view has been the ability of the bureaucracy to retract or recast its original demands, to make it appear as if the bureaucracy retained control over policy. Japanese energy policy in the 1950s and 1960s, for example, has been described by Martha Ann Caldwell as the work of "a small group of long-tenured and cooperating bureaucrats and businessmen. The policymaking system was in general quite insulated from the fracas of electoral or political debates."[81]

Caldwell thus reaffirms the orthodox view of Japanese economic policymaking as the product of ongoing, close, and cooperative efforts by major business organizations and MITI. Yet when she turns to particular policies and decisions, a very different picture emerges. When fishermen sought foreign exchange in 1954 to import heavy oil directly through the fisheries industry association [*Zengyoren*], they turned to the Diet. Once the Diet committee for maritime affairs began to consider the issue, a foreign exchange allocation was awarded despite vigorous objections by the oil industry. The dispute continued until a compromise was reached in 1957, under which Japan's fishing industry was enabled to import half of its needs.[82]

The oil procurement dispute provides a more accurate view of the realities of policymaking in Japan. Although Caldwell depicts the dispute as a reflection of the "weakness of the oil industry," more to the point is its demonstration of the political strength of fishing interests and the weakness of MITI, at least to the extent that MITI officials desired that the petroleum industry have exclusive rights over oil imports. The relative power of the Diet is manifest. Committee action in the Diet constituted an exercise of sufficient political muscle to force a significant change in policy. In the end, MITI officials were able to remain "in control" but only after compromise and accommodation. In the process, policies MITI desired at the outset were modified or abandoned as a result of outside political pressures.

This process of negotiation resulting in bureaucratic accommodation to economic interests that had access to the Diet or other sources of power exemplifies the predominant pattern of governance in Japan. Consensus was necessary to achieve compliance and compromise was necessary to achieve consensus. Although MITI maintained its central managerial role, it could not effectively dominate the policies that were pursued. Other examples include MITI's inability to withstand pressure in the mid-1950s from other firms to acquire foreign technology after a privileged "target" firm was permitted to conclude a license agreement or to prevent new entry in industries where concentration for economies of scale were desired. Compromise and accommodation thus characterized government plans for the textile, integrated steel, automobile, and electronics industries, to name the more prominent examples. As Yasusuke Murakami has written, "The crux of the administrative regulation in postwar Japan was ... the building of consensus for voluntary compliance in each industry,"[83] a consensus, he might have added, that required negotiated consent, mediation, and compromise.

Cabinet accountability to the Diet, the principal political reform of the postwar constitution, thus had an immediate if not apparent impact. Bureaucratic influence in making policy depended upon influence within the ruling LDP, but the political process in postwar Japan ensured the gradual decline of direct influence within both the party and the Diet. The position of political leaders with ties to the bureaucracy, such as former bureaucrats, inexorably weakened relative to career politicians with strong bases of local political support who had risen from local political offices. Far too little attention has been paid until recently to the importance of regional politics and to the power of local politicians, especially prefectural assemblymen, who in numbers have rivaled former bureaucrats in the LDP since its creation.[84] Relatively weak party identification by Japanese voters, as well as the electoral system of multimember districts, advantages those with local political influence, especially in lower house elections, over former bureaucrats despite the latter's trappings of national influence and prestige. Albeit gradual, political power in the Diet and the LDP steadily shifted away from the bureaucrat and toward the career politician. This shift is reflected not only in the numerical increase of career politicians relative to former bureaucrats in the party, as Fukui has noted,[85] but also in the variety of measures the bureaucratic establishment takes today to preserve influence, from the dispatch of rising bureaucrats to advise local governments to marital alliances between the sons and daughters of political leaders and senior bureaucrats—a more literal coupling of power with prestige.

The formal regulatory powers that Japanese administrations do exercise are also notably weaker than those of comparable governmental agencies in other industrial democracies. The regulatory statutes drafted under SCAP's aegis, such as Japan's antitrust legislation, almost invariably contain extensive investigatory and enforcement powers based on American practice. The lack of judicial contempt powers or any analogous coercive sanctions, as explained in Chapter 5, preclude effective formal enforcement. Despite what appear to be extensive powers to compel witnesses to testify and to obtain documents, no coercive mechanism exists to compel witnesses to respond truthfully or to release documents. Asked what the agency does when an industry association or company executive claims subpoenaed documents cannot be found, an FTC official replied, "In that case nothing can be done" [*shikata ga nai*].[86] For this reason the Japanese FTC is forced to rely almost exclusively on surprise searches or voluntary submissions.

Even Japanese tax authorities often experience difficulty in conducting audits of uncooperative taxpayers. One May several years ago in Tokyo over dinner a former Japanese student mentioned that his father, a psychiatrist, was exceptionally busy at this time of year. Asked why, he replied, "It is tax audit time." To the retort that taxpayers being audited may feel a need to see their psychiatrists, he quickly answered, "it's not the taxpayers but the auditors who see my father." He explained, when tax auditors attempt to enter the premises of many small companies, quite frequently they find the entrance blocked by members of a small business association. What do the auditors do then? "See my father," is his reply. No wonder Japanese businessmen and lawyers express shock and amazement at the U.S. Internal Revenue Service practice of assigning auditors on a continuing basis to major corporations, which must provide office space in their corporate headquarters.

Administrative Guidance: A Reflection of Authority without Power

As a result of the lack of formal legal powers and the weakness of the few legal penal fines that do exist for noncompliance with administrative orders, Japanese government officials have been forced by necessity to rely on informal, extralegal sanctions when coercion is required. Denied express legal powers to make and implement desired economic policies, Japan's economic ministries have had resort to indirect means of persuasion. Barely able to pressure much less expand any express legitimizing statutory powers, MITI, in the late 1950s and 1960s increasingly relied on controls bequeathed by the Occupation. Foremost among these were foreign exchange and foreign trade controls. The threat of denial of foreign exchange or an import license for essential raw materials in many instances was sufficient to achieve desired ends.

The promotional thrust of Japanese economic policy coupled with extensive bureaucratic involvement in the economic life of an industry or firm generally made overt threats unnecessary. The mechanisms of postwar economic policy ensured continual, cooperative relationships between Japan's leading corporations and government officials. Few adversarial issues arose, and those that did could be resolved cooperatively. For this reason, the inadequacy of formal legal sanctions seldom posed a problem. Most governmental actions were designed as benefits and therefore the question of how to compel compliance rarely surfaced. Even where an official request for action may have had some adverse consequences, in most instances the recipient could expect protection from major losses and thus could accommodate official policy. The prevalence of administrative guidance [_gyōsei shidō_] as an informal means of governmental persuasion by Japan's economic ministries is thus partially explained by the policies being implemented to foster economic growth and industrial development. Not all uses of administrative guidance fall into this category, however.

The economists and the lawyers tend to define the term administrative guidance differently. In the literature on Japan's postwar economy, administrative guidance is often equated with the content or substance of Japan's postwar industrial policy. For the lawyer, however, the term is descriptive of a process used to implement public policies as distinguished from the policies themselves. Administrative guidance is defined quite simply as advice or direction by government officials carried out voluntarily—that is, without formal legal coercion—by the recipient. By definition it does not involve either formal legal action on the part of the government or direct legal coercion. Compliance is voluntary therefore only in a narrow legal sense.

As noted in a recent Japanese study,[87] administrative guidance is an academic concept not a technical legal term. As such it has been the topic of considerable scholarly analysis in Japan, the United States, and Western Europe. Japanese legal scholars usually treat the subject in relation to more fundamental issues of administrative law, ranging from direct judicial review or other forms of redress by objecting recipients to the ultimate if more abstract question of the legality of particular instances of administrative guidance.[88]

These are, of course, critical questions for those concerned with the legal issues administrative guidance poses within the Japanese legal system. For instance, the restrictive approach adopted by Japanese courts in defining administrative measures subject to judicial review has insured that neither the recipients nor third parties adversely affected by administrative guidance have had access to the courts except in a few instances through damage actions.[89] Moreover, as a closed process of continuous interaction between government officials and a limited number of private parties, official resort to administrative guidance is also excoriated for exclusion of public participation and political review.[90]

At least in part because Japanese perceive the administrative process in the West to be a formal and more clearly defined procedural process, Japanese observers think of administrative guidance as a uniquely Japanese phenomenon. It is commonly regarded as the product of Japan's particular historical and social context and thus endemic as an aspect of the "Japanese climate."[91] Many western observers similarly emphasize the uniqueness of administrative guidance to Japan. Although all major studies in English and German recognize that practices analogous to administrative guidance can be found in the West, most emphasize the cultural factors that seem to explain administrative guidance as a peculiar Japanese institution. They find the underpinnings for administrative guidance in a neo-Confucian deference to authority and related desire to maintain harmony and cooperation and to avoid adversarial posturing, in other words, in the special social psychology of the Japanese. Paul Davis, for example, lists the persistence of patron–client relations, the continuity of traditional attitudes toward officials, a strongly held desire to avoid confrontation, and a weak "legal consciousness" as its main cultural props.[92] Elaborating upon these points, Wolfgang Pape is more sweeping:

> [T]he vertical structure of Japanese society allows open intercourse between those "above and below" and demarcates only in perpendicular fashion the interests of each group. This prevents formation of class consciousness and leads to a high degree of permeability in the traditional hierarchy from the Emperor to the common people (*shimojimo*). The structure of the smallest community of interest is transmitted to all other social units. Consequently, corresponding patterns of conduct are manifested be-

tween teacher and pupil, employer and employee, large firm and sub-con-
tractor and in like manner between public administrators and private
enterprises, without regard to any identity of interest on a horizontal
level.[93]

Pape adds the "average man's longing for *amae*" and "the reciprocal
obligatory effect [*giri*] of all kinds of favors or acts of benevolence [*on*]"[94]
to his list.

Such analyses cannot be dismissed out of hand. Some explanation is necessary
to explain what appears to be an extraordinary feature of the Japanese system of
governance—that informal requests to produce compliance—for Japanese and
Western commentators alike assert or seem to presume that administrative
guidance is an effective means of implementing policy. "Compliance," Jeffrey
Lepon claims, "is the typical Japanese corporate response to administrative
guidance."[95] Chalmers Johnson makes a similar claim, coining the term "developmental" as a new rubric under which administrative guidance as a cooperative
process for implementing economic policy is viewed as a cornerstone of Japan's
postwar recovery.[96] Although many duly note the role of private business in formulating economic policy and a Japanese stress on consensus, they appear
uniformly to believe that what officials want, officials get by voluntary compliance. Were this true, Japan would indeed be a unique case.

The mist clears and an array of fundamental misconceptions disappear,
however, when administrative guidance is viewed simply as a Japanese species
of informal enforcement. As such, administrative guidance is not peculiarly
Japanese, except perhaps for its ubiquity. Informal enforcement by official
suggestion, advice, recommendation, or pointed direction is not only common
to all legal systems, it is indeed the most common form of law enforcement.[97]
All legal systems depend upon voluntary compliance with the law from the
payment of taxes to regulatory control. No regime except perhaps one of absolute terror relies principally upon direct coercion, and even then compliance
is usually not involuntary in the narrow sense of a response to legally binding
orders backed by immediate and direct threats of compulsion. Fear is a formidable means of coercion.

Informal enforcement by United States antitrust authorities may contrast
starkly with MITI practice in policy but not as process. As described by William G. Shepherd of the University of Michigan:

> [T]he real influence of antitrust reaches much farther than the classic
> federal cases filed and litigated. Most of it occurs unseen through negotia-
> tions and threats that deter mergers and other actions. The antitrust agencies
> often intervene in regulatory cases through informal persuasion, by
> threatening to go to court or through testimony at formal public hearings.
> Such antitrust pressure was important in pushing forward every one of the
> seven major instances of deregulation in the 1970s, from airlines to
> stockbrokers' fees.[98]

Much the same could be said for Japanese antitrust enforcement. The vast
majority of all antitrust violations investigated by Japan's Fair Trade Com-

mission are resolved informally and without publicity either through negotiated settlement or at most the issuance of a warning.[99] Whether labeled administrative guidance or informal enforcement, and whether carried out by Japanese FTC and MITI or United States Federal Trade Commission and Justice Department officials, the process is the same.

What distinguishes Japan is the persuasive resort to informal enforcement in contexts that seem to require formal regulation in other industrial states. In Japan informal enforcement is not *a* process of governing, but has become *the* process of governing. It is used to implement nearly all bureaucratic policy, whether or not expressed in statute or regulation, at all levels of government and all administrative offices. Japanese officials use informal enforcement to implement policy in every conceivable situation from antitrust violations and price controls to regulation of financial institutions. Even bowling alley business hours have been informally curtailed by the police as a means of reducing juvenile crime.[100]

The emphasis on informal enforcement, as Japanese scholars have emphasized, leads to two separate concerns. First, informal enforcement seems in theory to permit Japanese officials significant autonomy in determining the policies to be enforced. Administrative guidance is law enforcement therefore only in the sense that law is equated with whatever policies the officials choose to implement. A series of antitrust decisions from the 1950 Hokkaidō Butter case through the 1980 Oil Cartel cases[101] illustrate MITI's use of informal enforcement to encourage business enterprises to engage in prohibited anticompetitive conduct for which MITI had little or no statutory authority. Second, the resort to informal enforcement appears at least superficially to be effective. If compliance were not forthcoming, would not, one asks, government officials turn to more coercive forms of law enforcement? Thus the persuasive use of administrative guidance itself suggests the effectiveness of informal enforcement in Japan to implement bureaucratic aims.

Analysis of the nature and consequences of informal enforcement in general raises doubt, however, as to the extent of official autonomy and the effectiveness of informal enforcement in Japan. To restate the conclusion, the persuasive resort to informal enforcement in Japan is best explained by two factors: the predominance of promotional as opposed to regulatory policies and the weakness of formal law enforcement. These two factors not only force reliance on administrative guidance as an informal means of implementing policy, but by the same token significantly curtail the autonomy of the bureaucracy in formulating policy. Both the aim of assisting industry and a lack of strong legal sanctions or other forms of formal legal coercion in effect compel officials in Japan to negotiate and compromise with respect to the policies they seek to implement. As a result in many instances—especially in economic policy—private parties possess more leverage in dealing with officials in Japan than in other industrial democracies, particularly the United States. The lack of procedural controls over discretion can thus be explained in that private interests with political influence do not gain by the introduction of formal procedures designed to limit official discretion. In addition, the increasing political influence of business interests relative to the economic ministries and the ruling political party in the Diet ensures that the bureaucracy is unable to acquire the legal powers necessary to overcome their reliance on informal persuasion. This is not to say that informal enforcement is necessarily ineffective or weak from the perspective of the enforcer. The argument is only that unless backed by formal legal powers it becomes a weaker and less effective means of enforcement than formal regulation.

The Consequences of Informal Enforcement

For a lawyer to delve into the causal factors of social behavior is a necessarily speculative venture. However, there is a least a certain commonsense reasonableness in an initial assertion that individuals or other decision-making units of society will ordinarily act in ways they perceive to be in their self-interest to act. The economist's assumption of rational behavior is surely a reasonable point of departure for all facets of social behavior so long as self-interest is defined broadly to include more than economic gain (or avoidance of economic loss) and "perception" of self-interest is acknowledged to be influenced by values and other impulses not subject to economic or other reasoned calculations. With this set of caveats, use of informal means of law enforcement, such as administrative guidance, can be explained as a rational choice by officials in implementing policy. Their decision involves the balancing of gains against costs. Informal enforcement is preferred to the extent it results in the desired conduct without the costs of formal procedures. Conversely, officials will resort instead to formal enforcement wherever the anticipated gains outweigh the costs of enforcement.

Many of the gains relate to the policies being implemented. Some laws or policies may not be particularly important to the enforcement authorities and thus are not enforced diligently or at all. In such instances, the costs of any enforcement are perceived to outweigh the gains. In addition, the importance of a particular policy is not left solely to the subjective judgment of the officials. The primary enforcement officials may not give a hoot about the policy itself but still be diligent law enforcers if they perceive they personally or institutionally have something to gain or lose by their conduct.[102] If, for example, the policies affect strongly held legislative views or the desires of supporters, and the law enforcer fears legislative or bureaucratic wrath if the policies are not enforced, then the gains of enforcement may be considerable.

The costs of enforcement also include a variety of factors. All law enforcement involves the direct costs of time, effort, and personnel. There are also political costs, as evidenced by the United States Federal Trade Commission's attempts to regulate used car sales and funeral home operations.

Compliance with formal law enforcement involves a similar balancing of gains and costs by the respondents. In deciding whether to comply with an informal, nonbinding request by government officials, the respondent balances the advantages against the disadvantages. Informal enforcement is most effective therefore to the extent that what is requested is viewed as ultimately beneficial or relatively more beneficial to the respondent or that failure to comply is perceived to be likely to result in greater disadvantage than would compliance. For example, taxpayers in the United States routinely comply with tax officials' nonbinding requests for audits. To refuse is viewed as a futile and possibly more costly gesture. (However, as noted above, with equal rationality the Japanese taxpayer's response may be quite different.)

Cultural factors are not irrelevant to these decisions. A community or individual sense of the legitimacy of government actions and policies may determine in particular instances whether a party will comply or not. Tax evasion, for instance, increases as taxpayers question the fairness of the tax system. Similarly, what is considered to be an illegitimate request by officials will be likely to produce greater efforts to avoid compliance. Consequently, the Japanese may be more tolerant of informal enforcement than Americans or Europeans, as both Japanese and non-Japanese observers suggest, because of shared attitudes or simply habit. Ultimately, however, such cultural factors do not displace other factors or lead to behavior that does not also serve self-interest except in situations, as posited in Chapter 5 with respect to litigation, where the official or the private party or both would have acted differently out of self-interest but for a cultural imperative. Only if, for instance, the respondent of an official request complies even though doing so runs counter to economic or other gain could an attitude of submission and deference to authority be viewed as determinative. A more realistic model of cultural influence, however, should distinguish deference to authority from submission to power. As explained, the authority of the government officials may not necessarily be questioned, yet their powers to act or to coerce may be effectively denied or challenged.

Because officials are more likely to resort to informal enforcement whenever it is more or equally effective in implementing policy—and it tends to be effective to the extent that the respondents perceive that they will gain by the policies or are likely to suffer greater disadvantage by failing to comply—the determining factors cluster around the nature of the policies being enforced and the certainty and severity of any penalties for noncompliance.

The sanctions for noncompliance may be extralegal. Informal enforcement is used in all systems where it is backed by the threat of formal sanctions or extralegal difficulties. American taxpayers submit to tax audits, as noted, in part because of the authority of the Internal Revenue Service to assess taxes unilaterally but also in part to avoid a closer scrutiny than a routine audit. Of course, the greater the officials' scope of permissible discretionary action, the greater the availability of informal sanctions.

The choice between informal and formal enforcement also involves a comparative calculation of which means is the *more* effective, not which is effective in any absolute sense. Law enforcement authorities must rely on informal means of implementing policy in circumstances where formal enforcement would be *less* or *no more* effective. In such cases, enforcement becomes a process of negotiation and compromise. Officials are forced to bargain and strike the best deal they can get. In this context official policy requires consensus and acceptance by those being regulated, and any demand by officials that is too costly to the respondent will not be implemented. That by virtue of tradition or cultural concerns the officials may put their best face forward, treating as official policy what has been produced by such negotiated consensus, does not alter the basic fact that the policymaker or policy enforcer has little if any real discretion to determine the ultimate conduct of those subject to regulation. Consequently, the discretionary powers of officialdom will not be a matter of any significant concern. Indeed, if anything, private parties gain by the lack of formal procedural restrictions in the decision-making process because they may be able to dominate in informal bargaining.

The availability and certainty of sanctions for failure to comply with government policies is therefore the single most important factor in determining the outcome of informal law enforcement. If sanctions against noncompliance are available and certain, informal enforcement will be used extensively as the most efficient and effective means for implementing policy. If not, informal means of enforcement also will be used, but the outcome will be a product of negotiation and compromise.

Why then, one might ask, would formal enforcement ever be used? The answer is quite simple. First, to be credible as a threat, formal sanctions must both be available and actually used. Unions, for example, must strike from time to time to preserve the efficacy of the threat of a strike for future contract negotiations. So, too, will formal sanctions be tested and applied. Second, as formal regulatory controls by government increase, demand for control over discretionary powers exercised by regulatory authorities also increases. Such demand tends to be satisfied in responsive political systems. In authoritarian political regimes, government officials have both broad legal enforcement powers and discretion. In more democratic or responsive political systems, there is usually less extensive formal governmental enforcement power or more control over official discretion. However, legal controls over discretion in fact reduce the certainty of sanctions and thus arguably produce greater resort to formal enforcement.

Consensual Governance

The avoidance of legal regulation and coercive state control must be viewed as among the most prominent characteristics of governance in postwar Japan. As Richard Samuels insightfully observes: "Although the Japanese state pervades the market, it does not lead, guide, or supervise private interests. There is little evidence that state actors have ever been able to resist political pressures in the absence of alliances with parts of the private sector."[103] He continues by asking:

In three hundred years of coal markets and a century of oil and electric power, where have state actors systematically denied access to particular groups in the policy process? Where have they ignored the demands of labor or small business with impunity? Where have state initiatives been adopted without evisceration and without guarantees? Transformations of energy markets have always preceded state intervention, and state intervention has always conformed to the reconfirmed evolving energy markets. Again we ask not why the Japanese state is so pervasive in the economy but why the pervasive state is so congenial to private firms.[104]

In answer to his own questions, Samuels concludes, "The Japanese bureaucracy does not dominate, it negotiates."[105]

Governmental decisions are not and cannot be unilateral. Legal ordering and state controls are accepted more often than not as a last resort. Individuals and private corporate interests alike seek governmental assistance and protection only out of necessity and the failure of extralegal, nongovernmental mechanisms for preserving a desired status quo or effecting a desired change. The jurisdictional authority of those with political and legal authority may seem pervasive and boundless in scope. However, a myriad of social and political arrangements—not the least of which is the postwar constitutional system of executive political accountability to the legislature and legislative accountability to the electorate—hem in those with any pretensions to authority by reducing and restraining their coercive powers. Authority to command thus may seem limitless in practice but not so the power to coerce.

This separation of power from authority in postwar Japan does not, however, render officials impotent. They remain managers whose capacity to perform their appointed tasks effectively depends upon their skills in achieving consensus and assent. Japan's postwar officialdom thus does not govern in any Western sense of the word. Instead they participate in the processes of governance as mediators, brokers, cajolers, and above all, presiding officials responsible for bargained-for, negotiated policymaking and implementation by reciprocal consent. To quote Samuels once more:

> Reciprocal consent is not uniquely Japanese. In Western Europe similar negotiations over the nature and extent of state intervention have resulted in a market presence for the state—often with considerable support from industry and labor. In Japan the state has been diverted away from market competition entirely. What makes Japan different is the routinization of economic policy which the durability of elites and their constituencies makes possible. Japan is not merely a vat of competing interests; neither is Japan a European government in an American business environment. Rather, the institutionalized routine of negotiation, reciprocal consent, is the tie that binds.[106]

The political, social, and economic consequences of this institutionalized routine are particularly significant for those outside the select enclosures of the system. Reciprocal consent does not work very well when there are too many players. Hence Japan's bureaucratic managers expend considerable efforts in reducing the number of participants. This means keeping outsiders out. Even within the system, hierarchical order prevails with those who have the greatest bargaining power taking lead roles. Above all, the process to work by necessity precludes transparency. By opening it to public participation or scrutiny, it becomes unmanageable and out of control. Frank Upham is surely correct therefore in his assessment that:

> [T]he bureaucracy does retain a surprising degree of control over the pace and course, if not the substance, of social change in Japan, and one of its major instruments for such control is the manipulation of the legal framework within which social change and its harbinger, social conflict, occur. . . . Just as the government uses institutionalized mediation, compensation systems, and affirmative-action grants to avoid or influence the course of conflict in the pollution and discrimination areas, MITI mediates interfirm and interindustry conflict with the goal of facilitating eventual agreement on policy that is satisfactory to the participants and also within government guidelines. The relative power of the bureaucracy vis-à-vis the private sector may be significantly less in industrial policy than in the other cases, but the underlying role of the government as mediator and facilitator within an informal process of conflict management remains unchanged.[107]

In the end, however, the pressures of the marketplace—be it political or economic—become determinative in the formation of policy and its implementation. Law, as most Japanese take for granted, does not control. But it does provide the framework within which consensual ordering occurs or a means of legitimating norms around which a consensus can be formed, and thereby channels behavior. Law is therefore only one of several factors that drive the mechanisms of societal ordering in Japan: social controls.

8

Hamlets and Hoodlums:
The Social Impact of Law without Sanctions

Few of the enigmas of Japan are as acute as the paradox it presents of a society so free from crime, rule abiding, and cohesive with such widespread flouting of law, virulent conflict, and overt thuggery. Although not the complete or even certain answer, such riddles begin to unravel by viewing Japan as a society of law without sanctions.

A legal order without effective legal sanctions need not grind to a halt. Legislators, bureaucrats, and judges may continue to articulate and apply, and thus legitimate, new rules and standards of conduct. The norms thus created and legitimized may have significant impact. To the extent that legal sanctions are weak, however, their validity depends upon consensus, and thus as "living" law, they become nearly indistinguishable from nonlegal or customary norms. As to those norms the community accepts as necessary or proper, the weakness of legal sanctions is likely to produce extralegal substitutes and to reinforce the viability of preexisting means of coercing behavior. The legal order will thus rely increasingly upon community consensus and the viability of the sanctions the community already possesses. The evolution of Japanese law exemplifies this process.

As explained in Part One, a coincidence in the seventeenth and early eighteenth centuries of emphasis within the Japanese governing elite on neo-Confucian values and the demands of polity ensured that justice would remain as inaccessible as possible, with the *mura* functioning as the principal paradigm of effective governance for the vast majority of Japanese. The fragile equilibrium of the early Tokugawa settlement and the centrifugal political forces that pulled power away from the center in the following decades made indirect rule and local autonomy a necessity. Each unit of the society, the lesser communities and the whole—whether *han*, hamlet, city ward, or family—were in effect left alone so long as taxes were paid and outward order and deference to Tokugawa hegemony were maintained. The aim was to preserve and maintain a balance of power that ensured political stability and fostered an expanding commercial economy. The contrast with Europe's island nation is stark. In Angevin England the monarchy achieved dominion by extending the king's justice through greater access to the king's courts and by fashioning new and more effective remedies. Through law the king provided protection for his subjects, thereby weakening the powers of manorial lords and, as a result of his subjects' newfound dependency, expanding the powers of the crown and the emerging state. In England the consequence was a common law for the nation and a vigorous judiciary, which served to mediate first between subject and sovereign and later between citizen and state. At least in England the rule of law thus embodied the combined functions of law both as a means for enforcement of state control and for containment of the authority and powers of monarch and state.

In Japan, notwithstanding the restoration and the transplanted institutions of the modern Western state, community autonomy and weak governance remained hidden behind a veil of ritualized deference to authority. Over time and in different ways and circumstances, the judicial, prosecutorial, and administrative instruments of state power and control were contained; past habits and patterns of social ordering were adapted to a changed political and economic environment. Western legal institutions continued paradoxically, however, to serve as a primary source for regulation and governance. Postwar Japan also witnessed the transference of the patterns of social control within the *mura* to the social and economic organizations of an industrial state with law and legal institutions functioning as vital components for defining legitimate norms and maintaining a framework for stable rule. As the cohesiveness and solidarity of village Japan weakened, the patterns of social control of the hamlet were adapted and strengthened within the firm and factory as well as other predominately urban communities of postwar Japan.

Patterns of Community Control

The carefully articulated penalties that adorned the *ritsuryō* and Tokugawa edicts that so appalled nineteenth-century Europeans were perhaps never as important as the simple community sanction of ostracism and expulsion, especially when joined with vicarious liability. Social control develops new dimensions when landlords are made responsible for the conduct of their tenants, village headmen for the activities of the village at large, or parents for the conduct of their children, and when expulsion from the community and its sustaining resources is an ever-present threat.

These patterns of traditional village—or more accurately hamlet—control persisted well into the postwar era. The hamlet or *buraku*, not the larger village, was in most instances the real locus of community cohesion, solidarity, and control. Without formal administrative or corporate status, the hamlet nonetheless existed by common assent and practice as a territorial unit. The mutual economic dependency of the cluster of households that constituted the hamlet on cooperative effort in maintaining common irrigation and drainage works and to assure access to their scattered landholdings compelled community; and from community, buttressed by shared pastimes and rituals, came the psychological satisfaction of belonging. Added to these centripetal pulls from within were also those from without. The households of the hamlet had learned centuries before that solidarity and cooperation also guaranteed a measure of freedom from outside control. The Japanese hamlet thus adapted quickly to a modern electoral system by voting as a unit after prior community agreement on the candidates most likely to serve hamlet interests.[1]

Submission to the hamlet community was neither an unwanted intrusion on individual autonomy nor an irrational response. Acting for the sake of the household or hamlet and putting the community's interests first seldom entailed denial of self or sacrifice of personal, individual interests. Avoiding self-assertion and yielding to the collective concerns of the community instead enabled the individual to exact greater control over the external environment and events than would have been feasible by individual effort and action. The economic interdependency of the hamlet nullified the first premise of the prisoner's dilemma. Failure to cooperate generally failed to bring even marginal gain and only increased the economic and social risks.

It would be a mistake, however, to characterize the hamlet as a conflict-free community in which coercive means of control were unnecessary or unavailable or to equate community consensus with an expression of unanimous individual consent. As Robert Smith points out in one of the few focused studies of informal, community sanctions in Japan,[2] the hamlet "reveals most clearly its essential character" in defining its collective interests, "for norms are clearly stated and closely sanctioned."[3]

Within the Japanese hamlet, like other closely knit, interdependent communities, a variety of constraints, some gentle, others harsh, ensured conformity to community norms. Smith quotes with approval Robin Williams' 1960 study of American society.[4]

> When in any group or social system there is a high consensus on the *standards* of conduct, ordinary social interaction continually reinforces conformity by precept, example, approval (respect, affection, etc.), and a great variety of complex and often unconscious mechanisms. Behavior is incessantly and subtly corrected by the responses of others; firmly interdependent expectations are integrated into mutually supporting self-other patterns. Incipient nonconformity is subject to immediate and unanimous attempts at control, and overt nonconformity occasions reaffirmation of the threatened norms through disapproval and the imposition of sanctions.[5]

Murahachibu, the ultimate sanction of the hamlet, is well-known. More than mere social ostracism, *murahachibu* deprived the offender and his or her household of the benefits of cooperative activity. Within a highly interdependent community, the penalty was economically and socially severe. As explained by John Embree:

> The most powerful local sanction against a buraku member who does wrong is to refuse him cooperation. This means that he receives no help at housebuilding or at transplanting. Neither can he belong to kō [the various voluntary and informal credit and social cooperatives within the community] and no one will help him bury his dead.[6]

Of uncertain etymology,[7] *murahachibu* represented the community's most extreme sanction. By ostracizing the entire household, the hamlet in effect imposed a form of vicarious liability, thereby inducing in turn the necessity within each household for effective means to control and constrain the behavior of its members. Especially noteworthy are the infractions most apt to incur such extreme community sanction. Above all others were exposure of the community to loss of face and disturbance of its harmony and peace.[8] More telling are the more specific actions understood by the community to produce these unwanted effects, also listed by Smith.

(1) Reporting any community decision or action with which one disagrees to the police or other formal authority, making it public in any way not ordinarily approved by the hamlet.

(2) Failing to maintain an established obligation with other hamlet households, including failure to participate in hamlet sacred and secular group observances such as shrine festivals, association meetings, and meetings of the mutual credit association where these exist.

(3) Failing to acquiesce in a decision of the hamlet association.

(4) Petty thievery, although this is by no means as universally sanctioned by eventual ostracism as are the first three.

(5) Exhibiting a tendency to hostility and to making deliberately critical and undiplomatic statements in public, thus shaming and disturbing others.[9]

As emphasized by nearly all outside observers,[10] the hamlet protected its own interests. The rules of hamlet life related to its immediate need for cohesion, cooperation, and consensus. Harmony was more than a valued ideal. Its breach was a punishable offense. Household obligations to participate in the ritual life of the community and to adhere to the consensual decisions of the community were subject to coercive enforcement. Above all, the legal rules of the state yielded to the customary rules of the community. For a member of the community to breach community mores by appeal to outside authorities, even state law, risked severe social condemnation and ostracism. As essayist Minoru Kida observed in his winsome account of life in the hamlet in the 1940s:

After living in the *buraku* for a time, I realized that it thinks and feels differently from the State about crime. The actions that are punished by ostracism are invariably actions that damage the *buraku* itself. As a rule, of course, most crimes against national law are also held to be criminal by the law of the *buraku*, and the *buraku* assists the police in prosecuting them. But if a violation of the national law does not happen to cause any harm to the *buraku*, the *buraku* is little concerned with it. For instance, blackmarketing, gambling, hunting out of season, and tampering with the election process are all illegal, but the *buraku* makes no attempt to stop them. These are all things that either have existed for centuries or are recognized as means of bringing money into the *buraku*, and the *buraku* will not cooperate with the police in their efforts to stop them. Indeed, when a person guilty of one of these crimes is caught by the police, everybody from the mayor of the village on down attempts to secure his release as soon as possible, and when he returns to the *buraku*, he is still regarded just as highly as before. The society of the *buraku* simply does not classify such actions as criminal.[11]

In other words, the hamlet would itself choose to enforce only those formal, legal rules expressing norms that affected immediate community interests. Unrelated legal rules were of little concern and would be generally ignored and allowed to atrophy unless a failure to report or to enforce them would subject the village to outside censure and shame. Even offenders could be welcomed back into the community's fold without stigma so long as the community was not implicated by their actions. Moreover, disclosure of crime or other legal infractions committed within the community with its approval or by those with authority or representative status headed the list of the most serious community offenses. The combined effect was to ensure not only that only those laws approved by community consensus were enforced but also that those the community or its leaders violated would remain carefully—and coercively—concealed.

Walter Ames completes the picture of hamlet independence from the law's domain in his description of the *chūzai* police assigned to rural communities.[12] As he says:

> There is a certain amount of tension in the role of a *chūzai san* enforcing the law within a social setting that stresses closeness between him and the surrounding community. Police officers by the nature of their job must formally intervene occasionally and invoke legal sanctions when violations of the law occur. Yet this can be at odds with the idea of rapport and understanding between the *chūzai san* and his tightly knit village neighbors. His dilemma is solved by the distinction between *tatemae* and *honne* referred to in the Introduction. The formal *tatemae* is that he enforces the law evenhandedly and rigorously, but in reality (the *honne*) the villagers neither expect nor want him to do so.[13]

Ames' stress on police "rapport" with the community can be misleading. It is important to keep in mind that the *chūzai* police are not members of the hamlet community. Generally rotated at regular intervals, rarely does a police officer serve more than two or three years in any post. Like other organizations of contemporary Japan, the police themselves constitute a separate hamlet-community, socialized to loyalty and solidarity and effectively isolated from the society at large and the urban neighborhoods as well as rural communities to which they are temporarily assigned.[14] Their involvement in the life of the community is artificial. However ubiquitous their presence, however ready to assist or counsel those in need over the most commonplace or intimate personal matter or to give ear to small talk and local gossip, all concerned tacitly understand that their attachment to the community and its concerns is contrived. The police do not belong. As representatives of outside governmental authority, like an occupying army, theirs is an imposed presence.

In response the community is outwardly cooperative and deferent. To the newly arrived *chūzai san* gifts are given and a place of honor at village festivities is reserved. These and other efforts are made to build "human relations" [*ningen kankei*] and are intended, as Ames explains, "to build good will with him so he will not intervene too frequently in their daily lives."[15] Thus the senior officer wisely admonishes the new arrival not to be too zealous in enforcing the law or to act against local customs and mores.[16] Thereby the hamlet manages to restrain the official outsiders it cannot otherwise eject. Their authority remains but their powers are carefully contained. Deference, overt cooperation, and hospitality are used as subtle forms of bribery, corrupting the authorities to allow the community within limits to do what it pleases. Dependent upon cooperation, the police are compelled to defer to community priorities and to enforce the legal rules it agrees to have enforced.

In the hamlet the paradigm of Tokugawa village governance is complete: a cohesive community as a consequence of economic interdependence that is largely self-governing by virtue of indirect rule and the community's capacity to ensure internal order and outward deference to the basic demands of outside authorities.

Commerce has caused this portrait of the Japanese hamlet gradually to fade. With Japan's postwar industrial growth the cohesion and self-governing solidarity of village Japan has dissipated. As nearby commercial opportunities have expanded, the number of part-time farmers and nonfarming households in the hamlet have increased. As rural households have become more heterogeneous in their economic pursuits, they have also become less dependent on the community and cooperation for vital economic needs. Increasingly fragmented, the hamlet is less and less able as a community to define common concerns or to compel compliance with community norms. As predicted by Tadashi Fukutake:

> This process of differentiation further weakens the constraints the hamlet exercises on the individual, and as each separate group of farmers pursues its own particular interests, co-ordinated action of the whole hamlet becomes increasingly difficult. The customary order inevitably changes, and this too weakens the spirit of conformity.[17]

Robert Smith, revisiting "his" hamlet of Kurusu twenty years after his initial study confirms the accuracy of Fukutake's observation.[18] Economic growth, the social and economic cleavage of land reform, an increase in the number of residents who used the hamlet as a place to live but not to work, combined to fragment the once cohesive community. The community was torn apart by a dispute over the acquisition of land by a large food-processing corporation for the purpose of building a broiler-processing factory. Past habits, the bonds of participation in community rituals and ceremonial observances, and affective ties among neighbors were sufficient to maintain a sense of community identity and a desire among most to restore most relationships. Nevertheless its solidarity was lost, absent the glue of mutual dependency and the constraints that held the community together.

It should also be emphasized that community consensus was not the product of unanimous individual assent. Given accepted hierarchies of status and influence, the views of some members of the community counted more than those of others. Habit, custom, and present perceptions of past practice also contributed with consequent advantage in influence to those old enough to speak with authority about past precedents. Cohesion and consensus thus should not be mistaken for an egalitarian homogeneity of authority or influence.

The *Mura* as Model

The Kurusu experience would appear to substantiate the vision of Takeyoshi Kawashima, Japan's internationally renowned legal sociologist. Kawashima posited an evolutionary, historical progression in which Japanese society would move in the direction of the West and "the Japanese attitude toward law, right, and social order will continue to undergo changes in the direction of the patterns of Western society . . . when the traditional social structure becomes disorganized as the process of industrialization proceeds."[19]

Thus far, at least with respect to urban Japan, Kawashima has not been proven correct. The pattern of disintegration evident in the rural hamlet is not representative of Japan as a whole. The *mura* itself may have changed, perhaps even in the direction Kawashima suggests, but not Japanese society at large. Lawsuits have not increased, crime rates continue to fall, and the state and its representative bureaucracies are even weaker than before. Legal controls have not replaced social controls. Quite the opposite has occurred. While cohesion and constraints within the hamlet itself have eroded, they have been introduced or strengthened within the urban political and economic organizations of postwar Japan. The patterns of community ordering of the *mura* have in effect become the models for corporate and bureaucratic organization and control. In the process the patterns of control of the *mura* have become the predominant patterns of governance for the nation.

The literature on organizational behavior in contemporary Japan is replete with examples of hamlet practices transferred into postwar industrial organizations. Writing in the late 1950s James Abegglen had identified three distinctive features of the Japanese factory: permanent employment, seniority-based wage scales, and employee participation in company decision making. Although justified by rhetoric that echoed shared values within the Japanese tradition, all were wartime or postwar innovations consciously adopted, usually as compromises, to deal with immediate needs. Andrew Gordon convincingly demonstrates that these features of "the postwar employment system emerged out of a decade-long contest between unions and managers, refereed by a government generally unfriendly to organized labor."[20] Others have also shown that most of the seemingly "traditional" practices of Japanese labor relations within large-scale enterprises date from the period between 1938 to 1955.[21]

Still culture mattered. Legitimated by shared experience and habit, the patterns of social control in the *mura* were readily available models that could be adopted with relative ease, particularly for the new postwar arrivals to Japan's industrial centers from rural hamlets throughout the country. Shared values and cultural expectations defined options that were socially acceptable and practices that could be imposed with relative ease. With industrialization Japan discovered in its tradition, rather than in the patterns of Western organization, workable, rational solutions that proved suitable in satisfying the particular economic and social needs of the postwar environment.

Take, for example, Thomas Rohlen's description of Uedagin, his pseudonym for the contemporary Japanese bank:

> A company's status and reputation are related to its size and power and also the quality of its personnel. Illegal or improper acts by Uedagin people reflect badly on their company and there is an implicit sense that the company should take responsibility, at least in part for such misconduct. Related is the fact that a high level of employee education, neatness, courtesy, and the like contributes greatly to any company's image and individuals are, in turn, judged by the prestige of their company. In such personal matters as marriage, the extension of credit, the rental of housing, and precedence in public places, one's company affiliation can speak as loudly as personal income, education, or family background.[22]

Substitute hamlet or village for bank or company and Rohlen's description will still be accurate. The company has become the village for its employees. The hierarchy of status and rank, the reliance on participatory, consensual decision making, the emphasis on seniority, and, above all, the subrogation of individual interests by those of the company. In return for the security of membership afforded by permanent employment, the certainty of the *nenkō* system of rewards based on seniority, and participation in the decision-making process, the company gains the loyalty and submission of its employees to its collective control. The postwar Japanese company thus evolved toward a replication of the mutual dependency and individual identification of personal interest with that of the hamlet community.

Like the hamlet the company, too, has two primary concerns—its collective reputation and "face" and internal harmony and cohesion. The slogan for Uedagin, "In harmony and strength," could have applied as easily to Embree's Suye *mura*, Beardsley, Hall, and Ward's Niike, or Smith's Kurusu. Like each of these hamlets, the preservation of harmony and strength implies an effort to preserve autonomy by keeping the authorities and other potentially intrusive outsiders at bay.

Concern for autonomy and the perception of outside intervention as a threat is another widely recognized characteristic of Japanese organizational behavior. Ezra Vogel in his observations on Japan's urban middle class juxtaposes the humility of the residents of Marunouchi in dealing with government officials on the one hand with their tendency "to avoid contact with government officials whenever possible" on the other.[23] As in the hamlet, "cheating and deceiving the government . . . is not considered reprehensible."[24] Collective rather than individual action enhances the ability of the individual to achieve such freedom from governmental control and, in the process of the subordination of individual interests to the group, it is not surprising that in all urban groups Vogel examines he finds that each "has virtually complete autonomy."[25]

Business enterprises display similar tendencies. One example is the reluctance on the part of Japanese companies to disclose any more information about their business activities than necessary to Japanese government officials and other outsiders. For many years, for example, Japanese firms regularly evaded foreign exchange control requirements to file and seek approval for guarantees extended to foreign lenders to support foreign loans, particularly for financing overseas business activities. Japanese law firms were routinely asked to issue opinion letters to foreign lenders on the validity of such unfiled and unapproved guarantees. The validity of these unapproved guarantees was uncertain until the Supreme Court's decision in a 1975 case[26] involving a guarantee by Tōkai Electric Construction K.K. for up to 250,000 U.S. dollars or (40,000,000 yen) for a loan made by the Okinawa Bank of the Ryūkyū. The Court reversed a lower court decision invalidating the guarantee inasmuch as it had not been approved by the Bank of Japan as required under the Foreign Exchange and Foreign Trade Control Law and related regulations. The Court accepted the lower court's view that the transaction violated the law but held that despite the violation the guarantee remained effective and enforceable between the parties. Asked why such approvals were not sought, Japanese company executives would invariably explain that they did not want to disclose the loan since it would invite governmental meddling in company affairs.

Another example—one that illustrates the fundamental difference in Japanese and American attitudes toward governmental assistance—is the propensity of Japanese exporters to seek private, nongovernmental resolution of trade disputes. In the early 1950s, for instance, as U.S. textile manufacturers began to protest with increasing vehemency over the increase of Japanese textile imports, representatives of the Japanese textile industry quietly proposed direct, private discussions with U.S. industry representatives to resolve the matter amicably without governmental interference on either side. The American side rejected the suggestion and proceeded to seek governmentally imposed legal solutions.[27]

The 1965 declaration by the *Keizai Dōyūkai* (Japanese Committee for Economic Development) Committee on Management Policy expressed the prevailing ideology of Japanese business leadership quite well. The leading recommendation called for a renewed emphasis on "independence and self-determination" by business leaders in their relationships with the government.[28] Interpreted in the Japanese context, the emphasis on "independence" was a plea for greater freedom from governmental intrusion, which by the standards of other industrial states, as explained previously, was hardly oppressive.

The impulse toward greater autonomy is also reflected in the response of Japanese business organizations to crimes committed by their employees. To an extent that is extraordinary at least from an American viewpoint, Japanese companies overwhelmingly tend—like the hamlet—to deal with the offender within the corporate community. Once apprehended the offender may be penalized by demotion and transfer or even termination—the company version of *murahachibu*—but once restitution is made and the requisite written apology is proffered, the matter stops. Only in cases involving serious offenses, particularly crimes against persons or property outside of the company, is the infraction likely to be reported to the authorities. A Japanese firm will go to considerable lengths to avoid any public exposure. "Such cases," notes Rohlen, "are usually hushed up."[29]

As in the case of the hamlet, this autarkic closure of the organization influences law enforcement in several ways. With an effective system of internal controls, it relieves law enforcing authorities—whether police, prosecutors, or an economic bureaucracy—of the additional burdens of policing behavior within the organization. Concern with the reputation of the organization and the desire to avoid outsider interference ensure that the organization will perform these functions effectively. It is therefore completely rational for Japanese to rely on the employer in extending credit or otherwise dealing with company employees even in transactions that are entirely personal. The wife of a visiting Japanese professor in Seattle, for example, related that she had decided to sell her car to an employee of the Seattle branch of a major Japanese bank because, she said, she could trust the bank to ensure that the employee acted responsibly and performed any agreed obligations. The aggregate effectiveness of these separate systems of control is reflected in the success Japanese criminal justice authorities have had in releasing offenders to the custody of family or firm once assurances are given that the deviant behavior will be controlled.

On the other hand, again like the hamlet, the organization often gains in this exchange a potentially determinative influence over what legal rules are actually enforced. So long as the infraction does not damage the firm, its principal concern will be to make certain that the infraction is not discovered. Indeed a company can be expected to expend considerable effort to cover up any violation it discovers and to discipline severely any employee that informs the authorities of wrongdoing by colleagues, especially those acting for the company itself.

Although buttressed by a variety of cultural supports, mutual economic dependency was the glue that held the hamlet together. As dependency on cooperative labor and effort among households lessened with the increase of nearby industry and commerce, the economic constraints that required community participation as well as the community's capacity to enforce cohesion weakened together. Economic interdependency is also the primary source of cohesion and constraint in Japan's contemporary urban workplace. Permanent employment combines both a guarantee by the employer of job security plus the curtailment of interfirm recruitment and thereby ties the worker to a single firm and its affiliates for an entire career. The consequence is the forced identity of individual with corporate interest. The worker's income and status are conditional to the employer's success. With few if any viable career alternatives, the worker has substantial economic incentive to make a long-term commitment to the firm and to cooperate to achieve its success. The magnitude of this contemporary form of collective interdependency is indicated in estimates that indicate that a fifth to a third of all gainfully employed Japanese are subject to the constraints of permanent employment. Even this estimate fails to assess the impact of perceived restrictions on interfirm mobility. Whether or not such restraints actually exist is less significant than *belief* that they do. The result is the same in either case: the worker accepts dependency on the community for his or her economic well-being. The ideological appeals to harmony and familial models help to reinforce this commitment, but without the more fundamental economic compulsion, they would not secure its realization.

Indicative of the acute sense of economic dependency is the resort to the threat of economic decline as a manipulative device to enhance employee commitment and productive effort. "Almost invariably," Rohlen observes, "the condition of the world, particularly the financial world, is portrayed as filled with threatening competition. Warnings about various economic hazards that endanger the existence of the institution are repeated often."[30] Despite apparent prosperity, workers are continuously reminded of the perils that only greater effort and sacrifice can overcome. For those who feel dependant on the group, the reminder that enemies are always out there or that other life-threatening dangers exist is as effective a way as any to keep the community together. Such appeals would have little impact if their audience did not already have an acute sense of individual insecurity.

As observed with respect to the *bengoshi*, there is convincing evidence that without a sense of insecurity Japanese tend to act quite independently. Acting alone outside of the framework of hamlet-like communities, Japanese exhibit an even greater degree of nonconformity than do Americans.[31] Group cohesion in Japan is not a product of voluntary action. As Chie Nakane points out, "In fact, in Japan it is very difficult to form and maintain the sort of voluntary associations found so often in Western societies."[32] She goes on to note the failure of postwar attempts to organize American-patterned voluntary welfare groups.[33] Studies also show that workers accept permanent employment out of necessity not choice. Their loyalty and commitment to one firm is a consequence of their economic dependency.[34] The ultimate goal for most Japanese is, like the *bengoshi*, freedom from control by others. Takie Lebra gives the example of the apprentice who "may suffer under a system of patronage and put up with all kinds of interpersonal conflict with his master or *oyabun* because he hopes to be able to stand on his own feet some day. Becoming *ippondachi*, 'independent,' is the ultimate reward."[35] The popular conception of Japanese "group-orientedness" as if it were some inbred psychological trait or immutable sociological condition approaches utter nonsense. Japanese do not function well in large groups or associations without the compulsion of perceived dependency or personal gain.

This said, however, from birth to adulthood, in home, school, and workplace, Japanese are socialized to the ways of individual submission to the community in order to achieve a greater degree of autonomy than would be possible through individual action. The effects of such socialization evidenced by the ability of individual Japanese to respond effectively to the group and to deal with a collective environment should not, however, be mistaken for personal preference. The repeated references to conformity and collective, cooperative, or collusive behavior in descriptions of Japanese society nearly always refer to examples of collective efforts to induce or compel conformity. Rewards and penalties are indeed used with little hesitation to create and maintain group solidarity and the priority of community interests above those of its individual members. The outwardly yielding but ambitiously competitive member of the group is the one who usually gets ahead.

The transformation of the Japanese firm in the early postwar period to a hamlet-like community occurred in the broader context of reinforcing changes in the legal system. The containment of legal controls, particularly in criminal and regulatory law enforcement, operated as an external stimulus. The salaried worker in Japan's large-scale industrial and financial enterprises were not the only Japanese disturbed by the disorder and insecurity of the immediate postwar period. Nor were business enterprises alone in their reluctance to invest new powers of social control in the state—especially one subject to the military occupation of an alien conqueror. Other Japanese, too, found in collective arrangements and controls a form of self-protection removed from state direction. The absence of legal sanctions and controls had direct impact on both the retention of earlier forms of social control as well as the creation of new ones. Boycotts, refusals to deal, and other forms of modern *murahachibu* became the most prevalent means by which social order was maintained.

Community or group cohesion is inexorably intertwined with such informal sanctions. Ostracism is not effective in a mobile society in which the benefits of membership in one group can be easily had by independence or by joining another. However, where one of the primary benefits of the community is its capacity to maintain stability and order, its ability to sanction reinforces its cohesion. Independent action becomes a risky alternative and access to other groups becomes more difficult.

Clientage, too, is the product of a demand for security by those who are unable to fend for themselves and whom the general community is unable to protect. In any society where the state fails to secure its citizens against social and economic risks there may be no choice but to attach oneself to those who can. The inability of the formal legal system in Japan to provide effective relief, to impose meaningful sanctions, thus tends to buttress the cohesion of groups and the lesser communities of Japanese society and to contribute to the endurance of vertical, patron–client relationships. The use of private mediators, reliance on banks and other large enterprises, the role of the *yakuza* and organized crime all fit this pattern of conduct. The features of postwar

Japanese society so often labeled as vestiges of a familial, neo-Confucianist, or feudal past tend upon closer examination to have been adaptations of social controls, legitimated perhaps by traditional symbols and ideological claims, designed to satisfy a basic need for security against risks the state is unwilling or unable to provide.

Consensual Sanctions

The demand for ways to reduce the risks and costs intrinsic to a volatile social and economic environment is also manifest in the prevalence of dependency and relational contracting. The oft-repeated Japanese penchant for informal, long-term contractual relationships, in which "goodwill" and personal trust are more important than written contracts, is symptomatic of transactional relationships in which the parties rely more on morals and markets than laws for enforcement. Without reliable legal sanctions, the words in a written contract are just words, no matter how carefully drawn. Although the party whose bargaining power remains strong perhaps need not be concerned, the weaker party has little choice but to rely on the "fairness" or "benevolence" of the other. Thus both sides—strong and weak—reach the same conclusion: if the agreement is reduced to writing at all, a vaguely worded document will suffice. On the other hand, when contracting abroad within legal systems Japanese believe are likely to enforce their agreements, they negotiate and draft with extreme care. Similarly, a Japanese firm will assiduously abide by adverse commitments to its contract partners in cases where sanctions—either informal, arising out of either their relative bargaining positions or the promise of an ongoing relationship, or formal, such as the likelihood of legal action—are perceived to be strong.

In a world of relational contracting, reputation and trust in one's constancy in performing obligations becomes essential. Trying to explain the difficulties of collecting debt in Japan to an exasperated foreign client who wanted to recover the sales price of goods sold to a small Japanese firm, a Japanese attorney finally said, "You should just write it off. The fellow was untrustworthy and that's that." A Japanese banker, asked about the problems the bank had faced in foreclosing security interests, retorted, "We don't lend to people who default."

Such incidents illustrate the nexus between reputation and weak law enforcement. When sellers and lenders cannot expect to obtain relief in the event of default, either they do not sell on credit or make loans, or they take great care to ensure that they are not selling or lending to "people who default." In other words, one's reputation for trustworthiness can become a necessity of commercial life. When community and patron provide the most important substitutes for formal sanctions, one's reputation will depend in large measure on affiliations and sponsorship. Thus in Japan, as most foreign businessmen and scholars know from personal experience, introductions are essential. Even law firms regularly, if politely, turn away potential clients who do not have proper introductions. Without introductions businessmen, government officials, libraries, and schools are often inaccessible.

Implied in such practice is a type of informal suretyship, that is, the reputation (but not formal legal liability) of the group and patron that depends in part on the conduct of the member and the client. In fact, few practices are more ubiquitous in Japan than the use of such suretyship. Letters of guarantee are unusually common as the prerequisite for an extraordinary variety of activities: immigration, loans, employment, and leases. One can hardly enter a legal relation in any context without having someone as guarantor. Such contracts have little legal significance despite (and to some extent because) of their breadth. Few would even think of enforcing most of these guarantees in court. They are demanded instead on the premise that the loss of reputation the guarantor suffers as a result of any misconduct of the person vouched for will itself restrain if not prevent such mischief. In other words, reputation too is vicarious.

The conduct and reputation of the members of the group or the client affect that of the group or patron. Thus the benefits of group membership and clientage come to depend in part on the capacity of the group (including the family in extreme cases) or patron to deny access or expel those who damage reputation. Again the pattern repeats: such needs reinforce the cohesion of the group and the power of the patron and thus the effectiveness of the informal sanctions they wield.

It should be apparent that in these cases the concern of the group or patron focuses on loss of reputation, not the conduct itself. To the extent that the group accepts the norm and wishes to enforce it for its own merits, there is no need to be concerned with reputation. To protect against loss of reputation, the group must enforce norms that other groups or the community at large see as legitimate and important regardless of its own attitude. As a result, as in the case of the hamlet, it is not the misdeed that is condemnable but the loss of reputation resulting from disclosure and outside knowledge of the misdeed. Thus, one discovers in Japan that failure to abide by the law may be known to, but not condemned by, the group. Yet as soon as the infraction becomes public, group condemnation follows. Again what emerges is a pattern of pervasive nonconformity, masked by outward conformity. Legal rules may be outrageously flouted so long as all appear to be punctilious in their observance.

One of the best examples of how effective the substitution of private contractual arrangements within a relatively small group of actors with a common, identifiable interest is the Japanese financial clearing house rule that member banks—that is virtually all commercial banking institutions in the country—must discontinue for two years to transact any type of business, deposits, or loans, with a customer that defaults twice within a six-month period on any promissory note or check. Since no firm can long stay in business without at least a bank account for deposits, promissory notes in Japan are nearly as secure as cash (and are in fact frequently required by creditors as a form of collateral). Japanese banks have in effect substituted a purely contractual mechanism for enforcement for a legal one. In Taiwan and Korea, for example, resort to the prosecutor and the criminal process is the principal threat against failure to pay a note when due or passing a bad check.[36] The clearing house rule itself is another "private" sanction. Any bank caught cheating by continuing to do business with a defaulting customer is itself subject to suspension.

Such sanctions only work—that is to say, the community can exercise coercive power—only when each member has something to gain by belonging or to lose by withdrawal. Dependency on the group—in the case of banks and promissory notes, dependency on the clearing house—and the willingness of the group to exclude or expel are required. Weak law enforcement and legal controls limit alternative means of protection and thereby foster such dependence. In turn, the strength of the community as defined by both the degree of dependency of its constituents and its solidarity in defending community over individual interest make possible its alternative to state-directed legal controls.

Another consequence is enforcement of formal legal rules without community consensus. As noted previously, to the extent that private litigation and especially the criminal process disclose violations of the law and thus damage reputation, the threat of a lawsuit or criminal complaint may produce a positive reaction. As explained in Chapter 5, the reluctance to be involved in a lawsuit operates to ensure the effectiveness of legal rules because the filing of a lawsuit produces a settlement that conforms to the likely outcome of a judicial decision. Hence the weakness of judicial enforcement powers does not necessarily make law irrelevant. The social stigma of the disclosure of wrongdoing can function as an equally effective and far more efficient substitute for state coercion.

The Dark Side of Social Controls

The vision of Japan as a society dominated by closely knit, interdependent communities and carefully cultivated, mutually supportive interpersonal networks enveloped in the rhetoric of harmony may perhaps beguile those who suffer from a sense of loneliness and isolation in environments that stress individual independence and the "spot" transaction. There is, however, a dark side to Japan's resort to social controls. Implicit in reliance on community rather than the state in maintaining social and economic order is the substitution of private for public means of direct coercion.

The obvious example is the gangster as enforcer. Japan's underworld of organized *yakuza*, *tekiya* street venders, and since the end of World War II, *gurentai* street gangs play an important role at the margin of mainstream society. In addition to business operations in prostitution, pornography, loansharking, and construction subcontracting, Japan's *yakuza* also provide enforcement services in aid of debt collection, leasehold evictions, and a wide range of other transactions. The boundaries between legitimate and illegitimate activities begin to blur, however, as enforcement turns to extortion in skimming money from bars, restaurants, and other establishments that use gangs to handle difficult customers or, in the case of the *sōkaiya*, paid gangster shareholders who have been hired by management to keep dissenting shareholders in line.[37]

The impact of reliance on social controls has even more troubling aspects than ensuring a societal need for organized crime. Japan's experience challenges the fundamental legal dichotomy between state and societal action. Constitutional and other legal constraints designed within the context of the Western legal and political tradition to secure freedom of the individual against the state have little relevance in a society in which the principal source of restraint is the community not the state. To paraphrase University of Tokyo constitutional law scholar Yōichi Higuchi, freedom from the political powers of the state receives wide public support, but freedom from the exercise of societal powers is offset by legal theories that deny the state the power to intervene. Not only are the constitutional and political protections against state restrictions not applicable in cases of "private" community restraints, but they themselves also become barriers preventing the state from intervening to protect the individual against the community.[38] Hence oppressive conduct by a private organization, whether school, company, or other institution, is beyond the reach of both constitutional guarantees designed to protect against state oppression and the state's power to provide redress. As Higuchi says, legal theories that recognize that juridical persons have the same civil rights against the state as individuals combined with policies that are designed to foster self-governing autonomy within the "segmented" communities of the society leave the individual without redress.[39]

Lawrence Beer strikes a similar discordant note in his exhaustive analysis of Japan's Supreme Court and lower court decisions involving free expression and related constitutional rights. "Free speech," he concludes, "seems regularly violated by private individuals and groups, as is the right not to be involuntarily exposed to another's views."[40] As Beer recognizes, "There is often little or nothing that law and government can and/or," he surprisingly adds, "should do to interfere with this aspect of the flow of private life."[41] He illustrates his point with the example of *Sōka Gakkai Free Speech* case. The *Sōka Gakkai*, one of Japan's best-known postwar religious movements, combines *Nichiren Shōshu* Buddhism with the educational views of schoolteacher Tsunesaburō Makiguchi and his protégés, Jōsei Toda and Daisaku Ikeda. During the sect's early proselytizing efforts, its members engaged according to most accounts in extreme forms of persuasion. These included bombarding the residence of a targeted family with as much noise as possible until at least one member of the family agreed to join. (This tactic is also used by gangster enforcers to force eviction of unwanted tenants or payment of an otherwise uncollectible debts.) In other cases the prospective member would be held involuntarily and subjected to continuous threats of the calamities that would come to those who resisted.[42] "The association and many of its activist members have been accused often," says Beer, "and sometimes justly, of violating individual rights by their aggressive methods of proselytizing, such as *shakubuku* ('to break and flatten'), and of silencing or attacking critics."[43] The *Free Speech* case involved such an attempt to silence critics. In 1969 two books were published attacking the *Sōka Gakkai* and its related political party, the *Kōmeitō* ("Clean Government Party"), one by Hirotatsu Fujiwara, a Meiji University political science professor, and the other by journalist Kunio Naitō. When advertisements announcing publication of Fujiwara's book appeared, various persons associated with the *Kōmeitō* or *Sōka Gakkai* began to pressure Fujiwara not to publish his book or at least delay publication until after the upcoming general elections and to limit the number of copies. Offers were also made to the author and publisher to buy up most of the copies. They were refused. However, when the book was printed, no distributors would market the book except on a specific order basis. Although distributors denied that they were bowing to pressure, a number of bookstores confirmed that they had been threatened with a *Sōka Gakkai* boycott. Both Fujiwara and the publisher were also subjected to a barrage of threatening letters and telephone calls.[44]

Beer quotes Kunio Naito's description of his experience:

> In spite of our secret editing work to preclude attempts to interrupt publication, the first galley proof somehow found its way into the hands of Komeito party leaders. [The] Chairman and Vice-chairman of the Komei Party demanded corrections and deletions. They told me they would not allow me to criticize President Ikeda. . . .
>
> Several distributors suddenly canceled contracts to distribute my book, saying that they did not want to be involved. . . . Ads for my book were also refused by the major newspaper publishing companies a day before the scheduled day of publication. . . . Several weekly magazine reporters interviewed me after learning about the attempts to suppress publication. Unfortunately, none of their stories got into print. . . .
>
> The situation became worse. Considerable copies of my book . . . disappeared from their [bookstore] bookshelves. The bookstore owners told me that men from the *Seikyo Shinbun* had asked them to take my book off their shelves.[45]

The controversy ultimately became a major political issue led by the Communist Party in both the national House of Representatives and the Tokyo Prefectural Assembly.

A similar example is the use of *kyūdan tōsō* [denunciation struggle] and other forms of what Frank Upham has aptly labeled "instrumental violence"[46] by the Buraku Liberation League. As described by Upham:

> Simply stated, denunciation is the attempt by a group of league members to convince one or more majority Japanese to adopt the BLL interpretation of a particular event, language, or policy that the BLL considers discriminatory. Although this tactic frequently consists of no more than two or three Burakumin explaining the BLL's wishes to a local bureaucrat, it differs from mere persuasion or the exercise of free expression in that implicit in all denunciation is the actual or threatened use of limited physical force by large groups of Burakumin.[47]

Upham goes on to describe the Yata incident in which members of the Liberation League forcefully kidnapped three teachers and subjected them to eighteen hours of continuous verbal and physical harassment and abuse.

Few university professors in Japan are unaware of the similar abuse inflicted upon a Tokyo University professor who in a speech given in West Germany used a common term for *Burakumin* that the league considers objectionable. Someone in the audience apparently taped the speech and sent it to the Liberation League, which then proceeded with the "denunciation" of the professor's conduct. The effect was immediate. Even when teaching abroad, Japanese university professors carefully avoid the forbidden word and even correct students who use it unknowingly.

Radical student tactics also fit the pattern of instrumental violence. The "trashing" of professors' offices was common in the late 1960s and for many years private and public university administrators have surrendered control over student dormitories to their politicized occupants, who ensure ideological continuity by carefully screening all applicants and rejecting any who do not satisfy rigid tests of political orthodoxy.

Such episodes can perhaps be explained by the indifference of governmental authorities to oppression and abuse within or between communities considered socially or politically marginal. A laissez-faire attitude toward conflict between the *Sōka Gakkai* or the *Burakumin* Liberation League and Communist Party members can be likened to tolerance of intergang conflict, or to use an example from George A. de Vos, sexual abuse by hoodlums of delinquent girls.[48] Such interpretation, however, leaves out the intimidation of Japanese from all walks of life, from university professors and students to corporate executives and small shopkeepers. Nor is such an explanation consistent with the failure of law enforcement authorities to intervene and deal effectively with the coercive pressures applied to government officials themselves. As in the case of the tax auditor, only a state without the power to protect or control could fail so completely to maintain civil order. Only the containment of legal controls and the resulting reliance on constraints imposed by the constituent communities of a segmented society—of authority without power, of legal command without legal coercion—suggest an adequate answer.

Law as *Tatemae*

Despite the relative weakness of law enforcement and state power, law and legal institutions remain vital. They have not atrophied from neglect. Quite the contrary, within the context of the peculiar mix of state authority and community controls, the institutions and processes of lawmaking and enforcement play an especially significant role. Law functions as *tatemae* in establishing the legitimate norms of principle that demark both ideals and boundaries. Although a violation of law may be condoned within a group and tolerated in fact by law enforcement officials and the society at large, public exposure of such infraction requires a response. As explained previously, the threat of a lawsuit, the filing of a criminal complaint, and even a formal appeal of a governmental decision commonly produce a quick response and a settlement that approximates the legal rule. This is not, it should be emphasized, akin to a double standard, one rule for public conduct and the other for private behavior. There is only one generally applicable rule, that articulated as law. Exposed infractions do therefore cause dishonor and shame not only upon the individual offender but also the community that tolerated or failed to prevent the offense.

Legal rules are relevant. They establish the norms of legitimate conduct and action. Although enforcement may be left to the community, the community is not totally free to ignore the law. Disclosure activates a process of general condemnation, including action by the appropriate law enforcing authorities. Depending upon societal perceptions of the seriousness of the offense, censure of the offender and his community may be stringent. Although ultimately a responsive apology and compensation may suffice, the stigma of shame and loss of face and reputation can be severe. In a society in which individual achievement depends heavily upon one's own reputation and that of the group to which one belongs, "face," like company goodwill, is a valued asset. Hiroshi Iyori, former commissioner and secretary-general of Japan's Fair Trade Commission, writes, for example, with complete candor and seriousness of the importance the denial of an imperial *kunshō* (national honors awarded annually to persons of outstanding merit) as a major deterrent to antitrust violations in Japan. Illegal collusion to restrict output or fix prices was reduced significantly after 1977, Iyori asserts, in part because of the introduction of an administrative surcharge on illegal profits but also, in Iyori's words:

> [B]ecause government conferral of a coveted decoration of honor on the president of a trade association that is involved in an antitrust violation is subject to suspension. Specifically, when an FTC decision finds an association to have violated the Antimonopoly Law, its president is considered ineligible for national honors for a period of three to five years.[49]

For the media such reactions serve as a major source of power. As the recent toppling of two prime ministers in rapid succession indicates, Japanese newspapers wield awesome influence in their capacity to expose and embarrass. Similarly, the legally mandated submission of the cabinet to questions in the Diet during parliamentary interpolation—which many American observers seem to ignore altogether or take to be of little importance—provides a major legislative check on executive power. As governmental officials readily acknowledge, the threat that a minister might be embarrassed by a question in the Diet implicating a ministry official in some sort of illegal activity or other misconduct functions as a powerful internal deterrent to official wrongdoing.

Litigation also acquires special significance in such an environment. As a forum for public disclosure of socially unacceptable conduct or as a process for developing public awareness and building consensus, litigation can be manipulated as an effective instrument in either community enforcement of existing legal rules or social change. Frank Upham's studies of a wide variety of litigated social disputes from the pollution cases to women's rights provide ample evidence of the effectiveness of lawsuits in influencing social and political change, less, however, with respect to the ultimate court judgment or award than in the influence of the lawsuits on public opinion and the political process. The suits brought by the victims of toxic waste and other forms of air and water pollution as well as by women seeking judicial redress for denial of equal employment opportunities were in the end far more significant for their political outcome than for the judicial judgments they produced.

The first major legislative initiative to deal with industrial pollution in Japan, for example, came in 1967,[50] the year in which the first of the "Big Four" pollution cases was filed.[51] Similarly, the major statutory scheme to aid victims of pollution was enacted in 1973[52] just as the first decisions in these cases were being handed down.[53] The evidentiary hearings in these cases, which were extensively reported in the media, stimulated and fostered public reaction and legislative response. The pollution suits were thus more effective as political instruments to effect a new consensus and thereby to influence the legislative process, than as a process through which the courts functioned as an institutional forum for making policy in redefining the applicable legal rules. All Japanese, including industrialists and government officials, surely shared a sense of horror at what unregulated industrial waste was doing to their land, air, and water. While the solutions adopted were bureaucratic, they surely made more sense and were more fair than incidental litigation with its costs, lack of uniformity, and delays. Few besides those who wished to use the pollution issue to achieve a radical transformation of Japanese society, with its unknowable consequences, have grounds to argue against the legislative outcome.

The steady recurrence of litigation challenging the constitutionality of Japan's Self-Defense Forces can be explained in similar fashion. Given the improbability of a Japanese Supreme Court decision invalidating Japan's defense policy, the purpose of bringing these actions is reasonably assumed to be to keep the issue before the public. Take, for example, the *Naganuma* litigation.[54]

The case involved a lawsuit brought in 1968 to challenge the redesignation of a forest preserve in order in the "public interest" to build a Nike-Zeus missile base near the town of Naganuma in Hokkaidō. The event presented an ideal case for an article 9 challenge to the constitutionality of Japan's Self-Defense Forces. The plaintiffs first sought a court decision to suspend the effect of the administrative redesignation necessary to build the base. They won in the district court but lost on appeal to the high court.[55] As the litigation continued to a decision on the merits in 1973, the base had been completed. Having lost whatever significance the case might have had in terms of either preventing or delaying the construction of the missile base, the lawsuit in American practice would have continued to be justified only by the possibility of a Supreme Court decision that the Self-Defense Forces were unconstitutional. However, the plaintiffs refused to accept the government's offer to make a special appeal to the Supreme Court, which would have by-passed the high court and prevented further delay of a final determination of the issue. This refusal to allow the special appeal was based on tacit recognition by the plaintiffs and their attorneys that they had no hope of winning on appeal. They knew they would lose but still persisted. Why? The *Naganuma* case and other lawsuits challenging the Self-Defense Forces that continue to be brought can be viewed as a form of political action. So long as the issue continues to be litigated in well-publicized cases, a political consensus against the Self-Defense Forces may be forged or at least one favoring their legitimacy remains in doubt.

Still another example of the use of lawsuits to achieve political aims is the litigation over legislative malapportionment. Lawsuits challenging the Japanese Diet's allocation of representative and councilors per district under the guarantee of equality of article 14, paragraph 1, of the postwar constitution are filed almost routinely after every national election. The applicable constitutional principles developed by the Japanese Supreme Court are reasonably clear. Beginning with the Court's 1964 decision rejecting the principle of absolute equality in *Koshiyama* v. *Chairman, Tokyo Metropolitan Election Commission*,[56] the first malapportionment case decided by the Court, through the Court's landmark 1976 judgment in *Kurokawa* v. *Chiba Election Commission*[57] and subsequent decisions in 1983,[58] the Court has articulated a rather precise standard. The constitutional mandate is considered to be satisfied so long as the maximum disparity between districts does not exceed a per voter ratio of representatives of roughly 1 to 3. Yet since the *Kurokawa* case, there has been little hope of positive judicial relief to remedy the chronic malapportionment of the Japanese Diet. Other than affirming the constitutionality of the electoral system the Supreme Court is likely to continue simply to issue declaratory judgments when the threshold level of "unreasonableness" is reached, holding that the electoral system is unconstitutional without invalidating elections or mandating action by the Diet. Why then do these cases continue to be brought? Again the answer seems to lie in the political impact of the judicial declaration, in other words, of law as *tatemae*. Protracted litigation calls into question the legitimacy of the political system with consequently greater likelihood—albeit no certainty—of a political response.

In like manner, conflict and social protest function as catalysts for political and social change in Japan. For those in authority whose legitimacy rests on an assurance of benevolent rule—that is, fairness and order—and oversight in the interest of the nation or society at large, any uncontained conflict and protest threatens. Accompanied by claims of illicit activities or other conduct in violation of the society's shared understandings regarding proper behavior, social protest is even more provocative. Exposure in this context of official neglect or active wrongdoing becomes more than a simple offense by individual actors. It is accepted by all concerned as evidence of failure by those in authority to satisfy the standards of proper governance and, especially in the case of official misconduct, is construed as a disturbing challenge to their legitimacy. When powerless to suppress or contain social conflict, governmental officials and others in authority respond by making every effort to eliminate its cause. By forcing such response to underlying social ills, social protest thereby becomes effective as an instrument of political action and change.

Power, Consensus, and Fairness

Karel van Wolferen may be the first foreign observer of contemporary Japan to have accurately analyzed in print the "riddle of power" in postwar Japan. In Japan, he writes, "power is diffused over a number of semi-self-contained, semi-mutually-dependent bodies which are neither responsible to an electorate nor, ultimately, subservient to one another."[59] "Japan," he continues, "is pushed, or pulled, or kept afloat, but not actually led, by many power-holders" in what he labels as an "elusive system."[60] Unfortunately, van Wolferen does not follow the logic of his analysis to conclusion. Excluded from "the system" as he describes it are opposition party leaders; pollution, consumer, and other social activists; as well as other antagonists who oppose it. Those who remain within the "system" turn out to be the familiar roster of bureaucrats, ruling party politicians, business leaders plus an establishment press and others who hold positions of authority and influence.

Those who seek villains and heroes and prefer to separate the black hats from the white by the quantum of power they wield are likely to doubt van Wolferen's analysis of the fragmentation of power but find comfort in his rather inconsistent conclusions. If so, they, too, are wrong. Take van Wolferen's initial proposition to its logical conclusion and indeed the riddle of power in Japan does begin to unravel. Power is diffused so widely among the many constituent groups of Japanese society—including even outcast and other socially marginal communities—that like the economist's model of economic power in highly fragmented, competitive markets, it can only be exercised with cooperation or collusion. Even then, the effective exercise of power is usually of short duration or limited scope. Van Wolferen's "system"—this "something, neither 'state' nor 'society' that nevertheless determines how Japanese life is lived and who obeys whom"[61]—reflects in reality a multitude of social, political, and economic bargains—give-and-take understandings, arrangements, spot and relational contracts by, between, and among competing groups forced to cooperate out of nationwide mutual dependency—and at times a perceived or imagined outside threat.

The aggregate is a remarkably resilient social and political order. To be sure, it appears to be fragile, a delicately balanced equilibrium held together by its own dynamics and always, it seems, in danger of collapse. Yet, again, like the extraordinary durability of the economic marketplace, however volatile, Japan's postwar consensual order self-adjusts and manages to endure.

The only real antagonists to van Wolferen's system, thus redefined, are those who seek either a concentration of power or its even greater diffusion through personal, individual empowerment—goals that, from the example of the concomitant rise of individualism and state power in the West, are not as inconsistent as they may at first appear. Care should be taken, therefore, not to misconstrue social and political conflict over authority in Japan as a contest between those who hold power and those who do not. Such struggles exist but seldom surface beyond the confines of the communities in which they take place. The power brokers of contemporary Japan are those who can manipulate best the community sanctions and the informal, consensual levers of coercion, however peripheral they may be in terms of Japan's hierarchical concentration of authority at the center. Japan's visible conflicts most often represent the last act in a successful play by those with power to force reform on those in authority.

With authority and power both constrained, consensus and fairness become essential aspects of the social glue that holds the system together. As Ronald Dore argues in a keenly perceptive little book, "Japan's competitive edge is not a matter of efficiency in the allocative sense," but rather in societal interrelationships and processes that "generate a sense of fairness which enables people to work cooperatively, conscientiously, and with a will." Whether or not founded, as Dore asserts, upon a Confucian premise of "original virtue"[62] or some other source, Dore correctly perceives that a myriad of social, political, and economic relationships induce those with either authority or power or both to behave more benevolently. In the Japanese cultural and institutional matrix fairness is "an efficient strategy for the retention" of both.[63] Governed less by coercive command than a participatory process of negotiation and bargained-for consent, postwar Japan has developed a set of social, political, and economic arrangements that must reflect a sense of what is fair by those whose consent to authority and power is necessary.

Any discussion of power defined to emphasize coercive force for purposes of analysis necessarily overstates its role. The impact of persuasion in many if not most instances may be far more crucial in determining the outcome of any decision or of social behavior and conduct. To slight the power of those in authority is not, therefore, to deprecate their influence, especially their capacity to manage the process of building consensus and thereby to exercise considerable control over the outcome. This is the primary lesson of Frank Upham's narratives on bureaucratic reaction to social protest and industrial policy. Nonetheless, neither power nor manipulation is the primary source of authority's influence. To let Ronald Dore have the last word: "A *persuasive* norm carries its own clout. Sanctions become less crucial if the norm is endowed with some morally compelling force which reduces the impulse to deviate and bring sanctions into play."[64] In a society in which coercion and sanction cannot easily be brought to bear to prevent deviation from established norms, it becomes all the more necessary for those norms to carry that "morally compelling impulse." They must be recognized as fair. For all the conflict, inefficiency, and dysfunction manifest in so many aspects of postwar Japanese social, political and economic life, Japan maintains a remarkably just as well as stable social order.

Conclusion: Command
without Coercion

Words fail to convey the nature and process of governance in Japan. No commonly accepted paradigm of how policy is made and enforced seems to fit. Terms like "regulation," "control," "freedom," and even "autonomy" and "consensus" seem oddly inappropriate. We can perhaps explain and thereby begin to resolve the quandary by examining what might be called an enthymeme of authority, an unstated premise in most other legal and political orders that with authority there must also be power, that the authority of the state to command necessarily implies its power to coerce in order to implement and enforce those commands. Divorce power from authority as in Japan, however, and the capacity of the state to direct and control, not just to intervene and participate, becomes principally a function of its ability to persuade, bargain, or cajole in order to induce consent. Without adequate means of coercion the state can only assure the effective enforcement of policy through influence and inducements to win consent.

In such contexts, to be effective governmental commands can seldom be unilateral or perceived as unfair. Even to describe them as governmental decisions is in many instances simply to locate the situs of the action but not the actor. This is because with only the authority to make policy, and without power to enforce it, those who govern need to have the consent of those whose cooperation or compliance is necessary for such policy to be implemented successfully. Consequently, those affected have a significant voice in the process of forming policy and an even greater opportunity to participate in its enforcement. The separation of power from authority in governance thus denies the state the capacity to choose to permit participation. It is forced upon it.

For Japan this process of rule—consensual governance—has been the product of institutional history and cultural environment, not intentional political choice. Buttressed by institutional and cultural props, the unstated premise of authority without power and consensual governance has thus become an inextricable feature of the Japanese legal order.

In both the West and the sinicized legal traditions of East Asia, law in effect defines the state's authority and its powers and is concomitantly the state's dominant instrument of social control. Consensual governance, on the other hand, implies a very different paradigm of the nature of law and its function, one that varies considerably from Japan's East Asian neighbors as well as its Western partners. We cannot then begin to understand the role of law and social controls in Japan without an appreciation of these contrasts.

First, as I have argued, the domination in Japan until the mid-nineteenth century of a concept of law derived from the imperial Chinese bureaucratic tradition was critically important in that it defined law narrowly in terms of state-made and bureaucratically enforced penal and administrative regulations, a definition that excluded the vast majority of the rules and standards that actually governed the lives of most Japanese. This implicit concept of law also explains the tension that resulted when Japan introduced continental European notions of law following the Meiji Restoration.

By subjecting more areas of private life and relationships to governmental control through law, Western legal orders were more inclusive. By East Asian standards the domain of law and therefore state control in the West was exceptionally broad. Yet by denying legitimacy to competing sources of social control, the legal orders of the West were also more exclusive, as illustrated by the tendency to regard self-help—even nonviolent self-help, such as refusals to deal—to be illegitimate unless authorized by law. In other words, in the West the state defined through law what forms of social sanctions, even for private transactions, were acceptable. In contrast, within the contours of either the traditional or the modern Japanese legal order, customary rules could be articulated and recognized as legal rules by adjudicating authorities— and thus become generally binding and enforceable—or be disregarded and denied even particularistic formal enforceability. Nevertheless, beyond the law's domain such rules or standards could continue to have whatever effect and impact may be permitted by extralegal systems of prescription and enforcement. Thus, for example, a customary rule regarding compensation for unforeseen consequences of economic conduct, as in the case of pollution, may be overridden by a requirement of negligence in the civil code (see article 709) and yet still be subject to undisputed extralegal enforcement by public condemnation and possibly political action.

Second, Japan has also lacked a universally applicable set of moral or ethical standards for social and political control that could serve either as a substitute for legal ordering or the foundation for a more inclusive legal order. The moral belief system of Chinese Confucianist thought embodied a cosmology that, whether effective or not, in theory at least subjected ruler and ruled alike to a set of definable standards of conduct, operating apart from the legal order to regulate all of society, including those who governed. Although much of this moral belief-system was introduced into Japan, like Western legal theory in the nineteenth century, it was a significant but still alien influence imposed from above, not evolved from within. Japan thus lacked the sort of pervasive and universally applicable moral standards that functioned in Chinese society as an alternative to law or in Western societies as a syncratic element of the legal order. In other words, custom and social convention only partially informed by either Confucianist or other "moral" principles or law have served as the principal sources of social standards for most Japanese communities. What then has been the dominant source for legitimacy in Japan? In a word, consensus. Legitimacy in Japan derives above all else from consent and consensus, as reflected in history as a shared, present perception of the past and custom.

Third, Japan also lacked an effective means of formal regulatory enforcement over its *mura*-like communities. As a result the means of coercion, including both the sanctions used and the manner they were applied, necessarily also became informal and equally dependent upon convention or custom. Unless an offense was perceived as likely to invite outside authorities to intervene and thus to interfere with the community's autonomous governance, even rules imposed from above by either traditional moral tenets or law could be effectively ignored unless internalized by the community as custom or convention. Thus two centuries ago the Tokugawa *mura* could generally expect to remain relatively free of direct, obtrusive governmental supervision or control by paying their rice tax when due, repairing roads and bridges as official regulations prescribed, and otherwise maintaining outward, visible conformity with official policies and community peace and harmony. Furthermore, by controlling the means and process of enforcement, the community thereby controlled the efficacy of any legal or moral rules imposed upon it. Yet to maintain order—a prerequisite for the preservation of autonomy—the community also had to ensure that the informal mechanisms for enforcement were effective. These were not hard to come by. In an environment in which both the economics of rice culture and the customary rituals of life required community cooperation, social censure was a formidable sanction. With such incentives, the Japanese managed to create an extraordinarily effective system of social controls.

Japanese villages thus evolved an elaborate system of consensual ordering among equals or near equals in legal status—what might well be labeled "government by contract." In a formal, legal sense, landholding members of the community were equal in status within a system in which formal inherited status distinctions determined the most basic differentiations of applicable legal rules and standards. Although significant inequalities in wealth and power existed as well as a hierarchy or authority based on village offices and custom, a large segment of the *mura* thus lived within an ideological framework in which they were formal equals. This factor further reinforced reliance on consensual means of governance. Japan was consequently largely governed by contract, with ostracism, fines, and other conventional village sanctions (including sanctioned violence), the principal means of coercion.

The consequence, of course, was an allocation of power. Those who control effective extralegal sanctions control the viability of whatever rules and norms are enforced and thereby the political, social, or economic order they produce. The interrelationships, conflicts, and tensions between Japan's legal order and competing systems of social control have had profound consequences for Japan's political and economic environment. Today, the Japanese *mura* and *mura*-like social organizations effectively preserve community autonomy insofar as they maintain at least an appearance of tranquility and law-abidingness.

Outward submission to authority does not, however, necessarily entail a diminution of community or individual freedom from control or result in compliance with legal rules. Rather, the system reflects a trade-off between submission and autonomy in that outward deference to authority ensures greater freedom from regulatory control by governing officials. Among other effects, it thereby diminishes the efficacy of formal legal controls while strengthening the need and use of informal, extralegal rules of conduct and sanctions to assure their compliance. To preserve autonomy the community must develop consensual controls to contain conflict and to maintain the order and stability in order to avoid direct intervention by the state.

The *mura*, however, was only one of two paradigms of governance in the Japanese tradition. The other was the castle town or *jōkamachi*. Whereas the *mura* was undergoverned at least by law, the *jōkamachi*, established as a means for facilitating control over samurai retainers, represented one of the more intensively regulated communities in the world. Although pockets of *mura*-like autonomy may have existed, here law governed in the form of regulatory, public law as understood within the context of the imperial Chinese administrative tradition with status and power relationships rigorously controlled.

Hardly compatible within either the paradigm of governance by contract of the *mura* or the regulatory legal order of the castle town was a third element of Japan's legal tradition—a sophisticated system of adjudication and judicial governance. Paralleling Western European experience, the political rulers of feudal Japan had early discovered in adjudication an efficient and effective means for establishing legitimacy and maintaining order. Judicial institutions were a predominant vehicle for both the recognition of legal rules and their enforcement. Judicial governance did not, however, fit comfortably within the framework of either the consensual or contract culture of the *mura* or the sinicized regulatory system of the castle town. Nevertheless, litigation and judicial institutions remained, although constrained by procedures for conciliation and other barriers.

Illustrative of these contrasts and their consequences are American criticisms of Japanese firms that have resisted efforts by American corporate investors to gain control or even representation on boards of directors as minority shareholders in light of Japanese investors' easy acquisition of majority interests in U.S. corporations. Some commentators express their inability to justify Japanese actions,[1] but they could reply that from a Japanese perspective the difference between the two situations is justification enough: The Americans consented but the Japanese did not.

To some such a retort may not be very satisfying, but one should pause to ask why. There is an unspoken premise in most demands for justification that commonly accepted principles or standards apply, against which the questioned conduct or activity can be judged or evaluated, irrespective of who is being judged and what their particular beliefs may be. In other words, there is an implicit reference to rules or standards applicable to all concerned. For the Americans, in this case, fairness requires equal, reciprocal treatment. From a purely Japanese cultural perspective, however, little if any justification would have been considered necessary. The issue is simply one of consent or disagreement among the parties. While the American owners may welcome Japanese investment, Japanese may not.

Another unstated premise also underlies such disputes: If the conduct of the Japanese is wrong, something should be done to make it right. If a Japanese company's efforts to exclude foreign investors are unjustified under some universal standard of fairness, the state—ours or theirs—should see to it that the rule of equal treatment is enforced, if not in this case then at least for the future. Thus Japanese officials have been, in the words of one American newspaper, "beseiged with complaints about Japan's unwillingness to offer reciprocity for its own overseas acquisition" and similarly pressed but equally resistant American officials publicly pledge "to keep the doors open to the Japanese" while pressuring the Japanese government to do more.[2] Lacking a similar sense of unfairness or an infraction of some universally applicable norm, the Japanese are less likely to seek state redress as a means of enforcement. Instead they are more likely to seek to use the state as leverage in achieving consent or a better bargain. Even then state intervention is used sparingly for it invites greater intrusion and loss of autonomy.

Such episodes illustrate the deep divisions between the United States and Japan in the most basic cultural assumptions about universal values, rules, and their application as well as the role of the state and fundamental patterns of social ordering. The cultural gap is less one of values themselves—in both societies fairness is defined to include equal treatment and reciprocity—than a difference over the source of these standards, how they apply, and who applies them. In other words, the two societies differ in their most basic assumptions regarding the sources of legitimacy and governance.

The complexity and institutional ambivalence in Japan's legal tradition also helps to explain the nature of Japan's early accommodation of Western law. That Japan had so little difficulty in adapting, first, continental European legal institutions and, later, American law models deserves special emphasis. Japan in fact readily absorbed new Western legal institutions, codes, statutes, and procedures with remarkable ease. No one argues, for instance, that European company law was ill-suited to Japan's cultural environment. Nor did it take Japanese entrepreneurs long to recognize and pursue the advantages of organizing themselves into limited liability partnerships or joint stock companies.

Law in Japan, as in the West, did provide an important source of legitimacy. Although, as noted above, legal rules did not represent moral commands and moral rules were not necessarily embodied in legal commands, codified law does seem to have had special legitimizing effect, especially when it could be argued to reflect tradition, quite apart from its instrumental use.

Needless to say, however, Japan did not fully replicate the legal orders of Western Europe. Conceptually, the definitions of law and the legal process were bound within the East Asian tradition. Official, sinicized notions of what rules or norms were "legal" did not encompass village agreements or judicial lawmaking, however similar they may have been in effect or function. Alien to that tradition was the idea of legal rules subject to private control over their application and enforcement—the essence of private law orders. Conceptually, law meant the regulatory commands of those who ruled. There was no concept of law as a means of private, autonomous ordering.

In summary, nearly all observers of postwar Japan have been struck by the pervasive strength of extralegal forms of social and market control. From administrative guidance to trade association cartels, informal, consensual methods of regulation and coercion have seemed to constitute the predominant mechanism of social and economic ordering. Japanese society is thus popularly characterized by Japanese and non-Japanese alike as remarkably free from effective legal regulation whether in the form of constitutional or statutory constraints on bureaucratic action or civil code rules for private behavior.

What is unusual about Japan's pattern of governance, however, is less dependency on consensus itself than the extent of that dependency and its legitimacy. Some level of societal consensus as to the legitimacy of the norms that legal rules reflect as well as the institutional processes for making and enforcing them is necessary in all legal orders—even the most repressive. Moreover, even regimes born of terror or fear may ultimately acquire legitimacy from habit and custom. In this sense, institutional or structural patterns become cultural phenomena by definition. Thus Japan's dependency on consensus can be argued to have acquired from habit and expectation a particular and self-reinforcing legitimacy. In this context, formal law making and law-enforcing processes—whether legislative, bureaucratic, or judicial—function in large measure as consensus-building processes rather than avenues for command and coercion.

In Japan, the legitimacy of governance by consensus allows—perhaps even requires—focus on the adequacy of processes for creating consensus. A bill passed by a bare majority in either a European parliament or the Japanese Diet becomes law. Because that law can be more effectively implemented in the European state than in Japan without consensus, majoritarian rule is more apt to be considered legitimate there than in Japan. By the same token, less attention need be paid in the European state than Japan to the role of legislative deliberations on a means of developing public consent to legislation. In contrast in Japan one must focus on the efficacy of the process in establishing consent. Thus opposition party denial of support is more effective politically in Japan as an expression of the denial of consensus for a particular legislative action and the failure of the party in power to achieve the requisite assent.

As a consequence, the equation of participation in legislative, party, or ministerial councils with political power in Japan is as misleading as the appearance of bureaucratic control. Access to the media and the courts has also assured influence over consensus and thus effective political participation. Postwar economic policies designed to limit new entry, promote concentration, or otherwise to foster economics of scale also had political justification in making consensus building more manageable. In the end, however, because the efficacy of legal rules has depended upon assent by those they are designed to regulate, political power has been increasingly diffused. The particular configuration of the postwar legal order in Japan has also in effect preserved a remarkable degree of autonomy for the lesser communities, or the modern *mura* of Japanese society, especially corporate business enterprises. As governmental controls have not fully penetrated into Japanese economic, political, and social life, overt deference to state officials has masked the reality of nonconformity. Consequently, societal order has been maintained in Japan more by a complex network of interpersonal and informal obligations and sanctions than those imposed by law. As a result, the predominant controlling norms of Japanese society have depended directly upon consensus and the structure of authority within particular groups as well as raw exercises of private power—both physical and economic.

In this context, Japan has enjoyed a special type of pluralism. Difficult perhaps to discern by those who define pluralism in terms of ethnic, religious, and ideological diversity, or of individual rather than group autonomy, Japanese pluralism is a product less of self-selection into voluntary associations than a cohesion born out of the necessity for security and order. Cohesion has meant that the values and norms shared within the firm, an industry, and other constituent communities of Japan carry more force and impact in determining the conduct of their members. Similarly, however, social recognition that legal rules do reflect consensus, gives them a special influence. As in the past, law continues to exert considerable legitimacy and didactic influence.

Law in postwar Japan thus presents another paradox. It serves as a means for legitimating norms while it remains relatively ineffective as an instrument of coercive control. Substantive legal norms thus operate as principles— *tatemae*—that both shape and reflect consensus. Without effective formal enforcement, they can only partially bind or command. They do not fully control or determine conduct but they do influence and restrain. Law as *tatemae* also promotes autonomy as outward compliance and the effectiveness of social controls lessen the need to develop stronger means of coercive law enforcement.

On the one hand, in a society in which consensus within both society at large and its constituent communities is critical to preserving order, formal legal rules have special significance in their capacity to establish basic standards for conduct. As *tatemae* legal norms may not command obedience, but they do demand respect and induce some level of outward conformity. As reflections of consensus, they establish the parameters of acceptable, legitimate behavior that subject those who violate them to the risk of the penalty of social condemnation. Yet, on the other hand, law's weakness as an instrument of control also promotes the development of cohesive constituent communities within society by reinforcing the need for attendant social controls to provide security and preserve social order.

Finally and perhaps most important, the paradox of law in Japan helps to explain the ultimate paradox of modern Japan as a society characterized by its solution to the fundamental challenge for all liberal states: How to create and preserve an ordered but free society. On the one hand, the containment of legal controls and forced reliance on rule without state coercion has ensured the Japanese notable freedom from state dominance despite pervasive state authority to participate actively in the economic and social life of the nation.

The lack of coercion has thus not caused an atrophy of state institutions or social disarray. Instead the consequence has been to strengthen the mechanisms of private social control and to give those who exert private power a greater voice in both the formation and implementation of public policy. For better or for worse, therefore, Japan is a society ordered more by extralegal and often quite coercive community and group controls than law or government power. Nevertheless, because of the legitimacy of pervasive state authority, the role of the state is more altered than diminished. State institutions still command but rarely without first establishing the necessary consent that assures compliance. The state remains active and interventionist, but its capacity to control or maintain order depends ultimately upon its ability to persuade and cajole in order to achieve consensus. In this context law and the formal mechanisms of law enforcement function more as tools for consensus building and leverage than coercive instruments of state control. Order is thereby maintained, and a rule of law by command without coercion prevails.

Notes

Introduction

1. Compare, e.g., Ezra Vogel, *Japan as Number One: Lessons for America* (Cambridge: Harvard University Press, 1979), especially Vogel's assertion (p. 72) that "MITI's aim is not to reduce competition among Japanese companies...," with the actions detailed in Kozo Yamamura, *Economic Policy in Postwar Japan* (Berkeley and Los Angeles: University of California Press, 1967), and Chalmers Johnson, *MITI and the Japanese Miracle* (Stanford: Stanford University Press, 1982). In contrast to Johnson's emphasis on the role of MITI and the developmental state, see David Friedman, *The Misunderstood Miracle: Industrial Development and Political Change in Japan* (Ithaca: Cornell University Press, 1988).

For contrary views of the contribution of free, competitive markets, see Milton Friedman, *Freedom to Choose* (New York: Harcourt, Brace, Jovanovich, 1980), and Leon Hollerman, *Japan, Disincorporated* (Stanford: Hoover Institution Press, 1988). For more moderate views that expose without resolving the paradox of persistent competition despite anticompetitive government policies, see Takafusa Nakamura, *The Postwar Japanese Economy: Its Development and Structure* (Tokyo: University of Tokyo Press, 1981), and Hugh Patrick and Henry Rosovsky (eds.), *Asia's New Giant* (Washington, D.C.: Brookings Institution, 1976).

2. See, e.g., *Report of the Review of the Joint Committee on Japanese Studies (JCJS) of the American Council of Learned Societies and the Social Science Research Council,* October 1989.

3. See Clyde V. Prestowitz, Jr., *Trading Places: How We Allowed Japan to Take the Lead* (New York: Basic Books, 1988).

4. See, e.g., Setsuo Miyazawa, "Taking Kawashima Seriously: A Review of Japanese Research on Japanese Legal Consciousness and Disputing Behavior," *Law & Society Review,* Vol. 21, No. 2 (1987).

5. H.L.A. Hart, *The Concept of Law* (Oxford: Clarendon Press, 1961), at pp. 77–96.

6. Roberto Unger, *Law in Modern Society* (New York: The Free Press, 1976).

7. For an insightful study of the contrast between adjudicative and administrative processes of law enforcement and their relationship to the role of the state, see Mirjan R. Damaška, *The Faces of Justice and State Authority: A Comparative Approach to the Legal Process* (New Haven: Yale University Press, 1986). Damaška posits two models of law enforcement, hierarchical and coordinate, which he views to be related to activist versus reactive states.

8. See, e.g., Rosser Brockman, "Commercial Contract Law in Late Nineteenth Century Taiwan," in J.A. Cohen, R.R. Edwards, and F.M. Chang Chen (eds.), *Essays on China's Legal Tradition* (Princeton: Princeton University Press, 1980), at p. 76; David Buxbaum, "Some Aspects of Civil Procedure and Practice at the Trial Level in Tanshin and Hsinchu from 1789 to 1895," *Journal of Asian Studies,* Vol. 30, No. 2 (1981), at p. 755; Chang Bin Liu, Commercial Law Under the Ch'ing Code (Ph.D. dissertation, School of Law, University of Washington, Seattle, 1984).

9. Hugh T. Scogins, for example, makes a persuasive case for state enforcement of contractual undertakings in traditional China in "Between Heaven and Man: Contracts and the State in Han Dynasty China," *Southern California Law Review,* Volume 63, No. 5 (July 1990), at pp. 1325–1404.

10. Max Weber, *Economy and Society: An Outline of Interpretative Sociology,* Vol. 2 (G. Roth and C. Wittich (eds.), New York: Bedminster Press, 1968), at p. 812.

11. See Carl J. Friedrich (ed.), *Authority* (Cambridge: Harvard University Press, 1958), especially the essays by Charles W. Hendel, Carl J. Friedrich, and Herbert Spiro, at pp. 3–57.

12. For a thoughtful exploration of the concept of power, see Kerry Schott, *Policy, Power and Order: The Persistence of Economic Problems in Capitalist Societies* (New Haven: Yale University Press, 1984), at pp. 16–18.

13. Karel van Wolferen, *The Enigma of Japanese Power* (New York: A.A. Knopf, 1989), at pp. 9, 10.

14. Judith N. Sklar, *Legalism: Law, Morals and Political Trials* (Cambridge: Harvard University Press, 1986 ed.).

15. Ibid., at 1.

16. See, e.g., Ronald Dworkin, *Taking Rights Seriously* (Cambridge: Harvard University Press, 1975).

Chapter 1

1. See, e.g., Shūzō Shiga, "Criminal Procedure in the Ch'ing Dynasty (II)" in *Memoirs of the Research Department of the Toyo Bunko*, No. 33 (Tokyo: 1975), at pp. 120–124.

2. A.F.P. Hulsewé, "The Legalists and The Laws of Ch'in," in W.L. Idema (ed.), *Leyden Studies in Sinology* (Leiden: E.J. Brill, 1981), at p. 2.

3. Herrlee Glessner Creel, "Legal Institutions and Procedures During the Chou Dynasty," in Cohen, Edwards, and Chen (eds.), *Essays on China's Legal Tradition* (Princeton: Princeton University Press, 1980), at p. 30.

4. A.F.P. Hulsewé, *Remnants of Han Law*, Vol. 1 (Leiden: E.J. Brill, 1955), at p. 41.

5. Wallace Johnson, *The T'ang Code: Volume I, General Principles* (Princeton: Princeton University Press, 1979), at pp. 278–291.

6. Shūzō Shiga, "Criminal Procedure in the Ch'ing Dynasty (I)," in *Memoirs of the Research Department of the Toyo Bunko*, No. 32 (Tokyo: 1974), at p. 3.

7. Ibid., at p. 44.

8. John Crook, *Law and Life of Rome* (Ithaca: Cornell University Press, 1967), at p. 82.

9. Rosser Brockman, "Commercial Contract Law in Late Nineteenth Century Taiwan," in Cohen, Edwards, and Chen, op. cit., at p. 94.

10. Ibid.

11. Derk Bodde and Clarence Morris, *Law in Imperial China* (Philadelphia: University of Pennsylvania Press, 1967), at p. 512.

12. See Brockman, op. cit., at p. 94; Jonathan K. Ocko, *Bureaucratic Reform in Provincial China* (Cambridge: Harvard University Press, 1983), at p. 68; Chang Bin Liu, Commercial Law Under the Ch'ing Code (Ph.D. dissertation, School of Law, University of Washington, Seattle, 1984), at pp. 225–256.

13. Hulsewé, "The Legalists," op. cit., at p. 2.

14. Johnson, op. cit., at pp. 61–83.

15. Shiga, op. cit., No. 33, at p. 116.

16. Niida Noboru, *Chūgoku hōseishi* (Chinese legal history) (Tokyo: Iwanami Shoten, 1963), at p. 107.

17. Kung-chuan Hsiao, *Compromise in Imperial China* (Seattle: University of Washington Press, 1979), at p. 16.

18. A. Arthur Schiller, *Roman Law* (New York: Mouton Publishers, 1978), at p. 555.

19. Ibid., at p. 556.

20. See, e.g., Harold J. Berman, *Law and Revolution: The Formation of the Western Legal Tradition* (Cambridge: Harvard University Press, 1983), esp. pp. 80–88.

21. Bodde and Morris, op. cit., at p. 10.

22. Joseph Needham, *Science and Civilization in China*, Vol. II (London: Cambridge University Press, 1956), at p. 564.

23. Ibid., at p. 582.

24. Leon Vandermeersch, "An Enquiry into the Chinese Conception of Law," in S.R. Schram (ed.), *The Scope of State Power in China* (Hong Kong: The Chinese University Press, 1985), at pp. 3–4.

25. Needham, op. cit., at p. 522.

26. Shiga, op. cit., No. 33, at p. 133.

27. Hahm Pyong-Choon, *The Korean Political Tradition and Law* (Seoul: Hollym Corporation, 1967), at p. 19.

28. Benjamin I. Schwartz, "The Primacy of the Political Order in East Asian Societies: Some Preliminary Generalizations," in S.R. Schram (ed.), *Foundations and Limits of State Power in China* (Hong Kong: The Chinese University Press, 1987), at p. 1.

29. Ibid., at pp. 1–2.

30. Ibid., at p. 3.

31. Niida Noboru, *Chūgoku hōseishi kenkyū: hō to shūkan, hō to dōtoku* (Research on Chinese legal history: law and custom, law and morality) (Tokyo: University of Tokyo Press, 2d ed., 1981), at pp. 530–531.

32. Schwartz, op. cit., at p. 4.

33. Ibid.

34. William P. Alford, "The Inscrutable Occidental? Implications of Roberto Unger's Uses and Abuses of the Chinese Past," *Texas Law Review*, Vol. 64, No. 5 (1986), at pp. 240–241.

35. See Ishii Ryōsuke, *Nihon hōseishi gaisetsu* (Survey of Japanese legal history) (Tokyo: Kōbundō, 2d ed. 1949), at pp. 9–57.

36. Ibid., at pp. 26–30.

37. Japanese historians refer to this period from A.D. 603 to 967 as *jōsei*. The date usually given for the Taika reforms is 645. See Ishii, op. cit., at pp. 4–5.

38. Hiramatsu Yoshirō, *Kinseihō* (Early modern law) Vol. II, *Iwanami kōza Nihon rekishi* (Iwanami lectures on Japanese history) [*Kinsei*, Vol. 3] (Tokyo: Iwanami, 1976), at p. 332. Translated in English as "Tokugawa Law" by Dan F. Henderson, in *Law in Japan: An Annual*, Vol. 14 (1981), at p. 1.

39. See, e.g., Morohashi Tetsuji, *Dai kanwa jiten* (Great Chinese character-Japanese dictionary), Vol. 2 (Tokyo: Daishūkan Shoten, 1984 ed.), at p. 834.

40. These included five degrees of flogging with a light bamboo rod; five degrees of flogging with a heavy bamboo stick; five degrees of penal servitude; three degrees of life exile; and two forms of capital punishment. Compare Johnson, op. cit., at pp. 55–61, with Inoue Mitsusada, Seki Akira, Tsuchida Naoshige, and Aoki Kazuo (eds.), *Ritsuryō* (Tokyo: Iwanami Shoten, 1976), at pp. 15–16.

41. They were rebellion; great sedition; treason; contumacy, e.g., beating or killing a lineal ascendant; depravity, e.g., plotting to kill three or more members of a household who had not committed a capital offense, to dismember someone, to possess poison or to practice sorcery; great irreverence, e.g., theft from temples or shrines or of imperial property; lack of filial piety, which included a variety of offenses against lineal ascendants and failure to abide by certain Confucian rituals; and unrighteous behavior, which

included specified offenses against officials and others in authority and failure to abide by mourning rituals. Johnson, op. cit., at pp. 61–83; Inoue, Seki, Tsuchida, and Aoki, op. cit., at pp. 16–19.

42. The Japanese included relatives of the emperor, imperial retainers, the morally worthy, and those with ability, high achievement or high position. Excluded were the T'ang Code "deliberations" for diligence and for guests of the state. Johnson, op. cit., at pp. 83–85; Inoue, Seki, Tsuchida, and Aoki, op. cit., at pp. 19–20.

43. For a description of the Yōrō *ryō* in English, see George B. Sansom, "Early Japanese Law and Administration," Part I, *Transactions of the Asiatic Society of Japan* [2nd Series], Vol. IX (1932), at pp. 67–109; Part II, *Transactions of the Asiatic Society of Japan* [2nd Series], Vol. XI (1934), at pp. 117–149.

44. See, e.g., Ishio Yoshihisa, *Nihon kodai hō shi* (History of Japan's ancient law) (Tokyo: Hanawa Shobō, 1964), at pp. 88–115.

45. See, e.g., Ishio Yoshihisa, *Nihon kodai hō no kenkyū* (Studies on Japan's ancient law) (Kyoto: Hōritsu Bunka Sha, 1961), at pp. 35–64. Ishio argues that early Japanese law was predominantly "charismatic" religious law, not customary law, and continued to influence Japanese practice after the introduction of Chinese law.

46. See, e.g., Ishio Yoshihisa's contrast between Chinese assumptions of rule by propertied bureaucratic command and a Japanese indigenous pattern of domination and control by a status elite, Ibid., at pp. 174–200.

47. Ishii, op. cit., at pp. 84–85. See also Rikō Mitsuo, *Nihon kodai hōseishi* (History of Japan's ancient legal system) (Tokyo: Keiō Tsūshin, 1986), at p. 47.

48. For a critique of such views, however, see, e.g., Hsu Dau-lin, "Crime and Cosmic Order," *Harvard Journal of Asiatic Studies*, Vol. 30 (1970), at pp. 111–125.

49. See Rikō, op. cit., at p. 97.

50. See Takikawa Masajirō, *Nihon hōseishi* (Japanese legal history) (Tokyo: Yūhikaku, 2d ed. 1930), at p. 154.

51. See Rikō, op. cit., at pp. 110–111; Ishii, op. cit., at pp. 134–138.

52. Rikō, op. cit.

53. See Inoue, Seki, Tsuchida, and Aoki, op. cit., at p. 665. See also Takikawa, op. cit., at pp. 169–175. For discussion of other views, see Okuno Hikoroku, *Ritsuryōsei kodai hō* (Ancient law under the *ritsuryō* system) (Tokyo: Sakai Shoten, 2d ed. 1968), at pp. 253–275.

Chapter 2

1. See G. Cameron Hurst III, "The Structure of the Heian Court: Some Insights on the Nature of 'Familial Authority' in Heian Japan," in J.W. Hall and J.P. Mass (eds.), *Medieval Japan: Essays in Institutional History* (Stanford: Stanford University Press, 2d ed. 1988), at pp. 39–59.

2. John Whitney Hall, "Feudalism in Japan—A Reassessment," in J.W. Hall and M.B. Jansen (eds.), *Studies in the Institutional History of Early Modern Japan* (Princeton: Princeton University Press, 1968), at p. 25, quoting from Rushton Coulborn, *Feudalism in History* (Princeton: Princeton University Press, 1956) at pp. 54–55.

3. Ishii, op. cit., at p. 257. See also Kan'ichi Asakawa, *The Documents of Iriki* (New Haven: Yale University Press, 1929), at p. 7.

4. See, e.g., Asakawa, op. cit., at pp. 29, 55–60; Hall, op. cit., at pp. 33– 34. Also, Jōuon des Longrais, *L'Est et L'Ouest* (East and West) (Tokyo and Paris: Maison Franco-Japonaise, Institut de Recherches d'Histoire Étrangère, 1958), at pp. 143–156.

5. Jeffrey P. Mass, *The Development of Kamakura Rule* (Stanford: Stanford University Press, 1979), at p. xv.

6. Marc Bloch, "The Rise of Dependent Cultivation and Seignorial Institutions," in W. Postan (ed.), *The Cambridge Economic History of Europe: Agrarian Life in the Middle Ages*, Vol. I (Cambridge: Cambridge University Press, 1966), at p. 290.

7. Satō Shin'ichi, *Kamakura bakufu soshō seido no kenkyū* (Research on the system of litigation under the Kamakura bakufu) (Tokyo, Unebō Shobō, 1943), at pp. 121–129, 166; Carl Steenstrup, "Sata Mirensho: A Fourteenth-Century Law Primer," *Monumenta Nipponica*, Vol. 35 (1980), at pp. 409–411.

8. Satō, op. cit., at p. 121; Steenstrup, op. cit., at p. 410. On dispute over the issue of when the *monchūjo* was established, see Mass, op. cit., at pp. 67–80.

9. Mass, op. cit., at p. 119.

10. Ibid., at p. 155.

11. Ibid., at p. 141. Although not as pervasive a feature of the trial as in Medieval Europe, the Japanese also on occasion might rely upon supernatural intervention to validate the veracity of testimony. Ishii points out that a witness whose testimony was subject to doubt could be required to take an oath and be confined in a Shinto shrine. If one of several designated events occurred during that period, the testimony would be treated as false or, if not, affirmed. Ishii, op. cit., at p. 291. See also Ishii Ryōsuke, *A History of Political Institutions in Japan* (Tokyo: University of Tokyo Press, 1980), at p. 47.

12. Mass, op. cit., at pp. 131–142.

13. Carl Steenstrup, Hōjō Shigetoki (1198–1261) and his Role in the History of Political and Ethical Ideas in Japan (Ph.D. dissertation, Department of East Asian Languages and Civilization, Harvard University, 1977), at p. 244.

14. Ibid., at p. 194.

15. See, e.g., Brian E. McKnight, *The Quality of Mercy: Amnesties and Traditional Chinese Justice* (Honolulu: University of Hawaii Press, 1981); William S. Shaw, *Legal Norms in a Confucian State* (Berkeley: Institute for East Asian Studies, University of California, 1981).

16. Ishii argues that a primary aim of the *ritsuryō* was to realize religious moral values and, similarly, the function of criminal penalties in medieval Japan was to enforce the ethical values of the warrior class. Ishii Ryōsuke, *Hōseishi* (Legal history) (Tokyo: Yamakawa Shuppansha, 1979), at p. 137.

17. Japanese legal historians generally describe the Kamakura period as an era of customary law and precedent. See, e.g., Ishii, *Hōseishi*, op. cit., at pp. 123–124. However, from description of the adjudicatory process, it appears that what they mean by the terms "customary law" and "precedent" is far narrower than the common usage of these terms in the West. Custom and precedent may have prevailed, but more in terms of procedural forms and reliance on past *legislated* rules than any articulate norms or principles. Takikawa appropriately refers to "administrative precedent" [*chōrei*]. See, e.g., Takikawa, op. cit., at p. 292. Documentary evidence rather than customary norms was apparently the determinative factor for most adjudicated cases.

18. Ishii, *Gaisetsu*, op. cit., at pp. 302–305.

19. Carl Steenstrup, "The Legal System of Japan at the End of the Kamakura Period from the Litigants' Point of View," in B. McKnight (ed.), *Law and the State in Traditional East Asia* (Honolulu: University of Hawaii Press, 1986), at p. 95.

20. Ibid., at p. 97.

21. Ibid. Haruyasu Sugiyama cautions, however, that, at least in the Kamakura period, *dōri* should not be equated with morality [*dōtoku*]. In practice, he notes, *dōri* tended to relate to accepted legal procedures not standards of conduct or behavior.

Sugiyama Haruyasu, *Nihon hōshi gairon* (Introduction to Japanese legal history) (Tokyo: Seibundō, 1980), at p. 182, fns. 3, 4.

22. Steenstrup, op. cit., at p. 97.

23. Ishii, *Hōseishi*, op. cit., at pp. 124–125.

24. Kenneth A. Grossberg, *The Laws of the Muromachi Bakufu* (Tokyo: Monumenta Nipponica, 1981), at p. 8.

25. See Ueki Naoichirō, *Goseibai shikimoku kenku* (Research on the *goseibai shikimoku*) (Tokyo: Iwanami Shoten, 1930), at pp. 1–10. For English translations, see John Carey Hall, "Japanese Feudal Laws I—The Institutes of Judicature, *Transactions of the Asiatic Society of Japan* [1st Series], Vol. 34 (Tokyo: 1906), at pp. 1–44; John Carey Hall, "Japanese Feudal Laws II—The Ashikaga Code," *Transactions of the Asiatic Society of Japan*, [1st series], Vol. 36 (Tokyo: 1908), at pp. 1–23; reprinted in John Carey Hall, *Japanese Feudal Law* (Washington, D.C.: University Publications of America, 1979), at pp. 3–71. For a translation of the *Kenmu* Formulary, with supplementary edicts, see Grossberg, op. cit.

26. Mass, op. cit., at p. 144.

27. Steenstrup, "The Legal System of Japan," op. cit., at p. 94. Steenstrup suggests that one of the functions of the system was to exhaust political challenges to *bakufu* rule by endless entanglement in litigation. Ibid., at p. 75.

28. Hall, op. cit., at p. 71.

29. By far the best account of Nobunaga's and above all Hideyoshi's statecraft is Mary Elizabeth Berry, *Hideyoshi* (Cambridge: The Council on East Asian Studies, Harvard University, 1982).

30. See Katsumata Shizuo (with Martin Collcutt), "The Development of Sengoku Law," in J.W. Hall, K. Nagahara, and K. Yamamura (eds.), *Japan Before Tokugawa: Political Consolidation and Economic Growth, 1500–1650* (Princeton: Princeton University Press, 1981), at pp. 103, 112–113.

31. Compare, e.g., articles 15 and 26 of the *Kenmu* Formulary distinguishing offensive and defensive warfare and the submission of disputes to the Muromachi *bakufu* for adjudication in the fourteenth century with article 520 added in the sixteenth century (translated in Grossberg, op. cit., at pp. 33, 40) and article 25 of the *Chōsokabe-shi okitegaki* of Tosa, translated in Marcus B. Jansen, "Tosa in the Sixteenth Century: The 100 Article Code of Chōsokabe Motochika," in Hall and Jansen, op. cit., at p. 105. See also, Tsujimoto Hiroaki, "*Ryōseibai hō no kigen ni tsuite*" (On the origins of the law to punish both parties to a quarrel), *Hōseishi kenkyū* (Studies in legal history), Vol. 18 (1968), at pp. 103–120.

32. See Katsumata Shizuo, *Sengoku hō seiritsushi ron* (Studies on the establishment of sengoku law) (Tokyo: University of Tokyo Press, 1982 ed.), at p. 257.

33. Katsumata, "Sengoku Law," op. cit., at p. 117. See also James Kanda, Japanese Feudal Society in the Sixteenth Century as Seen Through the Jinkaishū and Other Legal Codes (Ph.D. dissertation, Departments of History and East Asian Languages, Harvard University, 1974), at pp. 169, 350.

34. Ibid., at pp. 117–118.

35. Ibid., at p. 115.

Chapter 3

1. John Whitney Hall, *Government and Local Power in Japan* (Princeton: Princeton University Press, 1966), at pp. 341–343.

2. See Herman Ooms, *Tokugawa Ideology: Early Constructs, 1570–1680* (Princeton: Princeton University Press, 1985), at p. 170.

3. Ibid., at pp. 68–69.

4. Ibid., esp. pp. 289–296. This is Oom's principal thesis. For an excellent account of the ideological uses of neo-Confucianist reinterpretation of Japanese political history, see Kate Wildman Nakai, "Neo-Confucian Historiography: The Hayashi, Early Mito School, and Arai Hakuseki," in P. Nosco (ed.), *Confucianism and Tokugawa Culture* (Princeton: Princeton University Press, 1984), at pp. 62–91.

5. Quoted in Masao Maruyama, *Studies in the Intellectual History of Tokugawa Japan* (M. Hane, trans.) (Princeton: Princeton University Press, 1974), at p. 49.

6. See Anne Walthall, *Social Protest and Popular Culture* (Tucson: University of Arizona Press, 1986); Irwin Scheiner, "Benevolent Lords and Honorable Peasants," in T. Najita and I. Scheiner, *Japanese Thought in the Tokugawa Period* (Chicago: University of Chicago Press, 1978).

7. See, e.g., Susan B. Hanley and Kozo Yamamura, *Economic and Demographic Change in Preindustrial Japan, 1600–1868* (Princeton: Princeton University Press, 1977), at pp. 132, 137–139, 143–146.

8. David Magaley Earl, *Emperor and Nation in Japan: Political Thinkers of the Tokugawa Period* (Seattle: University of Washington Press, 1964).

9. Hall, *Government and Local Power*, op. cit., at p. 347.

10. For a description of the *myōreiritsu* of the Yōrō Code in comparison with the general provisions of the T'ang Code, see Chapter 1.

11. Dan Fenno Henderson, *Conciliation and Japanese Law: Tokugawa and Modern*, Vol. 1 (Seattle: University of Washington Press, 1965), at p. 58. *Dōri* is perhaps best understood to invoke whatever norms were considered by the magistrates of any particular period to conform to generally accepted values and perceptions of correct policy. As noted previously, in the Kamakura period *dōri* provided the underlying rationale in most adjudication and reflected the norms of the thirteenth and fourteenth century warrior community. Therefore Henderson is probably correct in assuming that by seventeenth and eighteenth centuries, *dōri* included a heavier emphasis on neo-Confucianist values and shogunate policy. Ibid.

12. For a detailed description of the administrative structure of the Tokugawa shogunate in English, see Henderson, *Conciliation*, op. cit., at pp. 63–77. In Japanese, see Ishii, *Gaisetsu*, op. cit., at pp. 414–424.

13. Nakada Kaoru and Ishii Ryōsuke, *Nihon hōseishi kōgi* (Lectures on Japanese legal history) (Tokyo: Sōbunsha, 1983), at pp. 168–169.

14. John Whitney Hall, "Tokugawa Japan: 1800–1853," in J.P. Crowley (ed.), *Modern East Asia: Essays in Interpretation* (New York: Harcourt, Brace & World, 1970), at p. 71.

15. See, e.g., Henderson, *Conciliation*, op. cit., at p. 101.

16. Ibid.

17. Okuno Hikoroku, *Osadamegaki no kenkyū* (Research on the Osadamegaki) (Tokyo: Shui Shoten, 1968), at p. 518.

18. Ishii, *Gaisetsu*, op. cit., at p. 478.

19. See Takikawa, op. cit., at p. 511.

20. See, e.g., John Henry Wigmore, *Panorama of the World's Legal Systems*, Vol. 2 (St. Paul: West Publishing Co., 1928), at pp. 503–520.

21. Hall, "Tokugawa Japan," op. cit., at p. 71.

22. Ishii, *Gaisetsu*, op. cit., at p. 425. For a detailed account of village life and law in Tokugawa Japan, see Kodama Kōta, *Kinsei nōmin seikatsushi* (History of early modern rural peasant life) (Tokyo: Yoshikawa Kōbunsha, 1957). For brief descriptions,

see Takikawa, op. cit., at pp. 445–450; Nakada and Ishii, op. cit., at pp. 174–180; Sugiyama, op. cit., at pp. 272–277.

23. See Harumi Befu, "Duty, Reward, Sanction, and Power: The Four-Cornered Office of the Tokugawa Village Headman," in B.S. Silberman and H.D. Harootunian (eds.), *Modern Japanese Leadership: Transition and Change* (Tucson: University of Arizona Press, 1966), at pp. 25–50.

24. Dan Fenno Henderson, *Village "Contracts" in Tokugawa Japan* (Seattle: University of Washington Press, 1975), Document 40.B, at pp. 164–166.

25. Ibid., Document 39, at pp. 159–161.

26. Ibid., Documents 41.A and 41.B, at pp. 167–170.

27. Kodama, op. cit., at p. 186.

28. Hanley and Yamamura, op. cit., at 322.

29. For an excellent summary in English of the *Kyōhō* reforms and compilation of the *Osadamegaki*, see Dan Fenno Henderson, "Introduction to the Kujikata Osadamegaki (1742)," in Hiramatsu Yoshirō Hakushi Tsuito Ronbunshū Henshū Iinkai (ed.), *Hō to keibatsu no rekishi-teki kōsatsu* (Historical studies on law and penal institutions) (Nagoya: Nagoya Daigaku Shuppankai, 1987), at pp. 489–544.

30. Nearly all sources rely on an official 1855 estimate of 61,549 villages. See, e.g., Takikawa, op. cit., at p. 442. For extended analysis of Tokugawa population estimates, see Hanley and Yamamura, op. cit., at pp. 38–68.

31. Henderson, *Village Contracts*, op. cit., at pp. 179–182.

32. Ibid., at pp. 137–159, esp. Documents Nos. 36 (pp. 143–146) and 38 (pp. 149–151).

33. Quoted in Maruyama, op. cit., at p. 246.

34. Dan Fenno Henderson, "Chinese Influences on Eighteenth Century Tokugawa Codes," in Cohen, Edwards, Chen, op. cit., at pp. 270–301; Dan Fenno Henderson, "Chinese Legal Studies in Early 18th Century Japan," *Journal of Asian Studies*, Vol. 30 (1970), at pp. 21–56.

35. Okuno Hikoroku, *Tokugawa bakufu to chūgoku hō* (The Tokugawa bakufu and Chinese law) (Tokyo: Sōbunsha, 1979), at p. 13.

36. Thomas B. Stephens, *The Disciplinary System of Order in China, A Case Study: The Mixed Court at Shanghai, 1911–1927* (Seattle: University of Washington Press, forthcoming).

Chapter 4

1. Insistence on Westernized law reforms as a condition to treaty revision is frequently argued to have been the catalyst for the Meiji legal reforms. See, e.g., Yoshiyuki Noda, "Comparative Jurisprudence in Japan—Its Past and Present, Part I," *Law in Japan, An Annual*, Vol. 8 (1975), at p. 12. Nonetheless nearly all Japanese scholars would agree that the Meiji legal reforms were not the product of a purely reactive response. The leaders of Meiji Japan genuinely wished to restructure what they themselves regarded as an archaic system. See, e.g., Hosokawa Kameichi, *Nihon hōseishi* (Japanese legal history) (Tokyo: Yūhikaku, 1961), at p. 167.

2. See Yokoyama Kōichirō, "*Keibatsu-chian kikō no seibi*" (Consolidation of penal and security institutions), in Fukushima Masao (ed.), *Nihon kindai hō taisei no keisei* (Formation of Japan's modern legal system), Vol. 1 (Tokyo: Nihon Hyōronsha, 1981), at p. 311.

3. Thomas C. Smith, *Political Change and Industrial Development in Japan* (Stanford: Stanford University Press, 1955), at p. 34.

4. Paul H.C. Chen describes this interlude in a superb study of the early Meiji reforms. Initially the Meiji government attempted to recreate the *ritsuryō* system. They went so far as to enact what was in effect a new *ritsuryō* code. Paul H.C. Chen, *The Formation of the Early Meiji Legal Order* (London: Oxford University Press, 1981). This attempt to resurrect the past was soon abandoned, however, in the enthusiasm for Western reform.

5. *Saibansho kōsei hō* (Law No. 6, 1890).

6. In English, see George M. Beckmann, *The Making of the Japanese Constitution* (Lawrence: University of Kansas Press, 1957). For a comprehensive treatment in Japanese, see Inada Masatsugu, *Meiji kenpō seiritsu shi* (History of the making of the Meiji constitution), 2 vols. (Tokyo: Yūhikaku, 1962).

7. See Ken Mukai and Nobuyoshi Toshitani, "The Progress and Problems of Compiling the Civil Code in the Early Meiji Era," *Law in Japan: An Annual*, Vol. 1 (1967), pp. 25-59.

8. See Ryōsuke Ishii, *Japanese Legislation in the Meiji Era* (Tokyo: Pan Pacific Press, 1958).

9. *Keiji soshō hō* (Law No. 96, 1890).

10. *Nihon teikoku kenpō* (Feb. 11, 1889).

11. *Minpō* (Laws Nos. 28 and 98, 1890). As detailed below, the 1890 Civil Code was never enforced. The second code, which is in effect as amended, was enacted in two parts, books I, II, and III in Law No. 89, 1896, and Books IV and V in Law No. 9, 1898.

12. *Shōhō* (Law No. 32, 1890). The 1890 code was replaced in 1899 by a second code, Law No. 48, 1899.

13. *Gyōsei saiban hō* (Law No. 48, 1890).

14. *Minji soshō hō* (Law No. 19, 1890).

15. For the intellectual change in the period after 1885, see Kenneth B. Pyle, *The New Generation in Meiji Japan: Problems in Cultural Identity, 1885–1895* (Stanford: Stanford University Press, 1969).

16. *Keihō* (Law No. 45, 1907).

17. *Japan Weekly Mail*, Oct. 29, 1897, pp. 530-533; Nov. 19, 1892, pp. 617-619; Nov. 26, 1892, pp. 656-661; Dec. 10, 1892, pp. 722-726.

18. *Japan Weekly Mail*, Dec. 10, 1892, at p. 726.

19. For a description in English, see John Henry Wigmore, *Law and Justice in Tokugawa Japan*, Part I (Tokyo: University of Tokyo Press, 1969), at pp. 113- 127.

20. Gustave E. Boissonade, *Les anciennes coutumes du Japon et le nouveau Code Civil* (Tokyo: Hakubunsha, 1894), at p. 12.

21. Ibid.

22. *Ginkō jōrei* (1872).

23. See Kozo Yamamura, *A Study of Samurai Income and Entrepreneurship* (Cambridge: Harvard University Press, 1974), at pp. 163-178.

24. Smith, op. cit., at p. 37.

25. Ryōsuke Ishii, *Japanese Culture in the Meiji Era: Volume IX Legislation* (Tokyo: Tōyō Bunko, 1958), at p. 600.

26. Robert Charles Epp, Threat to Tradition: The Reaction to Japan's 1890 Civil Code (Ph.D. dissertation, Departments of History and Far Eastern Languages, Harvard University, 1964), at p. 14.

27. Quoted in Ibid., at p. 16.

28. Masao Maruyama, *Thought and Behavior in Modern Japanese Politics* (London: Oxford University Press, 1963), at p. 5.

29. For detailed accounts in English of the code controversy, including the political process leading to the Diet actions, see Epp, op. cit., esp. pp. 44– 108; Ishii, *Japanese Culture*, op. cit., at pp. 577–598; and Richard W. Rabinowitz, "Law and the Social Process in Japan," *Transactions of the Asiatic Society of Japan*, Vol. 10 [3rd Series] (1968), at p. 30.

30. See Ishii, *Japanese Culture*, op. cit., at p. 596.

31. See Epp, op. cit., at 75–93.

32. Ishii Ryōsuke, *"Sain no minpō sōan"* (The peers' draft civil code), *Kokka gakkai zasshi*, Vol. 60, No. 1 (1946), at p. 39, cited in Epp, op. cit., at p. 30, fn. 41.

33. Epp, op. cit., at p. 77.

34. Rabinowitz, op. cit., at p. 30.

35. Sumu Miyagawa notes that prewar scholarship tended to describe the debate in terms of a factional dispute between the leading schools of Western jurisprudence. He cites, e.g., Ishida Shin, *Nihon minpōshi* (History of Japanese civil law) (Tokyo: Dōbunkan, 1928); Hoshino Tōru, *Minpōten ronsōshi* (History of the civil code controversy) (Tokyo: Nihon Hyōronsha, 1949); Hozumi Nobushige, *Hōsō yawa* (Conversations on the law) (Tokyo: Yūhikaku, 1920); Nakagawa Zennosuke, *Shihōshi* (History of private law) (Tokyo: Tōyō Keizai Shinbunsha, 1943), and Kobayakawa Kingo, *Kyūminpōten henshū katei to kyūminpōten ni kansuru ronsō ni tsuite* (The process of compiling the old civil code and the dispute concerning the old civil code) (Tokyo: Yamaguchi Shoten, 1943). Miyagawa Sumu, *Kyūminpō to Meiji minpō* (The old civil code and the Meiji civil code) (Tokyo: Aoki Shoten, 1965), at p. 78.

36. See, e.g., Ishii, *Japanese Culture*, op. cit., at p. 585.

37. Rabinowitz reaches the same conclusion. Rabinowitz, op. cit., at p. 38.

38. Carol Gluck, *Japan's Modern Myths: Ideology in the Late Meiji Period* (Princeton: Princeton University Press, 1985).

39. For details in English, see Epp, op. cit., at pp. 59–65.

40. Miyagawa, op. cit., at p. 214.

41. Beckmann, op. cit., at p. 84.

42. Constitution of the Empire of Japan, art. 55.

43. Ibid., art. 56.

44. Ibid., art. 57.

45. Ibid., art. 34.

46. Ibid., art. 35.

47. Ibid., art. 22.

48. Ibid., art. 23.

49. Ibid., art. 24.

50. Ibid., art. 25.

51. Ibid., art. 26.

52. Ibid., art. 27.

53. Ibid., art. 28.

54. Ibid., art. 29.

55. Hermann Roesler, "Commentaries on the Constitution of the Empire of Japan," in Johannes Siemes, *Hermann Roesler and the Making of the Meiji Constitution* (Tokyo: Monumenta Nipponica, 1966), at p. 43.

56. See James B. Crowley, *Japan's Quest for Autonomy* (Princeton: Princeton University Press, 1966), at pp. 66–78.

57. Maruyama, *Thought and Behavior*, op. cit., at p. 125.

Chapter 5

1. See *Dai-Nippon teikoku tōkei nenkan* (Japanese empire annual statistics) (Tokyo: Ōkurashō Insatsu Kyoku, 1920), at p. 404.

2. See Zentarō Kitagawa, *Rezeption und Fortbildung des europäischen Zivilrechts in Japan* (Reception and endurance of European civil law in Japan) (Frankfurt: Alfred Metzner Verlag, 1970).

3. See, e.g., Hirobumi Itō, *Commentaries on the Constitution of the Empire of Japan* (Tokyo: Chūō Daigaku, 1906); Nobushige Hozumi, *Lectures on the New Japanese Civil Code* (Tokyo: Maruzen, 1912).

4. See, e.g., comments by Japanese delegate to the 1922 Lausanne Conference to the Ismit Pasha, noted in Roderic H. Davison, "Turkey," in R.E. Ward and D.A. Rustow, *Political Modernization in Japan and Turkey* (Princeton: Princeton University Press, 1964), at p. 91.

5. Sonoda v. Sonoda, 7 Minroku (No. 6) 47 (Gr. Ct. Cass., June 20, 1909); Uta v. Uta, *Hōritsu shinbun* (No. 459) 8 (Nagasaki Ct. App., Sept. 28, 1907); Ikeda v. Ikeda, *Hōritsu shinbun* (No. 493) 17 (Osaka Ct. App., Mar. 26, 1908). For discussion of the "abuse of rights" doctrine, see Aoyama Michio, *"Wagakuni ni okeru kenri ran'yō riron no hatten"* (Development of the theory of abuse of rights in Japan), in *Kenri no ran'yō* (Abuse of rights), Vol. 1 (Tokyo: Yūhikaku, 1963), pp. 9–45; translated in John O. Haley and Dan F. Henderson (eds.), *Law and the Legal Process in Japan* (Asian Law Course Materials, University of Washington School of Law, Seattle, 1988 ed.), pp. 632–649.

6. See Taninaka v. Nozawa, 21 Minroku 49 (Gr. Ct. Cass., Jan. 16, 1915). For discussion in English, see Rex L. Coleman, "Japanese Family Law," *Stanford Law Review*, Vol. 9 (1956), at pp. 138–142; Yōzō Watanabe, "The Family and the Law: The Individualistic Promise and Modern Japanese Family Law," in A.T. von Mehren (ed.), *Law in Japan: The Legal Order in a Changing Society* (Cambridge: Harvard University Press, 1963), at pp. 365–366.

7. Tadao Hozumi, *"Hōritsu kōi no 'kaishaku' no kōzō to kinō II"* (Structure and function of the 'Interpretation' of juristic acts), *Hōgaku kyōkai zasshi*, Vol. 78, No. 1 (1961), at pp. 27–71, translated into English in *Law in Japan: An Annual*, Vol. 5 (1972), at pp. 132–164.

8. See Julian Gresser, Kōichirō Fujikura, and Akio Morishima, *Environmental Law in Japan* (Cambridge: MIT Press, 1981), at pp. 4–14.

9. *Tōkyō Asahi shinbun*, July 17, 1919, at p. 2.

10. Peter Duus, *Party Rivalry and Political Change in Taishō Japan* (Cambridge: Harvard University Press, 1968), at pp. 133–161.

11. Hozumi Shigetō, *"Chōtei hō,"* (Conciliation law), *Gendai hōgaku zenshū*, Vol. 38 (Tokyo: Nihon Hyōronsha, 1931), at p. 287.

12. *Shakuchi shakuya chōtei hō* (Law No. 41, 1922).

13. *Kosaku chōtei hō* (Law No. 18, 1924).

14. Ann Waswo, "The Origins of Tenant Unrest," in B.S. Silbermann and H.D. Harootunian (eds.), *Japan in Crisis* (Princeton: Princeton University Press, 1974), at pp. 387–388.

15. Ibid., at p. 389.

16. Civil Code, arts. 265–269.

17. Civil Code, arts. 270–279.

18. Civil Code, art. 604(1).

19. Civil Code, art. 278.

20. Civil Code, art. 268.

21. Yōzō Watanabe, *Tochi tatemono no hōritsu seido* (Legal institutions for land and buildings) (Tokyo: University of Tokyo Press, 1960), at p. 177.

22. Waswo, op. cit., at p. 397.

23. Watanabe, op. cit., at p. 176.

24. Waswo, op. cit., at p. 374

25. Hozumi, op. cit.

26. Saikō Saibansho (Supreme Court) (ed.), *"Wagakuni ni okeru chōtei seido no enkaku"* (Development of conciliation in our country) (Tokyo: Supreme Court of Japan, n.d. ca. 1951), at p. 21.

27. Waswo, op. cit., at p. 374.

28. Nagashima Hatasu, *Kosaku chōtei hō kōwa* (Discussion of farm tenancy conciliation law) (Tokyo: Shimizu Shoten, 1924).

29. Quoted in Byron K. Marshall, *Capitalism and Nationalism in Prewar Japan* (Stanford: Stanford University Press, 1967), at p. 60, from Kanda Kōichi, *Nihon Kōjōhō to rōdō hogo* (Factory law and protection of labor in Japan) (Tokyo: Dōbunkan, 1919), at p. 5.

30. See, e.g., Ron Napier, "The Transformation of the Japanese Labor Market, 1894–1937," in T. Najita and J.V. Koschmann (eds.), *Conflict in Modern Japanese History* (Princeton: Princeton University Press, 1982), at p. 350.

31. *Rōdō sōgi chōtei hō* (Law No. 57, 1926).

32. Saikō Saibansho, op. cit., at p. 34.

33. 48 Stat. 195. The provisions of the articles delegating authority for "cooperative action among trade groups" (§1) to establish "codes of fair competition" (§3a) were held to constitute an unconstitutional delegation of governmental authority in A.L.A. Schechter Poultry Corp. v. United States, 295 U.S. 495 (1935).

34. Ronald P. Dore and Tsutomu Ōuchi, "Rural origins of Japanese Fascism," in J.W. Morley (ed.), *Dilemmas of Growth in Prewar Japan* (Princeton: Princeton University Press, 1971), at pp. 201– 209.

35. *Senji minji tokubetsu hō* (Law No. 63, 1942).

36. Ibid., art. 19(2).

37. Land Lease and House Lease Conciliation Law, art. 5.

38. Ibid., art. 3.

39. Law No. 17, 1924, art. 4-2.

40. *Nōchi chōsei hō* (Law No. 67, 1938).

41. Ibid., art. 67.

42. See *Tōkyō Asahi shinbun*, Jan. 12, 13, 14, 15, 16, 17, 18, 1928, all at p. 2.

43. Koga Masayoshi, *Kenri ishiki ni tsuite* (On rights consciousness), *Hanrei taimuzu* (Special Issue No. 3, 1977), at p. 6.

44. Ibid., at p. 7.

45. Dore and Ōuchi, op. cit., at p. 203.

46. Henderson, *Conciliation*, Vol. 1, op. cit., at pp. 2-4.

47. *Kinsen saimu rinji chōtei hō* (Law No. 26, 1932).

48. See, e.g., Matsuo Kikutanō, *"Chōtei hō hatashite sonchi seshimu-beki ka"* (Should we continue to develop conciliation laws?), *Hōsō kōron* (No. 408) (July 1, 1934), at p. 5; *"Kinsen saimu chōtei narabi ni kakushu chōtei hō teppai mondai"* (Issue of abolition of the monetary claims conciliation law and other conciliation statutes), *Hōsō kōron* (No. 408) (July 1, 1934), at pp. 51-63; Narita Atsuo, *"Chōtei seido no bakko to shihō saiban no botsuraku"* (Proliferation of conciliation and the ruin of judicial trials), *Hōritsu shinbun* (No. 4066) (Dec. 15, 1936), at p. 3.

49. Matsuo, op. cit.

50. Ishibashi Magojirō, *"Chōtei hō to shokken shugi"* (Conciliation laws and authoritarianism), *Hōritsu shinbun* (No. 3101) (April 3, 1930), at p. 3.

51. See, e.g., Higashimoto Norikata, *"Kaikyū-teki ni mitaru kinsen saimu rinji chōtei hō"* (Temporary monetary claims conciliation law from a [Marxian] class perspective), *Hōritsu shinbun* (No. 3471) (Oct. 28, 1931), at p. 3; Miyoshi Shigeo, *"Gendai shakaishisō jōka no tame ni kakushu chōtei hō no haishi o nozomu"* (Hoping for the abolition of all conciliation laws for the purification of contemporary social theory), *Hōsō kōron* (No. 407) (June 1, 1937), at pp. 7–12.

52. Japan's rash of tenancy disputes in the 1920s and 1930s have recently generated considerable academic dispute in the United States as well. See Nishida Yoshiaki, "Growth of the Meiji Landlord System and Tenancy Disputes after World War I: A Critique of Richard Smethurst, *Agricultural Development and Tenancy Disputes in Japan, 1870–1940,"* *Journal of Japanese Studies*, Vol. 15, No. 2 (1989), at pp. 389–415; Richard J. Smethurst, "Challenge to Orthodoxy and its Orthodox Critics: A Reply to Nishida Yoshiaki," *Journal of Japanese Studies*, Vol. 15, No. 2 (1989), at pp. 417–437. All agree, however, that in both the 1920s and 1930s, tenants fared quite well before both the courts and conciliation committees.

53. Ann Waswo, *Japanese Landlords: The Decline of a Rural Elite* (Berkeley: University of California Press, 1977), at p. 108.

54. See Ronald P. Dore, *Land Reform in Japan* (London: Oxford University Press, 1959), at pp. 131, 147–148.

55. Wolf Ladejinsky, "Farm Tenancy and Japanese Agriculture," *Foreign Agriculture*, Vol. 1 (1937), at p. 425.

56. See, e.g., Higashimoto, op. cit., at p. 3; Miyoshi, op. cit., at p. 7.

57. See, Matsunaga Yoshiichi, *"Chōtei seido no kaizen"* (Reforming the conciliation system), *Hōritsu Shinbun* (No. 3365) (Feb. 3, 1932), at p. 7.

58. Ibid., at p. 8.

59. Miura Yagorō, *"Chōtei no shidō seishin"* (Guiding spirit of conciliation), *Hōritsu shinbun* (No. 3886) (Sept. 15, 1935), at p. 4.

60. Yamaguchi Yonachirō, *"Shakuchi shakuya chōtei hō no ran'yō to kaisei no ky'ūmu"* (Abuse of land lease and house lease conciliation and the urgency of reform), in *Hōritsu shinbun* (No. 3628) (Nov. 30, 1933), at p. 4.

61. Kishii Tatsuo, *"Chōtei kanken"* (Narrow view of conciliation), *Hōsō kōron* (No. 413) (Jan. 1, 1935), at p. 11.

62. Matsuo, op. cit., at p. 7.

63. See, e.g., Narita, op. cit., at p. 3.

64. See, e.g., Opinion of Inomata Kisei, in *Hōsō kōron* (No. 408), op. cit., at p. 52.

65. See, e.g., Matsuo, op. cit.

66. *Hōsō kōron* (No. 408), op. cit., at pp. 51–63.

67. Ibid., at p. 57.

68. Nomura v. Yamaki, 14 Minshū 1657 (Sup. Ct., G.B., July 6, 1960).

69. 10 Minshū 1355 (Sup. Ct., G.B., Oct. 31, 1956).

70. Ibid., at p. 1361.

71. Richard L. Abel, *The Legal Profession in England and Wales* (Oxford: Basil Blackwell, 1988), at pp. 446, 483.

72. Erhard Blankenburg and Ulrike Schultz, "German Advocates: A Highly Regulated Profession," in R.L. Abel and P.S.C. Lewis (eds.), *Lawyers in Society*, Vol. 2 (Berkeley: University of California Press, 1988), at pp. 124–125.

73. Ibid., at p. 150.

74. The initial policy of the Meiji government conformed to Tokugawa practice. In 1869 the government issued a notice prohibiting representation in litigation except in situations where the party was temporarily or permanently incapacitated. *Dajōkan tatsu*, Nov. 28, 1869, detailed in Tōkyō Bengoshi Kai (ed.), *Tōkyō bengoshi kai hyakunenshi* (Hundred year history of the Tokyo bar association) (Tokyo: Tōkyō Bengoshi Kai, 1980), at p. 13.

75. See article 42, *Shihō shokumu teisei (Dajōkan mugotatsu*, Aug. 3, 1873), in *Tōkyō Bengoshi Kai*, op. cit., at p. 10.

76. *Daigennin kisoku* (Shihōshō, *Futatsu* No. 1, 1876), in Tōkyō Bengoshi Kai, op. cit., Appendix, at p. 34.

77. Kenzō Ōtsubo, *Japan Federation of Bar Associations* (Tokyo: Asian Legal Research Institute, 1977), at p. 16; Richard W. Rabinowitz, The Japanese Lawyer: A Study in the Sociology of the Legal Profession (Ph.D. dissertation, Department of Social Science, Harvard University, 1955), at p. 119.

78. *Daigennin kisoku* (Shihōshō, *Futatsu* No. 1, 1880), in Tōkyō Bengoshi Kai (ed.), op. cit., at p. 42.

79. Ibid., arts. 3, 14.

80. Rabinowitz, Japanese Lawyer, op. cit., at p. 38.

81. *Bengoshi hō* (Law No. 7, 1893).

82. Ibid., art. 1.

83. Tadao Fukuhara notes that in 1929 alone foreign lawyers practicing in Yokohama and Kobe reportedly represented parties in 432 first instance trials, 39 *kōso* appeals, and 20 *jōkoku* appeals. Tadao Fukuhara, "The Status of Foreign Lawyers in Japan," *Japanese Annual of International Law* (1973), at p. 23.

84. The origin of the term is not certain (see Rabinowitz, *op. cit.*, at pp. 39-41), but by the early 1920s the label was attached to persons who provided assistance to litigants and helped in the out-of-court settlement of disputes for a fee. The bar repeatedly sought their prohibition. See *Tōkyō Bengoshi Kai*, op. cit., at pp. 323-326.

85. *Bengoshi hō*, art. 4(1) and (2).

86. See Ibid., art. 11.

87. Rabinowitz, Japanese Lawyer, op. cit., at pp. 59-60.

88. *Shihōkan shiho oyobi bengoshi no shikaku ni kansuru ken* (Cases concerning judicial officers' probation and qualification as lawyer), Law No. 52, 1923.

89. *Japan-Manchoukuo Year Book, 1937* (Tokyo: Japan-Manchoukuo Year Book Co., 1937), at p. 96.

90. *Bengoshi hō* (Law No. 53, 1933).

91. *Hōritsu jimu toriatsukai no torishimari ni kansuru hōritsu* (Law concerning the regulation of legal practice), Law No. 54, 1933.

92. *Bengoshi hō*, art. 6.

93. Rabinowitz, Japanese Lawyer, op. cit., at p. 63.

94. Peter Duus, "History of Japan (Taishō and early Shōwa history)," *Kodansha Encyclopedia of Japan*, Vol. 13 (Tokyo: Kodansha International, 1983), at pp. 119-120. Japan's 1930 census estimates that only 370,000 persons were unemployed. As noted by William W. Lockwood, however, this figure reflects "a good deal of underreporting" since large numbers of unemployed urban workers returned to rural comunities or found part-time employment. William W. Lockwood, *The Economic Development of Japan* (Princeton: Princeton University Press, 1954), at p. 156, fn. 11.

95. Andrew Gordon, *The Evolution of Labor Relations in Japan: Heavy Industry 1853-1955* (Cambridge: Harvard University Press, 1986), at p. 134.

96. Hugh T. Patrick, "The Economic Muddle of the 1920s," in Morely, op. cit., at Table 1, p. 214.

97. Lockwood, op. cit., at p. 467.

98. Gordon, op. cit., at p. 156.

99. See Lockwood, op. cit., at pp. 487–494.

100. Interviews with former Justice Shunzō Kobayashi and others, September 1979.

101. Letter to author from Masatsugu Mitsuki, Esq., March 27, 1978.

102. See, e.g., *Tōkyō Asahi shinbun*, March 2, 1928, p. 2 (Lawyer strangles beloved daughter and cuts wrists with scissors after conviction for larceny); April 9, 1928, p. 4 (Lawyer connected with rural tenancy rights goes mad on train, escaping from conductors, strips naked but runs into group of farmers, with whom he fights); April 13, 1930, p. 2 (Corrupt lawyer arrested); April 16, 1930, p. 2 (Another corrupt lawyer arrested on charges of extortion, "major round-up in the making"); April 18, 1930, p. 2 (Another corrupt lawyer arrested); April 20, 1930, p. 2 (Lawyer arrested for fraud); June 1, 1930, p. 2 (Five lawyers prosecuted for fraud); July 5, 1930, p. 7 (Lawyer reporting theft of brief case containing client's funds suspected of having stolen the money himself); Nov. 14, 1930, p. 11 (Lawyer arrested for fraud); March 6, 1931, p. 3 (Client sues his attorney for fraud); April 13, 1931, p. 11 (Drunken lawyer shot to death while breaking into house, later thought to have mistaken the house for his nearby office while intoxicated); May 6, 1931, p. 2 (Common for ugly disputes to break out between lawyers and their clients over fees because some lawyers take advantage of the weak or for other reasons); June 21, 1931, p. 11 (Lawyer about to be charged with fraud disappears but is discovered when he applies to practice with procurator's office in another district).

103. Justice Shunzō Kobayashi to author, September 1979.

104. Blakemore memo (undated draft), Code of Criminal Procedure File, Box 1477: SCAP, Legal Section, Legislation & Justice Division (National Archives, Suitland, Md.).

105. Ibid.

106. See *Bengoshi hō* (Law No. 205, 1949), arts. 8–19 (Registration with Japan Federation of Bar Associations); art. 12 (Right of individual bar associations to refuse to transmit request for registration on grounds of disqualification); arts. 13 and 18 (Right of individual bar associations to acquire cancellation of registration); art. 22 (Duty of lawyers to obey bar association rules); arts. 56–61 (Responsibility of bar associations for disciplinary action by bar associations). Constitution of Japan, art. 77, empowers the Supreme Court to make rules on "matters relating to attorneys." *Bengoshi hō*, art. 49, gives the Supreme Court supervisory authority over bar associations.

107. *Bengoshi hō*, art. 72 (Prohibitions against unauthorized practice of law and misrepresentation of qualification as lawyer); arts. 77–79 (Penal provisions for unauthorized practice and misrepresentation of qualification as lawyer).

108. Calculated from population figures in Statistics Bureau, Management and Coordination Agency, Prime Minister's Office, *Japan Statistical Yearbook* 1988, at pp. 23–24.

109. Nihon Bengoshi Rengōkai (Japan Federation of Bar Associations), *Shihō hakusho* (White paper on the judiciary) (Tokyo: 1974), pp. 326–327. For one of the first comments in English on the heavy caseload in Japanese courts, see Kazuaki Sono and Warren L. Shattuck, "Personal Property as Collateral in Japan and the United States," *Washington Law Review*, Vol. 39 (1964), at p. 571, fn. 6. This early observation was all but ignored in most discussions of litigation in Japan.

110. Nihon Bengoshi Rengōkai, op. cit.

111. Hideo Tanaka, *The Japanese Legal System: Introductory Cases and Materials* (Tokyo: University of Tokyo Press, 1976), at p. 476.

112. Ibid., at p. 477.

113. See Klaus F. Röhl, *"Gründe und Ursprünge aktuellen Geschäfts überlastung der Gerichte aus soziologischen Sicht"* (Causes and origins of the actual overload of courts: a sociological survey), and Peter Gottwald, *"Zur Bewältigung der Überlastung der Rechtsmittelgerichte"* (Managing overload in appellate courts), both in P. Gilles (ed.), *Effiziente Rechts verfolgung* (Efficiency in the pursuit of justice) (Heidelberg: C.F. Müllen Juristischen Verlag, 1987), at pp. 52, 53, 151.

114. See, e.g., Hozumi Shigeto, *"Shōgaku saibansho to hōritsu fujokai"* (Small claims courts and legal aid societies), Part 2, *Asahi shinbun,* January 13, 1928, at p. 3; also *Minji soshō gekisō su* (Dramatic increase in civil litigation) *Asahi shinbun,* Dec. 14, 1930.

115. In an otherwise very thoughtful series of articles in *Jiyū to seigi* (Liberty and justice), the Japanese Federation of Bar Associations' monthly periodical, on the problems of a "unified profession"—the expression for the postwar system of common qualifications for practicing attorneys, prosecutors, and judges through the Legal Research and Training Institute—no mention is made of the impact of this system on delay and court congestion. See *Jiyū to seigi,* Vol. 39, No. 2 (February 1988), at pp. 4–101.

116. See Marc Galanter, "Reading the Landscape of Disputes: What We Know and Don't Know (And Think We Know) About Our Allegedly Contentious and Litigious Society," *UCLA Law Review,* Vol. 31, No. 1 (1983), at pp. 4–71.

117. J. Mark Ramseyer, "Reluctant Litigant Revisited: Rationality and Disputes in Japan," *Journal of Japanese Studies,* Vol. 14, No. 1 (1988), at p. 112.

118. For an attempt at international comparison, see Austin Sarat and Joel B. Grossman, "Courts and Conflict Resolution: Problems in the Mobilization of Adjudication," *American Political Science Review,* Vol. 69 (1975), at pp. 1200–1217. Sarat and Grossman include data showing that Sweden, Finland, and Norway have less than half the number of civil cases per 100,000 population in comparison to Japan. Ibid., at p. 1208.

119. See, e.g., Takao Tanase, "The Management of Disputes: Automobile Accident Compensation in Japan," *Law & Society Review,* Vol. 24, No. 3 (1990), at pp. 651–691. Tanase does not fully endorse the notion that Japanese share an unusual aversion to litigation. Instead, he argues, low litigation rates reflect effective settlement of disputes through mediation. Nevertheless, he subscribes to the view that litigation rates in Japan are unusually low by virtue of reduced—albeit managed—demand.

120. See, e.g., David J. Danielski, "The Supreme Court of Japan: An Exploratory Study," in Glendon Schubert and David J. Danielski (eds.), *Comparative Judicial Behavior* (New York and London: Oxford University Press, 1969), at pp. 124–125; Alfred C. Oppler, *Legal Reform in Occupied Japan: A Participant Looks Back* (Princeton: Princeton University Press, 1976), at p. 107.

121. See, e.g., Tanase, op. cit.

122. The proposed rules were published in *Jiyū to seigi* (Liberty and justice), Vol. 39, No. 7 (1988), at pp. 57–62.

123. *Bengoshi hō* (Law No. 53, 1933), art. 27(2).

124. *Bengoshi hō* (Law No. 205, 1949), art. 30(3).

125. *Jiyū to seigi* (Liberty and justice), Vol. 32, No. 10 (1981), at p. 54.

126. Nihon Bengoshi Rengōkai Chōsa Shitsu, *Bengoshi gyōmu no jittai* (State of lawyers' practice) (Tokyo: Nihon Bengoshi Rengōkai, 1972), at p. 16.

127. Chie Nakane, *Japanese Society* (Berkeley: University of California Press, 1972), at pp. 48–49.

128. See Dan Fenno Henderson, *Foreign Enterprise in Japan* (Chapel Hill: University of North Carolina Press, 1973), at p. 128; Tasuku Matsuo, *U.S. and Japan Bankruptcy Law* (Tokyo: Sakai Publishing Co., 1971), at pp. 1–3, 197.

129. Yamanaka v. Kondō, *Hanrei taimuzu* (No. 495) 64 (July 1, 1983) (Tsu Dist. Ct., Feb. 25, 1983).

130. See, e.g., Discussion by Professors Eiichi Hoshino and Yoshimitsu Aoyama in *Rinjin soshō to hō* (Suits between neighbors and the law), *Hōgaku kyōshitsu* (No. 40) (January 1984), at p. 36.

131. Ryusaki Kisuke, *Saiban o meguru shimin to bengoshi* (Citizens who resort to court and lawyers), *Hanrei taimuzu* (No. 500) (Sept. 1, 1983), at pp. 42.

132. Mark A. Peterson, *Compensation for Injuries: Civil Jury Verdicts in Cook County* (Santa Monica, Calif.: Rand Corporation, Institute for Civil Justice, 1984), at p. 55.

133. David H. Bayley, *Forces of Order: Police Behavior in Japan and the United States* (Berkeley: University of California Press, 1976), at p. 87.

134. Henderson, *Conciliation*, Vol. 2, at p. 191.

135. Bayley, op. cit., at p. 88.

136. Zensuke Ishimura and Yuriko Kaminaga, "Attorneys and Cases Involving Automobile Accidents," *Law in Japan: An Annual*, Vol. 9 (1976), at p. 96.

137. Stewart Macaulay, "Non-Contractual Relations in Business: A Preliminary Study," *American Sociological Review*, Vol. 28 (1963), at pp. 55–67.

138. J. Mark Ramseyer and Minoru Nakazato, "The Rational Litigant: Settlement Amounts and Verdict Rates in Japan," *Journal of Legal Studies*, Vol. 18 (June 1989), at pp. 263–290.

139. Revenge as a motivating factor for litigation and the apology as the antidote are all too often neglected elements of any legal order. For a brilliant account of revenge as a catalyst for expanding a late eighteenth-century Chinese censorship campaign, see R. Kent Guy, *The Emperor's Four Treasuries: Scholars on the State in the Late Ch'ien-lung Era* (Cambridge: Harvard University, Council on East Asian Studies, 1987), at pp. 179–190. For a comparative view of apology, see Hiroshi Wagatsuma and Arthur Rosett, "The Implications of Apology: Law and Culture in Japan and the United States," *Law & Society Review*, Vol. 20, No. 4 (1986), at pp. 461–498; John O. Haley, "Comment: The Implications of Apology," *Law & Society Review*, Vol. 20, No. 4 (1986), at pp. 499–507.

140. See, e.g., Frank K. Upham, *Law and Social Change in Postwar Japan* (Cambridge: Harvard University Press, 1987), at Chapter Four; also Catherine W. Brown, "Japanese Approaches to Equal Rights for Women: The Legal Framework," *Law in Japan: An Annual*, Vol. 12 (1979), at pp. 29–56, reprinted in J.O. Haley (ed.), *Law and Society in Contemporary Japan* (Dubuque, Iowa: Kendall-Hunt, 1988), at pp. 197–220.

141. See, e.g., J. Mark Ramseyer, "The Costs of the Consensual Myth: Antitrust Enforcement and Institutional Barriers to Litigation in Japan," *Yale Law Journal*, Vol. 94 (1985), at pp. 604–645.

142. John Henry Merryman, *The Civil Law Tradition: An Introduction to the Legal Systems of Western Europe and Latin America* (Stanford: Stanford University Press, 2d ed. 1985), at p. 49.

143. Ibid., at p. 55.

144. See Ted L. Stein, "Contempt, Crisis, and the Courts: The World Court and The Hostage Rescue Attempt," *American Journal of International Law*, Vol. 76, No. 3 (July 1982), at pp. 504–512, esp. fns. 40–41.

145. *Zivilprozeß Ordnung* (Code of Civil Procedure), 30 Jan. 1877 (RGBl.S.83), as amended, art. 890.

146. See, e.g., Ernst Forsthoff, *Lehrbuch des Verwaltungsrechts* (Administrative law header) (Munich: C.H. Beck, 10th ed. 1973), at pp. 290–296.

Chapter 6

1. Procurators are, of course, assisted by clerical, administrative, and investigatory staff. However, they review all criminal files and remain responsible for any litigation.

2. Charles R. Fenwick, "Crime and Justice in Japan: Implications for the United States," *International Journal of Comparative and Applied Criminal Justice*, Vol. VI, No. 1 (Spring 1982), at p. 62. More complete statistics compiled by Loyola University (Chicago) economist David Merriman confirm Fenwick's conclusions. David Merriman, An Economic Analysis of the Post- World War II Decline in the Japanese Crime Rate (unpublished paper, November 1984), at Table 4, pp. 8–11. Merriman shows that between 1952 and 1982 the number of known homicides, rapes, bodily injury cases, robberies, and cases of fraud declined by more than 50 percent. Statistics on the number of cases reported for investigation to the procuracy and indictments filed indicate that except for criminal traffic violations and crimes under special statutes, overall crime rates per capita have been remarkably stable in Japan for over a half-century. Although the declines in the crime rates noted by Fenwick and Merriman may be somewhat exaggerated by the apparently aberrational increase in crime rates at the end of the 1960s, the total number of reported criminal code offenses per 100,000 population, 753.2, was only marginally less than the average for five years before wartime mobilization in 1937.

3. See, e.g., Hōmusho (Ministry of Justice), *Hōmu nenkan shōwa 62 nen* (Legal affairs annual report, 1987), at pp. 321–324, 326–329, for postwar statistics.

4. See Law No. 126, 1967, amending the Road Traffic Law (*Dōro kōtsū hō*), Law No. 105, 1960.

5. Ministry of Justice, *Summary of White Paper on Crime* (Tokyo: 1969), at p. 12.

6. Atsushi Nagashima, "The Accused and Society: The Administration of Criminal Justice in Japan," in A. von Mehren (ed.), *Law in Japan: The Legal Order in a Changing Society* (Cambridge: Harvard University Press, 1963), at Table 1, p. 322. At p. 312 Nagashima attributes delay in part to "prolonged statements by defendant—sometimes including political statements."

7. Ibid., at p. 322.

8. See, e.g., Richard Breuer, *Die Stellung der Staatsanwaltschaft in Japan* (The status of the procuracy in Japan) (Berlin: Junker & Dirnnhaupt, 1940).

9. Gerhard Casper and Hans Zeisel, "Lay Judges in the German Criminal Courts," *Journal of Legal Studies*, Vol. 1 (January 1972), at pp. 149–150.

10. Comments to author by Procurator Haruki Sugiyama, Seattle, June 1990.

11. Under the Inquest of Prosecution Law (*Kensatsu shinsakai hō*), Law No. 147, 1948, prosecution review commissions are designed to control the exercise of prosecutorial discretion by means of citizen advisory groups in each district. They are described with additional references in B.J. George, "Discretionary Authority of Public Prosecutors in Japan," *Law in Japan: An Annual*, Vol. 17 (1984), at pp. 64–65.

12. Conversations with Thomas L. Blakemore.

13. Keisatsuchō, *Hanzai tōkei shōwa 54 nen* (Crime statistics 1979) (Tokyo: 1979), at pp. 116-117.

14. George, op. cit., at fn. 94, p. 51.

15. Minoru Shikita, "Integrated Approach to Effective Administration of Criminal and Juvenile Justice," in *Criminal Justice in Asia: The Quest for an Integrated Approach* (Tokyo: UNAFEI, 1982), at p. 37.

16. Several studies on suspension of prosecution are available in English. One of the most thorough and most recent is George, op. cit. See also, Shigemitsu Dandō, "System of Discretionary Prosecution in Japan," *American Journal of Comparative Law*, Vol. 18 (1970), at pp. 518-531.

17. Code of Criminal Procedure (*Keiji soshō hō*), Law No. 131, 1948, arts. 461-470 provide for simplified proceedings by summary courts [*kan'i saibansho*], upon request by the prosecutor (art. 461) and acquiescence in writing by the accused (art. 461-2). Article 7(3) of the Penal Fine Temporary Special Measures Law (*Bakkin tō rinji sochi hō*), Law No. 251, 1947, as amended through Law No. 61, 1972, increased the maximum time from 5,000 yen to 200,000 yen.

18. As George, op. cit., at fn. 146, p. 57, notes, similar simplified procedures in which no defense is made are also available under art. 291-2 of the Code of Criminal Procedure in cases involving offenses for which the statutory penalty does not exceed a prison term of less than one year. However, in Table 6-3 such cases are included under the "Formal Trial" category. Consequently the number of noncontested cases allowed by the prosecutor in which the penalty is relatively minor is even greater than indicated in Table 6-3.

19. See Hōmushō (Ministry of Justice), *Hōmu nenkan* (Yearbook on administration of justice), for 1948-87.

20. Saikō Saibansho Jimu Sōkyoku (Supreme Court General Secretariat), *Shōwa 62 nen shihō tōkei nenpō; 2 keijihen* (1987 judicial statistics annual report: Vol. 2, criminal cases) (Saikō Saibansho, Tokyo, 1988), at p. 196.

21. In 1987, for example, guilt was not contested in 56,975 or 92 percent of 61,995 district court cases. Ibid., at p. 110.

22. Ibid., at p. 238.

23. See Ibid., 1964-87.

24. Haruo Abe, "The Accused and Society: Therapeutic and Preventive Aspects of Criminal Justice in Japan," in von Mehren, op. cit., at p. 334; Katsuyoshi Ōyama, Criminal Justice in Japan IV (unpublished paper, Tokyo, UNAFEI, c. 1978), at p. 9. The Ministry of Justice's 1989 *Summary of White Paper on Crime* (Tokyo, 1989) indicates that 18,130 of 32,893 (57%) offenders were released on parole before the expiration of their terms (at p. 117).

25. David H. Bayley, *Forces of Order: Police Behavior in Japan & the United States* (Berkeley: University of California Press, 1976), at p. 146.

26. Ibid.

27. Ministry of Justice *Summary of White Paper on Crime* (1989), op. cit., at p. 102.

28. See Japan, *Crime Prevention and Control National Statement* (The Fifth United Nations Congress on the Prevention of Crime and Treatment of Offenders, Sept. 1-12, 1975) (Tokyo), at p. 50. On controversy over use of detention, see Kazuo Itoh, "On Publication For Criticism of the 'Citizens' Human Rights Reports,'" *Law in Japan: An Annual*, Vol. 20 (1988), at pp. 64-65.

29. See, e.g., Richard S. Frase, "The Decision to File Criminal Charges: A Quantitative Study of Prosecutorial Discretion," *University of Chicago Law Review*, Vol. 47

(1980), at pp. 246–309. Frase estimates that U.S. attorneys prosecute 20 to 25 percent of all new criminal cases, a rate, he believes, considerably lower than state prosecutions. He indicates that, aside from consideration of the convictability of the accused or the availability of a more appropriate means of prosecution, such as state prosecution or civil or administrative proceedings, the decision not to prosecute is based on either the gravity of the offense or such personal characteristics of the accused as age and prior record. Ibid., at p. 264. Apparently neither the attitude of the accused nor the response of the victim is taken into account.

30. Shikita, op. cit., at p. 36. Walter Ames reports an estimate for Okayama prefecture that 95 percent of all suspects confess during police interrogation. Walter L. Ames, *Police and Community in Japan* (Berkeley: University of California Press, 1981), at p. 136.

31. Ibid., at p. 37.

32. Ibid.

33. Comment by Minoru Shikita in a 1980 Japan Society seminar held in New York City, quoted in Craig J. Parker, *The Japanese Police System Today: An American Perspective* (Tokyo: Kōdansha International, 1984), at p. 108.

34. Marsha E. Goodman, "The Exercise and Control of Prosecutorial Discretion in Japan," *UCLA Pacific Basin Law Journal*, Vol. 5, Nos. 1 & 2 (Spring and Fall 1986), at pp. 16–95.

35. Ibid., at p. 38.

36. Ibid., at p. 40.

37. See, e.g., Igarashi Futaba, "*Daiyō kangoku mondai ni tsuite*" (Concerning the problem of substitute jails), *Jurisuto* (No. 637) (May 1, 1977), at pp. 116–125; Igarashi Futaba, "*Nase keijiryūchijo' ga hitsuyō ka*" (Why are criminal detention centers necessary?), *Jurisuto* (No. 712) (March 3, 1980), pp. 85–91; see also, Futaba Igarashi, "Crime, Confession and Control in Contemporary Japan" (introduction and translation by Gavan McCormick), *Law in Context*, Vol. 2 (1984), at pp. 1–30.

38. See, e.g., Ames, op. cit.; Bayley, op. cit.; Parker, op. cit.; and William Clifford, *Crime Control in Japan* (Lexington, Mass.: Lexington Books, 1976).

39. Bayley, op. cit., at p. 152.

40. Ibid., at p. 153.

41. Ibid., at p. 154.

42. Ibid., at p. 150.

43. Miyazawa Setsuo, *Hanzai sōsa o meguru daiissen keiji no ishiki to kōdō* (The consciousness and practices of first-line detectives in criminal investigations) (Tokyo: Seibundō, 1985).

44. Ibid., at pp. 390–395.

45. Ibid., at pp. 235–264.

46. Chalmers Johnson, *Conspiracy at Matsukawa* (Berkeley: University of California Press, 1972), at p. 149.

47. Ibid., at 151.

48. See, e.g., Bayley's comparison, op. cit., at p. 151.

49. See cases analyzed in Daniel H. Foote, From Japan's Death Row to Freedom (unpublished manuscript).

50. Shigemitsu Dandō, *Japanese Criminal Procedure* (B.J. George, trans.) (Hackensack, N.J.: Fred B. Rothman, 1965), at p. 206.

51. Ibid., at p. 196.

52. Ibid., at pp. 205–206.

53. Shikita, op. cit.

54. See Johnson, op. cit., at pp. 11, 34–36, 201 (art. 37.1a).

55. Ibid.

56. See, e.g., Jerome Alan Cohen, *The Criminal Process in the People's Republic of China, 1949–1963: An Introduction* (Cambridge: Harvard University Press, 1968), at pp. 26 (Case No. 2), 30–33, 35, 554–555 (Item 261A).

57. Hulsewé notes the existence of an edict restricting the use of torture to assure the accuracy of coerced confessions as early as A.D. 84, Hulsewé, op. cit., p. 76. Shūzō Shiga, however, argues that confessions were not considered evidence. Shiga, op. cit., No. 32, at p. 120.

58. Paul H.C. Chen, *Chinese Legal Tradition under the Mongols: The Code of 1291 as Reconstructed* (Princeton: Princeton University Press, 1979), at pp. 51–61.

59. Ibid., at pp. 54–55.

60. Ishii, *Hōseishi*, op. cit., at p. 75.

61. Ibid., at p. 214.

62. As noted previously, under the *Legalitätsprinzip* or "legality principle" of German criminal procedure, the procuracy must by law prosecute all persons who, after investigation, are found to have committed criminal offenses. *Strafprozeßordnung* §§ 152(2). Minor exceptions are made.

63. See *Japan Weekly Chronicle*, March 16, 1922, at p. 389.

64. *Chian iji hō* (Law No. 46, 1925). See in English: Patricia G. Steinhoff, *Tenkō*: Ideological and Social Integration in Prewar Japan (Ph.D. dissertation, Department of History, Harvard University, 1969); and Richard H. Mitchell, *Thought Control in Prewar Japan* (Ithaca: Cornell University Press, 1976); see in Japanese: Okudaira Yasuhiro, *Chian iji hō shōshi* (Short history of the peace preservation law) (Tokyo: Chikuma Shobō, 1977).

65. See Okudaira, op. cit., at pp. 128–142; Mitchell, op. cit., at p. 111.

66. Okudaira, op. cit., at p. 135.

67. Quoted in Mitchell, op. cit., at pp. 98–99.

68. *Asahi shinbun*, June 7, 1936.

69. Both Ames and Bayley take note of the adoption of Little Red Riding Hood, which ends in the Japanese version with the wolf contritely asking to be forgiven. He is and all live happily ever after. Ames, op. cit., at p. 136; Bayley, op. cit., at pp. 139–140.

70. Bayley, op. cit., at pp. 138–140.

71. See, e.g., The Book of Jonah and the parable of the unforgiving servant, Matthew 18:21–35.

72. V. Lee Hamilton and Joseph Sanders, "Punishment and the Individual in the United States and Japan," *Law and Society Review*, Vol. 22, No. 2 (1988), at pp. 301–328.

73. Haruo Abe, for example, criticizes Japanese judges for a tendency toward excessive leniency in sentencing. Abe, op. cit., at p. 338

74. See, e.g., Miyazawa Kōichi (ed.), *Hanzai to higaisha: Nihon no higaishagaku* (Crime and victims: studies on victims in Japan), 2 vols. (Tokyo: Seibundō, 1970).

75. *Hōmu sōgō kenkyūjo kenkyūbu kiyō* 29 (Ministry of Justice Combined Research Institute Reesearch Division Bulletin No. 29) (Tokyo, 1986), at p. 20.

76. Katsuo Kawada, "Suspension of Prosecution in Japan" (unpublished paper, Tokyo, UNAFEI, n.d.), at pp. 19–20.

77. Dandō, "Discretionary Prosucution," op. cit., at pp. 527–528, noted in George, op. cit., at p. 59.

78. George, op. cit., at p. 59.

79. Bayley, op. cit., at pp. 140–141.

80. Ibid.

81. The works of Ellen Berscheid, Elaine Walster, and G. William Walster are particularly valuable in evaluating the Japanese approach. See, e.g., E. Walster, E. Berscheid, and G.W. Walster, "The Exploited: Justice or Justification," in J.R. Macaulay and C. Berkowitz (eds.), *Altruism and Helping Behavior* (New York: Academic Press, 1970); and Walster, Berscheid, and Walster, "When Does a Harm-doer Compensate a Victim," *Journal of Personality and Social Psychology*, Vol. 6 (1967), at pp. 435– 441. These and other works are summarized in Walster, Berscheid, and Walster, "New Directions in Equity Research," *Journal of Personality and Social Psychology*, Vol. 25, No. 2 (1973), at pp. 151–176, and Stewart Macauley and Elaine Walster, "Legal Structures and Restoring Equity," *Journal of Social Issues*, Vol. 27, No. 2 (1971), at pp. 173–195. I am indebted to Anne Marie Neugebauer, a University of Washington Law graduate, for introducing me to these materials.

82. See, e.g., G.M. Sykes and D. Matza, "Techniques of Neutralization: A Theory of Delinquency," *American Sociology Review*, Vol. 22 (1957), at pp. 664–670.

83. Abraham S. Goldstein, "Defining the Role of the Victim in Criminal Prosecution," *Mississippi Law Journal*, Vol. 52, No. 3 (Sept. 1982), at pp. 515–561.

84. Ibid.

85. Hamilton and Sanders, op. cit.

86. Citizens' Crime Commission of Philadelphia (ed.), *Tokyo: One City Where Crime Doesn't Pay* (Philadelphia: 1975).

87. Between 1950 and 1980 the percentage increase in crime rates in Sweden was even greater than in the United States. Steven Stack, "Social Structure and Swedish Crime Rates: A Time-Series Analysis, 1950–1979," *Criminology*, Vol. 20, Nos. 3 and 4 (November 1982), at p. 509. For example, burglary rates rose from 296 per 100,000 in 1950 to a rate of 1,679 in 1979 (a 468% increase) as compared to an increase in the United States from a rate per 100,000 of 312 in 1950 to 1,499 in 1979 (a 380% increase).

88. Fenwick, op. cit., at p. 66.

89. Ibid.

90. Ibid., at p. 67.

91. Ibid.

92. See, e.g., Kanehiro Hoshino, The Impact of Post-war Law Enforcement in Japanese Social Systems (unpublished paper, Conference on Contemporary Social Problems: Institutions of Change in Japanese Society, Center for Japanese Studies, University of California, Berkeley, Nov. 17, 1982), at p. 1.

93. Fenwick, op. cit., at pp. 64–65.

94. Yoshio Suzuki, "Crime," in *Kodansha Encyclopedia of Japan*, Vol. 2 (Tokyo: Kōdansha International, 1983), at p. 46.

95. Ibid.

Chapter 7

1. Robert E. Ward, *Japan's Political System* (Englewood Cliffs, N.J.: Prentice-Hall, 2d ed., 1978), at p. 163.

2. Henderson, *Foreign Enterprise* op. cit., at p. 195.

3. The person who coined the expression "Japan Incorporated" may now be lost to history, but one of the earliest published uses of the label appears in Eugene J. Kaplan, *Japan: The Government–Business Relationship* (Washington, D.C.: U.S. Department of Commerce, 1972).

4. William W. Lockwood, "Japan's 'New Capitalism,'" in W.W. Lockwood (ed.), *The State and Economic Enterprise in Japan* (Princeton: Princeton University Press, 1965), at pp. 447-522.

5. Chalmers Johnson, *MITI and the Japanese Miracle* (Stanford: Stanford University Press, 1982).

6. See, e.g., Joji Watanuki, *Politics in Postwar Japanese Society* (Tokyo: University of Tokyo Press, 1977), at p. 11.

7. Karel van Wolferen, *The Enigma of Japanese Power* (New York: Alfred A. Knopf, 1969), at pp. 43-44.

8. Although seldom analyzed, nearly all U.S. federal and state administrative agencies today have a similar role in advising and drafting legislation affecting areas under their jurisdiction. It is not uncommon for agency officials to sit informally with various congressional committees and work closely with their staffs in preparing legislation for Congress. See, e.g., Dennis C. Le Master, *Decade of Change: The Remaking of Forest Service Statutory Authority During the 1970s* (Westport, Conn.: Greenwood Press, 1984).

9. Johnson, *MITI*, op. cit., at p. 47.

10. Brian Smith, *Policy-making in the British Government: An Analysis of Power and Rationality* (Totowa, N.J.: Littlefield, 1976), at p. 86.

11. Ibid.

12. Gerhard Loewenberg, *Parliament in the German Political System* (Ithaca: Cornell University Press, 1967), at p. 267.

13. Henry W. Ehrmann, *Politics in France* (Boston: Little, Brown, 3d ed., 1983), at p. 307.

14. Ezra N. Suleiman, *Politics, Powers, and Bureaucracy in France: The Administrative Elite* (Princeton: Princeton University Press, 1974), at pp. 302-305.

15. See, e.g., Daniel I. Okimoto, "Ex-Bureaucrats in the Liberal Democratic Party," in D.I. Okimoto and T.R. Rohlen (eds.), *Inside the Japanese System* (Stanford: Stanford University Press, 1988), at pp. 187-190.

16. They include Shigeru Yoshida (Prime Minister 1946-47, 1948-54, Ministry of Foreign Affairs); Nobusuke Kishi (Prime Minister 1957-60, Ministry of Commerce and Industry); Hayato Ikeda (Prime Minister 1960-64, Ministry of Finance); Eisaku Satō (Prime Minister 1964-72, Ministry of Railways, later renamed Ministry of Transport); Takeo Fukuda (Prime Minister 1976-78, Ministry of Finance); Masayoshi Ōhira (Prime Minister 1978-80, Ministry of Finance).

17. Chalmers Johnson, "Japan, 'Who Governs?' An Essay on Official Bureaucracy," *Journal of Japanese Studies*, Vol. 2, No. 1 (1975), at p. 16.

18. See Stephen Reed, "Confused Voters and Contentious Politicians: The Five General Elections 1947-1955" (Paper presented at the Annual Meeting, Association for Asian Studies, Boston, Mass., April 1987), at p. 9; Satō Seisaburō and Matsuzaki Tetsuhisa, *Jimintō Seiken* (The LDP's political power) (Tokyo: Chūō Kōron, 1986), at p. 232.

19. Satō and Matsuzaki, op. cit..

20. Joel D. Aberbach, Robert D. Putnam, and Bert A. Rockman, *Bureaucrats and Politicians in Western Democracies* (Cambridge: Harvard University Press, 1987), at p. 277, fn. 16.

21. Haruhiro Fukui, "The Liberal Democratic Party Revisited: Continuity and Change in the Party's Structure and Performance," *Journal of Japanese Studies*, Vol. 10, No. 2 (1984), at p. 393.

22. Aberbach, Putnam, and Rockman, op. cit., at p. 277, note 16.

23. Henderson, *Foreign Enterprise*, op. cit., at p. 208.

24. Kenneth Culp Davis, *Administrative Law Treatise*, Vol. 1 (San Diego: K.C. Davis, 2d ed., 1982), at p. 17.

25. United States statistics from U.S. Bureau of the Census, *Statistical Abstract of the U.S. 1989* (Washington, D.C.: U.S. Government Printing Office, 1989), at Table 2, p. 7; U.S. Bureau of the Census, *Historical Statistics of the United States: Colonial Times to 1970*, Part 2 (Washington, D.C.: U.S. Government Printing Office, 1975), at Series Y308–317, p. 1102. Japanese statistics from Statistics Bureau, Management and Coordination Agency, Prime Minister's Office, *Japan Statistical Yearbook, 1949* (Tokyo: 1949), at Table 472, p. 873.

26. See Kent E. Calder, *Crisis and Compensation: Public Policy and Political Stability in Japan, 1949–1986* (Princeton: Princeton University Press, 1988), at p. 140, citing Johnson, MITI, op. cit., at p. 88.

27. Thomas Arthur Bisson, *Japan's War Economy* (New York: Institute of Pacific Relations, 1945), at p. 202.

28. Takafusa Nakamura, *The Postwar Japanese Economy: Its Development and Structure* (Tokyo: University of Tokyo Press, 1981), at p. 12.

29. Jerome B. Cohen, *Japan's Economy in War and Reconstruction* (Minneapolis: University of Minnesota Press, 1949), at p. 76.

30. Heinz Müller and Peter Giessler, *Kommentar zum Gesetz gegen Wettbewerbsbeschränkungen* (Commentary on the law against restraints of competition) (Frankfurt Lorch, 1st ed. 1958), at p. viii.

31. See George W. Stocking and Myron W. Watkins, *Cartels or Competition?* (New York: Twentieth Century Fund, 1948), at pp. 32–41.

32. Ibid., at pp. 93, 407.

33. Until mobilization and the advent of government procurement and raw material allocations in the mid-1930s Japan's *zaibatsu* did not enjoy significant gain in assets. See Cohen, op. cit., at p. 508. Unfortunately, however, statistics on *zaibatsu prices and profits are not available for the years before 1935*.

34. Yoshida Jinpū, *Nihon no karuteru* (Japanese cartels) (Tokyo: Tōyō Keizai Shinpō Kai, 1964), at p. 20.

35. Keizo Fujita, "Cartels and Their Conflicts in Japan," *Journal of the Osaka University of Commerce*, No. 3 (December 1935), at pp. 66–68.

36. *Jūyō yushutsuhin dōgyō kumiai hō* (Law No. 47, 1897, repealed by Law No. 35, 1900).

37. *Jūyō bussan dōgyō kumiai hō* (Law No. 35, 1900).

38. Yoshida, op. cit., at p. 21.

39. *Jūyō sangyō no tōsei ni kansuru hōritsu* (Law No. 40, 1931, decreed ineffective as of Aug. 11, 1942).

40. Lockwood, *Economic Development*, op. cit., at p. 230.

41. The subject of intense controversy within Japan's financial community, the issue required some partial resolution in the late 1970s to permit banks to distribute government bonds to the public. The question of whether sale of bonds to the public constituted business incidental to banking also involved interpretation of the 1927 Bank Law. The result was a compromise in the form of the authorizing provisions (arts. 10, 11) in the new 1981 Bank Law (*Ginkō hō*), Law No. 59, 1981, which became effective April 1, 1982. For an excellent analysis of the political context of this dispute, see Frances McCall Rosenbluth, *Financial Politics in Contemporary Japan* (Ithaca: Cornell University Press, 1989), and Frances Rosenbluth, "The Political Economy of Financial

Reform in Japan: The Banking Act of 1982," *UCLA Pacific Basin Law Journal*, Vol. 6, Nos. 1 & 2 (Fall 1989), pp. 62–102.

42. See Kōsei Torihiki Iinkai, (Fair Trade Commission) *Dokusen kinshi seisaku nijūnenshi* (Twenty year history of antimonopoly policy) (Tokyo: Kōsei Torihiki Iinkai, 1968), at pp. 152–153; Shōda Akira, *Dokusen inshi hō* (Antimonopoly law) (Tokyo: Nihon Hyōronsha, 1966), at p. 40.

43. See, e.g., Kozo Yamamura, *Economic Policy in Postwar Japan* (Berkeley: University of California Press, 1967).

44. *Gaikoku kawase oyobi gaikoku bōeki kanri hō* (Law No. 228, 1949).

45. The committee comprised three members of the SCAP's Economic and Scientific Section (Ryder as chair along with Hale and Allison), representatives of the International Monetary Fund (Mladek and Witchin) in addition to Japanese participants from the Ministry of Justice (Satō, Hayashi, and Nishimura), the Ministry of Finance (Ihara), MITI (Takeuchi and Seki), the Economic Stabilization Board (Tanibayashi and Yukawa), and the Foreign Exchange Control Board (Kiuchi and Okamura). Justin Williams, the principal representative from Government Section involved in the drafting process, apparently did not join the final committee. See Memo by Robert H. Neptune to Government Section, 1 Dec. 1949, Foreign Exchange Law File, Box 1477, SCAP, Legal Section, Legislation & Justice Division (National Archives, Suitland, Md.).

46. Ibid.

47. Ibid.

48. Mark Evan Mason, United States Direct Investment in Japan: Studies in Government Policy and Corporate Strategy (Ph.D. dissertation, Departments of History and East Asian Languages, Harvard University, 1988), at p. 320 fn. 16.

49. SCAP Circular No. 2, 1949.

50. Cabinet Order No. 51, 1949.

51. Ibid., art. 11.

52. Ibid., art. 3.

53. Ibid., art. 6.

54. Richard W. Rabinowitz, Law of Foreign Investment in Post-War Japan (Mimeographed materials for a course in Comparative Law, Harvard Law School, 1988), at pp. 2–48.

55. Mason, op. cit., at p. 370, citing 1986 Interview with Tristan Beplatt, a former Economic and Scientific Section official.

56. Ibid., citing Cohen Memorandum of July 14, 1948.

57. Ibid., at p. 371, citing SCAP Records, File Box 1040.

58. Ibid., at p. 377, fn. 148.

59. Eleanor M. Hadley, *Antitrust in Japan* (Princeton: Princeton University Press, 1970), at p. 370.

60. *Shiteki dokusen no kinshi oyobi kōsei torihiki no kakuho ni kansuru hōritsu* (Law No. 54, 1947).

61. *Eigyō dantai hō* (Law No. 191, 1948).

62. For an excellent study on this topic from the perspective of a Japanese scholar, see Masahiro Hosoya, "Economic Democratization and the 'Reverse Course' during the Allied Occupation of Japan, 1945–1952," *Kokusaigaku ronshū*, No. 11 (July 1983).

63. *Tokutei chūshō kigyō no antei ni kansuru hōritsu* (Law No. 294, 1952).

64. *Yushutsu torihiki hō* (Law No. 299, 1952).

65. The Japanese had before them the German 1952 Draft bill, which with some modification formed the basis for the 1957 *Gezetz gegen Wettbewerbsbeschränkungen* (Law against restraints of competition), 27 July 1957 (BGB1. I 1081).

226 *Notes*

66. Renamed and amended as the *Chūshō kigyō antei hō* (Law No. 140, 1953).

67. *Yushutsunyū torihiki hō* (Law No. 188, 1953).

68. Kozo Yamamura, "Success That Soured: Administrative Guidance and Cartels in Japan," in K. Yamamura (ed.), *Policy and Trade Issues of the Japanese Economy* (Seattle: University of Washington Press, 1982), at pp. 81–82.

69. See, e.g, Calder, op. cit.; Johnson, *MITI*, op. cit.; Okimoto, op. cit.

70. John M. Maki, "The Role of the Bureaucracy in Japan," *Pacific Affairs* (1947), at p. 396.

71. Ezra F. Vogel, *Japan As Number One: Lessons for America* (Cambridge: Harvard University Press, 1979), at pp. 56–57.

72. Johnson, *MITI*, op. cit., at pp. 26–29.

73. See Steven Kelman, *Regulating America, Regulating Sweden: A Comparative Study of Occupational Safety and Health Policy* (Cambridge: MIT Press, 1981), pp. 186–187.

In comparing American Occupational Safety and Health Administration (OSHA) inspectors and their counterparts in the Swedish Workers Protection Board (Arbtarkyddsstyrelsen, ASU), Kelman identifies a different orientation, which he describes as mission. The Americans, he writes, "know what they are supposed to do; most are go-getters about it, and a few are gung-ho. This gives the American inspectors an advantage over their Swedish counterparts, whose job is unclear." Steven Kelman, "Enforcement of Occupational Safety and Health Regulations: A Comparison of Swedish and American Practices," in K. Hawkins and J.M. Thomas (eds.), *Enforcing Regulation* (Boston: Kluwer-Nijoff Publishing, 1984), at p. 109. Kelman sees this as evidence that "a sense of mission is easier to infuse the clearer and more operationalizable [*sic*] the organization's goals are." Ibid. The contrasts between the American and Swedish inspectors, especially Kelman's finding of greater hostility by the OSHA inspectors toward private industry and the less rigid attitudes of the ASU inspectors, can be better explained by differences in what they perceive their mission to be rather than degrees of commitment to similar missions. The ASU inspectors also, however, have a regulatory orientation.

74. Yamanouchi Kazuo, *Gyōsei shidō* (Administrative guidance) (Tokyo, Kōbundō, 1977), at pp. 85, 121–22, cited in Johnson, *MITI*, op. cit., at p. 40, fn. 18.

75. Johnson, *MITI*, op. cit., at p. 40.

76. Letter of May 7, 1981, from His Excellency Yoshio Ōkawara, Ambassador of Japan, to William French Smith, Attorney General of the United States, reprinted in Mitsuo Matsushita and Lawrence Repeta, "Restricting The Supply of Japanese Automobiles: Sovereign Compulsion or Sovereign Collusion?, *Case Western Reserve Journal of International Law*, Vol. 14, No. 1 (Winter 1982), at pp. 78–79.

77. Kōsei Torihiki Iinkai, op. cit., at pp. 152–153.

78. Shōda, op. cit., at p. 40.

79. These events were described in detail by Kozo Yamamura in the 1960s and, more recently, Chalmers Johnson. Yamamura, *Economic Policy*, op. cit.; Johnson, *MITI*, op. cit. Neither author, however, fully analyzes the significance of the Diet's defeat on the *Tokushinhōan* and MITI's subsequent resort to antitrust evasion through administrative guidance. For a Japanese interpretation, see Shōda, op. cit., at pp. 42–45.

80. Chalmers Johnson, "MITI and Japanese International Economic Policy," in Robert A. Scalapino (ed.), *The Foreign Policy of Modern Japan* (Berkeley: University of California Press, 1977), p. 257.

81. Martha Ann Caldwell, Petroleum Politics in Japan: State and Industry in a Changing Policy Context (Ph.D. dissertation, Department of Political Science, University of Wisconsin-Madison, 1981), at p. 467.

82. Ibid., at pp. 78–79.

83. Murakami Yasusuke, "Toward a Socioinstitutional Explanation of Japan's Economic Performance," in Yamamura, *Policy and Trade Issues*, op. cit., at p. 42.

84. See in particular the works by Muramatsu Michio of Kyoto University, including "Center-Local Political Relations: A Lateral Competition Model," *Journal of Japanese Studies*, Vol. 12, No. 2 (Summer 1986).

85. Haruhiro Fukui, "The Liberal Democratic Party Revisited: Continuity and Change in the Party's Structure and Performance," *Journal of Japanese Studies*, Vol. 10, No. 2 (Summer 1984), at pp. 385–435.

86. Question and Answer Session, American Bar Association—Japan Society, Conference on Marketing in Japan, November 1978.

87. *Gyōsei shidō ni kansuru chōsa kenkyū hōkokusho* (Report on investigative study of administrative guidance) (Tokyo: Gyōsei Kanri Kenkyū Sentā, 1981) (hereafter *Administrative Guidance Research Report*). The report was prepared for the Administrative Management Agency [Gyōsei Kanri Chō] by a committee of Japan's leading legal scholars in administrative law and select businessmen and government officials.

88. See, e.g., Narita Yoriaki, "*Gyōsei shidō*," in *Gendaihō* (Contemporary law) Vol. 4 (Tokyo: Iwanami Shoten, Tokyo, 1966), at pp. 131–168, translated ("Administrative Guidance") in *Law in Japan: An Annual*, Vol. 2 (1968), at pp. 45–79.

89. See, for example, the summary of Japanese requirements for standing in Ichirō Ogawa, "Judicial Review of Administrative Actions in Japan," *Washington Law Review*, Vol. 43 (1968), at pp. 1075–1094. For a study of judicial review by means of damage actions, see Michael K. Young, "Judicial Review of Administrative Guidance: Governmentally Encouraged Consensual Dispute Resolution in Japan," *Columbia Law Review*, Vol. 84 (1984), at pp. 923–983, abstracted in "Administrative Guidance in the Courts: A Case Study in Doctrinal Adaptation," *Law in Japan: An Annual*, Vol. 17 (1984), at pp. 120–52.

90. See, e.g., Yamanouchi Kazuo, "Administrative Guidance and the Rule of Law," *Law in Japan*, Vol. 7 (1974), at pp. 22, 31–33. See also Watanabe Yoshifusa, "*Gyōsei shidō o meguru shomondai*" (Problems with administrative guidance), *Jurisuto*, No. 342 (1966), at pp. 46, 48–49.

91. *Administrative Guidance Research Report*, op. cit., at pp. ii–iii.

92. Paul A. Davis, *Administrative Guidance, Sophia University Socio-Economic Institute Bulletin*, No. 41 (1972), at pp. 7–11.

93. Wolfgang Pape, "Gyōsei shidō and the Antimonopoly Law," *Law in Japan: An Annual*, Vol. 15 (1982), at p. 15. See also Wolfgang Pape, *Gyoseishido und das Anti-Monopol-Gesetz in Japan* (Administrative guidance and the antimonopoly law in Japan) (Köln: Heymanns, 1980), at pp. 41–50.

94. Ibid., at p. 16.

95. Jeffrey M. Lepon, "Administrative Guidance in Japan," *Fletcher Forum*, Vol. 2 (1978), at p. 143.

96. Johnson, *MITI*, op. cit.

97. Kenneth Culp Davis estimates that in the United States "more than 90 percent of all administrative action [in the United States] is informal." Kenneth Culp Davis, *Administrative Law*, op. cit., Vol. 1, at §1.4, p. 14. As in Japan most informal action in the United States escapes judicial review. Ties outside of legislation also generally govern administrative procedures. See G. Robinson, E. Gellhorn, and H. Bruff, *The*

Administrative Process (St. Paul, Minn.: West Publishing Co., 2d ed. 1980), at p. 33. See also Thomas H. Austern, "Sanctions in Silhouette: An Inquiry into the Enforcement of the Federal Food, Drug, and Cosmetic Act," *California Law Review*, Vol. 51 (1963), at pp. 38–50, especially p. 41.

98. Letter to editor, *Regulation* (May/June 1983), at p. 2.

99. As Hiroshi Iyori notes in "Antitrust and Industrial Policy in Japan: Competition and Cooperation," in G.R. Saxonhouse and K. Yamamura (eds.), *Law and Trade Issues of the Japanese Economy* (Seattle: University of Washington Press, 1986), at fn. 36, approximately a third of all cases investigated end with a warning. Less than a tenth result in any formal action.

100. The *Administrative Guidance Research Report*, op. cit., includes detailed studies of administrative guidance by each of the economic ministries in transportation, petroleum, agriculture, forestry, fisheries, pharmaceuticals, labor and construction.

101. See In re Hokkaidō Batā K.K. et al., 1 Shinketsushū 103 (FTC Decision No. 28, Sept. 18, 1950); In re Noda Shōyu, 4 Shinketsushū 1 (FTC Decision No. 59, April 4, 1952); In re Tōyō Rēyon et al., Shinketsushū 17 (FTC Decision No. 2, Aug. 6, 1953), Kuni [Japan] v. Sekiyu Renmei et al., *Hanrei jihō* (No. 983) 22 (Tokyo High Court, Sept. 26, 1980), Kuni [Japan] v. Idemitsu Kōsan K.K. et al., *Hanrei jihō* (No. 985) 3 (Tokyo High Ct., Sept. 26, 1980). For a full discussion of these and related cases, see the symposium on the oil cartel cases in *Law in Japan: An Annual*, Vol. 15 (1982), at pp. 1–98.

102. See, e.g., Andras Sajo, "Why Do Public Bureaucracies Follow Legal Rules," *International Journal of the Sociology of Law*, Vol. 9, No. 1 (1981), at pp. 69–84.

103. Richard Samuels, *The Business of the Japanese State: Energy Markets in Comparative and Historical Perspective* (Ithaca: Cornell University Press, 1987), at p. 260.

104. Ibid.

105. Ibid.

106. Ibid.

107. Upham, op. cit., at pp. 17, 24–25.

Chapter 8

1. Robert J. Smith and John R. Cornell, *Two Japanese Villages* (Ann Arbor: University of Michigan Press, 1956), at p. 17. See also, Richard W. Beardsley, John W. Hall, and Robert E. Ward, *Village Japan* (Chicago: University of Chicago Press, 1959), at p. 7.

2. Robert J. Smith, "The Japanese Rural Community: Norms, Sanctions, and Ostracism," *American Anthropologist*, Vol. 63 (1961), at pp. 522–533.

3. Ibid., at p. 522.

4. Robin M. Williams, Jr., *American Society* (New York: A.A. Knopf, 2d ed., 1960).

5. Ibid., at p. 376, quoted in Smith, "Rural Community," op. cit., at pp. 522–523.

6. John F. Embree, *Suye Mura, A Japanese Village* (Chicago: University of Chicago Press, 8th ed., 1969), at p. 171.

7. Smith, "Rural Community," op. cit., at p. 525. Smith explains:

The etymology of this word is in doubt, but at least one authority . . . holds that it derives from the word *hajiku* [to repel, to reject, to snap]. There are, however, other folk-etymologies, one of which is worth noting here. It is often said that there are "ten parts" to relationships within a hamlet. These are occasions upon which some kind of aid or joint ceremonial participation among member households occur and are (1) rites of passage linked with the life-cycle, (2) marriage and wedding ceremonies, (3) death and funeral observances, (4) construction of buildings, (5) fires, (6) sickness, (7) floods or water damage, (8) leaving on a journey, (9) birth and related ceremonies, and (10) memorial observances for the ancestors.

The contention is that an ostracized household can expect help on only two of these ten occasions; thus, eight parts of the relationship with other member households are abrogated. In one prefecture, for example, it is reported that only in the event of death in a household or a natural disaster will other members of the hamlet rally round. In another area, the "two parts" remaining are extension of aid after a fire and attendance at weddings in the ostracized household. Ibid., at p. 525.

8. Ibid., at p. 527.
9. Ibid.
10. See, e.g., Beardsley, Hall, and Ward, op. cit., at p. 7.
11. Minoru Kida, "The Laws of the *Buraku*," *Japan Quarterly*, Vol. 4, No. 1 (1957), at p. 87.
12. Walter L. Ames, *Police and Community in Japan* (Berkeley: University of California Press, 1981).
13. Ibid., at p. 28.
14. Ibid., at pp. 151–162.
15. Ibid., at p. 29.
16. Ibid., at p. 28.
17. Tadashi Fukutake, *Japanese Rural Society* (London: Oxford University Press, 1967), at p. 215.
18. Robert J. Smith, *Kurusu: The Price of Progress in a Japanese Village, 1951–1975* (Stanford: Stanford University Press, 1978), esp. pp. 229–250.
19. Takeyoshi Kawashima, "The Status of the Individual in the Notion of Law, Right, and Social Order in Japan," in R. Moore (ed.), *The Status of the Individual in East and West* (Honolulu: University of Hawaii Press, 1968), at p. 440.
20. Andrew Gordon, op. cit., at p. 430.
21. See Robert E. Cole, *Work, Mobility, & Participation: A Comparative Study of American and Japanese Industry* (Berkeley: University of California Press, 1979), at pp. 11–12.
22. Thomas P. Rohlen, *For Harmony and Strength: Japanese White Collar Organization in Anthropological Perspective* (Berkeley: University of California Press, 1974), at p. 14.
23. Ezra F. Vogel, *Japan's New Middle Class* (Berkeley: University of California Press, 1967), at p. 96.
24. Ibid.
25. Ibid., at p. 141.
26. Bank of the Ryūkyū v. Tokai Electric Construction K.K., *Hanrei jihō* (No. 782) 19 (Sup. Ct., 3rd P.B., July 15, 1975).
27. John Lynch, *Toward an Orderly Market: An Intensive Study of Japan's Voluntary Quota in Cotton Textile Exports* (Rutland, Vt.: C.E. Tuttle, in cooperation with Sophia University, 1968), at p. 104.
28. Quoted in Michael Y. Yoshino, *Japan's Managerial System: Tradition and Innovation* (Cambridge: The MIT Press, 1968), at pp. 109–111.
29. Rohlen, op. cit., at p. 79.
30. Ibid., at p. 51.

31. See, e.g., Timothy P. Williams and Shunya Sogon, "Group Composition and Conforming Behavior in Japanese Students," *Japanese Psychological Research*, Vol. 24, No. 4 (1984), at pp. 231–234.

32. Chie Nakane, *Japanese Society* (Berkeley: University of California Press, 1972), at pp. 59–60.

33. Ibid., at p. 60.

34. Cole, op. cit., at p. 20, citing Cole's previous study of Japanese blue-collar workers, Robert E. Cole, *Japanese Blue Collar* (Berkeley: University of California Press, 1971), and Robert Marsh and Hiroshi Mannari, *Modernization and the Japanese Factory* (Princeton: Princeton University Press, 1976).

35. Takie S. Lebra, *Japanese Patterns of Behavior* (Honolulu: University of Hawaii Press, 5th ed., 1986), at pp. 65–66.

36. Discussions with judges and procurators in Taiwan and Korea.

37. For one of the best concise descriptions in English of *sōkaiya* activities, including the recent attempts at reform through amendment of the Commercial Code, see Lawrence W. Beer, *Freedom of Expression in Japan* (Tokyo: Kōdansha International, 1984), at pp. 379–380.

38. Yōichi Higuchi, "When Society is Itself the Tyrant," *Japan Quarterly*, Vol. 35, No. 4 (1988), at pp. 350–356.

39. Ibid., at p. 354.

40. Beer, op. cit., at p. 379.

41. Ibid.

42. Beer, op. cit., at p. 382, citing James W. White, *The Soka Gakkai and Mass Society* (Stanford: Stanford University Press, 1971), at p. 82.

43. Beer, op. cit., at p. 382.

44. Ibid., at pp. 383–385.

45. Ibid., at p. 385.

46. Frank K. Upham, "Instrumental Violence and Social Change: The Buraku Liberation League and the Tactic of 'Denunciation Struggle,'" in J. Haley (ed.), *Law and Society in Comtemporary Japan* (Dubuque, Iowa: Kendall-Hunt, 1988), at pp. 289–305; also in Upham, op. cit., at pp. 78–123.

47. Upham, *Social Change*, at p. 78.

48. George A. de Vos (with Keiichi Mizushima), "Organization and Social Function of Japanese Gangs: Historical Development and Modern Parallels," in G.A. de Vos (ed.), *Socialization for Achievement* (Berkeley: University of California Press, 1973), at p. 297.

49. Iyori Hiroshi, "Antitrust and Industrial Policy in Japan: Competition and Cooperation," in G. Saxonhouse and K. Yamamura, *Law and Trade Issues of the Japanese Economy: American and Japanese Perspectives* (Seattle: University of Washington Press, 1986), at pp. 61–62. Iyori explains the practice of honoring prominent individuals with a *kunshō* as follows:

> A national system of decorations of honor was established by government Directive No. 54 (Taiseikan), in April 1875. Its operation was suspended for a time by a Cabinet decision of 1946. In 1963, however, it was reinstated with honors conferred upon those, usually aged seventy or more, who have rendered meritorious service to the state or the public at large and those who have contributed to the public welfare or have worked for the prosperity of the economy or of industry. At present, about four thousand people receive decorations of honor in the spring and in the fall each year. The honors range over eight classes

of distinction within a number of categories.
Ibid., at p. 75, fn. 20.

50. *Kōgai taisaku kihon hō* (Basic Law for Pollution Control), Law No. 132 of 1967.

51. Ōno v. Shōwa Denkō K.K., *Hanrei jihō* (No. 642) 96 (Niigata Dist. Ct., Sept. 29, 1971) (filed in June 1967). The other three cases were Toyama *Itai-Itai* Case: Komatsu v. Mitsui Kinzoku Kōgyō, *Hanrei jihō* (No. 635) 17 (Toyama Dist. Ct., June 30, 1971), aff'd *Hanrei jihō* (No. 674) 25 (Nagoya High Ct., Aug. 9, 1972); Yokkaichi Industrial Asthma Case: Shiono v. Shōwa Yokkaichi Sekiyu, *Hanrei jihō* (No. 672) 30 (Tsu Dist. Ct., Yokkaichi Br., July 24, 1972); Kumamoto Minamata Disease Case: Watanabe v. Chisso K.K., *Hanrei jihō* (No. 696) 15 (Kumamoto Dist. Ct., March 20, 1973).

52. *Kōgai kenkō higai hoshō hō* (Law for Compensation of Pollution-Related Health Injury), Law No. 111 of 1973.

53. See Upham, *Social Change*, op. cit., at p. 58: "[The Law for the Compensation of Pollution-related Health Injury] was enacted in 1973 when the political and legal momentum created by the plaintiffs' successive victories in the Big Four convinced the government that preexisting legal and national schemes had failed to compensate the victims adequately or to slow the rush to litigation and protest."

54. Uno et al. v. Ministry of Agriculture, Forestry and Fisheries, 36 Minshū 1679 (Sup. Ct., 1st P.B., Sept. 9, 1982), affirming Ministry of Agriculture and Forestry v. Itō et al., 27 Gyōsai reishū 1175 (Sapporo High Ct., Aug. 5, 1976), reversing Itō et al. v. Ministry of Agriculture and Forestry, *Hanrei jihō* (No. 712) 26 (Sapporo Dist. Ct., Sept. 7, 1973).

55. Itō v. Ministry of Agriculture and Forestry, *Hanrei jihō* (No. 581) 5 (Sapporo High Ct., Jan. 23, 1970), reversing the Sapporo Dist. Ct. decision of Aug. 22, 1969, *Hanrei jihō* (No. 565) 23 (1969).

56. 18 Minshū 270 (Sup. Ct., G.B., Feb. 5, 1964).

57. 30 Minshū 223 (Sup. Ct., G.B., April 14, 1976).

58. Shimizu et al., v. Osaka Election Commission, 37 Minshū 345 (Sup. Ct., G.B., April 27, 1983). Tokyo Election Commission v. Koshiyama, 37 Minshū 1243 (Sup. Ct., G.B., Nov. 7, 1983).

59. van Wolferen, op. cit., at p. 42.

60. Ibid., at pp. 43, 49.

61. Ibid., at p. 44.

62. Ronald Dore, *Taking Japan Seriously: A Confucian Perspective on Leading Economic Issues* (Stanford: Stanford University Press, 1987), at p. 94.

63. Ibid., at p. 95.

64. Ibid., at p. 74.

Conclusion

1. "Global Village No Place for Japanphobia," *Wall Street Journal*, Nov. 29, 1989, at p. A17.

2. *Los Angeles Times*, November 6, 1989, at p. D-1.

References

Western Language Publications

Abel, Richard L., *The Legal Profession in England and Wales* (Oxford: Basil Blackwell, 1988).

Abel, Richard L., and P.S.C. Lewis (eds.), *Lawyers in Society*, 2 vols. (Berkeley: University of California Press, 1988).

Aberbach, Joel D., Robert D. Putnam, and Bert A. Rockman, *Bureaucrats and Politicians in Western Democracies* (Cambridge: Harvard University Press, 1987).

Alford, William P., "The Inscrutable Occidental? Implications of Roberto Unger's Uses and Abuses of the Chinese Past," *Texas Law Review*, vol. 64, no. 5 (1986), pp. 915–972.

Ames, Walter L., *Police and Community in Japan* (Berkeley: University of California Press, 1981).

Apter, David E., and Nagayo Sawa, *Against the State: Political and Social Protest in Japan* (Cambridge: Harvard University Press, 1984).

Asakawa, Kan'ichi, *The Documents of Iriki* (New Haven: Yale University Press, 1929).

Austern, Thomas H., "Sanctions in Silhouette: An Inquiry into the Enforcement of the Federal Food, Drug, and Cosmetic Act," *California Law Review*, vol. 51, no. 1 (March 1963), pp. 38–50.

Barshay, Andrew E., *State and Intellectual in Imperial Japan: The Public Man in Crisis* (Berkeley: University of California Press, 1988).

Bayley, David H., *Forces of Order: Police Behavior in Japan and the United States* (Berkeley: University of California Press, 1976).

Beardsley, Richard W., John W. Hall, and Robert E. Ward, *Village Japan* (Chicago: University of Chicago Press, 1959).

Beckmann, George M., *The Making of the Japanese Constitution* (Lawrence: University of Kansas Press, 1957).

Beer, Lawrence W., *Freedom of Expression in Japan* (Tokyo: Kodansha International, 1984).

Bellah, Robert N., *Tokugawa Religion: The Values of Pre-Industrial Japan* (Glencoe, N.Y.: Free Press, 1957).

Berman, Harold J., *Law and Revolution: The Formation of the Western Legal Tradition* (Cambridge: Harvard University Press, 1983).

Berry, Mary Elizabeth, *Hideyoshi* (Cambridge: The Council on East Asian Studies, Harvard University, 1982).

Birt, Michael A., "Samurai in Passage: The Transformation of the Sixteenth-Century Kanto," *Journal of Japanese Studies*, vol. 11, no. 2 (Summer 1985), pp. 369–399.

Bisson, Thomas Arthur, *Japan's War Economy* (New York: Institute of Pacific Relations, 1945).

Bodde, Derk, and Clarence Morris, *Law in Imperial China* (Philadelphia: University of Pennsylvania Press, 1967).

Boissonade, Gustave E., *Les anciennes coutumes du Japon et le nouveau Code Civil* (Tokyo: Hakubunsha, 1894).

Breuer, Richard, *Die Stellung der Staatsanwaltschaft in Japan* (The status of the procuracy in Japan) (Berlin: Junker & Dirnnhaupt, 1940).

Brown, Catherine W., "Japanese Approaches to Equal Rights for Women: The Legal Framework," *Law in Japan: An Annual*, vol. 12 (1979), pp. 29–56.

Bryant, Taimie L., "Sons and Lovers: Adoption in Japan," *The American Journal of Comparative Law*, vol. 38, no. 2 (Spring 1990), pp. 299–336.

Buxbaum, David, "Some Aspects of Civil Procedure and Practice at the Trial Level in Tanshin and Hsinchu from 1789 to 1895," *Journal of Asian Studies*, vol. 30, no. 2 (1971), pp. 255–279.

Calder, Kent E., *Crisis and Compensation: Public Policy and Political Stability in Japan, 1949–1986* (Princeton: Princeton University Press, 1988).

Caldwell, Martha Ann, Petroleum Politics in Japan: State and Industry in a Changing Policy Context (Ph.D. dissertation, Department of Political Science, University of Wisconsin-Madison, 1981).

Casper, Gerhard, and Hans Zeisel, "Lay Judges in the German Criminal Courts," *Journal of Legal Studies*, vol. 1, no. 1 (January 1972), pp. 135–191.

Chen, Paul H.C., *Chinese Legal Tradition under the Mongols: The Code of 1291 as Reconstructed* (Princeton: Princeton University Press, 1979).

——, *The Formation of the Early Meiji Legal Order* (London: Oxford University Press, 1981).

Citizens' Crime Commission of Philadelphia (ed.), *Tokyo: One City Where Crime Doesn't Pay* (Philadelphia: 1975).

Cohen, Jerome Alan, *The Criminal Process in the People's Republic of China, 1949–1963: An Introduction* (Cambridge: Harvard University Press, 1968).

Cohen, Jerome A., R. Randle Edwards, and Fu Mei Chang Chen (eds.), *Essays on China's Legal Tradition* (Princeton: Princeton University Press, 1980).

Cohen, Jerome B., *Japan's Economy in War and Reconstruction* (Minneapolis: University of Minnesota Press, 1949).

Coing, Helmut, et al. (eds.), *Die Japanisierung des westlichen Rechts* (Japanization of western law) (Tübingen: J.C.B. Mohr, 1990).

Cole, Robert E., *Japanese Blue Collar* (Berkeley: University of California Press, 1971).

——, *Work, Mobility, & Participation: A Comparative Study of American and Japanese Industry* (Berkeley: University of California Press, 1979).

Coleman, Rex L., "Japanese Family Law," *Stanford Law Review*, vol. 9 (1956), pp. 132–154.

Coulborn, Rushton, *Feudalism in History* (Princeton: Princeton University Press, 1956).

Crook, John, *Law and Life of Rome* (Ithaca: Cornell University Press, 1967).

Crowley, James B., *Japan's Quest for Autonomy* (Princeton: Princeton University Press, 1966).

Crowley, James B. (ed.), *Modern East Asia: Essays in Interpretation* (New York: Harcourt, Brace & World, 1970).

Damaška, Mirjan R., *The Faces of Justice and State Authority: A Comparative Approach to the Legal Process* (New Haven: Yale University Press, 1986).

Dando, Shigemitsu, *Japanese Criminal Procedure* (B.J. George, trans.) (Hackensack, N.J., Fred B. Rothman, 1965).

——, "System of Discretionary Prosecution in Japan," *American Journal of Comparative Law*, vol. 18 (1970), pp. 518–531.

Danielski, David, "The Constitutional and Legislative Phases of the Creation of the Japanese Supreme Court," in *The Occupation of Japan: The Impact of Legal Reform* (Proceedings of Symposium sponsored by the MacArthur Memorial, April 14 and 15, 1977).

Davis, Kenneth Culp, *Administrative Law Treatise*, vol. 1 (San Diego: K.C. Davis, 2d ed., 1982).

Davis, Paul A., *Administrative Guidance, Sophia University Socio-Economic Institute Bulletin*, no. 41 (Tokyo, 1972).

Dore, Ronald P., *City Life in Japan* (Berkeley: University of California Press, 1958).

———, *Land Reform in Japan* (London: Oxford University Press, 1959).

———, *Taking Japan Seriously: A Confucian Perspective on Leading Economic Issues* (Stanford: Stanford University Press, 1987).

———, (ed.), *Aspects of Social Change in Modern Japan* (Princeton: Princeton University Press, 1967).

Duus, Peter, *Party Rivalry and Political Change in Taishō Japan* (Cambridge: Harvard University Press, 1968).

Dworkin, Ronald, *Law's Empire* (Cambridge: Harvard University Press, 1986).

———, *Taking Rights Seriously* (Cambridge: Harvard University Press, 1975).

Earl, David Magaley, *Emperor and Nation in Japan: Political Thinkers of the Tokugawa Period* (Seattle: University of Washington Press, 1964).

Ehrmann, Henry W., *Politics in France* (Boston: Little, Brown, 3d ed., 1983).

Embree, John F., *Suye Mura: A Japanese Village* (Chicago: University of Chicago Press, 8th ed., 1969).

Epp, Robert Charles, Threat to Tradition: The Reaction to Japan's 1890 Civil Code (Ph.D. dissertation, Departments of History and Far Eastern Languages, Harvard University, 1964).

Eubel, Paul, *Das japanische Rechtssystem* (Japanese legal system) (Frankfurt: Alfred Metzner Verlag, 1979).

Fenwick, Charles R., "Crime and Justice in Japan: Implications for the United States," *International Journal of Comparative and Applied Criminal Justice*, vol. 6, no. 1 (Spring 1982), pp. 61–71.

Forsthoff, Ernst, *Lehrbuch des Verwaltungsrechts* (Reader in administrative law) (Munich: C.H. Beck, 10th ed., 1973).

Frase, Richard S., "The Decision to File Criminal Charges: A Quantitative Study of Prosecutorial Discretion," *University of Chicago Law Review*, vol. 47, no. 2 (Winter 1980), pp. 246–309.

Friedman, David, *The Misunderstood Miracle: Industrial Development and Political Change in Japan* (Ithaca: Cornell University Press, 1988).

Friedman, Milton, *Freedom to Choose* (New York: Harcourt, Brace, Jovanovich, 1980).

Friedrich, Carl J. (ed.), *Authority* (Cambridge: Harvard University Press, 1958).

Fujita, Keizo, "Cartels and Their Conflicts in Japan," *Journal of the Osaka University of Commerce*, no. 3 (December 1935), pp. 65–109.

Fukuhara, Tadao, "The Status of Foreign Lawyers in Japan," *Japanese Annual of International Law* (1973), pp. 21–44.

Fukui, Haruhiro, "The Liberal Democratic Party Revisited: Continuity and Change in the Party's Structure and Performance," *Journal of Japanese Studies*, vol. 10, no. 2 (Summer 1984), pp. 385–435.

———, "Studies in Policymaking: A Review of the Literature," in T. Pempel (ed.), *Policymaking in Contemporary Japan* (Ithaca: Cornell University Press, 1977), pp. 22–59.

Fukutake, Tadashi, *Japanese Rural Society* (London: Oxford University Press, 1967).

Galanter, Marc, "Reading the Landscape of Disputes: What We Know and Don't Know (And Think We Know) About Our Allegedly Contentious and Litigious Society," *UCLA Law Review*, vol. 31, no. 1 (October 1983), pp. 4–71.

George, B. James, "Discretionary Authority of Public Prosecutors in Japan," *Law in Japan: An Annual*, vol. 17 (1984), pp. 42–72.

Gilles, Peter (ed.), *Effiziente Rechts Verfolgung* (Efficiency in the pursuit of justice) (Heidelberg: C.F. Müllen Juristischen Verlag, 1987).

Gluck, Carol, *Japan's Modern Myths: Ideology in the Late Meiji Period* (Princeton: Princeton University Press, 1985).

Goldstein, Abraham S., "Defining the Role of the Victim in Criminal Prosecution," *Mississippi Law Journal*, vol. 52, no. 3 (September 1982), pp. 515–561.

Goodman, Marcia E., "The Exercise and Control of Prosecutorial Discretion in Japan," *UCLA Pacific Basin Law Journal*, vol. 5, nos. 1 and 2 (Spring and Fall 1986), pp. 16–95.

Gordon, Andrew, *The Evolution of Labor Relations in Japan: Heavy Industry 1853–1955* (Cambridge: Harvard University Press, 1985).

Gresser, Julian, Kōichirō Fujikura, and Akio Morishima, *Environmental Law in Japan* (Cambridge: MIT Press, 1981).

Grossberg, Kenneth A., *The Laws of the Muromachi Bakufu* (Tokyo: Monumenta Nipponica, 1981).

Guy, R. Kent, *The Emperor's Four Treasuries: Scholars on the State in the Late Ch'ien-lung Era* (Cambridge: Harvard University, Council on East Asian Studies, 1987).

Hadley, Eleanor M., *Antitrust in Japan* (Princeton: Princeton University Press, 1970).

Hahm, Pyong-Choon, *The Korean Political Tradition and Law* (Seoul: Hollym Corporation, 1967).

Haley, John O., "Administrative Guidance vs. Formal Regulation: Resolving the Paradox of Japan's Industrial Policy," in K. Yamamura and G. Saxonhouse (eds.), *Law and Trade Issues of the Japanese Economy: American and Japanese Perspectives* (Seattle: University of Washington Press, 1986).

———, "Comment: The Implications of Apology," *Law & Society Review*, vol. 20, no. 4 (1986), pp. 499–507.

———, "Confession, Repentance and Absolution," in M. Wright and B. Galaway (eds.), *Mediation and Criminal Justice: Victims, Offenders and Communities* (London: Sage Publications, 1989), pp. 195–211.

———, "The Context and Content of Regulatory Change in Japan," in K. Button and D. Swann (eds.), *The Age of Regulatory Reform* (Oxford: Clarendon Press, 1989), pp. 124–138.

———, "Governance by Negotiation: A Reappraisal of Bureaucratic Power in Japan," *Journal of Japanese Studies*, vol. 13, no. 2 (Summer 1987), pp. 343–357; also in *The Trade Crisis: How Will Japan Respond?* (Seattle: Society for Japanese Studies, 1987), pp. 177–191.

———, "Mission to Manage: The U.S. Forest Service as a 'Japanese' Bureaucracy," in K. Hayashi (ed.), *The U.S.–Japanese Economic Relationship: Can it be Improved?* (New York: New York University Press, 1989), pp. 196–225.

———, "The Myth of the Reluctant Litigant," *Journal of Japanese Studies*, vol. 4, no. 2 (Summer 1978), pp. 359–390; Japanese translation in *Hanrei Jihō*, no. 902 (Nov. 21, 1978), pp. 14–22, and no. 907 (Jan. 11, 1978), pp. 13–20.

———, "The Politics of Informal Justice: The Japanese Experience, 1922–1942," in R. Abel (ed.), *The Politics of Informal Justice*, vol. 2 (1982), pp. 125–147.

———, "The Role of Law in Japan: An Historical Perspective," *Kobe University Law Review*, no. 18 (1984), pp. 1–20.

———, "Sheathing the Sword of Justice in Japan: An Essay on Law Without Sanctions," *Journal of Japanese Studies*, vol. 8, no. 2 (Summer 1980), pp. 265–281.

———, "Toward a Reappraisal of Occupation Legal Reforms: Administrative Accountability," in Kōichirō Fujukara (ed.), *Eibeihō ronshū* (Essays on Anglo-American

Law) (Hideo Tanaka Festschrift) (Tokyo: Tōkyō Daigaku Shuppankai, 1987), pp. 543–567.

———, (ed.), *Law and Society in Contemporary Japan* (Dubuque, Iowa: Kendall-Hunt, 1988).

Haley, John O., and Dan F. Henderson (eds.), *Law and the Legal Process in Japan* (Seattle: Asian Law Course Materials, University of Washington School of Law, 1988 ed.).

Hall, John Carey, *Japanese Feudal Law* (Washington, D.C.: University Publications of America, 1979).

———, "Japanese Feudal Laws I—The Institutes of Judicature," *Transactions of the Asiatic Society of Japan* [1st Series], vol. 34 (Tokyo, 1906), pp. 1–44.

———, "Japanese Feudal Laws II—The Ashikaga Code," *Transactions of the Asiatic Society of Japan*, [1st Series], vol. 36 (Tokyo, 1908), pp. 1–23.

Hall, John Whitney, *Government and Local Power in Japan* (Princeton: Princeton University Press, 1966).

Hall, John Whitney, and Marius B. Jansen (eds.), *Studies in the Institutional History of Early Modern Japan* (Princeton: Princeton University Press, 1968).

Hall, John Whitney, and Jeffrey P. Mass (eds.), *Medieval Japan: Essays in Institutional History* (Stanford: Stanford University Press, 2d ed., 1988).

Hall, John Whitney, Keiji Nagahara, and Kozo Yamamura (eds.), *Japan Before Tokugawa: Political Consolidation and Economic Growth, 1500–1650* (Princeton: Princeton University Press, 1981).

Hamilton, V. Lee, and Joseph Sanders, "Punishment and the Individual in the United States and Japan," *Law & Society Review*, vol. 22, no. 2 (1988), pp. 301–328.

Hanley, Susan B., and Kozo Yamamura, *Economic and Demographic Change in Preindustrial Japan, 1600–1868* (Princeton: Princeton University Press, 1977).

Hart, H.L.A., *The Concept of Law* (Oxford: Clarendon Press, 1961).

Hein, Laura E., Energy and Economic Policy in Postwar Japan, 1945–1960 (Ph.D. dissertation, Department of Political Science, University of Wisconsin–Madison, 1986).

Henderson, Dan Fenno, "Chinese Legal Studies in Early 18th Century Japan," *Journal of Asian Studies*, vol. 30 (1970), pp. 21–56.

———, *Conciliation and Japanese Law: Tokugawa and Modern*, 2 vols. (Seattle: University of Washington Press, 1965).

———, *Foreign Enterprise in Japan* (Chapel Hill: University of North Carolina Press, 1973).

———, *Village "Contracts" in Tokugawa Japan* (Seattle: University of Washington Press, 1975).

Higuchi, Yōichi, "When Society is Itself the Tyrant," *Japan Quarterly*, vol. 35, no. 4 (October–December 1988), pp. 350–356.

Hiramatsu, Yoshirō, "Tokugawa Law," *Law in Japan: An Annual*, vol. 14 (1981), pp. 1–48.

Hollerman, Leon, *Japan, Disincorporated* (Stanford: Hoover Institution Press, 1988).

Hoshino, Kanehiro, The Impact of Post-war Law Enforcement in Japanese Social Systems (unpublished paper, Conference on Contemporary Social Problems: Institutions of Change in Japanese Society, Center for Japanese Studies, University of California, Berkeley, Nov. 17, 1982).

Hosoya, Masahiro, "Economic Democratization and the 'Reverse Course' during the Allied Occupation of Japan, 1945–1952," *Kokusaigaku ronshū*, no. 11 (July 1983).

Hozumi, Nobushige, *Lectures on the New Japanese Civil Code* (Tokyo: Maruzen, 1912).

Hsiao, Kung-chuan, *Compromise in Imperial China* (Seattle: University of Washington Press, 1979).

Hsu, Dau-lin, "Crime and Cosmic Order," *Harvard Journal of Asiatic Studies*, vol. 30 (1970), pp. 111–125.

Hulsewé, A.F.P., "The Legalists and The Laws of Ch'in," in W.L. Idema (ed.), *Leyden Studies in Sinology* (Leiden: E.J. Brill, 1981), pp. 1–22.

——, *Remnants of Han Law*, vol. 1 (Leiden: E.J. Brill, 1955).

Ichiro, Ogawa, "Judicial Review of Administrative Actions in Japan," *Washington Law Review*, vol. 43, no. 5 (June 1968), pp. 1075–1094.

Igarashi, Futaba, "Crime, Confession and Control in Contemporary Japan" (Introduction and translation by Gavan McCormick), *Law in Context*, vol. 2 (1984), pp. 1–30.

Irokawa, Daikichi, *The Culture of the Meiji Period* (Princeton: Princeton University Press, 1985).

Ishida, Takeshi, and Ellis S. Krauss (eds.), *Democracy in Japan* (Pittsburgh: University of Pittsburgh Press, 1989).

Ishii, Ryōsuke, *A History of Political Institutions in Japan* (Tokyo: University of Tokyo Press, 1980).

——, *Japanese Culture in the Meiji Era: Volume IX Legislation* (Tokyo: Tōyō Bunko, 1958).

Ishimura, Zensuke, and Yuriko Kaminaga, "Attorneys and Cases Involving Automobile Accidents," *Law in Japan: An Annual*, vol. 9 (1976), pp. 83–116.

Ito, Hirobumi, *Commentaries on the Constitution of the Empire of Japan* (Tokyo: Chūō Daigaku, 1906).

Itoh, Kazuo, "On Publication For Criticism of the 'Citizens' Human Rights Reports,'" *Law in Japan: An Annual*, vol. 20 (1988), pp. 29–73.

Jansen, Marius B., and Gilbert Rozman, *Japan in Transition: From Tokugawa to Meiji* (Princeton: Princeton University Press, 1986).

Japanese Government, *Crime Prevention and Control National Statement* (Fifth United Nations Congress on the Prevention of Crime and Treatment of Offenders, Sept. 1–12, 1975) (Tokyo).

JCJS, Report of the Review of the Joint Committee on Japanese Studies (JCJS) of the American Council of Learned Societies and the Social Science Research Council, October 1989.

Johnson, Chalmers, *Conspiracy at Matsukawa* (Berkeley: University of California Press, 1972).

——, "Japan, 'Who Governs?' An Essay on Official Bureaucracy," *Journal of Japanese Studies*, vol. 2, no. 1 (Autumn 1975), pp. 1–28.

——, *MITI and the Japanese Miracle* (Stanford: Stanford University Press, 1982).

Johnson, Wallace, *The T'ang Code: Volume I, General Principles* (Princeton: Princeton University Press, 1979).

Kanda, James, Japanese Feudal Society in the Sixteenth Century as Seen Through the Jinkaishū and Other Legal Codes (Ph.D. dissertation, Departments of History and East Asian Languages, Harvard University, 1974).

Kaplan, Eugene J., *Japan: The Government-Business Relationship* (Washington, D.C.: U.S. Department of Commerce, 1972).

Kawada, Katsuo, "Suspension of Prosecution in Japan" (unpublished paper, Tokyo: UNAFEI, n.d.).

Kawashima, Takeyoshi, "The Status of the Individual in the Notion of Law, Right, and Social Order in Japan," in C. Moore (ed.), *The Japanese Mind: Essentials to Japanese Philosophy and Culture* (Honolulu: University of Hawaii Press), pp. 262–287.

Kelman, Steven, "Enforcement of Occupational Safety and Health Regulations: A Comparison of Swedish and American Practices," in K. Hawkins and J.M. Thomas (eds.), *Enforcing Regulation* (Boston: Kluwer-Nijhoff, 1984), pp. 97–119.

——, *Regulating America, Regulating Sweden: A Comparative Study of Occupational Safety and Health Policy* (Cambridge: MIT Press, 1981).

Kida, Minoru, "The Laws of the *Buraku*," *Japan Quarterly*, vol. 4, no. 1 (1957), pp. 77–88.

Kitagawa, Zentaro, *Rezeption und Fortbildung des europäischen Zivilrechts in Japan* (Reception and endurance of European civil law in Japan) (Frankfurt: Alfred Metzner Verlag, 1970).

Krauss, Ellis S., Thomas P. Rohlen, and Patricia G. Steinhoff (eds.), *Conflict in Japan* (Honolulu: University of Hawaii Press, 1984).

Ladejinsky, Wolf, "Farm Tenancy and Japanese Agriculture," *Foreign Agriculture*, vol. 1, no. 9 (September 1937), pp. 425–446.

Lebra, Takie S., *Japanese Patterns of Behavior* (Honolulu: University of Hawaii Press, 5th ed., 1986).

Lebra, Takie Sugiyama, and William P. Lebra (eds.), *Japanese Culture and Behavior* (Honolulu: University of Hawaii Press, 1974).

Le Master, Dennis C., *Decade of Change: The Remaking of Forest Service Statutory Authority During the 1970s* (Westport, Conn.: Greenwood Press, 1984).

Lepon, Jeffrey M., "Administrative Guidance in Japan," *Fletcher Forum*, vol. 2, no. 2 (1978), pp. 139–157.

Liu, Chang Bin, Commercial Law Under the Ch'ing Code (Ph.D. dissertation, School of Law, University of Washington, Seattle, 1984).

Lockwood, William W., *The Economic Development of Japan* (Princeton: Princeton University Press, 1954).

Lockwood, William W. (ed.), *The State and Economic Enterprise in Japan* (Princeton: Princeton University Press, 1965).

Loewenberg, Gerhard, *Parliament in the German Political System* (Ithaca: Cornell University Press, 1967).

des Longrais, Jönon, *L'Est et L'Ouest* (East and West) (Tokyo and Paris: Maison Franco-Japonaise, Institut de Recherches d'Histoire Étrangère, 1958).

Lynch, John, *Toward an Orderly Market: An Intensive Study of Japan's Voluntary Quota in Cotton Textile Exports* (Rutland, Vt.: C.E. Tuttle, in cooperation with Sophia University, 1968).

Macaulay, J.R., and C. Berkowitz (eds.), *Altruism and Helping Behavior* (New York: Academic Press, 1970).

Macaulay, Stewart, "Non-Contractual Relations in Business: A Preliminary Study," *American Sociological Review*, vol. 28 (1963), pp. 55–67.

Macauley, Stewart, and Elaine Walster, "Legal Structures and Restoring Equity," *Journal of Social Issues*, vol. 27, no. 2 (1971), pp. 173–195.

Maki, John M., "The Role of the Bureaucracy in Japan," *Pacific Affairs*, vol. 20 (1947), pp. 391–406.

Marsh, Robert, and Hiroshi Mannari, *Modernization and the Japanese Factory* (Princeton: Princeton University Press, 1976).

Marshall, Byron K., *Capitalism and Nationalism in Prewar Japan* (Stanford: Stanford University Press, 1967).

Maruyama, Masao, *Studies in the Intellectual History of Tokugawa Japan* (Princeton: Princeton University Press, 1974).

———, *Thought and Behavior in Modern Japanese Politics* (London: Oxford University Press, 1963).

Mason, Mark Evan, United States Direct Investment in Japan: Studies in Government Policy and Corporate Strategy (Ph.D. dissertation, Departments of History and East Asian Languages, Harvard University, 1988).

Mass, Jeffrey P., *The Development of Kamakura Rule* (Stanford: Stanford University Press, 1979).

———, *The Kamakura Bakufu: A Study in Documents* (Stanford: Stanford University Press, 1976).

———, (ed.), *Court and Bakufu in Japan: Essays in Kamakura History* (New Haven: Yale University Press, 1982).

Matsuo, Tasuku, *U.S. and Japan Bankruptcy Law* (Tokyo: Sakai Publishing Co., 1971).

Matsushita, Mitsuo, and Lawrence Repeta, "Restricting The Supply of Japanese Automobiles: Sovereign Compulsion or Sovereign Collusion?," *Case Western Reserve Journal of International Law*, vol. 14, no. 1 (Winter 1982), pp. 47–81.

McKnight, Brian E., *The Quality of Mercy: Amnesties and Traditional Chinese Justice* (Honolulu: University of Hawaii Press, 1981).

———, (ed.), *Law and the State in Traditional East Asia* (Honolulu: University of Hawaii Press, 1986).

von Mehren, Arthur T. (ed.), *Law in Japan: The Legal Order in a Changing Society* (Cambridge: Harvard University Press, 1963).

Merryman, John Henry, *The Civil Law Tradition: An Introduction to the Legal Systems of Western Europe and Latin America* (Stanford: Stanford University Press, 2d ed., 1985).

Ministry of Justice, *Summary of White Paper on Crime* (Tokyo, 1969).

Mitchell, Richard H., *Thought Control in Prewar Japan* (Ithaca: Cornell University Press, 1976).

Miyazawa, Setsuo, "Taking Kawashima Seriously: A Review of Japanese Research on Japanese Legal Consciousness and Disputing Behavior," *Law & Society Review*, vol. 21, no. 2 (Fall 1987), pp. 219–241.

Morley, James W. (ed.), *Dilemmas of Growth in Prewar Japan* (Princeton: Princeton University Press, 1971).

Mukai, Ken, and Nobuyoshi Toshitani, "The Progress and Problems of Compiling the Civil Code in the Early Meiji Era," *Law in Japan: An Annual*, vol. 1 (1967).

Müller, Heinz, and Peter Giessler, *Kommentar zum Gesetz gegen Wettbewerbsbeschränkungen* (Commentary on law against restraints of competition) (Frankfurt: Lorch, 1st ed., 1958).

Murakami, Junichi, *Einführung in die Grundlagen des japanischen Rechts* (Introduction to the fundamentals of Japanese law) (Darmstadt: Wissenschaftliche Buchgesellschaft, 1974).

Muramatsu, Michio, "Center-Local Political Relations: A Lateral Competition Model," *Journal of Japanese Studies*, vol. 12, no. 2 (Summer 1986), pp. 303–327.

Najita, Tetsuo, and J. Victor Koschmann,(eds.), *Conflict in Modern Japanese History* (Princeton: Princeton University Press, 1982).

Najita, Tetsuo, and Irving Scheiner, (eds.) *Japanese Thought in the Tokugawa Period* (Chicago: University of Chicago Press, 1978).

Nakamura, Takafusa, *The Postwar Japanese Economy: Its Development and Structure* (Tokyo: University of Tokyo Press, 1981).

Nakane, Chie, *Japanese Society* (Berkeley: University of California Press, 1972).

Needham, Joseph, *Science and Civilization in China*, vol. 2 (London: Cambridge University Press, 1956).

Nishida, Yoshiaki, "Growth of the Meiji Landlord System and Tenancy Disputes after World War I: A Critique of Richard Smethurst, *Agricultural Development and Tenancy Disputes in Japan, 1870–1940*," *Journal of Japanese Studies*, vol. 15, no. 2 (Summer 1989), pp. 389–415.

Noda, Yoshiyuki, "Comparative Jurisprudence in Japan—Its Past and Present, Part I," *Law in Japan, An Annual*, vol. 8 (1975), pp. 1–38.

Nosco, Peter (ed.), *Confucianism and Tokugawa Culture* (Princeton: Princeton University Press, 1984).

Ocko, Jonathan K., *Bureaucratic Reform in Provincial China* (Cambridge: Harvard University Press, 1983).

Okimoto, Daniel I., and Thomas R. Rohlen (eds.), *Inside the Japanese System* (Stanford: Stanford University Press, 1988).

Ooms, Herman, *Tokugawa Ideology: Early Constructs, 1570–1680* (Princeton: Princeton University Press, 1985).

Oppler, Alfred C., *Legal Reform in Occupied Japan: A Participant Looks Back* (Princeton: Princeton University Press, 1976).

Ōtsubo, Kenzō, *Japan Federation of Bar Associations* (Tokyo: Asian Legal Research Institute, 1977).

Ōyama, Katsuyoshi, Criminal Justice in Japan IV (unpublished paper, Tokyo: UNAFEI, c. 1978).

Pape, Wolfgang, "Gyōsei shidō and the Antimonopoly Law," *Law in Japan: An Annual*, vol. 15 (1982), pp. 12–23.

——, *Gyosei shido und das Anti-Monopol-Gesetz in Japan* (Administrative guidance and the antimonopoly law in Japan) (Cologne: Heymanns, 1980).

Parker, Craig J., *The Japanese Police System Today: An American Perspective* (Tokyo: Kōdansha International, 1984).

Patrick, Hugh, and Henry Rosovsky (eds.), *Asia's New Giant* (Washington, D.C.: Brookings Institution, 1976).

Peterson, Mark A., *Compensation for Injuries: Civil Jury Verdicts in Cook County* (Santa Monica, Calif.: Rand Corporation, Institute for Civil Justice, 1984).

Postan, M.M., and H.J. Habarkuk (eds.), *The Cambridge Economic History of Europe: Agrarian Life in the Middle Ages*, vol. I (Cambridge: Cambridge University Press, 1966).

Prestowitz, Clyde V., Jr., *Trading Places: How We Allowed Japan to Take the Lead* (New York: Basic Books, 1988).

Pyle, Kenneth B., *The New Generation in Meiji Japan: Problems in Cultural Identity, 1885–1895* (Stanford: Stanford University Press, 1969).

Rabinowitz, Richard W., The Japanese Lawyer: A Study in the Sociology of the Legal Profession (Ph.D. dissertation, Social Science, Harvard University, 1955).

——, "Law and the Social Process in Japan," *Transactions of the Asiatic Society of Japan*, vol. 10 [3d Series] (1968), pp. 7–92.

——, Law of Foreign Investment in Post-War Japan (Mimeographed materials for a course in Comparative Law, Harvard Law School, 1988).

Ramseyer, J. Mark, "The Costs of the Consensual Myth: Antitrust Enforcement and Institutional Barriers to Litigation in Japan," *Yale Law Journal*, vol. 94, no. 3 (January 1985), pp. 604-645.

——, "Reluctant Litigant Revisited: Rationality and Disputes in Japan," *Journal of Japanese Studies*, vol. 14, no. 1 (1988), pp. 111-123.

Ramseyer, J. Mark, and Minoru Nakazato, "The Rational Litigant: Settlement Amounts and Verdict Rates in Japan," *Journal of Legal Studies*, vol. 18, no. 2 (June 1989), pp. 263-290.

Reed, Steven, "Confused Voters and Contentious Politicians: The Five General Elections 1947-1955" (Paper presented at the annual meeting, Association for Asian Studies, Boston, Mass., April, 1987).

——, *Japanese Prefectures and Policymaking* (Pittsburgh: University of Pittsburgh Press, 1986).

Robinson, Glen O., Ernest Gellhorn, and Harold Bruff, *The Administrative Process* (St. Paul, Minn.: West Publishing Co., 2d ed., 1980).

Roehl, Thomas, "A Transactions Cost Approach to International Trading Structures: The Case of the Japanese General Trading Companies," *Hitotsuhashi Journal of Economics*, vol. 24, no. 2 (1983), pp. 119-135.

Rohlen, Thomas P., *For Harmony and Strength: Japanese White Collar Organization in Anthropological Perspective* (Berkeley: University of California Press, 1974).

Rosenbluth, Frances McCall, *Financial Politics in Contemporary Japan* (Ithaca: Cornell University Press, 1989).

Rosenbluth, Frances, "The Political Economy of Financial Reform in Japan: The Banking Act of 1982," *UCLA Pacific Basin Law Journal*, vol. 6, nos. 1 and 2 (Fall 1989), pp. 62-102.

Sajo, Andras, "Why Do Public Bureaucracies Follow Legal Rules," *International Journal of the Sociology of Law*, vol. 9, no. 1 (1981), pp. 69-84.

Samuels, Richard, *The Business of the Japanese State: Energy Markets in Comparative and Historical Perspective* (Ithaca: Cornell University Press, 1987).

Sansom, George B., "Early Japanese Law and Administration," Part I, *Transactions of the Asiatic Society of Japan* [2d Series], vol. IX (1932), pp. 67-109; Part II, *Transactions of the Asiatic Society of Japan* [2d Series], vol. XI (1934), pp. 117-149.

——, *The Western World and Japan* (New York: Vintage Books, 1973).

Sarat, Austin, and Joel B. Grossman, "Courts and Conflict Resolution: Problems in the Mobilization of Adjudication," *American Political Science Review*, vol. 69 (1975), pp. 1200-1217.

Saxonhouse, Gary R., and Kozo Yamamura (eds.), *Law and the Trade Issues in the Japanese Economy* (Seattle: University of Washington Press, 1986).

Scalapino, Robert A. (ed.), *The Foreign Policy of Modern Japan* (Berkeley: University of California Press, 1977).

Schiller, A. Arthur, *Roman Law* (New York: Mouton Publishers, 1978).

Schott, Kerry, *Policy, Power and Order: The Persistence of Economic Problems in Capitalist Societies* (New Haven: Yale University Press, 1984).

Schram, Stuart R. (ed.), *Foundations and Limits of State Power in China* (Hong Kong: Chinese University Press, 1987).

——, (ed.), *The Scope of State Power in China* (Hong Kong: Chinese University Press, 1985).

Schubert, Glendon, and David J. Danielski (eds.), *Comparative Judicial Behavior* (New York and London: Oxford University Press, 1969).

Scogins, Hugh T., "Between Heaven and Man: Contracts and the State in Han Dynasty China," *Southern California Law Review*, vol. 63, no. 5 (July 1990), pp. 1325–1404.

von Senger, Harro, *Chinesische Bodeninstitutionen im Taihō Verwaltungskodex* (Chinese land tenure institutions in the Taihō administrative code) (Wiesbaden: Otto Harrassowitz, 1983).

Shaw, William S., *Legal Norms in a Confucian State* (Berkeley: Institute for East Asian Studies, University of California, 1981).

Shiga, Shūzō, "Criminal Procedure in the Ch'ing Dynasty (I)," in *Memoirs of the Research Department of the Toyo Bunko*, no. 32 (Tokyo, 1974), pp. 1–45.

Shiga, Shūzō, "Criminal Procedure in the Ch'ing Dynasty (II)" in *Memoirs of the Research Department of the Toyo Bunko*, no. 33 (Tokyo, 1975), pp. 115–138.

Siemes, Johannes, *Hermann Roesler and the Making of the Meiji Constitution* (Tokyo: Monumenta Nipponica, 1966).

Silbermann, Bernard S., and Harry D Harootunian. (eds.), *Japan in Crisis* (Princeton: Princeton University Press, 1974).

Silberman, Bernard S., and Harry D. Harootunian (eds.), *Modern Japanese Leadership: Transition and Change* (Tucson: University of Arizona Press, 1966).

Sklar, Judith N., *Legalism: Law, Morals and Political Trials* (Cambridge: Harvard University Press, 1986 ed.).

Smethurst, Richard J., *Agricultural Development and Tenancy Disputes in Japan, 1870–1940* (Princeton: Princeton University Press, 1986).

———, "Challenge to Orthodoxy and its Orthodox Critics: A Reply to Nishida Yoshiaki," *Journal of Japanese Studies*, vol. 15, no. 2 (Summer 1989), pp. 417–437.

Smith, Brian, *Policy-making in the British Government: An Analysis of Power and Rationality* (Totowa, N.J.: Littlefield, 1976).

Smith, Robert J., "The Japanese Rural Community: Norms, Sanctions, and Ostracism," *American Anthropologist*, vol. 63 (1961), pp. 522–533.

———, *Kurusu: The Price of Progress in a Japanese Village, 1951–1975* (Stanford: Stanford University Press, 1978).

Smith, Robert J., and John R. Cornell, *Two Japanese Villages* (Ann Arbor: University of Michigan Press, 1956).

Smith, Thomas C., *Political Change and Industrial Development in Japan* (Stanford: Stanford University Press, 1955).

Sono, Kazuaki, and Warren L Shattuck., "Personal Property as Collateral in Japan and the United States," *Washington Law Review*, vol. 39, no. 3 (August 1964), pp. 570–647.

Stack, Steven, "Social Structure and Swedish Crime Rates: A Time-Series Analysis, 1950-1979," *Criminology*, vol. 20, nos. 3 and 4 (November 1982), pp. 479–513.

Statistics Bureau, Management and Coordination Agency, Prime Minister's Office, *Japan Statistical Yearbook, 1949* (Tokyo, 1949).

Statistics Bureau, Management and Coordination Agency, Prime Minister's Office, *Japan Statistical Yearbook 1988* (Tokyo, 1988).

Steenstrup, Carl, *Hōjō Shigetoki (1198-1261) and his Role in the History of Political and Ethical Ideas in Japan* (Ph.D. dissertation, Department of East Asian Languages and Civilization, Harvard University, 1977).

———, "Sata Mirensho: A Fourteenth-Century Law Primer," *Monumenta Nipponica*, vol. 35 (1980), pp. 405–435.

Stein, Ted L., "Contempt, Crisis, and the Courts: The World Court and The Hostage Rescue Attempt," *American Journal of International Law*, vol. 76, no. 3 (July 1982), pp. 504–512.

Stephens, Thomas B., *The Disciplinary System of Order in China, A Case Study: The Mixed Court at Shanghai, 1911–1927* (Seattle: University of Washington Press, forthcoming).

Stocking, George W., and Myron W. Watkins, *Cartels or Competition?* (New York: Twentieth Century Fund, 1948).

Suleiman, Ezra N., *Politics, Powers, and Bureaucracy in France: The Administrative Elite* (Princeton: Princeton University Press, 1974).

Sykes, G.M., and D. Matza, "Techniques of Neutralization: A Theory of Delinquency," *American Sociological Review*, vol. 22 (1957), pp. 664–670.

Tanaka, Hideo, *The Japanese Legal System: Introductory Cases and Materials* (Tokyo: University of Tokyo Press, 1976).

——— , "The Role of Law in Japanese Society: Comparisons with the West," *University of British Columbia Law Review*, vol. 19, no. 2 (1985), pp. 375–388.

Tanase, Takao, "The Management of Disputes: Automobile Accident Compensation in Japan," *Law & Society Review*, vol. 24, no. 3 (1990), pp. 651–691.

UNAFEI, *Criminal Justice in Asia: The Quest for an Integrated Approach* (Tokyo: UNAFEI, 1982).

Unger, Roberto, *Law in Modern Society* (New York: The Free Press, 1976).

Upham, Frank K., "After Minamata: Current Prospects and Problems in Japanese Environmental Litigation," *Ecology Law Quarterly*, vol. 8, no. 2 (1979), pp. 213–268.

——— , *Law and Social Change in Postwar Japan* (Cambridge: Harvard University Press, 1987).

——— , "Litigation and Moral Consciousness in Japan: An Interpretative Analysis of Four Japan Pollution Suits," *Law & Society Review*, vol. 10, no. 2 (Summer 1976), pp. 579–619.

U.S. Bureau of the Census, *Historical Statistics of the United States: Colonial Times to 1970*, Part 2 (Washington, D.C.: U.S. Government Printing Office, 1975).

U.S. Bureau of the Census, *Statistical Abstract of the U.S. 1989* (Washington, D.C.: U.S. Government Printing Office, 1989).

Vogel, Ezra F., *Japan As Number One: Lessons for America* (Cambridge: Harvard University Press, 1979).

——— , *Japan's New Middle Class* (Berkeley: University of California Press, 1967).

de Vos, George A. (ed.), *Socialization for Achievement* (Berkeley: University of California Press, 1973).

Wagatsuma, Hiroshi, and Arthur Rosett, "The Implications of Apology: Law and Culture in Japan and the United States," *Law & Society Review*, vol. 20, no. 4 (1986).

Walster, Elaine, Ellen Berscheid, and G. William Walster, "New Directions in Equity Research," *Journal of Personality and Social Psychology*, vol. 25, no. 2 (1973), pp. 151–176.

——— , "When Does a Harm-doer Compensate a Victim," *Journal of Personality and Social Psychology*, vol. 6, no. 4 (1967), pp. 435–441.

Walthall, Anne, *Social Protest and Popular Culture* (Tucson: University of Arizona Press, 1986).

Ward, Robert E., *Japan's Political System* (Englewood Cliffs, N.J.: Prentice-Hall, 1967).

————, (ed.), *Political Development in Modern Japan* (Princeton: Princeton University Press, 1968).

Ward, Robert E., and Dankwart A. Rustow (eds.), *Political Modernization in Japan and Turkey* (Princeton: Princeton University Press, 1964).

Waswo, Ann, *Japanese Landlords: The Decline of a Rural Elite* (Berkeley: University of California Press, 1977).

Watanuki, Joji, *Politics in Postwar Japanese Society* (Tokyo: University of Tokyo Press, 1977).

Weber, Max, *Economy and Society: An Outline of Interpretative Sociology*, vol. 2 (G. Roth and C. Wittich [eds.], New York: Bedminster Press, 1968).

White, James W., *The Soka Gakkai and Mass Society* (Stanford: Stanford University Press, 1971).

Wigmore, John Henry, *Law and Justice in Tokugawa Japan*, Part I (Tokyo: University of Tokyo Press, 1969).

————, "New Codes and Old Customs," in *Japan Weekly Mail*, Oct. 29, 1897, pp. 530–533; Nov. 19, 1897, pp. 617–619; Nov. 26, 1897, pp. 656–661; Dec. 10, 1897, pp. 722–726.

————, *Panorama of the World's Legal Systems*, vol. 2 (St. Paul: West Publishing Co., 1928).

Williams, Robin M., Jr., *American Society* (New York: A.A. Knopf, 2d ed., 1960).

Williams, Timothy P., and Shunya Sogon, "Group Composition and Conforming Behavior in Japanese Students," *Japanese Psychological Research*, vol. 26, no. 4 (1984), pp. 231–234.

van Wolferen, Karel, *The Enigma of Japanese Power* (New York: A.A. Knopf, 1989).

Yamamura, Kozo, *Economic Policy in Postwar Japan* (Berkeley: University of California Press, 1967).

————, *A Study of Samurai Income and Entrepreneurship* (Cambridge: Harvard University Press, 1974).

————, (ed.), *Policy and Trade Issues of the Japanese Economy* (Seattle: University of Washington Press, 1982).

Yamanouchi, Kazuo, "Administrative Guidance and the Rule of Law," *Law in Japan: An Annual*, vol. 7 (1974), pp. 22–33.

Yoshino, Michael Y., *Japan's Managerial System: Tradition and Innovation* (Cambridge: MIT Press, 1968).

Young, Michael K., "Judicial Review of Administrative Guidance: Governmentally Encouraged Consensual Dispute Resolution in Japan," *Columbia Law Review*, vol. 84 (1984), pp. 923–983, abstracted as "Administrative Guidance in the Courts: A Case Study in Doctrinal Adaptation," *Law in Japan: An Annual*, vol. 17 (1984), pp. 120–152.

Japanese Language Publications

Aomi Shunichi, *Hō to shakai* (Law and society) (Tokyo: Chūo Kōron Sha, 1967).

Aoyama Michio, "*Wagakuni ni okeru kenri ran'yō riron no hatten*" (Development of the theory of abuse of rights in Japan), in *Kenri no ran'yō* (Abuse of rights), vol. 1 (Tokyo: Yūhikaku, 1963), pp. 9–45.

Arai Kōjiro, "*Seisai*" (Sanctions), in *Nihon Minzokujaku Taikei* (Outlines of Japanese ethnology), vol. 4 (Tokyo: Heibonsha 1959), pp. 173–188.

Dai-Nippon teikoku tōkei nenkan (Japanese empire annual statistics) (Tokyo: Ōkurashō Insatsu Kyoku, 1920).

Fukushima Masao (ed.), *Nihon kindai hō taisei no keisei* (Formation of Japan's modern legal system), vol. 1 (Tokyo: Nihon Hyōronsha, 1981).

Gyōsei shidō ni kansuru chōsa kenkyū hōkokusho (Report on investigative study of administrative guidance) (Tokyo: Gyōsei Kanri Kenkyū Sentā 1981).

Hata Ikuhito, *Kanryō no kenkyū* (Studies of bureaucracy) (Tokyo: Kōdansha, 1983).

Higashimoto Norikata, "*Kaikyū-teki ni mitaru kinsen saimu rinji chōtei hō*" (Temporary monetary claims conciliation law from a [Marxian] class perspective), *Hōritsu shinbun* (No. 3471) (Oct. 28, 1931), at p. 3.

Hiramatsu Yoshirō, *Kinseihō* (Early modern law) vol. II, *Iwanami kōza Nihon rekishi* (Iwanami lectures on Japanese history) [*Kinsei*, vol. 3] (Tokyo: Iwanami, 1976).

Hiramatsu Yoshirō Hakushi Tsuito Ronbunshū Henshū Iinkai (ed.), *Hō to keibatsu no rekishi-teki kōsatsu* (Historical studies on law and penal institutions) (Nagoya: Nagoya Daigaku Shuppankai, 1987).

Hōmu sōgō kenkyūjo kenkyūbu kiyō 29 (Ministry of Justice Combined Research Institute Research Division Bulletin No. 29) (Tokyo: Hōmushō, 1986).

Hōmushō (Ministry of Justice), *Hōmu nenkan* (Yearbook on administration of justice) (Tokyo: Hōmushō, 1948–1987).

Hoshino Tōru, *Minpōten ronsōshi* (History of the civil code controversy) (Tokyo: Nihon Hyōronsha, 1949).

Hosokawa Kameichi, *Nihon hōseishi* (Japanese legal history) (Tokyo: Yūhikaku, 1961).

Hozumi Nobushige, *Hōso yawa* (Conversations on the law) (Tokyo: Yūhikaku, 1920).

Hozumi Shigetō, "*Chōtei hō*," (Conciliation law), *Gendai hōgaku zenshū*, vol. 38 (Tokyo: Nihon Hyōronsha, 1931), pp. 225–290.

Hozumi Tadao, "*Hōritsu kōi no 'kaishaku' no kōzō to kinō II*" (Structure and function of the 'Interpretation' of juristic acts), *Hōgaku kyōkai zasshi*, vol. 78, no. 1 (1961), pp. 27–71, translated in *Law in Japan: An Annual*, vol. 5 (1972), pp. 132–164.

Igarashi Futaba, "*Daiyō kangoku mondai ni tsuite*" (Concerning the problem of substitute jails), *Jurisuto* (No. 637) (May 1, 1977), pp. 116–125.

———, "*Nase 'keijiryūchijo' ga hitsuyō ka*" (Why are 'criminal detention centers' necessary?), *Jurisuto* (No. 712) (March 3, 1980), pp. 85–91.

Inada Masatsugu, *Meiji kenpō seiritsu shi* (History of the making of the Meiji constitution), 2 vols. (Tokyo: Yūhikaku, 1962).

Inoue Mitsusada, Seki Akira, Tsuchida Naoshige, and Aoki Kazuo (eds.), *Ritsuryō* (Tokyo: Iwanami Shoten, 1976).

Ishibashi Magojirō, "*Chōtei hō to shokken shugi*" (Conciliation laws and authoritarianism), *Hōritsu shinbun* (No. 3101) (April 3, 1930), p. 3.

Ishida Shin, *Nihon minpōshi* (History of Japanese civil law) (Tokyo: Dobunkan, 1928).

Ishii Ryōsuke, *Hōseishi* (Legal history) [*Taikei Nihonshi sōsho*, vol. 4] (Tokyo: Yamakawa Shuppansha, 1979).

———, "*Kamakura bakufu seiritsuki no futatsu no mondai*" (The problem of the date of the establishment of the Kamakura *bakufu*), *Hōseishi kenkyū* (Legal history review), vol. 17 (1967), pp. 1–32.

———, *Nihon hōseishi gaisetsu* (Survey of Japanese legal history) (Tokyo: Kōbundō, 2d ed., 1949).

———, "*Sain no minpō sōan*" (The peers' draft civil code), *Kokka gakkai zasshi*, vol. 60, nos. 1 and 6 (1946), pp. 26–47, 361–383.

Ishio Yoshihisa, *Nihon kodai hō no kenkyū* (Studies on Japan's ancient law) (Kyoto: Hōritsu Bunka Sha, 1961).

———, *Nihon kodai hō shi* (History of Japan's ancient law) (Tokyo: Hanawa Shobō, 1964).

Kageura Tsutomu, *Matsuyama han hōreishū* (Laws and regulations of the Matsuyama domain) (Tokyo: Kintō Shuppansha, 1978).

Katsumata Shizuo, *Sengoku hō seiritsushi ron* (Studies on the establishment of sengoku law) (Tokyo: Tōkyō Daigaku Shuppankai, 1982 ed.).

Kawashima Takeyoshi, *Nihonjin no hōishiki* (Legal consciousness of Japanese) (Tokyo: Iwanami, 1967).

Kenjo Yukio, *"Edo bakufu no nengu shūnō hōshin"* (Policy on *nengu* tax assessment of the Edo *bakufu*), *Hōseishi kenkyū* (Legal history review), vol. 17 (1967), pp. 33-74.

"Kinsen saimu chōtei narabi ni kakushu chōtei hō teppai mondai" (Issue of abolition of the monetary claims conciliation law and other conciliation statutes), *Hōso kōron* (No. 408) (July 1, 1934), pp. 51-63.

Kishii Tatsuo, *"Chōtei kanken"* (Narrow view of conciliation), *Hōso kōron* (No. 413) (Jan. 1, 1935), p. 11.

Kobayakawa Kingo, *Kyūminpōten henshū katei to kyūminpōten ni kansuru ronso ni tsuite* (The process of compiling the old civil code and the dispute concerning the old civil code) (Tokyo: Yamaguchi Shoten, 1943).

Kodama Kōta, *Kinsei nōmin seikatsushi* (History of early modern rural peasant life) (Tokyo: Yoshikawa Kōbunsha, 1957).

Koga Masayoshi, *Kenri ishiki ni tsuite* (On rights consciousness), *Hanrei taimuzu* (Special Issue no. 3, 1977).

Matsunaga Yoshiichi, *"Chōtei seido no kaizen"* (Reforming the conciliation system), *Hōritsu Shinbun* (No. 3365) (Feb. 3, 1932), p. 7.

Matsuo Kikutanō, *"Chōtei hō hatashite sonchi seshimu-beki ka"* (Should we continue to develop conciliation laws?), *Hōso kōron* (No. 408) (July 1, 1934), p. 5.

Minamoto Ryōen, *Giri to ninjō* (Giri and ninjō) (Tokyo: Chūo Kōron Sha, 1969).

Miura Yagorō, *"Chōtei no shidō seishin"* (Guiding spirit of conciliation), *Hōritsu shinbun* (No. 3886) (Sept. 15, 1935), p. 4.

Miyoshi Shigeo, *"Gendai shakaishisō jōka no tame ni kakushu chōtei hō no haishi o nozomu"* (Hoping for the abolition of all conciliation laws for the purification of contemporary social theory), *Hōso kōron* (No. 407) (June 1, 1934), pp. 7-12.

Miyagawa Sumu, *Kyūminpō to Meiji minpō* (The old civil code and the Meiji civil code) (Tokyo: Aoki Shoten, 1965).

Miyazawa Kōichi (ed.), *Hanzai to higaisha: Nihon no higaishagaku* (Crime and victims: Studies on victims in Japan), 2 vols. (Tokyo: Seibundō, 1970).

Miyazawa Setsuo, *Hanzai sōsa o meguru daiissen keiji no ishiki to kōdō* (The consciousness and practices of first-line detectives in criminal investigations) (Tokyo: Seibundō, 1985).

Morohashi Tetsuji, *Dai kanwa jiten* (Great Chinese character-Japanese dictionary), vol. 2 (Tokyo: Daishūkan Shoten, 1984 ed.).

Nagashima Hatasu, *Kosaku chōtei hō kōwa* (Discussion of farm tenancy conciliation law) (Tokyo: Shimizu Shoten, 1924).

Nakada Kaoru and Ishii Ryōsuke, *Nihon hōseishi kōgi* (Lectures on Japanese legal history) (Tokyo: Sōbunsha, 1983).

Nakagawa Gō, *Nihonjin no hō kankaku* (Sense of law of the Japanese) (Tokyo: Kōdansha, 1989).

Nakagawa Zennosuke, *Shihōshi* (History of private law) (Tokyo: Tōyō Keizai Shinbunsha, 1943).

Narita Atsuo, *"Chōtei seido no bakko to shihō saiban no botsuraku"* (Proliferation of conciliation and the ruin of judicial trials), *Hōritsu shinbun* (No. 4066) (Dec. 15, 1936), p. 3.

Narita Yoriaki, *"Gyōsei shidō,"* in *Gendaihō* (Contemporary law), vol. 4 (Tokyo: Iwanami Shoten, 1966), pp. 131-68, translated in *Law in Japan: An Annual*, vol. 2 (1968), pp. 45-79.

Nihon Bengoshi Rengōkai (Japan Federation of Bar Associations), *Shihō hakusho* (White paper on the judiciary) (Tokyo, 1974).

Nihon Bengoshi Rengōkai Chōsa Shitsu, *Bengoshi gyōmu no jittai* (State of lawyers' practice) (Tokyo: Nihon Bengoshi Rengōkai, 1972).

Niida Noboru, *Chūgoku hōseishi* (Chinese legal history) (Tokyo: Iwanami Shoten, 1963).

———, *Chūgoku hōseishi kenkyū: hō to shūkan, hō to dōtoku* (Research on Chinese legal history: law and custom, law and morality) (Tokyo: Tōkyō Daigaku Shuppankai, 2d ed., 1981).

Nitta Ichirō, *"Nihon chūseihō seishi kenkyū no dōkō kara—'chūseihō' no kōsei o chūshin ni"* (Recent research on Japanese medieval law—centering on the structure of 'medieval law'), *Hoseishi kenkyū* (Legal history review), vol. 36 (1986), pp. 181-210.

Ōhira Yūichi, *"Kinsei ni okeru 'kanekuji' saiken no hogo ni tsuite"* (On protection of 'moneysuit' obligations in the early modern period), in Otake H. and Harafuji H. (eds.), *Bakuhan kokka no hō to shihai* (Law and control by the state in the Tokugawa period) (Tokyo: Yūhikaku, 1984), pp. 289-330.

Ōki Masao, *Nihonjin no hō kannen* (Japanese concept of law) (Tokyo: Tōkyō Daiyaku Shuppansha, 1983).

Okudaira Yasuhiro, *Chian iji hō shōshi* (Short history of the peace preservation law) (Tokyo: Chikuma Shobō, 1977).

Okuno Hikoroku, *Osadamegaki no kenkyū* (Research on the *Osadamegaki*) (Tokyo: Shui Shoten, 1968).

———, *Ritsuryōsei kodai hō* (Ancient law under the *ritsuryō* system) (Tokyo: Sakai Shoten, 2d ed. 1968).

———, *Tokugawa bakufu to chūgoku hō* (The Tokugawa *bakufu* and Chinese law) (Tokyo: Sōbunsha, 1979).

Riko Mitsuo, *Nihon kodai hōseishi* (History of Japan's ancient legal system) (Tokyo: Keiō Tsūshin, 1986).

Rokumoto, Kahei, *"Nihonjin no hōishiki saiho"* (Japanese legal consciousness reconsidered), in Mochizuki, et al. (eds.), *Hō to hōkatei* (Law and legal process) (Tokyo: Seibundō, 1986).

Ryusaki Kisuke, *Saiban o meguru shimin to bengoshi* (Citizens who resort to court and lawyers), *Hanrei taimuzu* (No. 500) (Sept. 1, 1983), pp. 27-43.

Saikō Saibansho (Supreme Court) (ed.), *"Wagakuni ni okeru chōtei seido no enkaku"* (Development of conciliation in our country) (Tokyo: Saikō Saibanshsho, n.d. ca. 1951).

Saikō Saibansho Jimu Sōkyoku (Supreme Court General Secretariat), *Shōwa 62 nen shihō tōkei nenpō; 2 keijihen* (1987 judicial statistics annual report: vol. 2, criminal cases) (Tokyo: Saikō Saibansho, 1988).

Satō Seisaburō and Matsuzaki Tetsuhisa, *Jimintō seiken* (The LDP's political power) (Tokyo: Chūō Kōron, 1986).

Satō Shin'ichi, *Kamakura bakufu soshō seido no kenkyū* (Research on the system of litigation under the Kamakura bakufu) (Tokyo: Unebō Shobo, 1943).

Shiomi Toshitaka, *Nihon no bengoshi* (Japanese lawyers) (Tokyo: Nihon Hyōronsha, 1972).

————, (ed.), *Gendai no bengoshi* (Contemporary lawyer) (Tokyo: Iwanami Shoten, 1966).

Sugiyama Haruyasu, *Nihon hōshi gairon* (Introduction to Japanese legal history) (Tokyo: Seibundo, 1980).

Takikawa Masajirō, *Nihon hōseishi* (Japanese legal history) (Tokyo: Yūhikaku, 2d ed., 1930).

Taniguchi Sumio, *Okayama han* (Okayama domain) (Tokyo: Yoshikawa Kobunkan, 1964).

Tōkyō Bengoshi Kai (Tokyo Bar Association) (ed.), *Tōkyō bengoshi kai hyakunenshi* (Hundred year history of the Tokyo bar association) (Tokyo: Tōkyō Bengoshi Kai, 1980).

Tsujimoto Hiroaki, "*Ryōseibai hō no kigen ni tsuite*," (On the origins of the law to punish both parties to a quarrel), *Hōseishi kenkyū* (Studies in legal history), vol. 18 (1968), pp. 103-120.

Ueki Naoichirō, *Goseibai shikimoku kenkyū* (Research on the *goseibai shikimoku*) (Tokyo: Iwanami Shoten, 1930).

Watanabe Yoshifusa, "*Gyōsei shidō o meguru shomondai*" (Problems with administrative guidance), *Jurisuto*, no. 342 (March 15, 1966), pp. 46-50.

Yamaguchi Yonachirō, "*Shakuchi shakuya chōtei hō no ran'yō to kaisei no kyūmu*" (Abuse of land lease and house lease conciliation and the urgency of reform), *Hōritsu shinbun* (No. 3628) (Nov. 30, 1933), p. 4.

Yamanouchi Kazuo, *Gyōsei shidō* (Administrative guidance) (Tokyo: Kobundō, 1977).

Yoshida Jinpū, *Nihon no karuteru* (Japanese cartels) (Tokyo: Tōyō Keizai Shinpō Kai, 1964).

Yōzō Watanabe, *Tochi tatemono no hōritsu seido* (Legal institutions for land and buildings) (Tokyo: Tokyō Daigaku Shuppansha, 1960).

Index